This important new study describes how English people defined and attempted to control misbehavior during the later medieval and early modern periods. Professor McIntosh argues against the suggestion that social regulation was a distinctive feature of the decades around 1600, resulting from Puritanism. Instead, through an examination of public court proceedings from 255 villages and small towns distributed throughout England, she demonstrates that concern with wrongdoing mounted gradually between 1370 and 1600. In an attempt to maintain harmonious relations, preserve order, and lessen the social damage of poverty, local leaders prosecuted people who slandered or quarreled with their neighbors, engaged in sexual misdeeds, operated unruly alehouses, or refused to work. Professor McIntosh also explores who the offenders were as well as the factors that led to misbehavior and shaped responses to it. More generally, her findings shed light on the transition from medieval to early modern patterns and open up little-known sources and new research methods. This novel study will be of interest to medievalists and early modernists, with interests ranging from social and economic history to legal and religious history.

Controlling misbehavior in England, 1370–1600

Cambridge Studies in Population, Economy
and Society in Past Time 34

Series Editors

ROGER SCHOFIELD
ESRC Cambridge Group for the History of Population and Social Structure
RICHARD SMITH
ESRC Cambridge Group for the History of Population and Social Structure
JAN DE VRIES
University of California at Berkeley
PAUL JOHNSON
London School of Economics and Political Science

Recent work in social, economic and demographic history has revealed much that was previously obscure about societal stability and change in the past. It has also suggested that crossing the conventional boundaries between these branches of history can be very rewarding.

This series exemplifies the value of interdisciplinary work of this kind, and includes books on topics such as family, kinship and neighbourhood; welfare provision and social control; work and leisure; migration; urban growth; and legal structures and procedures, as well as more familiar matters. It demonstrates that, for example, anthropology and economics have become as close intellectual neighbours to history as have political philosophy or biography.

For a full list of titles in the series, please see end of book

Controlling misbehavior in England, 1370–1600

MARJORIE KENISTON McINTOSH

University of Colorado at Boulder

CAMBRIDGE
UNIVERSITY PRESS

PUBLISHED BY THE PRESS SYNDICATE OF THE UNIVERSITY OF CAMBRIDGE
The Pitt Building, Trumpington Street, Cambridge CB2 1RP, United Kingdom

CAMBRIDGE UNIVERSITY PRESS
The Edinburgh Building, Cambridge CB2 2RU, United Kingdom
40 West 20th Street, New York, NY 10011–4211, USA
10 Stamford Road, Oakleigh 3166, Australia

First published 1998

Printed in the United Kingdom at the University Press, Cambridge

Typeset in 10/12 pt Palatino [VN]

A catalogue record for this book is available from the British Library

Library of Congress cataloguing in publication data applied for

ISBN 0 521 621771 hardback

To the archivists
of England's county, national, and local record offices,
in appreciation of
their professional competence,
their helpful service to their diverse clientele,
and their careful protection of the documents
in their custody

Contents

Part I   The history of social regulation

Part II   Factors that influenced social regulation

Illustrations

List of illustrations

Graphs in Appendices

Tables and lists

Tables

Tables and lists in Appendices

Acknowledgements

It is a great pleasure to thank the many people and institutions that have contributed to this project. Between May of 1990 and September of 1995 I traveled to 83 archives in England plus one in North America and used microfilm provided by three others. During the months when it was still light after 5:00, I drove to see the communities whose records I had read that day, and wherever possible I stayed in farmhouse bed and breakfast places where I could chat with my host and hostess about rural life in the 1990s. Hospitable friends welcomed me on weekends. I am fortunate to have gained such an extraordinary exposure to England's diversity, today as well as in the past.

As the dedication of this volume makes clear, I am deeply indebted to the archivists and other staff members of England's county, national, and local record offices. Although I was a foreigner asking to consult large numbers of awkward and little-used documents, the staff provided consistently helpful service. Record offices have responded with admirable flexibility to their changing roles over the past generation. The number of users is now far larger than when I was a graduate student in the mid-1960s and the clientele much more diverse, including many people who were attracted to a study of the past through curiosity about their own family, house, or community. The expertise of staff members is therefore focused primarily and rightly upon more recent historical periods. Increased physical demand upon documents has required the use of new technologies to ensure that the records will survive into future generations. Changes in governmental structures and funding have forced many record offices into financial competition with swimming pools and other "leisure activities" or, even more difficult, with essential social services. It is impressive that their staffs have maintained their equanimity and their commitment to providing fine service to all their users in the face of such profound transitions. I – and many thousands of others – acknowledge their assistance with gratitude.

My research has benefited from involvement with a number of academic institutions and has received generous financial backing. I began exploring this project in 1983–4, when I was honored to be the Visiting Research Fellow in the Arts at Newnham College, Cambridge, supported by a Research Fellowship from the (US) National Endowment for the Humanities. Serious work in the archives began in 1990–1, when I held a Faculty Fellowship from the University of Colorado and enjoyed an affiliation with Jesus College, Oxford. I was fortunate to receive a Visiting Research Fellowship from the Borthwick Institute for Historical Research at the University of York in the summer of 1992; during that and several other summers through 1995, research in England was supported by grants from the Council on Research and Creative Work and the Graduate Committee on the Arts and Humanities at the University of Colorado. In 1995–6 I had the great luxury of writing this book during twelve months of uninterrupted concentration, thanks to a Fellowship from the John Simon Guggenheim Memorial Foundation. I have also profited from participation in various seminars offered at the Institute of Historical Research in London and appreciate having access to its library and to the British Library. A number of graduate students at the University of Colorado capably assisted me with aspects of the research process.

The ideas in this book and its presentation have been influenced by many other scholars. Preliminary versions of my argument were presented in seminars given at Oxford University in November, 1990, at the Cambridge Group for the History of Population and Social Structure in May, 1991, and at the Institute of Historical Research in June, 1992, at each of which I received valuable comments. Teaching an interdisciplinary graduate seminar with Margaret Ferguson of the English Department at the University of Colorado improved my ability to read texts and utilize critical theory. Jeremy Goldberg, Conrad Russell, Roger Schofield, Margaret Spufford, and Keith Wrightson offered thoughtful suggestions about an initial attempt to lay out my thoughts in written form, and I learned from the audience at my plenary address at the Western Conference on British Studies in October, 1994. The final form of the book has been considerably improved by the reactions of Elaine Clark, Margot Finn, Paul Glennie, Thomas Green, Richard Hoyle, Richard M. Smith, Dorothy Owen, Margo Todd, and Robert Woods, who provided detailed comments far beyond the call of normal collegial or editorial assistance. In many respects this book is a testi-

mony to the generosity that exists within the Anglo-American historical
community.

Completed at the sign of the Grizzly Trail,
Bar-K Ranch, Jamestown, Colorado
January, 1997

Abbreviations

AO   Archive(s) Office
EETS   Early English Text Society
OED   *The Oxford English Dictionary*, 2nd edn., 20 vols., ed. J. A.
        Simpson and E. S. C. Weiner, Oxford, 1989–
PRO   Public Record Office, London
RO   Record Office
Stats *The Statutes of the Realm*, 12 vols., London, 1810–28
Realm
STC   *Short Title Catalogue*, ed. Pollard and Redgrave (= *A
        Short-Title Catalogue of Books Printed in England, Scotland,
        and Ireland and of English Books Printed Abroad, 1475–1640*,
        first compiled by A. W. Pollard and G. R. Redgrave, 1926;
        2nd edn. by W. A. Jackson, F. S. Ferguson, and K. F.
        Pantzer, 3 vols., London, 1976–91)
Tudor *Tudor Royal Proclamations*, 2 vols., ed. Paul L. Hughes and
Royal James F. Larkin, New Haven, Conn., 1964 and 1969
Procls.
VCH   *The Victoria County Histories*, issued in multiple volumes by
        county, mid-nineteenth-century through the present, by
        various presses

Introduction

The debate over social regulation

During the decades around 1600, many English communities were deeply troubled by social misbehavior.[1] In an attempt to maintain good order and enforce ethical conduct, local officials reported and punished sexual wrongdoing, excessive drinking, and the playing of illegal games, especially among the poor.[2] Sometimes they addressed verbal abuse known as "scolding," described as a characteristically female offence.[3] If the campaign for reform was led by fervent Puritans, it might include an attack upon older traditions of popular culture as well – customary village recreations like morris dancing and seasonal rituals

---

[1] For a thoughtful discussion of the historiography of social regulation, see Keith Wrightson's "Postscript" to the paperback edition of his and Levine's *Poverty and Piety*. This Introduction will not reassess the literature and interpretive problems he considers there.

[2] Works that discuss social regulation around 1600 and are not cited specifically below include Richardson, *Puritanism in North-West England*, Peter Clark, *English Provincial Society*, Rosen, "Winchester in Transition," Wrightson, *English Society*, Hunt, *The Puritan Moment*, Underdown, *Revel, Riot, and Rebellion*, Kent, *The English Village Constable*, Mayhew, *Tudor Rye*, Levine and Wrightson, *The Making of an Industrial Society*, Marcombe, *English Small Town Life*, and Ingram, "Reformation of Manners."

[3] Scolds quarreled with others or spread malicious gossip. For recent studies of scolding and/or defamation, see Haigh, "Slander and the Church Courts," de Bruyn, *Woman and the Devil*, ch. 5, Sharpe, "Defamation and Sexual Slander," Gregory, "Slander Accusations and Social Control," Underdown, "The Taming of the Scold," Amussen, *An Ordered Society*, esp. p. 123, Boose, "Scolding Brides and Bridling Scolds," Gowing, "Gender and the Language of Insult," her "Language, Power and the Law," and her *Domestic Dangers*, Ingram, "'Scolding Women Cucked or Washed'," and Hindle, "The Shaming of Margaret Knowsley."

1

like May Day festivities.[4] Efforts to contain misconduct were generally led by the male heads of well-established families of yeomen, the more prosperous craftsmen and traders, and occasionally some of the resident gentry. In addition to informal means of control, these men were able to employ the authority of the English legal system: they could include social wrongdoing among the problems they reported as jurors in their local courts, as lay parish officials in the church courts, or as local spokesmen summoned before county Sessions of the Peace. The punishments imposed upon offenders (a monetary fine, some form of public confinement *cum* ridicule, whipping, open confession of error, or religious excommunication) depended upon the nature of their offence and the type of court.

While historians agree that anxiety about misbehavior was widespread around 1600, the reasons for concern are not fully understood. One explanation suggests that attempts at "a reformation of manners" were influenced in some communities by the Puritan ideology of "the middling sort" who dominated local offices. Ardent Puritans, eager to create a truly Christian community on earth and to eliminate what they regarded as sinful cultural traditions, used the secular and ecclesiastical courts to impose their own, more demanding standards of moral behavior upon all members of their village or town. This argument, offered initially by Keith Wrightson in his 1973 Ph.D. thesis and supported by his and David Levine's pathbreaking study of the Essex village of Terling, has been illustrated more recently within both a southern county town and another small Essex community.[5] An approach that emphasizes the impact of religious ideology upon social practices is part of a distinguished historiographic tradition: influenced by the work of Christopher Hill, it can be traced back to the venerable debate about the relationship between religious, social, and economic changes triggered by Max Weber and R. H. Tawney, who were themselves responding in part to the suggestions of Karl Marx.[6] Unfortunately, a simplistic and more sweeping application of the proposed

---

[4] Most fully, Hutton, *The Rise and Fall of Merry England*, esp. ch. 4; see also Ingram, "Ridings, Rough Music, and the 'Reform of Popular Culture'" and "From Reformation to Toleration." For continental parallels, see Muchembled, *Popular Culture and Elite Culture*, and Oestreich, *Strukturprobleme der frühen Neuzeit*.

[5] Wrightson, "Puritan Reformation of Manners" and his and Levine's *Poverty and Piety*; Underdown, *Fire from Heaven*, and von Friedeburg, *Sündenzucht und sozialer Wandel*, which supercedes his "Reformation of Manners."

[6] For Hill, see, e.g., *Society and Puritanism* and *Change and Continuity*; for the earlier debate, see Weber, *The Protestant Ethic and the Spirit of Capitalism* (New York, 1926, but originally issued as articles during the first two decades of the century), and Tawney, *Religion and the Rise of Capitalism*; Marx, *Das Kapital*.

importance of Puritanism has slipped into some historical thinking: social control around 1600 was caused by Puritanism, and hence regulation of conduct was a new phenomenon.

The precise role played by Puritan concerns as compared with other influences remains unclear. Of the scholars who have looked carefully at early modern responses to misbehavior, none has argued that Puritanism was in itself either a necessary or a sufficient cause of efforts to control wrongdoing. Wrightson and Levine, for example, note the importance of a cluster of demographic and economic changes in Terling that led to population pressure and severe problems with poverty as well as to cultural differentiation between middling families and the poor; these issues worked together with Puritan goals in shaping the pattern of social regulation.[7] Conversely, Cynthia Herrup has shown that East Sussex experienced virtually no attempt to reform conduct during the Elizabethan and early Stuart periods despite a Puritan presence.[8] Thanks to the studies of Martin Ingram we know that some smaller villages and towns were controlling misbehavior around 1600 even when Puritanism was not at work.[9] Ingram points instead to other kinds of motives: a general Christian ethical sense about the need for responsible marriages and the evils of blatant sexual immorality; economic concerns about the creation of new households among the poor and the problem of bastard children, leading to higher parish taxes; and eagerness to contain disorderly or immoral conduct that might be disruptive of village harmony.

A number of studies have highlighted the distinctive features of the decades around 1600, thereby raising the possibility that vigorous social regulation was tied to those particular conditions. In practical terms, the 1590s experienced high population density, bad harvests and food shortages, acute poverty, unusual amounts of migration, disruption of normal marriage patterns, and potentially violent unrest.[10] Such factors were likely to have increased the amount of wrongdoing and anxiety about it. So too were the cultural contrasts between local leaders and the poor visible in some communities by the end of the sixteenth century, manifested in differing levels of literacy and involvement in

---

[7] Wrightson and Levine, *Poverty and Piety*. A similar combination of factors is visible in the village of Earls Colne, Essex (von Friedeburg, *Sündenzucht und sozialer Wandel*).

[8] In *The Common Peace*.

[9] "Religion, Communities and Moral Discipline" and *Church Courts, Sex and Marriage*, esp. pp. 166–7 and 233–7. Examples of Puritanism's variable influence upon social regulation are McIntosh, *A Community Transformed*, pp. 250–7, and Richard Dean Smith, "Social Reform in an Urban Context."

[10] See, e.g., Walter and Schofield, eds., *Famine, Disease and the Social Order*.

popular culture.[11] Political and administrative developments likewise had important consequences for social regulation. James A. Sharpe has noted that efforts to contain misbehavior in the later Elizabethan and Jacobean periods were shaped by the presence of "an aggressive central and local governmental system" that was "anxious and (within limits) capable of intervening to alleviate" the demographic, economic, social, and cultural problems that threatened the stability of local communities.[12]

Evidence from medieval England, however, demonstrates that attempts to curtail wrongdoing had occurred in other periods and circumstances as well. Margaret Spufford, writing from the vantage-point of a Stuart historian but with information furnished by several medievalists, has suggested that the decades around 1300 witnessed control over the sexual misconduct of the poor in a fashion similar to that seen around 1600.[13] After noting the resemblances between the demographic and economic conditions of the later thirteenth and the later sixteenth centuries and between the village elites of the two periods, Spufford looked at the role of the church courts in enforcing sexual morality and at the reports made to manor courts concerning *leyrwite* and *childwite*, the payments owed to the lord by villein women who committed fornication or bore bastard children. Arguing that medieval courts were attempting to regulate sexual misconduct, especially among poor women, three centuries before the early modern manifestation of concern, she concluded that social control could not be "in any way peculiar to puritanism."[14] While her summary of what early modern historians have said about Puritanism as a motivating force for social regulation does not do full justice to the multifaceted nature of many of their studies, her discussion of the parallels in control over misconduct is nevertheless intriguing.

Pockets of social regulation have been documented in the fifteenth century too. My own previous research showed that between 1460 and 1500 local courts in some of England's bustling market centers tried energetically to control the same kinds of misbehavior and the same kinds of people as were the focus of attention around 1600.[15] In wrestling with such problems as scolding, sexual misconduct, disorderly

---

[11] E.g., Cressy, *Literacy and the Social Order*, Wrightson, "Two Concepts of Order," and Hutton, *The Rise and Fall of Merry England*.
[12] Sharpe, *Crime in Early Modern England*, esp. p. 173.
[13] "Puritanism and Social Control?" Her paper emphasizes the similarities between the periods but does not discuss the many significant contrasts.   [14] *Ibid.*, p. 57.
[15] McIntosh, "Local Change and Community Control" and *Autonomy and Community*, pp. 250–61.

alehouses, taking wood from hedges, and playing illegal games, leaders of these communities concentrated on the actions of the poor, young people, and newcomers to the community. Shannon McSheffrey has recently described strenuous control over behavior in London in the later decades of the fifteenth century; records of many other urban communities similarly document anxiety about social wrongdoing.[16] Church courts were active too, dealing with sexual wrongdoing and verbal abuse.[17]

The relationship between earlier manifestations of control over misconduct and the outburst of concern around 1600 has not yet been established. Wrightson, in his "Postscript" to the 1995 paperback edition of the Terling study, acknowledges that medieval manor courts had undertaken some degree of social regulation, especially over sexual matters, but he stresses that early seventeenth-century control was unusual in two respects other than the contribution of Puritanism: an entirely different *scale* of concern as compared with the previous half-century, and the recourse made in the later period to "extra-parochial courts of Church and State" which had formerly been little used in social regulation.[18] This raises another problem. If control over misconduct was handled by different types of courts in various periods, what appear to be changing levels of concern with wrongdoing over time may to some extent be artificial, deriving from an inconsistent use of records across the medieval and early modern eras.

Viewed more generally, our ability to trace the course of social regulation has been hampered by the structural definitions conventionally used in academic institutions when teaching and studying history. Lack of information about possible precedents for Elizabethan/Jacobean regulation derives in part from the unnatural chasm created by the continuing pedagogic use of 1485 as a cut-off date between periods, obscuring awareness of the continuities between later medieval and early modern England. Many historians of the sixteenth and seventeenth centuries received little training in the issues and sources important during the generations before Henry VII's accession, while medievalists are often poorly informed about developments after the fifteenth century. Another arbitrary division, the separation of insular from continental European history, contributed to a sense

---

[16] In "Sexual Misconduct and the Regulation of Behaviour" (I am grateful to Dr. McSheffrey for a copy of this excellent study, which shows great sensitivity to language and individual circumstances); for other cities, see Chapter 1, section one below, and the records cited in Appendix 1.1.

[17] E.g., Karras, *Common Women*, and Poos, "Sex, Lies, and the Church Courts."

[18] Wrightson and Levine, *Poverty and Piety*, p. 201.

among some scholars that social regulation was a characteristically English phenomenon. We now have an excellent set of studies of German, French, Dutch, and Italian communities during the Reformation and Counter-Reformation periods showing that a willingness to control social behavior appeared at least sporadically on the continent during the generations before the Reformation as well as during the sixteenth and seventeenth centuries in Lutheran, Calvinist, and Catholic Reformation settings.[19] Control over wrongdoing in England was without doubt part of a pan-European phenomenon.

The approach and arguments of this study

To answer the questions that surround English social regulation, we need a broader study – one that spans the transition between the medieval and early modern periods, examines developments throughout the country, and draws upon a diverse array of court records and other texts. In attempting to fill that need, this book explores four issues between 1370 and 1600: what were the forms through which misconduct could be addressed, what was the history of regulation during that period, what attitudes underlay efforts to control wrongdoing, and what factors influenced the amount of misbehavior and local responses to it? A starting date in the later fourteenth century allows us to establish a baseline of limited concern with misconduct during the first few generations after the 1348–9 plague.[20] By extending until 1600, the project provides a link into the better studied episodes of intense regulation during the late Elizabethan and Jacobean periods.[21]

[19] E.g., Moeller, *Imperial Cities*, Ozment, *The Reformation in the Cities*, Burke, *Popular Culture*, Hoffman, *Church and Community*, Hsia, *Social Discipline*, Roper, *The Holy Household*, Schilling, *Civic Calvinism*, Mentzer, ed., *Sin and the Calvinists*, and Prodi and Penuti, eds., *Disciplina dell'anima*.

[20] Originally I hoped to start in the later thirteenth century so as to include the period of concern with misconduct around 1300, but this plan proved infeasible. The method used in this study requires that long runs of records be employed, covering as much of the full period as possible, but relatively few courts offered documents extending from the later thirteenth into the sixteenth centuries. If the starting date were moved to the later fourteenth century, a much wider array of documents became available.

[21] My initial plan was to go into the seventeenth century, to trace the full history of the period of heightened concern around 1600, but the nature of the sources again intervened. Because the lesser local courts in many parts of the country no longer bore the brunt of responsibility for social regulation by 1600, their records reveal only part of the full picture. Yet attempting a systematic analysis of the now extensive records of the other jurisdictions throughout the country was too ambitious. Further, several other scholars are working on social regulation during the seventeenth century, drawing upon the wider range of records available by 1600, including contemporary books and

The first question to be investigated concerns the mechanisms through which social wrongdoing was addressed.[22] What were these vehicles and how did they operate, how did their efforts interact with each other, and how did their roles change over time? Here we find that regulation formed part of a complex network designed to resolve conflict and curtail behaviors deemed socially harmful. As with personal disputes between individual local people, wrongdoing could be addressed through entirely informal means or through institutions like the pre-Reformation confessional, parish fraternities, urban guilds, and the developing system of poor relief. These units worked in tandem with more formal legal bodies to limit problems that seemed damaging to their communities. Four types of courts handled misconduct between 1370 and 1600: at the local level, the public courts held in England's villages, market centers, and hundreds (the administrative units into which most counties were divided), plus the legal bodies of the cities and larger towns; and at the intermediate level, the church courts operating within dioceses or archdeaconries, plus county Sessions of the Peace. Distribution of responsibility between these bodies shifted considerably over time: whereas the two kinds of local courts were assigned primary authority over all social offences except sexual misconduct during the fourteenth and earlier fifteenth centuries, the intermediate-level courts came to play a more important role across the later fifteenth and sixteenth centuries in some parts of the country. Here we encounter the issue of regional variation, a major theme within this study. Many of the lesser public courts in East Anglia, the Southeast, and the lower Midlands were actively concerned with social regulation from the 1460s through the mid-sixteenth century, but during the following fifty years control over wrongdoing in those areas was largely transferred to the church courts and county Sessions of the Peace. In the North, West, and Southwest, by contrast, most lesser courts did not begin to address misconduct aggressively until the sixteenth century but remained actively engaged with such problems right through 1600. The rhetorical and in some cases practical influence of Parliament and the crown likewise grew from the 1530s onwards. Hence this work supports in broad terms the argument of Sharpe and Wrightson that institutions at the county and national level were more significant to social regulation around 1600 than they had been previ-

pamphlets and the detailed depositions given before some of the church courts and a few of the Sessions. (See, e.g., Ingram, "'Scolding Women Cucked or Washed'" and Gowing, *Domestic Dangers*.)

[22] Because the rest of this section summarizes the detailed discussion in subsequent chapters, references will not be provided here.

ously. Yet it modifies that assessment in two respects: it establishes that this was the result of a slow shifting of power, and it adds a regional dimension to the analysis.

Of particular interest is the essential role played by the public courts convened in the country's smaller communities and by the jurors within them. In these little known institutions, established residents of middling status were sworn onto "presentment juries" to report about problems that affected the well-being of their community and to determine appropriate penalties.[23] The jurors were neither powerful and highly educated men nor the landless poor but rather yeomen, husbandmen, and local craftsmen and traders. Further, the same kinds of men were likely to serve as churchwardens in their parish, responsible for notifying the ecclesiastical courts about certain kinds of social wrongdoing, and as jurors or constables summoned before county Sessions of the Peace. They thus wielded considerable discretionary power through their decisions about which particular offences and offenders to report and which courts to use in addressing problems.

A second goal of this project is to determine the history of concern with wrongdoing between 1370 and 1600. To do so, reports of misconduct were analyzed from 267 public courts held in 255 villages, market centers, and hundreds.[24] These courts offer long chronological runs of records from communities distributed throughout England, permitting systematic assessment across our period. Only those instances of misbehavior that came to the attention of the courts through the unanimous reports of presentment juries are included in the study, for issues raised in private suits between parties may reflect individual problems rather than more widely held community concerns. It must be emphasized that these records do not allow us to distinguish between objective changes in the level of social wrongdoing within a given community and shifting attitudes on the part of the jurors towards whatever misdeeds did occur. Thus, if we observe that a particular court started to report sexual wrongdoing for the first time during the 1460s, we cannot tell whether such misbehavior was only now beginning to occur, perhaps due in part to the arrival of immigrants with different standards of conduct, or whether established local families had become more wor-

---

[23] "Middling" as used here with reference to the socio-economic range of local communities differs from the higher level implied by that word in most of the articles in *The Middling Sort of People* (ed. Barry and Brooks). The occupational terms below apply primarily to the sixteenth century; during the medieval period, such men came from the central and upper ranks of the peasantry.

[24] These places all had fewer than c. 3,000 inhabitants. For how the courts were selected and the data analyzed, see Chapter 2 below.

ried about sexual issues and therefore decided to mention to the court problems which in the past they would have overlooked. In most cases both factors were probably at work, but only detailed local studies can sort out the relative contribution of each.[25]

Conduct regarded as socially harmful or disruptive by jurors has been classified here into eleven offences, ten of which are grouped for analytic convenience into clusters based upon the goals or anxieties that underlay them. The Disharmony cluster contains three offences often said in local records to be damaging to local harmony, goodwill, and peaceful relations between neighbors. Verbal misconduct known as "scolding" could take the form either of argumentative, quarrelsome speech or of malicious/untrue statements made behind another person's back. Eavesdropping, as its name implies, involved standing outside the walls of a house to listen to what was being said within. Nightwalkers wandered around after dark with no obvious reason for being out and hence were suspected of ill intent. A second grouping has been labeled the Disorder cluster, for its offences were commonly described as violating order, control, and discipline. This set includes sexual misconduct, unruly alehouses, and a set of imprecise charges in which a person was said to be of bad governance, suspicious life, or evil reputation. The third cluster revolves around the social problems that stemmed from poverty. While many local people continued to assist the needy in traditional charitable fashion or helped the deserving poor through the developing institutions of formal poor relief, a growing number of community leaders in the later fifteenth and sixteenth centuries decided to tackle the undesirable consequences of poverty through

---

[25] The closest we can come to an objective measure comes from information about bastardy, which presumably provides some reflection of the amount of sexual activity outside marriage. Adair's detailed analysis of illegitimacy rates by region indicates that between 1538 and 1599 the western part of the country had generally higher bastardy rates than did the East; the peak seen in the northwestern counties was roughly three times that found in the Southeast (*Courtship, Illegitimacy and Marriage*, figs. and tables 2.2–2.7). (I am grateful to Dr. Adair for a copy of his Ph.D. thesis and for detailed county figures.) If presentments for sexual misconduct in the 267 local courts studied here are grouped into the same regions used by Adair, we find that the Northwest did indeed demonstrate more attention to this issue than did the Southeast between 1540 and 1599, but the contrast is far less than in the bastardy rates. Adair's study shows that the stigma associated with extra-marital births was less in the North and West than in the South and East, due to differing definitions of betrothal and marriage; this may explain why regional contrasts in presentments concerning sexual wrongdoing are more muted than the bastardy levels might imply. Conversely, the apparent regional difference seen here may be influenced by the fact that the lesser public courts remained more active during the late sixteenth century in the Northwest than in the Southeast.

the courts. The Poverty cluster consists of taking wood from common hedges for use as fuel, called "hedgebreaking," feeding or sheltering vagabonds, refusing to work if poor, or allowing subtenants to move into one's holding.

These ten forms of behavior were chosen precisely because they were not expressly against the law or at least were not assigned to the lesser public courts for correction. The freedom of the jurors in dealing with such issues may be contrasted with those illegal actions which juries were required to report as part of the common law's nationwide system for maintaining the peace (like physical assaults, theft, or rape) and those which were indisputable crimes in the eyes of the church – and later the state (like witchcraft). While personal and local factors of course shaped jurors' decisions even in the latter areas, they were definitely *supposed* to report the more serious offences, whereas they had a choice about whether or not to prosecute social wrongdoing. A report about misbehavior therefore presupposes genuine concern among community leaders, providing a glimpse into how misbehavior was constructed. To examine the impact of explicit illegality upon local court reactions, a final issue was added to the list as a special case: playing any of a wide range of games proscribed by Parliamentary legislation.

Quantitative analysis of how many of these eleven offences were reported to local courts over time reveals a gradual rise in concern between the late fourteenth century and the end of the sixteenth. During the baseline period of 1370–99, only 14 percent of the lesser courts under observation reported any types of wrongdoing, but by the 1460s–70s the figure had risen markedly to 40 percent. (Duodecades are used as the chronological unit of analysis from 1400 onwards.) This evidence supports previous suggestions that social regulation was a serious concern within certain settings during the later fifteenth century. In the 1520s–30s the proportion of courts that addressed misbehavior climbed to 54 percent before reaching a peak of 59 percent in the 1580s–90s. Even when we add to this pattern the increasing contribution of the intermediate courts to controlling misconduct during the Elizabethan period, it is difficult to conclude that vigorous regulation around 1600 was a new phenomenon, altogether different in scale from what had come before.

If the evidence is broken down by cluster – by the type of concern that led to court action, interesting chronological variations emerge. Offences in the Disharmony cluster (scolding, eavesdropping, and night-walking) were reported to the local courts at a fairly consistent rate between the 1420s–30s and the 1520s–30s, dropping somewhat thereafter. Although attention to scolding/defamation in the church courts may have risen during the later sixteenth century, it is unlikely that this was sufficient to compensate for the diminished concern with maintaining local goodwill seen in all other types of courts. A declining emphasis on peaceful interactions is observable in other settings and texts as well.[26] In a different pattern, reports of offences in the Disorder cluster (sexual misconduct, disorderly alehouses, and people described in such terms as being badly governed) became a serious issue in the 1460s–70s, moving to a higher plateau between 1500 and 1539 and falling back later. Decreased attention to such problems at the local level during the second half of the sixteenth century almost certainly resulted from a jurisdictional shift: jurors apparently preferred to take some of these cases to the intermediate-level courts, with their more effective forms of control over sexual wrongdoing and alehouses. The ideological context confirms serious attention to problems of order and control through the end of Elizabeth's reign. The Poverty cluster followed yet another course. Worry about hedgebreaking, giving hospitality to vagabonds, refusing to labor, and receiving subtenants mounted after 1460 and continued to rise right through the end of Elizabeth's reign. Here the local response was paralleled by growing concern in other institutions, by increasingly sophisticated analysis of the problems of poverty among more educated people, and by the actions of Parliament as it began to implement methods for assisting the needy poor while forcing idlers to work. Reports of illegal gaming grew quite steadily across the fifteenth and sixteenth centuries. Analysis of the gender of those presented for wrongdoing and of the procedures and punishments employed similarly demonstrates significant changes over time. We must thus recognize that "social regulation" as a catch-all phrase could contain pronounced chronological as well as regional variations in the particular kinds of offences and people controlled. This helps to explain the lack of consensus among historians with respect to social regulation – previous studies have revealed only scattered pieces of a complex and shifting process.

A third focus of this book is the attitudes that shaped local responses. A wide range of texts has been used in exploring this issue. Some of the local court records employed for the quantitative analysis provide brief explanations of why particular actions or people constituted a threat to their communities. Such statements may be compared with material from other bodies that regulated misconduct (urban institutions, the

---

[26] For this and subsequent statements about the broader ideology, see Chapter 8 below; for political factors, see Chapter 5.

church courts, and Sessions of the Peace) and with several dissimilar sources: the ordinances of almshouses and hospitals founded in the fifteenth and sixteenth centuries, and descriptions of social wrongdoing contained in petitions submitted to the Lord Chancellor. To place these texts into a broader ideological context, we also consider Parliamentary statutes, royal proclamations, and other political writings as well as a variety of moral, poetic, and dramatic works.

This examination reveals considerable consistency within any given period in how social wrongdoing was perceived and conceptualized across the range of sources examined. The attitudes of jurors in local courts were widely shared by their peers operating in other settings and by people of higher social/economic/educational status. Yet, as we have seen, the concerns were by no means stable over time. In addition to the changing emphases placed upon the three central issues (harmony, order, and poverty), a set of more focused worries is visible. Local people, like those above them, felt that it was vital that they and their neighbors be able to defend their reputation, credit, or good name, for upon these qualities rested a person's ability to function as a trusted member of the social community and an effective participant in market transactions. Malicious rumors had therefore to be curtailed and private conversations and actions kept free from observation. Conversely, because the quality of a person's speech helped to shape his or her reputation, jurors were more likely to present people for other offences if they were known to use "bad conversation." Starting in the later fifteenth century, jurors worked to maintain a disciplined labor force, particularly in communities experiencing the transition to larger-scale and more highly capitalized forms of agricultural or industrial production or craftwork. Although most judgments about regulation of conduct seem to have been based on a desire to maintain the quality of the community's social and economic life coupled with general moral considerations, overtly religious factors played an occasional role, as seen in efforts to clamp down on certain forms of wrongdoing during divine services.

Jurors' decisions about whether to report an offence were influenced further by the kinds of people engaging in that behavior, a process clearly visible from the 1460s–70s onwards. The actions of young people, including servants and apprentices, were scrutinized with particular closeness.[27] Here the primary issues appear to have been fear of

---

[27] Many, perhaps most, young men and some young women spent time between their mid-teens and their mid-twenties in service or, less often, as apprentices, living and working in another household until they had sufficient occupational skills and could afford to marry and set up their own independent household. See Chapter 6, section two below.

disorder associated with how they used their free time, especially sexuality and drinking, and worry about economic issues – both the frittering away of servants' limited incomes (or their masters' goods) through inappropriate leisure time activities, and the developing of bad habits among the junior members of the labor force. Newcomers to the community were inherently suspect unless they arrived as comfortable landholders/craftspeople or married into an accepted local family. Anxiety about rising poverty often led to supervision of the actions of people with limited means. Those who lived idly without working were inherently upsetting: they might resort to illegal means to support themselves and use their spare time in inappropriate ways. Jurors were also troubled when the laboring poor wasted their resources in ale-houses or betting on games. When confronted with poverty-ridden strangers traveling aimlessly from place to place, local leaders tried to make the reception of these "vagabonds" sufficiently unwelcoming that they would keep moving right on out of the community. Even more worrisome was any attempt on the part of poor outsiders to settle locally, especially after the passage in 1552 and 1563 of Parliamentary statutes that ruled newcomers eligible for local poor relief, supported by more prosperous residents, if they stayed in one place for three years or more. Finally, the evidence assembled here shows that women formed a higher fraction of all those reported for wrongdoing between 1460 and 1539 than either before or after. We cannot be sure whether this was due to more female misbehavior on a per capita basis, to a rising proportion of women in certain types of communities, or to male fear of possible disorder among women, particularly in places undergoing rapid economic restructuring at that time.

The final question is what factors influenced a community's problems with and reactions to misbehavior. Various potential causes are explored separately: political considerations, geographical/demographic/economic features (a quantitative assessment based largely upon tax information), and ideological/religious influences. This examination, related wherever possible to the experience of the same 255 communities whose court records were analyzed previously, reveals considerable regional variation and marked changes across time. Local regulation of behavior operated quite independently of political developments at the national or county level during the later fourteenth and fifteenth centuries. Although the uncertainties deriving from instability in higher institutions of government and law between c. 1450 and 1485 may have increased the determination of local leaders to maintain control within their own communities, and although jurors may have drawn upon the language used by those above them in stressing the need for order and discipline, there were few shifts in broader social attitudes or ideas about the specific types of wrongdoing that were likely to have affected regulation of misconduct within the lesser courts. In practical terms those communities that expressed broad concern about social wrongdoing during the later fifteenth century were characterized by distinctive geographic, demographic, and economic features and often had a tradition of local "self-government."

Across the sixteenth century, however, circumstances changed markedly. As anxiety about misbehavior and a willingness to prosecute it spread to a wider range of communities, the influence of localized factors weakened. By the 1580s-90s the most common features were population pressure and a high and rising fraction of poor people, observations that agree with the detailed studies of Wrightson and Levine and von Friedeburg. Yet such influences were now compounded by other significant factors, especially the expansion of the power of national and county government during the Tudor period, the effort of Parliament and the crown to define and transmit political and social ideas, and the success of the Elizabethan church in communicating its teachings about moral behavior to the laity. By the later sixteenth century local regulation of misbehavior was working in parallel with the concerns of higher authorities. In those communities that reported social misconduct during the decades around 1600 for a mixture of practical and general ethical reasons, as described by Ingram, regulation constituted a continuation of the rising trajectory documented in this study. It is only in places where such considerations were joined by a more urgent call for social reformation as led by ardent Puritans that we encounter an intensity and divisiveness that may be regarded as new. In an ironic ideological inversion, some committed Puritans were so sure of the godliness of their cause that they were prepared to destroy at least temporarily the very social values that had in the past underlain and been used to justify correction of wrongdoing. While this study therefore supports Wrightson's emphasis on the distinctiveness of social regulation when implemented by committed Puritans, it offers a rather different perspective upon the social costs of such campaigns.

Several additional topics of current historical interest are considered as well, though this project does not claim to resolve them. The evidence presented here challenges the suggestion made by Lyndal Roper, David Underdown, and Anthony Fletcher that the sixteenth (and early seventeenth) centuries experienced a crisis in gender relations, seen in efforts to control female sexuality and/or speech.[28] This study's rich

---

[28] Roper, *The Holy Household* and Underdown, "The Taming of the Scold"; cf. Roper, *Oedipus and the Devil* and Fletcher, *Gender, Sex and Subordination*. This issue is discussed in Chapter 3, sections two and one below.

information about local jurors and their concerns disagrees with several aspects of the proposed interaction between centers and peripheries during the period of emergence of the nation state.[29] In emphasizing the agency of jurors, the book extends recent discussion of how "popular opinion" was created and under some circumstances brought to the attention of legal bodies for formal action.[30] It also stresses the importance of the concept of personal credit, showing in this case how it affected the definition and prosecution of socially harmful behavior.[31] The study demonstrates that new problems and solutions to them might well emerge first at the lowest level of government and courts, moving only gradually into the attention of higher authorities, an observation that reverses the directionality assumed by many analyses of national politics and law during the early modern period.[32] Finally, we gain a fine illustration of how lags could develop between practical developments and revised ideological statements during periods of rapid change, thereby highlighting the difficulties faced by theorists like Pierre Bourdieu when trying to explain how new realities are introduced into a set of inherited values, language, and behaviors.[33]

This study forms a complement to the insights gained from existing studies of social regulation within particular communities or of certain types of courts operating in a single diocese or county. To gain deep and specific understanding of the nature and causes of social misbehavior and attempts to control it, we must have that kind of focused research, able to utilize a variety of local materials to trace the role of localized pressures and the contributions of individual players. The types of records used in this project seldom document human experience at such depth. Most notably, they provide little if any information about the offenders as people and why they may have chosen or been forced to violate the dominant standards of behavior. Nor do they shed light on underlying social issues like the construction of gender, reflected, for example, in the predominance of women among those presented for scolding. Yet detailed studies will be more useful when they can be placed into a wider context, compared with what was happening in other communities and regions of the country to assess whether devel-

[29] E.g., Ankarloo and Henningsen, eds., *Early Modern European Witchcraft*, and Tilly, ed., *The Formation of National States*, as discussed in Chapter 1, section two below.

[30] Gowing, *Domestic Dangers*, Holmes, "Women: Witnesses and Witches," and Sharpe, "Witchcraft and Women"; Herrup, *The Common Peace*. For this issue, see Chapters 1 and 3 below.

[31] Muldrew, "Interpreting the Market"; see Chapters 1 and 3 below.

[32] As discussed in Chapters 1, 3, section four, and 5 below.

[33] E.g., Bourdieu, *Outline of a Theory of Practice* and cf. de Certeau, *The Practice of Everyday Life*, as discussed in Chapter 8, section one below.

opments observed in one setting were part of a broader pattern or
something distinctive to that particular situation. This project creates a
general framework while at the same time opening up additional topics
to be explored in future research.

The past and present

Before turning to the period after 1370, we may look briefly at the
history of social regulation during the preceding century. As Margaret
Spufford has brought to our attention, the decades on either side of 1300
witnessed considerable concern with sexual wrongdoing in both
church and manorial courts.[34] Whereas Spufford's use of *leyrwite* and
childwite evidence from manor court rolls is inconclusive, as it may
reflect the financial interest of the lord rather than the social interest of
fellow tenants, there is ample evidence of the latter's concern in the
statements of manorial juries summoned to identify problems that
affected the good order of their communities.[35] Jurors reported those
who engaged in sexual misconduct or gave hospitality to people of "ill
repute"; female sexual offenders and the men who supported them
were sometimes banished from the manor (by the court) or removed
from their holdings (by the lord). In a broader display of social regulation, jurors named those who were out at night without cause, ran
disorderly alehouses, or through their speech created ill-will among
their neighbors.

Misbehavior by the poor – many of whom were finding it difficult to
reach the level of economic subsistence in this period of overpopula-
tion, heavy taxation, and rising prices – was apparently seen as a
particular problem. Research on individual communities that enables
us to identify the status of people accused of social misdeeds indicates
that the poor received disproportionate attention. Richard M. Smith
and Zvi Razi, for example, have shown that peasant women who were
named for engaging in sexual activity before marriage or for giving
birth to illegitimate children were drawn heavily from among the
poorest villein families.[36] Spufford has argued that there is no reason to

---

[34] Spufford, "Puritanism and Social Control?"

[35] E.g., in manors of the Abbey of Bec and Ramsey Abbey (*Select Pleas in Manorial and
Other Seignorial Courts*, pp. 26 and 96–8); in the manor of Wakefield (*Court Rolls of the
Manor of Wakefield*, vol. II, p. 191, and vol. III, pp. 108, 113, 122, and 166); in the manor of
Horsham St. Faith, Norfolk (Elaine Clark, ed., "The Court Rolls of Horsham St. Faith,"
entries 1910–14, 2098, 2115, 2117, 2175, and 3111–13); and in the manor of Halesowen
(Hilton, "Small Town Society," and Zvi Razi, personal communication).

[36] As cited by Spufford in "Puritanism and Social Control?"

assume that the level of actual sexual misbehavior differed between poor and wealthier families: what we see in these presentments is instead a reflection of the relative difficulties faced by the poor in concealing premarital sexual activity or arranging a hasty marriage once pregnancy was discovered.[37] Though court evidence does not permit us to discriminate between those two possibilities, it would be surprising if the actions of people who were socially and economically marginalized did not deviate at times from the norms of appropriate conduct held by established and financially secure families.[38] Yet we know about wrongdoing only when it has passed through the filter of what juries of middling-level men decided to report to the local courts. Jurors may well have felt less need to publicize and punish misbehavior among the families of their peers, for they knew that the pregnant daughter of a prosperous local family would be given a dowry to ensure her marriage before the baby's arrival and that excessive drinking by the son of a respectable family would be curtailed by his own relatives.[39]

Wrongdoing by immigrants lacking land or a trade was also worrisome. The decades around 1300, when the total population of England was almost certainly even higher than it was to be in 1600, were marked by intense pressure on land and tiny holdings for many of the poor. Hence there was considerable selective movement of people out of densely packed villages into towns and those rural areas that offered a lower ratio of labor to land.[40] Such migration, which began in some areas around 1280 and became more pronounced in the opening decades of the fourteenth century, led to a rise in the number of poor newcomers in many urban centers and market communities. The problems and responses seen around 1300 thus bear strong resemblances to what occurred around 1600, despite fundamental differences in the economic, cultural, legal, and political contexts.

From the later 1320s through the end of the century, relatively few reports of misbehavior were submitted to local courts.[41] This drop was

---

[37] *Ibid.*

[38] In Terling, Essex, nearly three-quarters of the mothers of illegitimate children between 1570 and 1609 came from the ranks of the poorest families or were unknown outsiders (Wrightson and Levine, *Poverty and Piety*, pp. 126–34), though this was affected by disruption of planned marriages among the poor.

[39] Local leaders were probably thinking within a framework of "community law," with their attention directed as much toward the person as toward the offence (Lenman and Parker, "The State, the Community and the Criminal Law").

[40] Richard M. Smith, "Demographic Developments in Rural England."

[41] The church courts, however, continued to receive some reports of sexual problems: see Chapter 1, section one below.

probably affected initially by terrible weather in the 1310s, causing massive food shortages and ultimately a major population crisis in England as elsewhere in Europe. Famine leading to the death of perhaps 10 percent of the residents of many communities lessened the shortage of land and must have caused such severe social disruptions that misbehavior probably seemed trivial to both tenants and lords by comparison, not worth bringing to the attention of the courts. The arrival of bubonic plague in 1348–9, creating a still greater demographic collapse followed by lesser epidemics in the coming decades, magnified these economic and social consequences. Not until the fifteenth century did worry about wrongdoing begin to emerge once more as a serious issue in the lesser courts.

It is the period between 1370 and 1600 that we henceforth address. Chapter 1 introduces the forms through which wrongdoing could be controlled, while the next chapter lays out the method employed here for exploiting the rich records of the lesser public courts held in villages, market centers, and hundreds. The history of social regulation in 255 smaller communities is described in Chapter 3, together with the attitudes that underlay that response. Chapter 4 shows that the concerns about wrongdoing seen in these lesser courts were shared by people operating in other contexts. The second part of the study explores the factors that influenced the changing patterns of social regulation. Political issues are investigated in Chapter 5, while the next two chapters analyze the geographic, demographic, and economic characteristics of the same 255 communities over time: Chapter 6 considers those places that addressed an unusually broad array of different social problems as compared with those that expressed no concern with wrongdoing at all; Chapter 7 groups the communities on the basis of the types of offences they reported and then examines the features of each set of places. The final chapter considers ideological and religious influences, ending with a discussion of the particular role played by Puritanism around 1600 and its consequences. All dates are given in the old style used in England at the time, except that the year is taken to begin on 1 January. Quotations from Latin have been translated into modern English, and the spelling of quotations in English from fifteenth- and sixteenth-century manuscripts has been modernized; for passages taken from modern editions, the original spelling has been maintained except that the "thorn" and "yogh" characters are represented here as "th" and either "gh" or "y."

Striking parallels are apparent throughout this study between the problems and attitudes of the fifteenth and sixteenth centuries and those found at the end of the twentieth century in Western Europe and

North America. We too are troubled by misbehavior that seems to threaten good order and decency, especially when it is committed by people who lie at the edges of our social and economic structures. The actions of young people, outsiders, and the poor are scrutinized more closely than is the conduct of established and familiar neighbors. For us, issues of race and ethnicity commonly reinforce these attitudes, but we shall get at least a glimpse of comparable feeling about the Irish and Scots in fifteenth- and sixteenth-century England. Yesterday's "vagabonds" bear more than a superficial resemblance to today's "street people" or "travelers"; contemporary law enforcement officials might envy the ease with which their predecessors could simply order wrongdoers to move out of the community. A call to restore social discipline and moral values serves as a convenient slogan for some of our politicians and religious activists just as it did for some leaders in the past. For readers of this study, the parallels between the experiences of medieval/early modern English people and their own experiences in the present may well create a recurring sense of *déjà vu*. These similarities suggest that knowledge of the past can help to provide a more thoughtful context and perhaps greater human understanding in confronting contemporary problems.

PART I

The history of social regulation

1

The forms of control

Between the Black Death of 1348–9 and the end of the sixteenth century, residents of English communities experienced profound changes in local demographic, economic, and social structures and in the broader legal, political, ideological, and religious world around them. Because many of the disruptions and the new patterns that emerged from them threatened familiar social relationships and traditional economic interactions, they were likely to create problems with misbehavior – either increasing the amount of actual wrongdoing or at least raising concern among respectable people about whatever misconduct did occur. While in many cases wrongdoing must have been handled in informal and hence undocumented ways, village and town leaders sometimes decided to report offenders to local or intermediate-level courts, where they could be publicly named and punished. The surviving records of those courts permit historical study of social regulation, revealing the changing patterns of concern with misconduct in later medieval and early modern England. As was seen in the Introduction, the decades around 1300 witnessed active attention to certain kinds of wrongdoing in both church and manorial courts. Anxiety had dropped by around 1330 and remained low during the central and later decades of the fourteenth century. During the fifteenth and sixteenth centuries, however, the number of reports of misbehavior submitted to legal bodies rose once more, reaching a peak in the decades around 1600. Throughout this extended period, social regulation changed gradually over time because it was organically related to the particular circumstances of individual communities as well as to broader developments.

This chapter begins by examining the forms through which control over misbehavior could be implemented, showing that regulation was shared between a variety of institutions and that the balance of responsibility between them changed over time. It then describes the lesser public courts whose records provide much of the evidence used in later chapters, focusing upon the discretionary agency of the presentment jurors and upon geographical variations in the level of activity of these courts.

Mechanisms of social regulation

Local leaders and other respectable men and women worried by any of the eleven types of wrongdoing included in this study could employ various forms of control. Regulation of misconduct formed part of a complex reticulum designed to resolve conflict and minimize forms of social behavior seen as damaging to the community. Some misdeeds, especially sexual misconduct, were sins in the eyes of the church, so pre-Reformation priests were in a position to administer admonishment and correction privately through the confessional. At a more public though informal level, local channels of communication spread news about any wrongdoing and shaped the community's sense of how serious the problem was and how it might best be tackled. Women were active participants in this formation of "public opinion." They helped to define in practical daily terms what constituted appropriate social behavior for women and for men in their interactions with women; they discussed problematic situations and decided when a case should be brought to the attention of male officials for formal prosecution.[1] For some wrongdoers, simply the realization that people were aware of their actions and that their reputation was imperiled would have been sufficient to bring about improvement, for one's social and economic standing depended upon having a good name. For other offenders, a well-timed reprimand by a more powerful person – the head of the family, a landlord or employer, or a Protestant clergyman – may have carried considerable weight. These informal means cannot be studied in any systematic fashion since they left little evidence in the records.[2]

If personal correction proved insufficient, or if the magnitude of the offence was clearly beyond the scope of private action, the issue might be brought before some kind of an institution authorized to provide a public airing of the problem and to impose punishments. Many groups controlled misbehavior among their own members just as they tried to settle personal disputes between them, including the pre-Reformation

---

[1] Deal, "Whores and Witches," Holmes, "Women: Witnesses and Witches," Sharpe, "Witchcraft and Women," and Amussen, *An Ordered Society*, esp. pp. 130–1.

[2] Such techniques are sometimes mentioned in an ancillary fashion in statements submitted to the central equity courts like Chancery and Requests and in depositions made by parties or witnesses in private suits heard by the church courts.

religious fraternities operating at the parish level and the urban guilds.[3] Proper conduct was also a criterion for receiving assistance from most of the private charitable foundations of the fifteenth and sixteenth centuries.[4] From 1552 onwards, a new weapon was added to the arsenal: as parish officials began to aid legitimately needy residents through payments collected from their wealthier neighbors, they were in a position to refuse relief to anyone whose moral behavior was inadequate or who did not display suitable deference.[5] Able-bodied poor people who refused to work could be sent to bridewells for some mixture of training and punishment as early as the 1550s if they lived in London or a few of the other urban centers; from 1576 a growing number of counties had their own bridewells or houses of correction.[6] Although the full panoply of the Elizabethan Poor Laws was not in place until 1598 (modified slightly in 1601), the preliminary forms of the system provided considerable opportunity for regulation of behavior.

The English legal system too offered mechanisms for dealing with misconduct, at both local and intermediate levels. At the bottom of the system lay two main types of courts: the generally more powerful bodies held within cities and major towns, and the public courts held in smaller places. (Throughout this study, England's urban communities, classified here as six cities and thirty-two larger towns with populations of over c. 3,000 inhabitants, are distinguished from its c. 715 market centers and many thousands of villages.[7]) The lesser public courts consisted of those manor courts with "leet" jurisdiction, the smaller borough courts, and the hundred courts convened by sheriffs for the administrative/legal subdivisions of their counties. Within these bodies juries of established, middling-level residents were sworn to "present" or report problems of concern to the community. While most of the issues were agricultural or economic in nature, some juries between 1370 and 1600 mentioned social misbehavior as well, even though they were not formally empowered to do so. At an intermediate level, two other kinds of courts served larger geographical areas: the church courts, in which churchwardens or other lay officers and the clergyman of the parish submitted reports of offences which were then

[3] See, e.g., McRee, "Religious Gilds and Regulation of Behavior," and Hanawalt and McRee, "The Guilds of *Homo Prudens*"; for conflict resolution, see Chapter 8, note 11 below. Women as well as men were participants in most fraternities.
[4] See Chapter 4, section two below. For two elderly widows removed from an almshouse in (the) Devizes, Wilts. in 1583 for their "abuses and disorderly behavior," see Wilts. RO G20/1/15, fol. 23r.
[5] Slack, *Poverty and Policy*, and McIntosh, "Local Responses to the Poor."
[6] Innes, "Prisons for the Poor."
[7] See the Notes to Appendices 1.1 and 2.1 for how these categories were defined.

prosecuted "ex officio" by the court's convener; and Sessions of the Peace, held by county Justices of the Peace but resting upon information provided by juries and constables from the local communities.[8] (Cities and some of the larger towns had their own Sessions.) These four types of courts worked in tandem to address wrongdoing, though the distribution of authority between them shifted over time. Moreover, their promotion of community well-being through jury reports was reinforced in many cases by their hearing of private suits between individuals, a process intended to resolve conflict peacefully.[9]

The upper stratum of the law played only an indirect role in social regulation. The central courts of the common law system, based in Westminster, did not normally address petty issues like social misbehavior; the Assize justices who came through the counties hearing felonies and other capital crimes rarely dealt with misconduct before the late sixteenth century.[10] The equity courts, functioning as an arm of the crown's prerogative, might be told about wrongdoing in the course of the petitions submitted to them and the resulting hearings, but few forms of social misconduct received their express attention.[11] Parliament of course had the sole right to create statutes, but few laws dealt with social issues nor were they always enforced locally as their framers had intended.[12]

This range of institutions offered choices to people concerned about misbehavior. Individuals who felt themselves personally aggrieved by wrongdoing could select among several options. Let us say that Will-

---

[8] Church courts were normally held for archdeaneries within the dioceses. Another potential institution, the county courts, heard only private suits during the period covered by this study: e.g., PRO SC 2/153/62, SC 2/183/69, and SC 2/200/30, and Palmer, *The County Courts.*

[9] Private suits were heard by many local courts until at least around 1500, and the church courts heard certain types of private disputes as "instance cases." The rise in civil litigation in the central courts during the sixteenth century probably stemmed in part from the declining use of the lesser courts (Brooks, *Pettyfoggers and Vipers*).

[10] Of the eleven offences considered here, the Assize justices became important only in the attack on vagrancy during the Elizabethan period. Otherwise, they heard a few charges of "scandalous words" (all involving attacks on the established church, ministers or prelates, the queen, or her friends) or of "barratry" (nearly all coupled with other crimes); in some areas they dealt with an occasional unlicensed alehouse. See, e.g., the *Calendars of Assize Records* for the Elizabethan period for the counties of Essex, Herts., Kent, Surrey, and Sussex (ed. Cockburn).

[11] See Chapter 4, section two below. Some of the central courts, especially Chancery, may have exerted a limited influence over local court treatment of misconduct in the course of responding to appeals from people who alleged that they had not received proper justice in the lesser courts. (See, e.g., McIntosh, *A Community Transformed*, pp. 335–40.)

[12] See Chapter 3, section four below.

iam's (or Margaret's) social and economic credit was being jeopardized by a malicious rumor about his dishonest practices, spread by a hostile neighbor. William's primary goal would be to get the issue heard and resolved publicly so that his good reputation could be re-established. Although his friends and neighbors might be willing to serve as arbitrators of the dispute, and although his religious fraternity or town guild perhaps offered mechanisms for resolving the conflict, some kind of formal legal action may well have seemed preferable as it offered a more public forum and greater visibility for the clearing of his name. William would then need to decide whether to lodge his grievance in the form of a private suit against the person who was defaming him, a case probably heard by his local village or urban court, or to bring the problem to the official attention of the jurors in that court.[13] If he could persuade the jurors that this instance of verbal wrongdoing was harmful to the community at large, or that his opponent had a history of causing trouble through false speech, they might be willing to name the person for scolding in their formal presentment, thereby achieving still greater publicity together with official punishment. If Mary (or Thomas) faced comparable loss of standing through false statements about her sexual misconduct, she faced similar choices: she could pursue a private suit for defamation in an ecclesiastical court (which dealt with sexual slander), or she could attempt to convince the jurors or churchwardens that this problem was of wider consequence so that her adversary should be included in their public listing of wrongdoing. Occasionally an aggrieved person might resort to one of the central courts.[14] Because private suits, regardless of the venue in which they were heard, were primarily a reflection of the individual concerns of the parties, not necessarily focused upon the well-being of the community as a whole, this study will henceforth concentrate upon misbehavior as reported publicly to the courts.

Local leaders, the kinds of men who served as jurors in the local courts or before county Sessions or were chosen as churchwardens in their parishes, likewise had a number of options when attempting to curtail wrongdoing. The first decision was which offences and people to report. Problems might come to their attention through their own or their families' sources of information or through a complaint submitted by someone else. If the complainant was a person well regarded by his or her peers and had compelling evidence, or if several reliable people mentioned the same issue, jurors/churchwardens were probably pre-

---

[13] See Chapter 3, note 15 below for the forms of action for defamation.
[14] *Select Cases on Defamation* and see Chapter 4, section two below.

pared to consider the case, but the concerns of more marginal members of the community may not have found their way into jury deliberations with equal ease. Other offenders were reported by constables, who had caught them in the act of wrongdoing.[15] After gathering information about these alleged instances of misbehavior, community leaders decided which ones to pursue. Their thinking was presumably affected by the nature of the offence, who the offenders were (their age, whether they were long-term residents of the community or newcomers, their economic condition, and their gender and marital status), and the likelihood that the wrongdoers would respond to the various potential forms of chastisement.

If they felt that a problem should be tackled through the legal system, they had then to decide which institution to use. The local courts had several advantages. They were physically close at hand and functioned directly through information provided by the jurors, who acted as spokesmen for the dominant social values of that community. Set against the benefits of these courts, however, were limitations in their ability to prosecute people who refused to cooperate with their authority or were not residents of that place and, in the case of the smaller places, in the forcefulness of the punishments they could impose. Sometimes, therefore, local officials concluded that it was worth the extra effort of taking misbehavior before a church court or the Sessions. Although bringing an offender before an intermediate court had several drawbacks (one generally had to travel elsewhere to submit the complaint, and it was hard to be sure how the higher officials of the church or the Justices of the Peace who presided over the courts and determined the punishments would react), these institutions had greater authority to compel offenders to appear and could order more emphatic physical or financial penalties. In part because the efficacy of the intermediate courts was attractive to local leaders under certain circumstances, these bodies became increasingly important to the prosecution of wrongdoing over the course of the fifteenth and sixteenth centuries.

An ideal study of social regulation would determine the precise role played over time by each of the four main legal institutions responsible for controlling wrongdoing. If we had long runs of records from the two types of local courts plus the church courts and Sessions of the Peace spread throughout the country during the later medieval and early modern periods, we could analyze in a systematic fashion the particu-

---

[15] Occasionally constables or other officers submitted their own presentments directly to the court.

lar offences addressed by each category of court, assess how energetic each institution was in addressing misconduct, examine chronological and regional patterns, and trace the distribution of authority between the bodies.

Unfortunately, for three of these courts, the nature and quantity of the surviving records make a large-scale study of changing responses to wrongdoing difficult or impossible. Some of the larger urban centers have very rich archives, but the documents do not lend themselves to the formulation of a broad account of concern. Social regulation was often dispersed between many different institutions in urban areas, so it is hard to trace the complete pattern; the type of evidence is seldom consistent between communities, nor do the surviving records necessarily span the later medieval/early modern eras. Although some of the fine secondary studies of individual cities or towns include discussion of social regulation, they are by definition specific. At the intermediate level, we have a number of sets of church court records, but many document the activities of archiepiscopal institutions rather than the courts held within archdeaneries that were primarily responsible for supervising lay behavior; relatively few of the latter span the interval between 1370 and 1600, nor are they well distributed throughout the country.[16] For Sessions of the Peace, evidence exists only about urban Sessions until 1538, apart from a few scattered county records from the second half of the fourteenth century; it is likely, however, that the types of offences heard by urban Sessions in earlier periods provide a reasonable indication of what their county brethren were doing since all Sessions had similar jurisdictions. During the second half of the sixteenth century continuous runs of some county Sessions become available. Existing secondary accounts of particular church courts or Sessions do not provide interpretable quantitative evidence about changing levels of concern or cover a long enough period.[17]

It is only with respect to the fourth kind of court, the public bodies

---

[16] See, e.g., Woodcock, *Medieval Ecclesiastical Courts*, Owen, *The Records of the Established Church* and "Ecclesiastical Jurisdiction," and Donahue, ed., *The Records of the Medieval Ecclesiastical Courts*. Visitation articles and injunctions, another potentially valuable source, likewise provide limited and uneven coverage.

[17] For studies that include discussion of social conduct, see Wunderli, *London Church Courts*, Marchant, *The Puritans and the Church Courts*, Houlbrooke, *Church Courts and the People*, and Ingram, *Church Courts, Sex and Marriage*; Sharpe, *Crime in Seventeenth-Century England*, and Woods, *Forging a Culture of Law and Order*, which makes effective use of central court records in the absence of direct local evidence. A few of these works give some indication of the number of cases heard over time, but they do not relate those figures to population levels, making them impossible to assess. See Chapter 2 for a discussion of this methodological problem.

held in England's smaller communities, that we find sufficient documentary evidence to support a systematic analysis over time. The
courts of manors, the smaller boroughs, and hundreds not only shouldered the primary burden of social regulation through at least the
middle of the sixteenth century, they also left a vast body of largely
untouched records about how local leaders perceived wrongdoing and
attempted to control it. This project will therefore focus upon social
regulation as implemented by the lesser courts.

Though a full study of the other three types of institutions could not
be attempted, I have prepared a rough overview of what sorts of
wrongdoing they were addressing at various stages within the later
medieval and early modern periods. For urban areas, I sampled evidence starting as early as the later fourteenth century from two of the
six communities classified here as cities and from nineteen of the
thirty-two towns.[18] A few of these records contained court presentments but most were the orders and memoranda in urban "Assembly
Books." Since directives were not always carried out, this evidence may
exaggerate the amount of actual correction in urban courts. For the
church courts, I sampled the offences reported by lay officials and/or
the parish clergy from twenty-eight different courts between 1435 and
1599[19]; for Justices of the Peace, including both county and city bodies, I

---

[18] See Appendix 1.1 for the method and sources used. By the end of Elizabeth's reign,
urban institutions were dealing, or had dealt, with all eleven offences studied here. Of
the Disharmony cluster, scolding was an issue from the later fourteenth century
onwards, with declining concern after the late fifteenth century. Eavesdropping and
nightwalking were likewise present from the earliest records used, but here attention
dropped after around 1520. In the Disorder cluster, sexual problems were addressed
vigorously until around 1500, with a pronounced drop thereafter. Alehouses too were
of concern even before 1400, with an apparent decline in interest between 1460 and
1540 and a rise again later in the century. People said to be badly governed were
mentioned from the mid-fifteenth century through the end of that century. Offences in
the Poverty cluster emerged more gradually. Hedgebreaking appeared first around
1440 and remained at a low level from then on. An occasional vagabond was mentioned in the later fourteenth and earlier fifteenth centuries, but serious concern started
only about 1480, remaining high through the end of Elizabeth's reign. Subtenants
emerged as an active issue after 1560. Gaming was mentioned now and then prior to
around 1460, when concern rose sharply, staying high through the end of the sixteenth
century.

[19] See Appendix 1.2 for the method and sources used. Private suits ("instance cases") are
not included in this analysis. Of the eleven offences, church courts were dealing with
five by the end of the sixteenth century. They appear to have paid relatively little
attention to scolding and/or defamation until around 1460, with some interest thereafter and a higher level during Elizabeth's reign. All the records used indicate strong
concern with sexual misdeeds; drunkenness received occasional notice after around
1500, with more at the very end of the sixteenth century. Loose descriptions of being

sampled presentments from twenty-eight Sessions between 1351 and 1599.[20]

When material from this exploratory survey is coupled with the far more comprehensive information from the lesser local courts to be discussed below, we see pronounced changes over time both in the types of wrongdoing considered by the various institutions and in the balance of authority between the courts. During the later fourteenth century, when concern with misbehavior was relatively low in most settings, the courts at the bottom of the system were responsible for the great majority of whatever regulation did occur. Some of the large urban centers were reporting the offences in the Disharmony cluster plus sexual wrongdoing, alehouses, and gaming; these issues were less prevalent in the smaller communities, where only 14 percent of all courts under observation reported any social problems at all. (See Appendix 3.1.) The church courts were presumably attending to sexual issues as they did both before and after this period, and Sessions of the Peace heard a few cases of nightwalking.

Attention to misbehavior mounted across the fifteenth century. By the 1450s urban institutions and the lesser public courts alike were dealing at least occasionally with all the offences studied here except for admitting subtenants. In the smaller communities the fraction of courts addressing wrongdoing rose from 17 percent in the 1400s–10s to 38 percent in the 1440s–50s. During this period the church courts started hearing an occasional report of gaming during services and some began to deal with scolding/defamation, while Sessions of the Peace added

badly governed appeared around 1500, remaining at a fairly low level for the rest of that century. Playing games during services received a rare mention as early as the mid-fifteenth century and was reported now and then from around 1520 onwards.

[20] See Appendix 1.3 for the method and sources used. Sessions were hearing all eleven offences by the end of the sixteenth century. Within the Disharmony cluster, scolding began to appear around 1480 and was mentioned quite commonly until around 1560, when the level declined. Nightwalking was of major concern from the 1350s through about 1540, after which it virtually disappeared. Of the Disorder cluster, sexual misconduct or bastardy was reported frequently from around 1440 onwards, with an apparent drop between 1540 and 1580. Problems with alehouses or drunkenness were seen occasionally around the mid-fifteenth century but became more common during the sixteenth, with a great rise in the last two decades. Charges of being badly governed were frequent between 1460 and 1520 and continued for the rest of the sixteenth century at a lower level. Within the Poverty cluster, hedgebreaking was not mentioned until around 1560 and then only at a very low level; vagabonds were of occasional concern between 1440 and 1520, with attention rising from then until the end of the century. Subtenants were not an issue until the final two decades, and then only minimally. Gaming was a major problem from 1460 through 1540, with a gradual decline thereafter.

sexual problems, alehouses, and vagabonds to their range of offences. After around 1460, the proportion of urban communities reporting concern mounted though no new offences were added. The lesser public courts now received a few reports of subtenants, and the total fraction of these courts that reported social issues increased slightly. Church courts became actively involved with scolding/defamation, while Sessions added scolding, being badly governed, and gaming to their jurisdictional range.

The patterns visible in the sixteenth century are more complex. Attention to offences in the Disharmony cluster declined after the middle of the century in urban communities, the lesser courts, and Sessions alike. Although several secondary studies describe rising numbers of presentments and/or private suits for defamation in the church courts during the later Elizabethan period, and although actions of "trespass on the case" alleging defamation heard by the common law courts may also have increased, it seems unlikely that those changes were sufficient to offset the loss of interest in the public consequences of scolding within the very large number of other courts.[21] Concern with problems in the Disorder cluster remained high across the century in urban areas, though not always at the level of the late fifteenth-century peak, but dropped somewhat in the lesser courts. Church courts began to deal with drunkenness early in the sixteenth century, and secondary accounts suggest more ecclesiastical concern with sexual problems at the end of this century than before.[22] Sessions addressed all the problems in this cluster, with generally rising concern especially during the Elizabethan period. Increased attention to issues of Disorder in the intermediate-level courts and continued concern in urban areas almost certainly served to counterbalance the decline in the lesser courts. It is only with respect to the Poverty cluster that we see increasing anxiety among both kinds of lesser courts and Sessions right across the century. Urban institutions began dealing with subtenants in the Elizabethan period, and by the end of the century a high fraction of all larger communities expressed serious worry about problems associated with

---

[21] E.g., Haigh, "Slander and the Church Courts," and *Select Cases on Defamation*. See Chapter 2 below for the impossibility of interpreting a rising number of cases in the absence of information about population. Further, because private actions of defamation were intended primarily to clear the individual name and reputation of the plaintiff, not to restore harmony to the community as a whole, they do not form an exact parallel to public reports of scolding. For a parallel weakening of the emphasis upon community harmony within the broader ideological context, see Chapter 8, section one below.

[22] Ingram, *Church Courts, Sex and Marriage*, chs. 7–9, which poses the same problems of assessment as do reports of increased scolding.

the poor. Of the lesser courts, the fraction reporting issues within this cluster rose from 24 percent in the 1500s–10s to 47 percent by the 1580s–90s. While such issues never came within the jurisdiction of the church courts, Sessions began to accept reports of hedgebreaking after 1560 and of subtenants after 1580; attention to vagabonds also rose sharply in the Elizabethan period. Gaming was a major problem in urban areas until at least 1560, while in the smaller places concern continued to mount throughout the century. Church courts heard only occasional reports of gaming during services, but Sessions maintained a keen interest throughout Elizabeth's reign.

Even this cursory account makes clear the pronounced chronological changes in the particular kinds of offences heard by the various courts and in the distribution of authority between them. It also demonstrates that as early as the 1460s–70s local leaders were able to choose between their own courts, ecclesiastical bodies, and Sessions of the Peace as vehicles for addressing scolding/defamation and sexual problems; in dealing with nightwalking, alehouses, people who were badly govern-ed, vagabonds, and gaming they could turn either to local courts or the Sessions. By the later sixteenth century nearly all offences could poten-tially be heard by either local or intermediate courts, emphasizing the agency of community officials in deciding how to prosecute those offenders deemed worthy of public attention and correction.

A final component must be added to this survey of the forms of control: the part played by political institutions.[23] From the late fif-teenth century the crown was potentially in a position to influence local attitudes and sometimes the actions of lower and intermediate courts through its proclamations, orders that carried the force of law until Parliament next met. From the 1520s–30s onwards, a flow of dramati-cally worded royal proclamations on such problems as vagrancy, joined by comparable rhetoric in some Parliamentary statutes, may have increased the emotional charge with which these issues were discussed around the country. The expansion of political and adminis-trative control at the county level contributed to closer supervision of the actions of the lesser courts while also involving in the government a growing number of people of higher social status – gentry and merchants especially – rather than the economically comfortable but modestly placed men who had always dominated local bodies. A willingness to assume office among wealthier, more powerful people was presumably influenced by their increasing awareness that social misbehavior and the problems of poverty were potential sources not

---

[23] For a fuller discussion, see Chapter 5 below.

only of conflict within individual communities but also of wider public disorder. At the county level such concern manifested itself in the expanded role of JPs sitting in formal Sessions and in a new willingness among the Justices to act individually – assisting local constables, for example, by requiring potential offenders to post bond, backed by two other people, guaranteeing that they would stay out of trouble for a stipulated period of time.[24] Similar worries within the House of Commons contributed to the social legislation enacted by some sixteenth-century Parliaments. Members of the nobility may have become more conscious of social problems through debates in the House of Lords or through holding county offices like the Lord Lieutenancy. Control over misbehavior by around 1600 was thus simultaneously more intense and more widely dispersed among various institutions and social groups than it had been during the later fourteenth century.[25] Yet this situation resulted from an extended process of development and, as we will see, was marked by significant regional differences.

The lesser public courts

Because England's lesser courts have received little scholarly attention, general historical accounts do not give adequate credit to the key roles they played in the lives of many medieval and early modern people. Manorial courts, the most numerous of these bodies, provided a venue within which the lord could enforce his seigneurial rights, disputes between the tenants could be resolved, and issues of wider concern to the community raised and addressed. Most manors had their own individual courts, but in some cases groups of them were pulled together into composite units held as lay Honours/Liberties or by ecclesiastical bodies, with a common court for the whole unit. Similar sorts of functions were performed by the courts of boroughs, most of which were located in small market centers with fewer than 3,000 people rather than in major urban communities, and by the courts of the hundreds (termed "wapentakes" in some parts of the country). Since the majority of English people lived within areas served by these bodies, the courts' records provide a valuable but underutilized source of information about the past. The material about social regulation to be presented in Chapters 3, 6, and 7 derives from these records, so we need to understand the lesser courts and their operation and be aware of

---

[24] While bonds for good bearing had been used in the past, their numbers rose sharply during the later sixteenth century.

[25] For a calendar of all legal records from a single county at the beginning of the seventeenth century, see *Kent at Law, 1602: The County Jurisdiction* and the planned successor volumes on other kinds of courts.

pronounced regional variations in their vitality during the sixteenth century.

Ordinary manor courts, known as "baronial" courts, had three main duties.[26] They functioned as vehicles for seigneurial control – the setting in which lords exercised their economic and social rights with respect to their tenants. Based upon information provided by juries of the tenants, medieval courts recorded such information as the transfer of land and the payments that accompanied it, failure to perform labor services on the lord's own pieces of land within the manor, and fees paid by villein tenants for permission to marry, enter the clergy, or leave the manor. These seigneurial functions gradually diminished as a result of the changes initiated by the 1348–9 plague. The lord was also obliged to provide a forum within which local people could bring suit against each other concerning disputes stemming from problems like unpaid debts and animals that damaged another person's crops. In this sense baronial courts operated as the bottom layer of the common law system. Finally, by the fourteenth century even the most limited manorial courts swore in juries which reported on agricultural problems within the community, such as people who had put their animals into the common fields outside the designated times. Manorial juries also elected officials to function between court sessions, men who acted usually in a capacity required by the lord (such as being his bailiff) but sometimes in a shared agricultural vein (such as being the common shepherd).

Some manor courts, however, as well as most of the borough courts and all the hundred courts had additional rights that may be described as public or "leet" jurisdiction. Leet courts rested upon presentment juries, a body of twelve or more men sworn to "present" or submit a collective report concerning problems of interest to the community as a whole. (Ancestor to the modern grand jury, the presentment jury as an institution derived primarily from the practice initiated by the Assize of Clarendon of 1166 whereby jurors from the townships and hundreds were sworn at the tourns held by sheriffs to report upon criminal offences; presentment juries became common in manorial leet courts during the later thirteenth and early fourteenth centuries.[27]) Leet courts

---

[26] There is no thorough recent study of manor courts and their public jurisdiction. For earlier works, all of which focus on the pre-plague period, see *Select Pleas in Manorial and Other Seignorial Courts*, Hearnshaw, *Leet Jurisdiction*, Morris, *The Frankpledge System*, and Homans, *English Villagers*; see also Beckerman, "Customary Law." For the later period, see Crowley, "Frankpledge and Leet Jurisdiction" and, for the sixteenth century, McIntosh, "Social Change and Tudor Manorial Leets."

[27] See Dawson, *A History of Lay Judges*, and Beckerman, "Procedural Innovation and Institutional Change."

had a broad jurisdictional range. They were responsible for punishing
those who broke the king's peace, electing constables to keep order
between court sessions. They enforced the Assize of Bread and Ale, an
order instituted originally in 1266–7 and updated periodically thereafter that specified the weight, size, quality, and price of certain foodstuffs and beverages throughout the country.[28] Keeping highways
passable and bridges in adequate repair was another duty. In many
parts of the country, they also oversaw the operation of the tithing
groups or frankpledges, groups of men collectively responsible for the
good behavior of their members.

   Although public courts were convened by the steward of the manor,
the bailiff of the borough, or the sheriff or his deputy within the
hundred, the presiding officer exercised little control over their proceedings. Once a jury was sworn, the convener read aloud the
"charge," the list of items upon which it was supposed to report.[29] The
jurors then deliberated, submitting their list of problems and offenders
(which had to be unanimous) either later that session or at the next
meeting. People accused of certain kinds of wrongdoing were in theory
free to challenge the presentment, bringing in oath helpers to swear to
their honesty, but in practice this almost never happened, so the presentment functioned in effect as a conviction. At the end of the session, a
small group of men elected by the jurors or appointed by the court's
convener determined the punishment to be imposed upon wrongdoers.
In most courts and periods, and for most types of offences, the penalty
was a small money fine, of anywhere between a few pence and a
shilling or two. Under some circumstances, however, larger cash fines
or more physical means of punishment were employed.

   Power within these public courts thus lay in the hands of the men
who formed the presentment juries and were selected as officers. They
were normally able to get their own judgments accepted, to see that
what mattered to them became policy for the community.[30] The rolls
seldom specify how jurors were chosen, but local studies indicate that
they were the heads of established tenant families, either holding a
comfortable unit of land as a yeoman or husbandman or working as a

---

[28] Special officers called ale tasters were chosen to supervise the manufacture and sale of
such wares.
[29] For examples of the articles contained in charges, see Hearnshaw, *Leet Jurisdiction*,
pp. 43–64, Beckerman, "The Articles of Presentment," *Modus tenend[i] cur[iam] baron[is]
cum visu[m] franem [sic] plegii* (1510, STC #7706), *Modus tenendi curiam baronis, cum visum
franci plegii* (1536, STC #7713), and Adames, *The Order of Keeping a Courte Leet*.
[30] For this "political" role, see Goheen, "Peasant Politics?"

crafts- or tradesman.[31] They in turn elected, usually out of their own ranks, the other local officials. Shouldering increasing responsibility for the common life of their community during the later medieval period as seigneurial control over the courts declined, these men may be seen as predecessors of the even more autonomous leaders who shaped local life in England and the colonies during the seventeenth and eighteenth centuries. Though jurors were asked to think in terms of the good of the whole community, to report people and problems that disrupted its tranquillity or order, their presentments were of course influenced by their own attitudes and goals. Their decisions and the reasons they gave for prosecuting offenders thus open for us a window into the concerns of middling-level local people.

Of particular importance for this study, local court jurors sometimes went beyond their charge, the list of specific offences about which they were instructed to report, by addressing types of social misbehavior that were not assigned to their courts for correction at all. Few of the eleven offences considered here appeared in sample lists of the charge prior to the 1590s and some were never included at all. If they were mentioned, their first reference usually came several decades *after* such problems started to be reported to the lesser courts.[32] The common law, Parliamentary statutes, and royal proclamations rarely addressed social wrongdoing, and if they did, responsibility for controlling it was assigned to bodies other than the lesser courts. Sexual misconduct violated the church's law, but ecclesiastical institutions, not the lower secular courts, were supposed to deal with any transgressions. In reporting most forms of misconduct, jurors were therefore on extremely shaky legal ground.

We do not know how they defended their widespread decision to proceed with social regulation in the absence of formal jurisdictional authority. It is not simply that they were ignorant of what the law said,

---

[31] For their status, see, e.g., the works cited in note 44 below. Only men were supposed to be sworn onto these juries, but in a rare exception from 1585 Joan Craddock, widow, was elected to represent her frankpledge in the manor court of Newcastle-under-Lyme, Staffs. during the following year (PRO DL 30/237/22).

[32] A charge from c. 1340 names only tavern-haunters out of the various types of misconduct in this study; charges from c. 1400 and 1510 include only nightwalkers (Hearnshaw, *Leet Jurisdiction*, p. 60; Beckerman, "The Articles of Presentment," and *Modus tenend[i]" cur[iam] baron[is] cum visu[m] franem [sic] plegii*, [1510, STC #7706], fol. B4r). Over the course of the sixteenth century the list expanded: scolds, eavesdroppers, and nightwalkers were mentioned in 1536, and vagabonds, keepers of brothels and gaming houses, and hedgebreakers by 1593 (*Modus tenendi curiam baronis, cum visum franci plegii* [1536, STC #7713], fol. 6r–v, and Adames, *The Order of Keeping a Courte Leet*, pp. 12–18).

for when they presented people for playing certain games declared illegal by Parliament they were careful to mention the statutory prohibition. In some cases they may have been emulating other courts, believing that since the church courts, Sessions, and/or urban bodies had the right to deal with certain kinds of wrongdoing, it was legitimate for their community's court to act in a similar fashion. Because the jurors were often key figures in their parishes as well, they may have seen a parallel with those institutions, which during the later medieval period were assuming a variety of new practical as well as spiritual roles.[33] Or perhaps the forms of social wrongdoing resembled so closely other misdeeds that were assigned to the lesser courts for correction that jurors felt entitled to present them. Did they argue, for example, that since they were charged with punishing people for physical attacks, why should they not report equivalently damaging verbal attacks as well? Some jurors may have accepted that their punitive role had no authorization but decided to tackle misconduct anyway because it constituted such a peril to their community.

In an effort to strengthen the legality of their presentments and the severity of the punishments which they could impose, some of the lesser public courts reworked and expanded a procedure which was to be of considerable significance for later English and colonial history, the byelaw.[34] By this technique, jurors at a given court session proscribed a certain type of behavior from that time forward, specifying also the penalty to be imposed upon any subsequent offenders. Thereafter they were free to present and punish people accordingly. Whereas byelaws binding upon all members of the community had been used in some manorial courts for tenurial or agricultural matters as early as the late thirteenth century, their application to social problems and the imposition of more severe penalties began to emerge only around 1460.[35] During every duodecade between 1500 and 1599, 16–20 percent of all courts under observation in this study passed byelaws for the regulation of social misconduct. It seems remarkable that local bodies were allowed to develop this procedure so extensively and with no outside

[33] E.g., Scarisbrick, *The Reformation and the English People*, Duffy, *The Stripping of the Altars*, Burgess and Kümin, "Penitential Bequests and Parish Regimes," and Kümin, *The Shaping of a Community*.
[34] Byelaws proved ideally suited to the needs of small, often isolated communities of English settlers in other parts of the world. See, e.g., Konig, *Law and Society*.
[35] For the earlier history of byelaws, see the pioneering works of Ault, "Some Early Village By-laws," *The Self-Directing Activities of Village Communities*, and "Village Assemblies in Medieval England," Cam, "The Community of the Vill," and Beckerman, "Customary Law." While manorial lords may have promoted the passage of byelaws for matters that affected their seigneurial rights, there is no evidence that they influenced ordinances concerning social wrongdoing.

supervision, for byelaws gave to a court the power to create its own local statutes. Although such ordinances posed a potential threat to the legislative authority of Parliament and to the upper- and intermediate-level courts of the common law, there seems to have been scant objection to or even discussion of these new local weapons, probably because they were being used to address issues which more powerful people too viewed as disruptive.

In a parallel move, some of the most active local courts began in the later fifteenth century to utilize forms of punishment more effective than the traditional small cash fine. They turned first to forms of confinement accompanied by display and probably ridicule. Males might be sent to the stocks or pillory, which locked them to a frame or post as they stood in some public place, while women found guilty of verbal abuse were sometimes sentenced to sit in a tumbrel, later called a cuckingstool.[36] In the most categorical of all punishments, a rising number of lesser courts ejected permanently from their communities those people found guilty of grievous social offences or whose presence seemed especially worrisome. Eviction emerged around 1460, and between 1500 and 1539, 12–14 percent of the courts studied here used it as a weapon in each duodecade, with somewhat lower levels later in the century. While we cannot trace what happened to people who were banished, it seems likely that in an era of limited transmission of news from one place to another, even on an official level, miscreants had a reasonable chance of starting life afresh in a new setting if they chose – or of resuming their wrongdoing elsewhere. Like other poor migrants, many of them probably ended up in the cities and larger towns.

Even this brief introduction should establish that regulation of social misconduct by the lesser public courts was by no means a simple "top down" phenomenon. If a type of behavior was causing trouble in their community, local jurors reported it, whether or not they had been authorized to do so. They were not dutifully carrying out the instructions issued by their superiors, for rarely had such orders been given. For some offences, like scolding, being badly governed, and those within the Poverty cluster, the lesser courts began to tackle problems well before intermediate-level institutions took notice of them; the decision of the church courts and Sessions to prosecute such misconduct may indeed have been affected by the local courts' activities. Although Parliament rarely took any notice of behavioral problems, when it did pass a statute, as in the case of gaming, local jurors were highly selective in their enforcement of it.[37] It must also be emphasized

---

[36] See Chapter 3, section one, and Chapter 4 below for tumbrels/cuckingstools.
[37] See Chapter 3, section four below.

that Parliamentary legislation almost invariably followed rather than preceded the beginnings of vigorous regulation at the local level. While studies of government, law, and politics at the national and county levels commonly assume that influence moved outwards and downwards from central institutions, this material reminds us that local communities often confronted new problems first and generated practical responses to them that subsequently served as models for policy at a higher level.[38]

But neither is it true that local courts operated in a vacuum, free from outside influences. Local jurors seem to have been aware of the jurisdiction and punishments of other kinds of courts, copying them when it served their own interests. Their willingness to attempt control over sexual wrongdoing, for example, may have been influenced by their own experiences as parish officers testifying before the church courts or by what they heard from those who did serve as churchwardens or sidesmen. As jurors before Sessions they may have observed that nightwalking was being prosecuted there; when visiting larger urban communities they perhaps learned that eavesdropping and rowdy alehouses were reported to those courts and that forms of physical punishment were used. Moreover, at least by the later sixteenth century, changes in the broader political and ideological climate presumably had some effect upon jurors' decisions about what and whom to report.[39]

The role of these jurors fails to conform to several suggestions made by theorists using center–periphery analysis to study the process of state-building during the early modern period. Arguing that social integration (initiated by central authorities) was a precondition for the emergence of the nation state, such scholars propose that local jurymen and tax collectors served as mediators between individual communities and authority at the national level; through this process members of the peripheries came to accept values defined at the center as part of their own self-images.[40] Our study offers scant evidence of changing values or identities among the lesser courts' jurors prior to 1600. Further, targeted transmission of ideas about the desired legal and social order from central authorities to local leaders was rare before the late sixteenth century and occurred within the intermediate courts rather than at the level of villages and market centers. Jurors or constables

---

[38] This process is clearly visible in the evolution of poor relief: see Slack, *Poverty and Policy*, and McIntosh, "Local Responses to the Poor."

[39] See Chapters 5 and 8 below.

[40] See, e.g., Ankarloo and Henningsen, eds., *Early Modern European Witchcraft*, esp. the intro. and ch. 5, and Tilly, ed., *The Formation of National States*, esp. Rokkan's "Dimensions of State Formation."

summoned before county Sessions of the Peace and parish representatives called before the church courts came into more immediate contact with representatives of central institutions and by the later Elizabethan period were exposed to explicit ideological messages generated by the national government or church.[41] If altered values/identities among local court jurors and deliberate social integration were both limited prior to 1600, it may be that state-building in England should be seen primarily as a development of the later seventeenth and eighteenth centuries, resulting from very different causes.[42]

Since the lesser public courts played such a vital role in the regulation of misconduct, it is particularly fortunate that their records survive in abundance. Spread among England's public record offices – county, national, and local – as well as in private collections, vast quantities of manuscript rolls and later of court books on parchment or paper have been preserved, for thousands of courts.[43] In some cases only bits and pieces still exist, while for others we have continuous records over hundreds of years, a few starting as early as the mid-thirteenth century and occasionally extending into the twentieth. These records are not instantly accessible to the potential user. Written normally in highly abbreviated medieval Latin, daunting at first but decipherable with practice, they are entered in a variety of local hands which become progressively less uniform and often messier as one moves into the later fifteenth and early sixteenth centuries before improving again thereafter. By the mid-Elizabethan period, some presentments were recorded in English. Local court documents have been fruitfully employed in studies of particular communities or topics. Historical demographers have used manor court rolls to trace changes in population over time within certain villages, while social historians have examined such topics as kinship relations and provisions for the elderly and orphans.[44] Scholars interested in economic issues have delved into

---

[41] See, e.g., the speeches delivered by Sir William Lambarde as Custos Rotulorum of Kent to Quarter Sessions juries during the 1580s–90s: *William Lambarde and Local Government*.

[42] As argued by Brewer, *The Sinews of Power*.

[43] A survey of these records for the medieval period was prepared at the University of Birmingham by Judith Cripps and Janet Williamson, under the direction of R. H. Hilton (see the following note); they can also be approached through the manorial listings of the National Registry of Archives in Quality Court, Chancery Lane, London, arranged by county.

[44] Here as below, only a few examples are given for each type of study. For demography, Razi, *Life, Marriage and Death*, and Poos, *A Rural Society*; for social topics, Richard M. Smith, "Kin and Neighbors," and Elaine Clark, "Some Aspects of Social Security" and "The Custody of Children." More generally, see Razi and Smith, eds., *Medieval Society and the Manor Court*, which includes as an appendix the Birmingham listing of medieval manor court rolls.

these manuscripts in pursuit of information on landholding patterns and local credit networks.[45] Other research explores local power structures and gender issues within individual communities.[46] Court records of some of the smaller boroughs have been studied in similar fashion, but the hundred courts have received no historical attention in this period.[47]

Previous research has not, however, taken full advantage of the potential of the records left by the lesser public courts. In a geographic sense, nearly all the work done thus far has focused on a single community or small group of them; only a few scholars have utilized sources from more than a single area, and their attention was not directed primarily at regional variations.[48] Moreover, most earlier projects examined places in the Midlands, East Anglia, or the Southeast, a concentration which has led to the erroneous assumption that patterns observed in those areas pertained throughout the country. The broader vantage-point offered by this study, based upon information from every county in England, demonstrates that very different patterns were present in the West, Southwest, and North.[49] In chronological terms, many scholars have wrongly concluded that local court records are of little value after c. 1400 or 1450 and that the courts were largely moribund by c. 1500. It is true that over the course of the later fourteenth and fifteenth centuries, as the influence of the lords weakened, the rolls become less useful in studying elements of seigneurial control. The post-plague records also provide progressively less detail about the pleadings in private suits, statements that furnish such important material for economic and social historians prior to 1348–9; in the sixteenth century few courts recorded private suits at all, though some continued to hear them.[50] But in the area of public business most local bodies remained active into the sixteenth century and sometimes right

---

[45] E.g., P. D. A. Harvey, ed., *The Peasant Land Market*, Elaine Clark, "Debt Litigation," and McIntosh, "Money Lending."

[46] The first works to tackle the former were prepared by J. A. Raftis and his students at the Pontifical Institute of Mediaeval Studies in Toronto: e.g., Raftis, *Warboys*, Britton, *The Community of the Vill*, E. B. DeWindt, *Land and People*, and Anne DeWindt, "Peasant Power Structures." For the latter, see, e.g., Bennett, *Women in the Medieval English Countryside*.

[47] E.g., Hilton, "Small Town Society," and Raftis, *A Small Town*.

[48] E.g., Elaine Clark and Hilton: see notes 44 and 47 above.

[49] For evidence that private suits were still being heard in some manor courts around 1600 even if not recorded on the rolls, see McIntosh, *A Community Transformed*, pp. 301–3.

[50] See Map 2.1 and note 11 to Chapter 6 for the counties included within the regions defined here.

through the Elizabethan period. This continuity of public jurisdiction allows us to bridge the gap between the main bodies of medieval and early modern records, particularly the documentary hole that renders many aspects of fifteenth-century life obscure. Since we have almost no records other than tax assessments that allow us to examine developments on a comparative basis across the country during these centuries, it is exciting to identify a rich new source.

For East Anglia, the Southeast, and the lower and central Midlands, this research supports what we have learned from previous studies of particular communities or courts. The public courts of manors, boroughs, and hundreds alike were generally titled Views of Frankpledge, while sessions that combined public and baronial matters were often termed General Courts.[51] At public sessions the tithingmen or Chief Pledges of the tithings normally constituted the presentment juries, although the jurors could also be described as "the twelve men sworn for the king" (a body that might in practice include more than just a dozen members). The common historical impression that the activity of public courts declined across the sixteenth century is substantiated by manorial and hundred courts from this part of England: most of them were carrying out little or no leet business by 1600. They might have had a surge of activity in the later fifteenth century and in some cases a burst of energy in the 1520s–30s, but by the end of Elizabeth's reign their enthusiasm was gone. This was not the result of any formal restriction of their jurisdictional rights – they were still allowed to present and punish the full range of public business, but they seldom chose to do so. Because no higher courts cared whether they were active or not, there was no pressure on them to continue in the public sphere. Hence they subsided into simple manorial courts, alongside the traditional "baronial" institutions that had never enjoyed fuller powers. By the end of the sixteenth century they might still deal with an occasional matter of local agricultural interest and enforce the Assize of Bread and Ale in desultory fashion, but otherwise they were prepared to let the church courts and Sessions of the Peace attend to any problems within their territory.

This general decline in public activity included issues of social misbehavior. As will be discussed more fully in Chapters 6 and 7, these regions contained very few local courts that were dealing aggressively with misconduct after c. 1560, and by the end of the sixteenth century they showed unusually low interest in each of the three clusters of

---

[51] The term Leet court (or *Leta*) was sometimes used in Cambs., Essex, Norf., and Suff., while courts in Lincs. and Notts., like their northern neighbors, might be designated Great Courts or Tourns.

offences. Barely more than a third of the courts in this part of England passed byelaws about wrongdoing between 1370 and 1600. The relative passivity of these courts by the later sixteenth century may be linked both to the early demise of manors and hundreds as institutions in the region and to the strong role assumed by the intermediate-level courts. Borough courts remained more vigorous, as did many public courts of all kinds in Lincolnshire, Derbyshire, and Nottinghamshire, some of which became more active during Elizabeth's reign.[52]

Divergent patterns are apparent in other parts of the country. In the West and Southwest, a wider range of terms was employed for the public courts and their jurors.[53] In the West/Southwest, some lesser leet courts remained energetic throughout the sixteenth century. Many courts in Wiltshire, Somerset, Devon, and Cornwall, as well as in Gloucestershire, Herefordshire, Staffordshire, and Shropshire, were dealing vigorously with a wide array of public issues until 1600, sometimes expanding their involvement across the sixteenth century. By the Elizabethan period the region contained an unusually large fraction of courts that reported social wrongdoing, and nearly half of all courts studied in these areas passed byelaws about misconduct. It is clear that during the sixteenth century the lesser public courts shouldered a greater share of the entire burden of social regulation in the West/Southwest than did their counterparts in the Midlands/Southeast.

In the North and Northwest too, the lesser public courts maintained their vitality. Virtually all the courts studied in Cumberland, Durham, Lancashire, Northumberland, Westmorland, and Yorkshire were actively engaged in public matters during the Elizabethan period, in some cases more so than in the years around 1500. We encounter interesting variations in terminology and in specific areas of jurisdiction as well.[54]

[52] This includes not only manor and borough courts but also hundred courts, which remained lively in Derby. and Notts.

[53] While View of Frankpledge was sometimes used, they were more commonly described as Legal courts or Legal hundreds, Courts leet, Tourns, Halmotes, or Law hundreds. The jurors were similarly given varied titles: the inquisition, the homage, the twelve men named/sworn for the king, or the free jurors.

[54] Yorks. resembled its southern neighbors in calling a few of its public courts Views of Frankpledge, but the others were Great Courts, Courts with leet, or Tourns; the composite courts of Durham and Lancs. labeled themselves Halmotes. In courts not designated as Views, the jurors were normally called the inquisition or just labeled by township or area. The three northernmost counties used no special terminology of any kind for public courts: all manorial bodies were simply designated as Courts (or occasionally Great Courts), at some of which presentment juries were sworn to report on public issues. Further, courts in Cumb. and Westml. which carried out all other types of public business did not handle enforcement of the Assize of Bread and Ale.

By the end of Elizabeth's reign courts in this area displayed an utterly unparalleled level of concern with the Disharmony cluster. The North also saw the highest use of byelaws for misconduct, with more than half of the courts passing such ordinances. The unusually vigorous role of these courts presumably stemmed from such factors as the different systems of landholding found in the North, including border tenure, the presence of powerful ecclesiastical lords who enjoyed unusual legal and political as well as spiritual rights, and the comparable lay influence of the duchy of Lancaster and the palatinate of Chester.

When the experiences of the individual regions are aggregated to the national level, we see that increasing attention to misconduct in local courts of the West, Southwest, and North more than offset the growing lassitude of those located in the Midlands, East Anglia, and Southeast. Despite the fact that the latter areas account for about three-fifths of all the courts included in this project, concern with wrongdoing rose gradually over the course of the fifteenth and sixteenth centuries for the country as a whole. Whereas only 14–17 percent of all courts under observation reported any social offences during the decades on either side of 1400, the figure increased gradually from 31 percent to 39–40 percent between 1420 and 1499 (see Graph 3.12 and Appendix 3.1). In the 1500s–10s, 47 percent of the courts under observation reported people for one or more of these offences, a value that rose throughout the century to a peak of 59 percent in the 1580s–90s. Problems with social harmony, good order, and poverty were obviously still acute in the eyes of many local jurors at the end of Elizabeth's reign, and in many sections of the country they continued to use their local courts to address those issues.

2

Methodological underpinnings

The information to be presented in Chapters 3, 6, and 7 about social regulation in 255 smaller communities derives from an unfamiliar method of working with local court records. Since that technique has implications for the patterns observed, it needs to be described in some detail. As long as the methodological constraints of the approach are kept firmly in mind, it offers some significant benefits, enabling us to utilize a large mass of records previously employed only for local research to trace responses to misbehavior in all parts of the country over more than two centuries, including the especially obscure fifteenth century.

It was necessary first to establish criteria for the types of communities and courts to include. My decision to focus upon courts held in villages and market centers with fewer than about 3,000 inhabitants, excluding England's urban communities, stemmed from both intellectual and practical factors.[1] The great majority of the population lived in the smaller places, so their experience was characteristic, yet we know very little about them as compared to the better studied urban areas. Moreover, voluminous masses of records survive for some of the bigger places, more than I could reasonably tackle. Because my approach required that I be certain that each court included did indeed exercise public jurisdiction and thus had the potential authority to handle social misconduct, I eliminated all courts with only baronial status. The type of court as indicated on its own rolls was not in itself a reliable guide to whether it could deal with public matters, especially in the northern part of the country, for there was considerable variation in how even a

---

[1] For the criteria used to define these categories, see the Notes to Appendices 1.1 and 2.1.

46

given court titled itself over time.[2] A functional definition was therefore adopted: any court that enforced two forms of control expressly confined to leet bodies could be safely assumed to have the power to regulate social conduct as well. These tests were whether the court reported violations of the peace (such as assaults and rescues from the constable), and whether it enforced the Assize of Bread and Ale, reporting local bakers, brewers, and sometimes other craftspeople who had ostensibly produced goods of inferior quality or who sold at excessive price.

I looked also for long runs of surviving records. Use of short sets from many different places would make it impossible to determine whether changes observed over time concerning social issues stemmed from actual shifts in what the jurors of those places chose to report or whether they derived from contrasts between the courts studied in various periods. Wherever possible, therefore, I picked records that spanned a minimum of 100 years between 1370 and 1599: 88 percent of all courts selected covered that length, and nearly two-thirds extended for 150 years or more.[3] In geographical areas where few records survive, however, it was necessary to settle in some cases for shorter runs in order to gain at least some information about the region. Because I analyzed the data within twenty-year periods between 1400 and 1599 and within a thirty-year period in the late fourteenth century, and because a sampling procedure was utilized, the sets did not have to be uninterrupted so long as they included entries from at least two or three years within the duodecades observed.[4] If more than enough courts with long series of records were available for a given area, I selected diverse types of places from among the possibilities.

---

[2] This was particularly true for hundred or wapentake courts based in a community that also had a manorial or borough court. In analyzing these courts, I placed them into the categories most commonly used in the records themselves: see Appendix 2.1.

[3] For the 267 courts studied, the distance from the earliest to the latest record used spanned 200–230 years for 34 percent; for 30 percent it spanned 150–199 years; for 24 percent it spanned 100–149 years; and for 13 percent it spanned less than 100 years. The mean was 162 years, the median 169. See Appendix 2.1 for the list of courts used for this project, with their dates and references.

[4] The records of 18 percent of the full set covered 9–11 duodecades (not necessarily consecutive); 30 percent covered 7–8 duodecades; 34 percent covered 5–6 duodecades; and 17 percent covered fewer than 5 duodecades. The mean for the full group was 6.4 duodecades, the median 7. Wherever possible, I concentrated my sampling in one of the decades within each unit, to increase the comparability of the evidence. The number of observations made in each decade is: 1370s, 36; 1380s, 82; 1390s, 61; 1400s, 71; 1410s, 61; 1420s, 101; 1430s, 68; 1440s, 105; 1450s, 55; 1460s, 110; 1470s, 91; 1480s, 80; 1490s, 112; 1500s, 82; 1510s, 93; 1520s, 76; 1530s, 140; 1540s, 89; 1550s, 114; 1560s, 110; 1570s, 98; 1580s, 79; 1590s, 132.

The final set includes 255 communities, of which 58 percent were villages, 29 percent market centers, 8 percent hundreds, and 5 percent composite manorial estates (Honours, Liberties, or combined units held by an ecclesiastical body).[5] Map 2.1 displays the communities by type, indicating also the geographic regions into which they have been grouped for analysis in Chapters 6–7; Appendix 2.1 lists the places and dates used, giving document references.[6] This distribution reflects an intentional weighting in favor of market centers at the expense of rural villages, for my earlier work had indicated there was a more aggressive response to social issues in the secondary commercial centers.[7] For twelve places information was obtained about two different types of courts: manorial plus borough, or hundred plus one of the others. Of the resulting total of 267 courts, 77 percent were manor courts, 8 percent borough courts, 10 percent hundred courts, and 5 percent courts of composite manorial estates.

In order to achieve a fairly consistent distribution throughout the country, I initially hoped to find for each county a minimum of five places with individual public courts or two big sets of composite manorial records, with at least 100 years under observation for each court. This goal was reached for 34 of the 41 counties – defining each of Yorkshire's three ridings as a separate county – all located in the Midlands, East Anglia, Southeast, Southwest, or Yorkshire.[8] For the remaining seven counties, situated mainly in the West and North, I was unable to find enough good sets of records.[9] (The insurmountable

---

[5] The set contains 147 villages (of which 3 were also the center of hundred courts for the surrounding area), 74 market centers (of which 3 also had hundred courts and 6 had both manor and borough courts), 20 hundreds (of which 6 also had courts for villages or market centers), and 14 manorial estates.

[6] This and the maps in Chapters 6–7 were produced by converting the data files prepared in SPSS (Statistical Package for the Social Sciences) software into computer mapping files using MapInfo software. See Chapter 6, section one below for a listing of counties by region and a discussion of the uneven distribution of type of community.

[7] Everitt's list of market towns, 1500–1640, includes a total of c. 715 places, out of a total of c. 9,000 parishes (see Notes to Appendix 2.1). If we use the very crude equivalency of one community per parish, those figures yield a ratio of 1:11.6 for market towns to villages. The equivalent ratio for the communities studied here is 1:2.2.

[8] For these counties I have between five and nine places each: either five to eleven individual courts (including two types of courts for several places) or a mixture of individual and composite courts.

[9] Those counties are: Heref. (only three individual courts, all spanning at least 100 years); Shrops. (only four individual courts, of which just three spanned 100 years); Ches. (two composite units, just one of which spanned 100 years); Westml. (only two individual courts, just one of which spanned 100 years); the East Riding of Yorks. (only three individual courts, just two of which spanned 100 years); and Notts. (five individual courts and one composite unit, just three of which spanned 100 years).

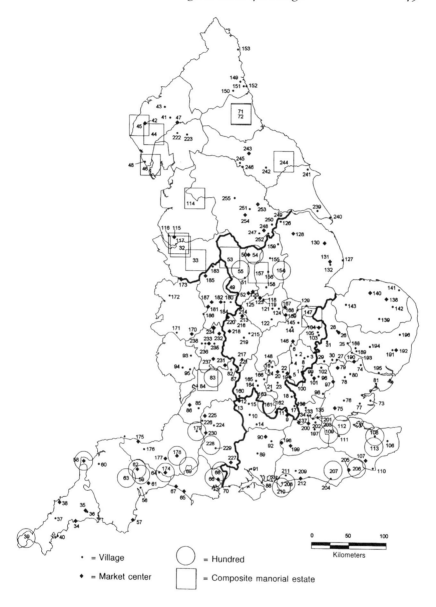

Map 2.1   The 255 places included in this study, showing type of community and region

See App. 2.1 for identification numbers by place.

Table 2.1. *Number and type of courts under observation by duodecade, with median sizes of communities*

		Number and percentage of courts under observation (row percentages)				
	Villages (all manor courts)	Market Centers			Composite manorial estates	Total
Dates		Manor courts	Borough courts	Hundreds		
1370–99	82=55%	38=26%	10= 7%	12= 8%	6=4%	148
1400–19	73=57%	30=23%	10= 8%	12= 9%	3=2%	128
1420–39	73=51%	36=25%	10= 7%	17=12%	7=5%	143
1440–59	71=50%	35=25%	13= 9%	14=10%	8=6%	141
1460–79	89=54%	42=25%	14= 8%	15= 9%	6=4%	166
1480–99	81=54%	39=26%	12= 8%	11= 7%	8=5%	151
1500–19	77=52%	32=22%	14=10%	14=10%	10=7%	147
1520–39	96=52%	42=23%	18=10%	16= 9%	12=7%	184
1540–59	89=55%	39=24%	15= 9%	11= 7%	8=5%	162
1560–79	84=51%	45=27%	11= 7%	15= 9%	11=7%	166
1580–99	92=52%	46=26%	15= 9%	11= 6%	12=7%	176
Total set	147=55%	58=22%	22= 8%	26=10%	14=5%	267

		Median sizes of communities				
No. of hectares in parish or hundred, early 19th century	1,166 (= 2,882 a.)	2,428 (= 5,999 a.)	1,973 (= 4,876 a.)	(8,569= 21,173 a.)	–	
Projected population in 1524/5 (using multiplier of 6.5)	231	533	845	2100	–	

shortage of evidence for the West and North may actually produce a reasonable reflection of the true distribution of the population in later medieval and sixteenth-century England.)

Table 2.1 shows the distribution of places by duodecade, together with the median area of each type of community according to censuses of the early nineteenth century – the first figures available for England as a whole – and their estimated population in 1524/5.[10] The manors in

---

[10] The hectares given here are those of the parish within which the court lay, based upon acreages from the censuses, as provided for many counties by the *VCH* and otherwise by volumes of the *Kelly's County Guides*; these figures are probably fairly accurate for

this set ranged in area and population from places with fewer than 400 hectares (= c. 1,000 acres) and no more than 100 residents to great "extended" manors containing thousands of hectares, multiple townships or parishes, and large populations.[11] Of the market centers, those with manorial courts were somewhat larger in area but smaller in population than those with borough courts. The size of hundreds varied, but they were nearly always larger than individual parishes: in this set they had a median area of about 8,600 hectares (= c. 21,000 acres). The estimated average population of the hundreds in the 1520s was two and a half times that of the next largest type. The composite manorial estates ranged even more widely in area, in the extent to which they were physically concentrated in one area as opposed to scattered over a much wider region, and in the number of communities and people included. (Because they were dispersed, information about their areas and populations could not be obtained.) While in a few cases they included only a handful of manors within a fairly contained region, most were larger and the greatest were very large indeed. The Honour of Peveril in Nottinghamshire, for example, comprised eight manors, two hundreds, and 114 individual parishes as well as Sherwood Forest; the estate of the Bishop of Durham included 85 communities in northeast England.[12]

Information was entered into computer files using the Statistical Package for the Social Sciences software. Set up by place and decade, with a summary entry for each duodecade to be used for the main analyses, the files record whether the jurors of a given court expressed concern with each of the types of misbehavior studied. This could take the form either of reporting people for misbehavior or of passing a byelaw that proscribed a particular action in the future. For each community, duodecade, and offence, I entered also the gender of those named (men only, women only, or both men and women), whether

rural parishes but less so for urban or suburban areas, where the original parishes may have been subdivided into smaller units before the time of these values. Estimates of population are based upon the number of taxpayers assessed for the 1524–5 Subsidy, multiplied by a standard figure of 6.5 (as used by Alan Dyer, *Decline and Growth*, Appendix 5); these figures too are only approximate, since we are sure neither of the amount of under-registration in individual communities nor of the proper multiplier. Information on the number of hectares was obtained for 231 places (= 91 percent); population figures from 1524/5 survive for 181 places (= 71 percent).

[11] While most of these extended manors were found in the North and West, within a mere 25 km of London lay the royal manor of Havering (-atte-Bower), Essex, which comprised 6,400 hectares (= 16,000 acres) and at least 1,500 people in the 1520s, distributed between three parishes. See McIntosh, *Autonomy and Community* and *A Community Transformed*.

[12] Deering, *Nottinghamia vetus et nova*, pp. 354–5; Durham Univ. Libr., Archives and Special Collections, 5 The College, HC I/9 and I/34, *passim*.

byelaws were imposed, and whether eviction was employed as a penalty.[13] If the records used from a given court during a given duodecade
revealed no presentments or byelaws concerning a given type of misbehavior, I entered a "O" for that place and period. Because I was noting
"negative evidence" of this kind, I avoided published records as much
as possible, for often I could not be entirely confident that the editor had
included all entries and had translated some of the more obscure Latin
terms correctly.[14]

Two aspects of how the documents were used and material entered
for analysis affect the nature of the resulting data. In order to gain
information from a wide and diverse set of courts throughout the
country over a long chronological period, I was obliged to sample their
records. (The alternative was to use all surviving documents from a
much smaller number of places.) Within each duodecade, I normally
observed four to six consecutive leet court sessions. Since most public
courts met twice per year, this resulted in two to three years of evidence. In some cases, a larger number of sessions was examined, and in
a few cases I had to settle for fewer. Duodecades were employed
because my previous work with local courts had indicated that when a
community became seriously concerned about social misconduct, its
period of increased control rarely lasted for more than 20–25 years. By
sampling within duodecades, I was therefore unlikely to overlook a
period of heightened regulation. Records of the purely baronial meetings of these courts were not used, for they rarely dealt with public
matters, and if a social issue was raised in a baronial session it would
almost always be mentioned at a public court as well.

This sampling technique means that the data presented in Chapters
3, 6, and 7 constitute systematically gathered minimum values for the
amount of social regulation in the lesser courts, not accurate reflections
of the total amount of concern. For some and perhaps many courts, the
years that were not examined must have included attention to additional types of behavior. While there is no reason to expect systematic
distortion between various types of offences, there may well be a
skewing between types of communities: because jurors in a small
manorial court might submit only occasional reports of social problems
within a given duodecade, my sampling method was more likely to
have missed those presentments than in the more consistently active

---

[13] Throughout this study the term "gender" is used in a general sense, as a synonym for
"sex." It does not imply, more specifically, the social construction of male and female
roles as contrasted to biological sex differences.

[14] As Appendix 2.1 displays, I used published sources for eight of the 267 courts; for three
of these I looked at original documents too.

courts of larger communities. This doubtlessly exaggerates to some extent the contrast in my data between levels of concern in villages as compared with market centers.

Further, in entering the data, I decided for reasons of methodological rigor not to record the number of people reported per year or duo-decade, although I had noted the numbers when working with the records. Information on the numeric level of concern can only assist comparison if one knows the total population of the area within the jurisdiction of that court. In the absence of per capita rates of present-ment, simple numbers can be highly misleading. Thus, one would expect *a priori* that a market center with 2,500 people would report many more people for social problems than would a rural village with 250 people. The larger number of presentments in the bigger commu-nity does not in itself tell us anything about the level of concern on a per capita basis. Similarly, a court that reported more people for social misconduct at the end of the sixteenth century than at the end of the fifteenth may not have been experiencing a heightened concern with social regulation but rather simple population growth, with no change in the per capita levels of wrongdoing. Only through detailed local studies can one attempt to estimate changing populations over time and then calculate per capita rates. Since this was impossible for a national survey, I decided not to utilize the number of individuals presented at all. Hence the data presented below do not reveal vari-ations in the intensity with which behavior of a particular sort was addressed in different communities; neither do they document changes in intensity over time within a given community. A report in Court A of one person for scolding during a particular duodecade looks the same as five scolds presented in Court B during the same period; a single presentment of a scold in Court A during the 1420s-30s looks the same as five reports of scolds in Court A at some later time. The method thus reveals breadth or range of concern among various offences but not depth within a given type.

3

Social regulation in England's smaller communities

As part of their efforts to limit social disruption, leaders of England's lesser communities during the later medieval and early modern period decided in some cases to utilize the public courts held for their manor, borough, hundred, or composite estate.[1] The reports they made to such courts as members of presentment juries together with the byelaws they passed allow us to investigate two central questions of this study: what was the history of social regulation over time, and what attitudes underlay local responses to wrongdoing, shaping the social construction of misbehavior? We can look also at issues of gender, examining the changing distribution of men and women among those reported for the various offences. Another theme is the discretionary powers of jurors, the remarkable independence with which they interpreted and extended formal law. Few of the forms of misconduct that worried them were proscribed by the common law, ecclesiastical law, Parliamentary statute, or royal injunction, and even when the offence was deemed illegal, responsibility for punishing malefactors was rarely assigned to the lesser public courts. Yet because such wrongdoing threatened local stability, jurors proceeded anyway. Equivalent autonomy is seen in their response to the playing of certain indoor and outdoor games banned by Parliamentary statute. In this case jurors were quite prepared to ignore illegal gaming in their communities unless it constituted a problem in their own eyes; when they did report and punish gamesters, they usually did so in a fashion different from that ordered in the statutes themselves. Material from the lesser courts thus provides forceful evidence of the agency of local jurors.

---

[1] Hundreds were the administrative/legal units into which most counties were divided, called "wapentakes" in some regions; composite estates consisting of multiple manors were held by large lay or ecclesiastical lords. For other methods of confronting wrongdoing, see Chapter 1 above.

The first major question, the history of concern with wrongdoing, is traced through the records of 267 courts held in 255 villages and market centers between 1370 and 1599.[2] Ten specific types of misconduct are analyzed within three clusters, based upon deep-seated attitudes that shaped local concern (anxiety about disharmony, disorder, and the problems of poverty); illegal gaming is discussed as a special case. Though the boundaries around these clusters were not impermeable (some offences were described primarily in terms of the concerns of one cluster but contained secondary elements characteristic of another), they provide a convenient structure for analysis.[3] To relate the lesser courts to other bodies, a brief comparison is made for each offence with the role of the intermediate-level courts described more fully in Chapter 1. For most topics this account describes the evidence for England as a whole: regional variations and contrasts between types of communities will be discussed in Chapters 6 and 7 below.

Quantitative evidence about levels of concern and gender is laid out in graphical form, arranged by duodecades so as to reveal changes over time. These graphs are of two types. The first kind displays information about the extent of the response to misconduct, showing the percentage of those courts under observation in each duodecade that expressed concern about the various offences.[4] Attention could be manifested either through reporting one or more wrongdoers or by passing bye-laws about the problem. In the 1520s–30s, for example, 42 of the 184 courts under observation recorded presentments or byelaws about scolding, so Graph 3.1 shows 23 percent for scolding in that duodecade. The second type of graph presents information about the gender of the people reported. Only those courts that named offenders for a given form of wrongdoing have been analyzed, with the presentments then broken down by gender: men only, women only, or any combination of one or more men plus one or more women. Thus, among the 42 courts that reported people for scolding in the 1520s–30s, 12 percent presented men only, 50 percent presented women only, and 38 percent presented both men and women. Those percentages are displayed on Graph 3.2 for that duodecade. The impact of two methodological decisions discussed in Chapter 2 should be noted here. Sampling records within

---

[2] See Chapter 2 above for how these courts were selected; see Appendix 2.1 for a list of the records used and Appendix 3.1 for a tabular summary of the evidence about regulation. For the offences and clusters, below, see the Introduction.

[3] Scolding, for example, was seen primarily as a threat to harmony but in some cases might disrupt good order as well; unruly alehouses clearly threatened order and control, but attention was often focused in practice upon their poorer patrons.

[4] For the number of courts under observation per decade, see Appendix 3.1.

duodecades rather than using all surviving documents means that the numbers of communities shown to have been involved in social regulation are minimum values; and because the types of offences but not the number of people reported for each offence form the basis of the analysis, we can assess the *range* of behaviors that were troublesome but cannot measure changing *intensity* of concern within a given court about a particular offence.

For the second question, the attitudes that influenced local responses to wrongdoing, information comes from statements in the lesser court records about why such misconduct was seen as troubling or harmful.[5] Unlike the brief and formulaic descriptions of wrongdoing normally found in the upper- and intermediate-level courts of the common law system, jurors in the lesser public courts often described in their own words why a given action or offender constituted a threat to the public good and hence should be punished. These statements were sometimes included in the clerk's written account of the presentment. (In most cases he first translated them from late medieval/sixteenth-century English into Latin, thereby adding an additional filter, so they cannot be taken as literal transcriptions of the jurors' words.) These textual passages are provided in only some of the rolls and never extend to more than a few sentences in length, so they are by no means as valuable as the rich narratives contained within some of the depositions taken by the church courts and Sessions of the Peace. Since, however, we have so few sources that reveal the social and economic concerns of local families of middling status, we may welcome the insights furnished by these documents.

The Disharmony cluster

Like the leaders of smaller settlements in many cultures, the heads of established families in English local communities were concerned about social harmony and tranquillity. Peaceful relations between neighbors contributed to a social mood marked by generally amicable interactions, and an attitude of goodwill and trust was conducive to untroubled economic dealings. In a perfect community, people spoke

---

[5] The great majority of this evidence comes from the court rolls of the 255 communities, but occasional examples are taken from the "Assembly Books" of thirty-one other market centers: town books, ordinances, or documents expressing the decisions and policy of town leaders. Because there was often a disparity between orders made by local governments and what was actually enforced by the courts, the two types of records cannot be compared directly. Appendix 3.2 lists the places whose "Assembly Books" were used.

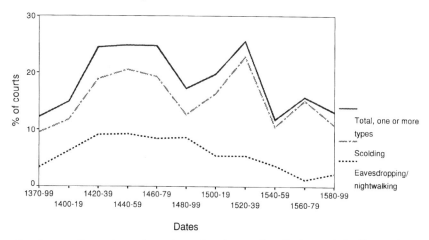

Graph 3.1   Percentage of courts under observation that reported offences in
the Disharmony cluster

cheerfully and openly with their neighbors, rather than arguing heated-
ly or causing ill will by spreading malicious gossip. If problems arose,
they were resolved directly by the antagonistic participants themselves
or with the help of friends or neutral third parties, so that resentment
was not allowed to fester. Likewise, people respected the privacy of
their neighbors' houses, avoiding the temptation to listen to or watch
what was happening inside. They also respected the need for local
security, refraining from wandering around at night without cause.

Although many communities presumably found it possible to maintain adequate harmony and goodwill through entirely informal means,
jurors in some settings between 1370 and 1599 decided to use their local
courts to draw attention to and punish the misdeeds of disruptive
people. As Graph 3.1 and Appendix 3.1 display, maintaining tranquillity within the community appears to have been a fairly constant goal of
local jurors from the early fifteenth century until around 1540: during
five of the six duodecades between 1420 and 1539, 20–26 percent of all
courts under observation reported people who had engaged in scolding, eavesdropping, or nightwalking.[6] Whereas each of these offences
was embedded within a long tradition of moral analysis and social
condemnation, none was a clear violation either of the common law of
England/Parliamentary statutes or of the ecclesiastical laws. In most

[6] All figures are based on the number of courts under observation, not the number of
places, since we have records of two different types of courts for twelve communities.
This graph, and all others, were generated directly from the computer-based data files,
using SPSS software.

cases local jurors took advantage of this legal fluidity and simply sidestepped the fact that they had no clear legal authority. Rather than attempting an explicit justification of their right to handle such problems, they offered only a brief statement that such conduct was against the peace. Frequently they associated the maintenance of local peace as between neighbors with "the peace of the lord king," thus serving a double purpose: they stressed that peace was a social virtue supported by the weight of the crown while also suggesting that these actions should indeed be punished since they violated the generic legal requirement of maintaining the peace.

Scolding

By far the most common presentment within this cluster was scolding or misuse of the tongue, either being quarrelsome/argumentative or spreading false or private information about other people behind their backs. Scolding might occur with a specific other person but more often it was presented as "common," occurring frequently and with unnamed people. As Graph 3.1 displays, during most duodecades between 1420 and 1579, the proportion of courts under observation that reported scolding or enacted byelaws about it was between 15 percent and 21 percent, with a slightly higher peak in the 1520s–30s. Even in the duodecades showing lower concern, at the far ends of the period, about 10 percent of the courts mentioned this offence. Comparison of this pattern with what was happening in the intermediate courts suggests that verbal disruption became a serious issue in these smaller communities before it appeared at higher levels of the law.[7] Although the reported rise in concern with defamation in the church courts in the later sixteenth century and the new use of the action "trespass on the case" as a means of prosecuting private suits alleging defamation in the common law courts may have offset some of the decline seen in the lesser institutions, it is unlikely to have compensated fully for that decrease. We are probably seeing here a reflection of broader practical and ideological changes: as will be discussed in Chapter 8, attention to social harmony, to amicable dealings between neighbors, seems to have diminished in a number of settings and texts over the course of Elizabeth's reign.

As reported by local court jurors, scolding was an overwhelmingly female offence from the later fourteenth century through the 1510s. (See

[7] For this and subsequent comparisons with the intermediate courts, see Chapter 1, section one, and Appendices 1.2–1.3.

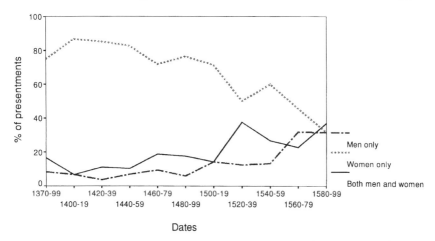

Graph 3.2   Courts that reported scolding: percentage of presentments by gender

Graph 3.2.) In each of those duodecades, 71–86 percent of the courts that mentioned scolding named women only, many of whom were married; the rest of the courts presented either men only or both men and women. From 1520 onwards, however, the proportion of courts reporting only women scolds fell – to 46–60 percent between 1520 and 1579, and to just 32 percent in the 1580s–90s. This is a surprising observation in light of the focus upon female scolds by prescriptive writers and the church courts around 1600: the assumption of many early modern historians that scolding was almost inevitably a female offence needs to be reexamined.[8] (We have no means of telling whether the local court presentments reflected the actual gender distribution of verbal misuse, but the pronounced changes over time in the extent to which men too were named indicate at least that any bias was not a constant.) This evidence does not accord with Underdown's suggestion that "a preoccupation with scolding women" was a characteristic feature of the century after 1560, seen as part of a wider crisis in gender relations stemming ultimately from the spread of capitalism.[9]

While most presentments of scolding offer only a minimal description of the offence, a few provide an indication of what was actually involved and why it was seen as harmful to harmonious social relation-

[8] For references, see note 3 to the Introduction.
[9] In "The Taming of the Scold," esp. pp. 126–7, and see Amussen, *An Ordered Society.* Note that other scholars emphasize the importance of Protestant social thought to conflicts in gender relations: see, e.g., note 59 below.

ships.[10] Such wordings enable us to distinguish between two varieties of scolding. In the first, a scold was quarrelsome, casting insults or engaging in heated arguments with others, thereby breaking the peace of the neighborhood. The harmful impact of this verbal combativeness is suggested by frequently used terms like *litigator/-trix* and *rixator/-trix* (both originally meaning "a contentious person") and by less common descriptors like *conviciator/-trix* (from "abusive") and *contrabator/-trix* (from "beating against").[11] A presentment that makes clear the aggressive nature of some episodes of scolding comes from Badbury hundred in Dorset in 1422, where the jurors reported Agnes Chapman of Horton not only for scolding but, more explicitly, for attacking Richard Maule and others "with contumelious words," in disturbance of the peace.[12] Hot arguments could also draw others into the controversy. Jurors in (Saffron) Walden, Essex said in 1384 that Richard Stephens and his wife were common scolds and perturbers of the king's peace: "through their insulting words they bring about dissension among the people."

[10] Several of the most common Latin descriptors, including *objurgator/-trix* and *garrulator/-trix*, do not specify what kind of spoken offence had taken place. Excluded from this analysis are presentments of people, mainly men, as *barrators/-trices*. In the fourteenth and fifteenth centuries this term usually referred to people who brought vexatious suits against others or in other ways used the law disruptively (*OED*, and cf. 34 Edward III, c. 1: *Stats. Realm*, vol. I, p. 364). By the end of the sixteenth century it normally referred to someone who had incited others to violence, although occasionally it was used for people who were simply argumentative. Since there is no way to distinguish between the possible meanings, all such presentments have been omitted. The number of presentments for barratry in these courts was small, so exclusion of the offence has not had a significant impact upon the total numbers. Swearing, an offence handled by the church courts, almost never appeared in the lesser leet courts and has not been counted as scolding. Also excluded here are presentments of people for making specific derogatory statements about local officers, a matter of concern to the officials and their authority but not necessarily to the general well-being of the community.

[11] For examples of the latter two terms, see Liverpool RO 920 SAL 1/9 (West Derby, 1492) and Lincs. AO Crowle Manor I/65 (Crowle, 1424–5). Other presentments include such verbs as *maledicant* ("revile") and *redarguit* ("reprove" or "rebuke"): Durham Univ. Libr., Archs. and Spec. Colls., Prior's Kitchen, DCD Halmote Court, autumn, 1389 (Ferry[hill?], Durham), and PRO DL 30/5/71 (Halton Fee, Ches., 1465). In the later fourteenth and fifteenth centuries the various Latin terms employed for a scold may have been translations of the English word "shrew," applied to evil-disposed or malignant men from the later thirteenth century and to railing or turbulent women by the late fourteenth (*OED*); by the later sixteenth century, some version of the term "scold" is nearly always used in those presentments given in English. In some of the Cumberland courts during the second half of the fifteenth century, people were said to be *irr[ationale] in lingua* (e.g., Cumbria RO, Carlisle, D/Lec/299/1472–3 and 1487–8, and DRC/2/62).

[12] Dorset RO D/BKL CF 1/1/32. For below, see Essex RO D/DBy M1.

From the later fifteenth century through the 1530s, the argumentative version of scolding was seldom reported unless it accompanied other forms of misbehavior. On two occasions in 1469 pairs of male scolds in Crowle, Lincs. who started out arguing with each other moved on to more violent fighting: one case resulted in bloodshed, while in the second, one of the quarrelers followed the other man into his house before attacking him.[13] In Horsham St. Faith, Norf., Beatrice Beddes, wife of William, was said in 1501–2 to scold commonly but especially with Alice Amys, Richard's wife; as the verbal enmity between the two women escalated, Beatrice broke into Alice's house. Later in the sixteenth century quarrelsome speech again began to be presented in its own right, in many cases practiced by men.[14]

The second meaning of scolding involved the deliberate spreading of malicious or false gossip, aptly described in fifteenth-century English as "back-biting."[15] Because of its ability to shatter good social relations within the community, backbiting was seen as a particularly damaging sort of misconduct, and it was often described somewhat more fully in the court records. In 1467 Richard Whyng was presented by the court of Badbury hundred, Dorset as "a lying disturber and maker of evil gossip about his neighbors and a slanderer of his said neighbors and the people of the lord king, and he is a causer of divers insults with malicious words."[16] In 1473–4 the jurors of Cawston, Norf. reported Isabel Famme and John Howes as "common creators of false tales" between their neighbors; this was not only against the peace but also caused social disturbance. Jurors normally focused on the disruptive consequences of malicious gossip for the harmony of the neighborhood or community as a whole. A concern with social tranquillity underlay the order issued in 1465 by the jurors at the halmote court of the Prior and Convent of Durham, who enjoined William Raper's wife, of Billing-

---

[13] Lincs. AO Crowle Manor I/120. For below, see Norf. RO N.R.S. 19511, 42 C 3.

[14] The level would have been slightly higher if the term "barratry" had been counted within this offence (see note 10 above).

[15] This contrasts with private suits for defamation in the ecclesiastical courts, where the validity of the allegation was irrelevant to the offence: defamation could be alleged even if the damaging statement was true, so long as it was made in public and stemmed from malice. In the local courts, where the accuracy of a charge did matter, jurisdiction over private suits for defamation had been lost during the fourteenth century; during the sixteenth century defamation could be prosecuted as "trespass on the case" in both local and central common law courts (see Helmholz's introduction to *Select Cases on Defamation*). For studies of defamation/slander, see Haigh, "Slander and the Church Courts," Sharpe, "Defamation and Sexual Slander" and "'Such Disagreement betwyx Neighbours'," Gowing, *Domestic Dangers*, and Deal, "Whores and Witches."

[16] Dorset RO D/BKL CF 1/1/49. For below, see Norf. RO N.R.S. 6024, 20 E 2.

ham, Durham, to stop scolding with her neighbors and instead "to be well disposed and bear herself honestly towards the tenants."[17] In 1481 Margaret Akrede was said by the court of Spilsby cum Eresby, Lincs. to be a common scold with her tongue, "provoking controversy in poisonous fashion [*venemose*] between her neighbors."

This kind of scolding had the power to destroy another person's individual reputation or credit, thereby damaging not only their social but also their economic trustworthiness.[18] Jurors in a few of the lesser public courts, especially in northwestern England, not only reported people for scolding but also proceeded to investigate the allegation. In Cockermouth, Cumb., Thomas Byglande was presented in 1502 for scolding and defaming Thomas Dogeson, junior, and his son. The court had inquired into the charges, concluding that Dogeson and his son "are well conducted and of good fame," whereupon the jurors fined Byglande 40d.[19] The Cockermouth court remained concerned about false accusations in later years as well, presenting several men in the 1530s for unlawfully scolding and upbraiding others: one called his opponent a sheep stealer while another charged that his enemy was a cuckold. Since neither scold could prove his claim, both were fined. Indeed, jurors in Cumberland and Westmorland showed deep concern with the damaging power of false accusations right through the sixteenth century, joined by Northumberland at least by the 1560s.[20]

Byelaws were infrequently used for scolding, with just 5 percent of all courts that reported scolding in any duodecade passing ordinances against this behavior. The wording of these fairly rare orders can be illuminating. In 1519 jurors in Methley, West Yorks. enjoined that "no one shall permit or give any insulting or shameful words to any of his neighbors without reasonable cause, under a penalty of forfeiting 12d. to the lord for each time so offending."[21] A byelaw passed by the court of Earl Soham, Suff. in 1566–7 ordained and concorded "by the advice

---

[17] Durham Univ. Libr., Archs. and Spec. Colls., Prior's Kitchen, DCD Halmote Court, summer, 1465. For below, see Lincs. AO ANC 3/14/55.

[18] Private suits involving credit in market terms were heard by these same local courts in another facet of their jurisdiction. Cf. Muldrew, "Interpreting the Market."

[19] Cumbria RO, Carlisle, D/Lec/299. For below, see *ibid.*

[20] E.g., for Cumb., Cumbria RO, Carlisle, D/Lec/299/1/1/27, D/Lec/299, books for 1567–9 and 1596–7, and D/Lons/W8/8; for Westml., Cumbria RO, Carlisle, D/Lons/L5/2/2/1–31 and D/Lons/L MM 4–5; for Northumb., Northumb. RO 2795/1–2 and cf. 1 DE/2/4.

[21] Darbyshire and Lumb, *The History of Methley*, p. 196. For below, see Suff. RO, Ipswich, V 5/18/1.11.

both of the Chief Pledges and of the jurors that every person of whatever sort that lives and remains within this vill shall be of good fame and conversation ... with one another, viz., not to contend by words through which the friendship between neighbors may be broken, under penalty for each person so offending of 20s."

While the most common form of punishment for scolding was a cash fine, female offenders (though apparently not men) were occasionally ordered to face the mixture of confinement and public ridicule that accompanied being locked into a structure of display for a stated period of time. The chair-like tumbrel, also known as a thew or cuckingstool, might either be permanently fixed in a conspicuous location or be movable, placed in front of the offender's house or on a cart which carried her around the commmunity.[22] Initially the tumbrel was employed only for scolds who repeated their offence. Jurors in the Dorset manor of Abbotsbury presented Rose Mouryng, married to Thomas, for scolding against two other married women in 1424–5; because she had been presented for a similar fault before, it was ordered that she be seated in the tumbrel for one hour.[23] Margery Smyth of Minehead, Som., wife of Thomas, was presented in 1444 as a common scold; when she was reported for the same offence the following year, the jurors ordered that she "have the tumbrel." By the second half of the fifteenth century, even women presented for the first time might be sent to the tumbrel. A draft presentment in mixed English and Latin preserved in the borough records of Droitwich, Worcs. from the 1460s names [Muchel?] Gylle as "a common scold" and prays that she may be "set on the thew."[24] A particularly interesting wording is found in a byelaw passed by the borough of Northallerton, N. Yorks. in 1510: "It is ordered that henceforth no woman, neither married nor otherwise, shall commonly scold with her neighbors nor be rebellious at any time, under the penalty that those found acting badly shall be put in the tumbrel at their door [*collistrigam ad hostium illarum*]. And that they be

---

[22] A tumbrel first appears as a punishment in the Assize of Bread and Ale of 1266–7, to be used against female offenders (*Stats. Realm*, vol. I, pp. 199–200, made more explicit in "The Judgment of the Pillory" of the same year, *ibid.*, pp. 201–2). In the later fourteenth century Langland urged that female providers of food and drink who violated the Assize be punished in "py[n]yng stolis" (Langland, *Will's Visions of Piers Plowman*, p. 232, Passus III, ll. 67–8). Men sentenced to equivalent forms of display for other kinds of wrongdoing were locked to a pillory post or placed in the stocks.

[23] Dorset RO D/FSI Box 2, Abbotsbury, roll for 1424–5. For below, see Som. RO DD/L P27/11.

[24] Worcs. RO (Headquarters, County Hall) 261.4/31, BA 1006/#298 (Box 31). Apparently spelled "yew," this is almost certainly a late use of the "thorn" character.

seated there wearing a crown [*corunati*] according to the mode of the pillory until pardoned."[25]

By the 1540s the term "cuckingstool" was coming into use. At least through the end of the sixteenth century, this word seems in most cases to have been just another name for the object previously described as a tumbrel.[26] In 1540 Hacker's wife of Basingstoke, Hants. was warned to leave off scolding "upon the pain to suffer upon the 'cockingstool,'" while ten years later jurors in the borough court of Dartmouth, Devon reported that "we have a fault that we have not a 'coken stole' for scolds that ought to be."[27] Because the cuckingstool was used by other types of courts as a punishment for sexual offenders, women sentenced to it for scolding might feel particularly shamed. There is only a single reference in all the records consulted from these smaller communities suggesting that a cuckingstool was used for ducking or dropping scolds in water, as was sometimes done in the larger towns and cities, especially during the seventeenth century. At the surprisingly early date of 1490–1 jurors in (Saffron) Walden, Essex reported that "one pit with water called 'le Cokestolepet' is overflowing and full of sand," whereupon the inhabitants were ordered to clean it out.[28] These documents likewise contain no mention of the scold's bridle, or brank, used in at least a few northern English communities during the seventeenth century.[29]

Eviction from the community was rarely used for scolds except during the 1520s–1530s. John Dix, sen., of Chippenham, Cambs. was presented in 1535 for giving hospitality to "a certain Felicia," an immigrant whose harmful speech caused "many disputes and great discord to grow between the inhabitants of this vill"; Felicia was ordered to move away from Chippenham within the coming week under penalty of 6s 8d.[30] The following year the jurors of Kirtlington, Oxon. presented

---

[25] N. Yorks. County RO, Northallerton, ZBD 1/53/13 (I am grateful to Christine Newman for access to these records). *Collistrigium* is usually translated as "pillory" but here and in certain other instances when it was applied to women, the tumbrel seems clearly to have been intended. The crown, which heightened the element of ridicule, was used in other shaming rituals as well.

[26] Thus, in Basingstoke, Hants. in 1586 the jurors reported that their stocks and pillory were not in repair, and that "there is no tumbrel, called a cucking stool, in the town" (Baigent and Millard, *A History of Basingstoke*, p. 349).

[27] *Ibid.*, p. 330, and Devon RO *f.009.4, 64743, both in English. In (the) Devizes, Wilts. the Mayor and Brethren first determined in 1583 that "there was no honesty" in Edith Marten's statement that Elizabeth Webb was a whore and then ordered that Marten "ride in the cucking stool from the Guildhall unto the dwelling house of the said Marten and the Cookingstole to stand at her door" (Wilts. RO G20/1/16, fol. 58r, an "Assembly Book"). For the association with sexual misconduct, see Chapter 4 below.

[28] Essex RO D/DBy M11.   [29] See, e.g., Boose, "Scolding Brides and Bridling Scolds."

[30] Cambs. RO, Cambridge, R55/7/1f. For below, see Oxon. Archs. Dash I/i/53.

Alice Adams as a common scold "who is likely every day to cause disputes, discord, and other damage between her neighbors. Therefore it is ordained by the whole court that Alice shall withdraw from the vill of Kirtlington before the feast of St. Thomas the Apostle next coming under penalty of forfeiting 40d."

Eavesdropping and nightwalking

Eavesdroppers stood outside other people's houses, often at night, listening to their conversations or sometimes observing their private acts, while nightwalkers, found wandering around after sunset with no reason that seemed legitimate to respectable people, were suspected of having more nefarious intent. Because these offences were less common but related, they have been grouped together on Graph 3.1, which shows relatively low concern throughout our period and a decline after the end of the fifteenth century. Sessions of the Peace too responded to these issues from a fairly early period but displayed diminishing interest after the earlier sixteenth century.[31] In terms of gender, eavesdroppers were more likely to be male than female, and nearly all nightwalkers were men. Graph 3.3 displays these offences in combined form, showing that among those courts that reported such problems, men only (as opposed to women only or both men and women) constituted half to three-quarters of the people charged in most duodecades; female involvement was higher between 1460 and 1519 than previously.[32]

Eavesdroppers normally listened to people's private conversations while standing outside their houses (sheltered by the overhanging roof); sometimes they spied upon events inside. Eavesdropping, never the topic of legislation, was usually described in minimal language. If any justification was given for the presentment, it was said to cause social harm, either violating privacy or disturbing peaceful relations between neighbors. In 1425 the jurors of Harrow, Middx. reported John Rexheth as a common "'Evesdroppere,'" "listening at night and snooping into [*explorans*] the secrets of his neighbors."[33] Agnes Nevell of Colerne, Wilts. was said in 1517 to be "a perturber of the peace in her neighborhood in that she lies under the windows of Edward Node and hears all things being said there by the said Edward." As it provided

---

[31] The decline in attention to nightwalking seen in all courts by the second half of the sixteenth century may stem in part from a decision to present such offenders as vagrants, for which the punishments were more severe.

[32] After c. 1520 so few courts reported these offences that the gender distributions have less validity; further, even a small change in the number of places reporting women can result in apparently wide fluctuations in the percentages. See Appendix 3.1.

[33] Greater London RO Acc.76/2416. For below, see New College Oxford MS 2736.

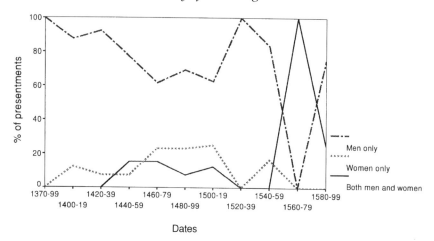

Graph 3.3   Courts that reported eavesdropping/nightwalking: percentage of
presentments by gender

prime material for salacious or detrimental gossip, eavesdropping was
clearly linked to scolding. Margaret Masam of Ely Barton, Cambs. was
said in 1442–3 to be "a common listener at night who follows the said
listening by increasing disputes," while in East Stonehouse, Devon,
John Ewen and Cornelius, the servant of Robert Matthew, were described in 1509 as "common listeners at windows and sowers of discord
between their neighbors."[34]

The small number of presentments for nightwalking suggests that
this was not a major problem in the eyes of jurors in the lesser communities. The Statute of Winton of 1285 had called for the arrest of strangers walking around at night in towns, while legislation of 1331 authorized local constables to arrest suspicious strangers passing in the night as
well as anyone suspected of manslaughter or other felonies.[35] Neither
empowered local juries to report and punish residents of their own
community who were merely out at night without cause, but this
offence was generally included in the jurors' charge and under some
circumstances presentments were made. A man accused of wandering
at night was usually described prior to 1500 as a *noctivagator*. The verb
vagare/vagari (dep.) stressed that the offender lacked a good reason for
being out, as contrasted with someone walking purposefully and legitimately from one place to another. Wandering at night was normally
said merely to be against the (king's) peace or to the harm of the

[34] Cambridge Univ. Libr. E.D.R.C/6/6, and Corn. RO ME 1747.
[35] 13 Edward I, c. 4; 5 Edward III, c. 14 (*Stats. Realm*, vol. I, pp. 97 and 268). The latter
specified that those arrested were to be delivered to the *sheriff* for trial and punishment.

neighbors. Somewhat more fully, John Key of Brigstock, Northants. was reported in 1464 for "wandering at night through the streets and common areas, to the harm of all his neighbors and a dangerous example to others."[36] In the sixteenth century, the term *vigilator* was often used. This word, meaning literally someone who keeps watch at night, implied a destructive inversion of the responsible role played by those who maintained the official night-time patrol of the community, known as the *vigilatio*. Thus, Thomas Swifte, Thomas Kelsey, and William Robynon were said by the jurors of Kirton Lindsey, Lincs. in 1548 to be "of bad bearing in that they watch/walk [*vigilant*] at night-time, to the grave harm of their neighbors."[37]

In practice, however, nightwalking was seldom presented as an offence unless it was linked with another form of wrongdoing. It might be associated with eavesdropping, as in the case of Thomas Ian of Ottery St. Mary, Devon, said in 1393 to be a common walker by night "in order to hear the secrets of his neighbors."[38] Sexual motives are suggested in the presentment of John Baker and William Newton of Padstow, Corn. in 1576 for "leading a lascivious [*liciviosa*] life and being 'common night watchers.'" Those out at night might be looking for a chance to do some casual stealing, as was Richard Tylke of the hundred of Hayridge, Devon, reported in 1489 as a watcher at night and a "holecrop" (a dialect word for a petty thief) among his neighbors.[39] Frequenting an alehouse or playing illegal games were frequently associated with nightwalking. If a person found wandering at night was bearing a weapon, suspicion increased.[40] In their attempts to control eavesdropping and nightwandering, jurors in only 3 percent of all courts that reported any instances of these offences promulgated bye-laws against such actions. A cash fine of various sizes was the standard punishment; neither corporal punishment nor eviction was normally employed.

Combined figures for the percentage of all courts that reported one or more of the types of misbehavior in this cluster are shown at the top of Graph 3.1. The pattern is relatively flat in two respects. There is no single peak (four of the six central duodecades between 1420 and 1539 share a value of 25–26 percent), and the distance between the highest and the lowest values per duodecade is only 14 percent. Nor are dramatic changes seen in the 1460s–70s or the 1520s–30s, periods when new patterns were appearing in other areas of social regulation.

[36] Northants. RO Buccleugh MSS, Box X.367, 14.8.
[37] Lincs. AO K.R. 499. None of the men had any goods through which they could be made to pay a fine.   [38] Devon RO CR 1288. For below, see Corn. RO PB/4/49.
[39] Devon RO CR 122.   [40] E.g., PRO DL 30/48/568 and Corn. RO ME 1747.

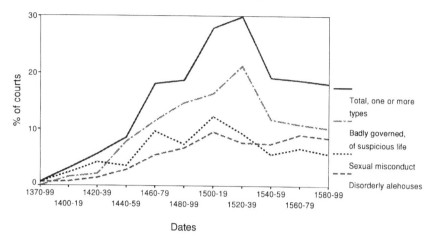

Graph 3.4   Percentage of courts under observation that reported offences in the Disorder cluster

The Disorder cluster

By around 1460 the lesser public courts were displaying heightened interest in sexual misbehavior, disorder in alehouses and inns, and less clearly defined offenders who were said to be "badly governed or ruled," "of suspicious life," "of evil repute," or even just "suspect." The terms used to characterize all these offences suggest that they violated good order, control, appropriate rule or governance, and discipline: both self-control over one's own behavior and the discipline that should be exercised by people in authority over their charges. As Graph 3.4 displays, these offences were unimportant in the decades around 1400 but were reported by nearly a fifth of all courts in the latter part of the fifteenth century; presentments reached a peak of 28–30 percent in the first four decades of the sixteenth century before dropping somewhat thereafter. Problems in this cluster were often described by jurors in fuller language than were offences in the Disharmony category, sometimes with a certain rhetorical flourish. Intriguingly, in rolls from market centers during the later fifteenth and earlier sixteenth centuries such presentments commonly followed reports of problems with sanitation, such as privies that were polluting other people's drinking water, hides being tanned in a common stream, or clothes washed in a common well. This suggests that jurors felt a connection between good social order and public cleanliness.[41] In trying to regulate these kinds of misbehavior, none of which was formally assigned to local court juris-

---

[41] Cf. Thomas, "Cleanliness and Godliness."

diction, jurors experimented with new procedures and punishments.[42] Byelaws were sometimes imposed, the stocks and tumbrel were tried, and for the most severe cases, a new form of punishment – expulsion from the community – was employed.[43] Banishing a wrongdoer from the community seems to have been especially tempting when he or she was a newcomer and poor.[44]

The timing of this powerful emphasis on control and governance is of considerable interest. The first surge of concern, between 1460 and 1499, occurred during the Wars of the Roses and the decades when Edward IV and Henry VII were attempting to rebuild the power of the monarchy and the force of the common law. It is perhaps no coincidence that the language used by local jurors in describing offences during that period is similar to that found in works addressed to the king, promoting the use of royal authority to restore order and discipline.[45] The zenith of local concern in the 1520s–30s came just as Thomas Cromwell, assisted by the Reformation Parliament, was trying to establish more effective control by all branches of the national government. It seems extremely unlikely that the local jurors were merely acceding to Parliament's wishes. More probably, their independent efforts to tighten discipline within their own communities ran in parallel with those of their superiors. Further, the rhetoric used in the lesser courts when describing problems in the Disorder cluster between 1460 and 1539 bears interesting resemblances to the idealistic view of society and political control advocated by the "commonwealth" approach of the mid-sixteenth century.[46]

Sexual misconduct

When they brought up sexual matters, jurors were on questionable legal ground since the church courts, not secular ones, had jurisdiction over such issues. Although as individuals they may have felt that sexual wrongdoing violated Christian morality, and although churchwardens were encouraged to report such problems to the ecclesiastical

---

[42] See Chapter 1 above for a fuller discussion of byelaws and eviction.

[43] Physical violence like whipping (as opposed to restraint cum ridicule) was not used as a punishment by the lesser public courts; constables were authorized to whip vagrants by a statute of 1531 (22 Henry VIII, c. 12, *Stats. Realm*, vol. III, p. 329). For punishments in other courts, see Chapter 4, section one below.

[44] Only detailed local studies can establish how generally this was true. Virtually all those expelled from the manor and Liberty of Havering, Essex during the later fifteenth century because of sexual wrongdoing or for keeping unruly alehouses frequented by the poor were recent arrivals: McIntosh, *Autonomy and Community*, pp. 250–61.

[45] See Chapter 5, section one below.   [46] See Chapter 8, section three below.

courts, jurors were not supposed to use religious criteria as the basis for secular court decisions. Yet, as Graph 3.4 indicates, during three of the four duodecades between 1460 and 1539, 9–12 percent of all courts presented sexual misconduct, with lower figures both before and after. Jurors seldom reported casual fornication and adultery, which they presumably left to the church courts, but focused instead on prostitutes, their male procurers, and brothel keepers. The ecclesiastical courts and Sessions of the Peace appear to have started addressing such problems before the village and market centers became involved, and the level of concern in the church courts may have increased at the end of the sixteenth century. Here again we need further studies to establish whether ecclesiastical attention to sexual wrongdoing was increasing at a sufficient rate to balance the decline seen in the lesser courts and probably in Sessions too.

In virtually all communities prior to around 1460, even prostitutes seem to have been ignored unless they had done something else wrong too. Marian Bocher of Kingston-upon-Thames, Surrey, the wife of Thomas, was presented in 1434 as "a common whore who illegally keeps in her house a common tavern at all hours of the night."[47] In 1483 jurors in the hundred court of Knowlton, Dorset presented Edith Helpryn als. Miller as "a common whore who lives suspiciously," with her husband acting as a common procurer for her; they also named both Edith and her husband Henry as holecroppers. Alehouse keepers were sometimes charged with offering the services of whores as a side attraction, while some brothel keepers offered illegal games as an extra enticement.[48] In other instances, local standards of decency had obviously been violated by more than the simple presence of prostitution.[49]

During the later fifteenth and early sixteenth centuries, the language used to describe sexual misconduct in many courts changed as the number of presentments rose. Especially in market centers, the jurors now attempted to characterize sexual offences as constituting a threat to good order within their communities.[50] It was of course easy to do so

---

[47] Surrey RO, Kingston-upon-Thames, KF 1/1/1. For below, see Univ. of Nottingham Libr., MSS Dept. Mi 5/164/30.
[48] E.g., Ely Barton, Cambs. in 1502–3 (Cambridge Univ. Libr. E.D.R. C/6/17) and Hayridge hundred, Devon in 1562 (Devon RO CR 147).
[49] In the borough of Thornbury, Gloucs. the jurors reported in 1381 that "Thomas Edward receives Margery, the concubine of William Kyng, to the scandal of the vill," while jurors in Downton, Wilts. seem to have been shocked in 1465 that Eve Pykenet kept a brothel in which her daughter Agnes was one of the whores (Staffs. RO D641/1/4E/4 and Wilts. RO 490/1169).
[50] For the impact of type of community upon social regulation, see Chapters 6 and 7 below.

in general terms, for whores violated conventional social expectations and might enjoy unusual independence through living outside normal families and having their own sources of income. Yet the jurors' descriptions of wrongdoing suggest several more specific concerns. The terms used to describe such problems frequently indicate an inversion or distortion of customary virtues and relationships. Heads of households, for example, together with the keepers of any kind of public establishment, were expected to receive and care for visitors but also to maintain discipline among their families and guests. Two of the verbs most commonly used for keeping a whorehouse (or an alehouse) were *hospitere* ("to entertain or give hospitality to") and the less readily translatable term *fovere* (meaning originally "to keep warm," thence "to tend" or "to nourish").[51] Thus, John Wurre and Katherine his wife of Fakenham (Lancaster), Norf. were charged in 1503–4 with keeping a brothel and "giving hospitality to divers badly governed persons at night time, to the bad example and grave harm of others"; Edith Dene of Downton, Wilts., the wife of William, nourished (*fovet*) a common brothel in 1465 in partnership with John Clerk, a chaplain, while another man served as their procurer.[52] The indignation that permeates this language suggests that the jurors felt that these sorts of wrongdoing not only represented a breakdown in governance but also made a mockery of socially beneficial behaviors and institutions.

Another reason for discomfort with sexual wrongdoing by around 1500 was its ability to cause controversy within the community, thus linking it with concerns about social harmony. Margery Binche of Cawston, Norf. was described in 1493–4 as the keeper of a brothel who "gives hospitality to divers suspect persons, causing controversy and discord between her neighbors."[53] She herself was then presented as a scold. Jurors in the Honour of Clitheroe, Lancs. claimed in 1511 that Nicholas Grymeshagh of Accrington operated a house called "a borthel house," in which he kept a single woman who was the mistress of a married man; through this arrangement "strife and discord have arisen" between the latter and his wife. The exchange of information between local people that must have underlain many presentments is implied by the wording of two allegations in the manor of East Stonehouse, Devon in 1588. The jurors first charged (in English) that John Merefylde "gives hospitality to and receives a certain man called Robert Ha[che], who doth keep company with Joan the daughter of the

---

[51] For the language and symbolism of hospitality, see Heal, *Hospitality*, esp. ch. 1.
[52] Norf. RO N.R.S. 20743, Box 41 D 4; Wilts. RO 490/1169.
[53] Norf. RO N.R.S. 6025, 20 E 3. For below, see *The Court Rolls of the Honor of Clitheroe*, vol. III, p. 19.

said Merifeld, very disorderly and suspiciously, being a man married and his wife living."[54] They went on to present Sibbela Parkinge who "doth lodge and entertain one Thomas Colle, and they do accompany and lodge together not being married."

Only a handful of records, all from the first half of the sixteenth century, suggest an explicitly moral or religious objection to sexual misconduct. Jurors in Ely Barton, Cambs. in 1502–3 ordered that John Walshman and Christopher Walker "shall not keep nor hold common hospitality in brothels in their houses, where divers men and women satisfy their fleshly lust [*carnavit concupisc'*] so much that neighbors living both nearby and far away are often disturbed by their abominable deeds [*nefand' opera*]."[55] This is one of the few instances when one suspects that the steward or clerk named by the lord of the manor, the Bishop of Ely, may have had some influence over the language used. Two courts separated by a considerable distance and located in very different kinds of communities used identical wordings when describing sexual misconduct in the 1530s. The roll for Great Brickhill, Bucks. says in 1535 that "all the inhabitants" present a certain whore named Elizabeth [blank] who is living there "against the law of God and the peace of the lord king."[56] (Perhaps rather naively, the jurors ordered that no tenant of the area was to go to her under penalty of 6s 8d.) Four years later William Color als. Dyer of the borough of Tiverton, Devon was reported for living "lecherously [*luxuriose*] and suspiciously, to the bad example of others and against the law of God and the peace of the lord king."

Byelaws were rarely used when addressing sexual problems. Only 7 percent of the courts reporting such problems imposed their own local ordinances, with the few examples concentrated between 1460 and 1539. Sexual wrongdoing involving local people was normally punished through money fines. If, however, the offence was serious, many communities beginning in the later fifteenth century seized the opportunity to evict the malefactor from their territory.[57] Further, at least a few of the market centers by the Elizabethan period and possibly earlier were using forms of public humiliation, including "rough music."[58]

[54] Corn. RO ME 1764. For below, see *ibid.*
[55] Cambridge Univ. Libr. E.D.R. C/6/17. For the limited impact of the lord of the manor, see Chapter 6 below.
[56] Bucks. RO D/BASM/10/1. For below, see Devon RO CR 250.
[57] Thomas Green has suggested that this may imply a (possibly subconscious) link with excommunication of sexual offenders in the church courts (personal communication).
[58] Officials in (the) Devizes, Wilts., for example, ordered in 1559 that William Smyth and Agnes Atkyns be "punished in the open stocks for playing the knave and the whore together"; in 1584 a man and woman were to be "led about the town with basons,"

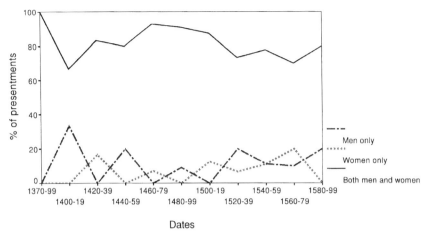

Graph 3.5   Courts that reported sexual misconduct: percentage of
presentments by gender

The material presented here is not consistent with several theoretical proposals about sexuality in the early modern period. Lyndal Roper suggested initially that a concern with sexual problems in sixteenth-century European cities was an attempt to control female sexuality, part of a broader crisis in gender relations deriving from new Protestant social values; later she and Anthony Fletcher each argued that male anxiety about the gender order during the early modern period stemmed ultimately from men's fear of female assertiveness, independence, and sexuality as well as from doubts about their own manhood.[59] Although the kinds of sources used in this study say little about the construction of gender, it is important to note that the majority of the lesser English courts that reported sexual problems presented both men and women at the same time, with women named alone in no more than a fifth of all courts in any duodecade (see Graph 3.5). The proportion of women did not rise during the periods when early Protestant and then Puritan social ideals were being introduced into England. It seems, therefore, that local jurors were not concerned prin-

with a marginal notation in the town book, "Sounding basons carried before him for her evil carriage" (Wilts. RO G 20/1/11, fol. 4r, and G 20/1/16, fol. 65r, both "Assembly Books"). "Basons" were probably basins, hit with a stick like a drum. In 1575 Sudbury, Suff. ordered that any persons found guilty of fornication or adultery by the mayor and aldermen should be "set in a cart and so to be carried about the town with papers set upon their heads declaring the matter and cause of offence" (Suff. RO, Bury St. Edmunds, EE 501 C141 B/1, fol. 117d, an "Assembly Book").

[59] In *The Holy Household*; her *Oedipus and the Devil* and his *Gender, Sex and Subordination*. For the possible impact of capitalism upon gender relations, see note 9 above.

cipally with female sexuality but rather were attempting to regulate disorderly sexual behavior wherever it occurred, among both men and women.[60] Further, we see no sign in these records either of an obsessive, prurient interest in sexuality among those responsible for controlling it nor of excessive valorization of sexual counter-ideals, expressed, for example, in carnival-like activities.[61]

Disorderly alehouses

Unruly alehouses, taverns, and inns were described in terms similar to those used for sexual wrongdoing. Reports of these problems rose gradually across the fifteenth century and remained fairly level, at 7–10 percent, across the sixteenth.[62] If we compare this pattern with the intermediate-level courts, the most striking feature is the increasing involvement of Sessions of the Peace between 1540 and the end of the century. This probably reflects the greater powers of the JPs, especially their right to require a large financial bond from any potential alehouse keeper plus two guarantors before a license was granted. Local jurors concerned about a disorderly public house in the second half of the sixteenth century may therefore have preferred to take the case before the Sessions, where the JPs could use the bond to enforce good behavior, rather than presenting it to their local court. Because the people reported to the lesser public courts were almost always the keepers of public houses, not their patrons, and because the proprietors of most establishments were male, it is not surprising that women were seldom named in the village and market center courts (see Graph 3.6).

---

[60] For a parallel argument, see Cressy, "Gender Trouble and Cross-Dressing."

[61] Roper, *Oedipus and the Devil*, esp. ch. 7; e.g., Bakhtin, *Rabelais and His World*, and Stallybrass and White, *Politics and Poetics*. The only ritualized but disorderly response to sexual issues found within English popular culture was the "skimmington" or "charivari," directed against women who dominated their husbands or cuckolded them (Ingram, "Ridings, Rough Music and the 'Reform of Popular Culture'"). Since female domination was not regulated by the courts at all and cuckolding only if reported as adultery, the rituals are unlikely to have been a reaction to official discipline.

[62] Included within this category are presentments of people described as keepers of public establishments for maintaining bad rule, order, or governance in their houses. (In some cases the person was not said to be a keeper in the presentment but was included in the list of those fined at the same session for violations of the Assize of Bread and Ale as an alehouse or inn keeper.) Presentments concerning the Assize of Bread and Ale have not been counted within this category, as they often functioned as licensing lists in this period, nor have reports of proprietors operating without a formal license from the JPs. Several other studies have taken the latter as a mark of concern with disruptive alehouses, but since we cannot tell whether a given presentment was a simple administrative issue or a reflection of worry about misrule within that establishment, it seemed wiser not to count them.

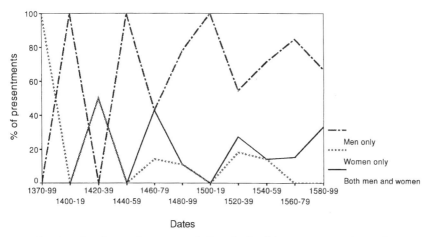

Graph 3.6   Courts that reported disorderly alehouses: percentage of presentments by gender

Insofar as the local courts had any statutory power in dealing with alehouses, it did not include monitoring their good order and rule. The Assize of Bread and Ale stipulated that the local courts were to supervise the price, weight or volume, and quality of certain kinds of food and drink.[63] Some courts extended this jurisdiction to cover other kinds of craftwork as well. Although the Assize itself specified punishment in the pillory or tumbrel for offenders, in practice local courts imposed small money fines instead. (For many communities, the names of those craftspeople assessed at public court sessions provide a *de facto* list of everyone working in those trades, suggesting that the fines had become in effect a licensing procedure.) Local authorities were also supposed to see that alehouses and inns displayed some kind of pole or sign that indicated they were public houses, not "blind" or concealed establishments. The only statutes authorizing control over the quality of order maintained within alehouses were to be enforced by the JPs, not the lesser public courts.[64]

Undeterred by lack of formal authority, local jurors proceeded to report and punish the proprietors of unruly alehouses and inns. Some

[63] "Assisa panis et cervisie," *Stats. Realm*, vol. I, pp. 199–200. For punishments, see "Judicium Pillorie," *ibid.*, pp. 201–2.

[64] A statute of 1495 ordered that alehouses be licensed by JPs after their keepers had provided appropriate sureties for good behavior; it also authorized JPs to close badly run houses (11 Henry VII, c. 2, modified only slightly in 19 Henry VII, c. 12, *Stats. Realm*, vol. II, pp. 569 and 657). An act of 1551–2 confirmed that all keepers of public houses must be licensed, assuring through their bond that they would maintain "good order and rule" and allow no illegal games (5 & 6 Edward VI, c. 25, *Stats. Realm*, vol. IV, pp. 157–8).

presentments claimed that inappropriate people frequented such houses and/or that they were open at improper times. In an unusually early case, jurors in the borough of Thornbury, Gloucs. presented Juliana Fox in 1379 as a common aleseller who "receives priests and others into her house at illegal times, viz. around the middle of the night."[65] In 1483 William Jonson, an alehouse keeper of Tooting Bec, Surrey, was presented for "keeping divers men and women who are suspect and of bad condition." Drunkenness was almost never mentioned, jurors apparently choosing to hand that problem over to the church courts. If any concern was expressed about the personal impact of spending too much time in alehouses, it was couched in terms of its financial consequences. Thomas Dewell als. Borke of Great Cummersdale, Cumb. was presented (in English) by the court of Dalston in 1574 because "he is a common haunter of alehouses and daily giveth himself to wasting and expending more than he is able to maintain."[66]

Many presentments from the later fifteenth and sixteenth centuries display special concern with servants and apprentices. Simon Jacob of Little Downham, Cambs. was reported in 1491–2 for "giving hospitality to servants of the tenants" at his alehouse, causing them to "subtract their service from their masters."[67] In 1516 the jurors of Basingstoke, Hants. sent an order to all alehouse proprietors that "they keep no man's apprentice in their house after seven o'clock, nor no man's servant after nine of the clock of the night," with a penalty for every offence of 20s.[68] William Firthe, a brewer of Aston, Derby., was presented in the court of Scarsdale hundred in 1582 because he "keeps apprentices, boys, and servants in his house at night."

Several new concerns become apparent after around 1500. Alehouses were viewed with special disfavor if they provided service to vagabonds. Andrew Taylor als. Laurance of Maidenhead in the manor of Cookham, Berks. was said in 1508 "to keep a common house and keep bad rule in giving hospitality to vagabonds, to the great harm of the neighborhood."[69] Jurors in Hales(owen), Worcs. ordered in 1573 that no innkeeper or alehouse keeper "shall from henceforth give hospitality to or keep in their houses any traveling [*itinerant*] people from outside beyond the space of one day and one night unless there is cause due to sickness." Respectable families also disliked the kind of speech

[65] Staffs. RO D641/1/4E/4. For below, see Greater London RO M95/BEC/9.
[66] Cumbria RO, Carlisle, DRC/2/68.   [67] Cambridge Univ. Libr. E.D.R. C/11/3.
[68] Baigent and Millard, *A History of Basingstoke*, p. 320. For below, see Notts. AO DDP 59/7.
[69] Berks. RO D/ESk M28. For below, see Birmingham Central Libr., Archs. Dept., Hagley Hall MS 377991, Box 78.

used in alehouses. Jurors of the borough of Clare, Suff. reported Robert Wasyll in 1523 because "he gives hospitality in his inn to vagabonds and suspect people who are of bad conversation, to the harm of his neighbors."[70] Nicholas May of Chippenham, Cambs., keeper of a victualling house, was said by jurors in 1560 to "maintain in it divers suspect persons of bad conversation, both by day and by night."

During the middle and later sixteenth century, jurors in Devonshire and a few other places attempted to ensure that alehouses closed during religious services.[71] Joan Stotte and Margery Gerret of the borough of Dartmouth were reported in 1550 because "they keep suspect alehouses both on Sundays and holidays and during other services of God."[72] In 1569 three men were said to have played at dice during service time in the public house of John Armestronge, a brewer of Monkleigh, Devon, while an alehouse keeper in East Stonehouse, Devon "did maintain and keep men a drinking in his house in the time of prayer" in 1588.

Disorderly public houses were associated with a variety of other problems. The presence of female tapsters, or ale servers, raised concerns about sexual liaisons. Jurors in Sherborne hundred in Dorset ordered in 1496 that four innkeepers "shall henceforth not receive or give hospitality in their houses to any women called 'Tapcesters' beyond one day and one night."[73] Indeed, some houses probably did serve as informal brothels. Innkeeper Geoffrey Mayle of Maidenhead in the manor of Bray, Berks. was reported in 1494 because "he keeps divers women of illegal condition called 'comen wymen.'"[74] Alehouses were also frequently the site of illegal gaming. In 1563 John Huddell, a licensed aleseller of Monkleigh, Devon, was reported because he "permits divers persons to play with playing cards in his house," while the previous year Robert Salter, a brewer from the area of Payhembury in the hundred of Hayridge, Devon, was fined for keeping "one court for playing at handball [*pilam palmaria*], which divers people frequent."[75] An exceptionally colorful charge (in English) from c. 1594 against Edward Harvye and his wife, alehouse keepers of Berwick-upon-Tweed, Northumb., pulls together many of

---

[70] PRO DL 30/116/1797. For below, see Cambs. RO, Cambridge, R55/7/1g.

[71] For the playing of illegal games during divine services, see section four below.

[72] Devon RO *f.009.4, 64743. For below, see Devon RO CR 1108 and Corn. RO ME 1764, the latter in English.

[73] Dorset RO Old Museum Ref. KG 9. For a female tapster in Romford, Essex, said to be "of bad condition" and therefore expelled in the 1490s, see PRO SC 2/172/37, m. 4d.

[74] Berks. RO D/EG M41.

[75] Devon RO CR 1107 and CR 147. For below, see Berwick-upon-Tweed RO C.1/1, fol. 28v, an "Assembly Book."

these issues, adding to them characteristic mistrust of those coming from over the border: to their alehouse "resort Scots, shepherds, tinkers, rogues, and other disordered and unlawful company and use drinking, gaming, playing at cards, and other misdemeanors as well in service time on the Sabbath day as at other times, and ... [Harvye's] wife hath been always wonderfully suspect to be a privy harlot."

Byelaws were frequently used against those who operated unruly alehouses or inns. Of all courts reporting this problem, 21 percent issued local ordinances about the quality of order expected and the penalties to be faced by those who violated local standards; this is the most extensive use of byelaws within the first two clusters of offences. But as they tried to develop more effective punishments, jurors faced a serious problem. The customary cash fine was of little use against the keepers of many smaller alehouses and inns, who were too poor to pay. Further, local officials hesitated to shut down entirely the lesser public houses which played such an important economic and social role among the poor.[76] In 1574–5 William Barrett of Wivenhoe, Essex was presented because "he keeps a common inn and at diverse times and places has allowed people to play illegal games and to observe bad rule in the same."[77] For this offence he was fined 12d. The following year, Barrett was again presented for keeping a hospice (this time called an alehouse) and permitting illegal games, but the record notes that "because he is exceedingly poor [*valde pauper*] the penalty is remitted" under the condition that he not offend similarly in the future. A few courts experimented with forms of physical detention.[78]

Badly governed, living suspiciously, or of evil reputation

The last category within this group of offences is a composite of various loosely defined presentments that refer to the poor quality of the offender's governance or life. Some of the statements implied sexual misconduct, while in others the charge of poor control seems to have been associated with disorder in alehouses.[79] Such cases were counted

---

[76] Peter Clark, *The English Alehouse.*   [77] Essex RO D/DBm M105. For below, see *ibid.*

[78] E.g., in Broughton, Hunts. in 1465, where the constable was told by the manor court that if he found people seated in an alehouse after 8 o'clock at night, he should put them into the stocks (PRO SC 2/179/70).

[79] An example of such language overtly associated with sexual wrongdoing comes from Alciston, East Sussex in 1535, where the jurors presented Thomas Osbarn and his wife Joan for "keeping a suspect and badly governed house called a 'bawdry house'" (East Sussex RO SAS G18/55). Jurors might also imply sexual misconduct without actually referring to it: in Mitchell, Corn., they ordered in 1498 that "if any resident or inhabitant within the said borough receives into his house any woman who is suspect or badly

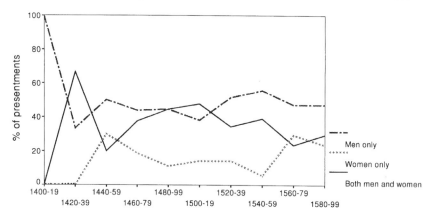

Dates (no entry for periods in which no presentments)

Graph 3.7   Courts that reported being badly governed: percentage of
presentments by gender

under those headings in the quantitative analysis. In other instances,
unprovable suspicion of theft seems to have underlain the presentments, while in the remainder we cannot tell what the jurors found
objectionable.[80] Nevertheless, unspecific charges like these, tallied under the "bad governance" heading, were common. The percentage of
courts reporting people in such terms started rising in the 1440s–50s
and grew steadily to a surprising zenith of 21 percent of all courts under
observation in the 1520s–30s; it then dropped to 10–12 percent after
1540. The church courts and Sessions of the Peace used similar sorts of
language in reporting problems, but their response started slightly later
than in village and market centers. As shown in Graph 3.7, the gender
distribution of people reported within this category in the lesser courts
was weighted somewhat towards men.

governed for 3 days and 3 nights, he shall forfeit for each time 40d" (Courtney Libr.
Royal Institution of Corn., Truro, HH/14A/9). Brewer John Holemede of the Westexe
region of Tiverton hundred, Devon was charged in 1456 with "receiving suspect men
who are not well governed," while as late as 1597–8 Thomas Yonges, an innkeeper in
Fakenham, Norf., was reported for allowing four men "to keep bad governance at
night time in his said house to the great disturbance of his neighbors" (Devon RO CR
341 and Norf. RO N.R.S. 20745, 41 D 4).

[80] The wrongdoers who frequented Thomas Weser's brothel in Minehead, Som. in 1467
were "men ... of bad living by whom the neighbors' goods are stolen and carried
away," while Richard Stoner of Westbury in the Surrey manor of Godalming was said
in 1538 both "to give hospitality to men of bad fame and conversation" and "to consort
with whores and thieves and other malefactors" (Som. RO DD/LP28/13 and Surrey
RO, Guildford, LM 215).

By the early sixteenth century, such accusations were coming to be associated with the related issues of a person's general reputation or "fame" and the quality of his or her speech. James Coke and his wife were ordered to move out of Great Horwood, Bucks. in 1515 because "they are of bad fame and commonly keep bad rule, to the harm of their neighbors," while the court of Cookham, Berks. evicted Robert William and his wife Margaret from Maidenhead in 1524 because "they are badly governed and of bad reputation."[81] John Downer and his wife Margaret, alesellers in Harrow, Middx., were ordered in 1530 to cease operating their public house under the huge penalty of £5 because "they give hospitality to and keep in their house men and women of bad conversation and governance."

As was true for many other offences during the sixteenth century, bad rule was commonly attributed to vagabonds and those who received them. John Grey, tailor, was described by the jurors of Ely Barton, Cambs. in 1507–8 as a vagabond, of evil disposition, who was "unwilling to govern himself well."[82] That same year an innkeeper of Maidenhead, Berks. was said "to keep bad rule in giving hospitality to vagabonds, to the great harm of the neighborhood and the inhabitants of the same." Jurors in the Honour of Halton, Ches. ordered in 1535–6 that anyone in the borough of Halton "who keeps any suspect persons, vagabonds, and other misruled, disquieting, or disorderly persons who are not of good name and fame among their neighbors" should move away from the community.[83]

Sometimes, however, we have no idea of why such people or their conduct were regarded as objectionable. When no specific offence was even implied, one suspects that the jurors indeed did not have evidence of any more concrete misdeed or they would have reported that as more likely to lead to punishment. William Merssh was presented by the court of Langtoft and Baston, Lincs. in 1466–7 because he "receives, gives hospitality to, and maintains in his house badly governed people and of suspicious life, to the great disturbance of the total vill of Baston."[84] Jurors for the area of Shields, Durham in the halmote court of the Prior and Convent of Durham ordered in 1491 "that no tenants shall keep or give hospitality within their holding to Margaret Burrell nor

---

[81] New College Oxford MS 3920, and Berks. RO D/ESk M41. For below, see Greater London RO Acc.76/2421.
[82] Cambridge Univ. Libr. E.D.R. C/6/17. For below, see Berks. RO D/ESk M28.
[83] PRO DL 30/8/103.
[84] Lincs. AO 6.Ancaster 1/85. For below, see Durham Univ. Libr., Archs. and Spec. Colls., Prior's Kitchen, DCD Halmote Court, spring, 1491.

any other person of dishonest governance." John Bene and his wife Agnes of Hexton, Herts. were labeled outrageous (*enormia*) in 1511–12 for "keeping bad rule to the harm of their neighbors."[85]

In prosecuting these issues, local court officials rarely promulgated their own ordinances. Only 10 percent of the courts reporting problems with bad governance imposed byelaws, with most of the instances occurring between 1460 and 1539. This probably stems from the jurors' inability to describe precisely what types of behavior should be pro-scribed: presentments made in such terms seem often to have stemmed from mistrust of particular individuals rather than forming part of an effort to control definable categories of behavior. Nor is it surprising that eviction was often the punishment of choice in dealing with people reported in these terms.

Combined figures for those courts that reported one or more of the problems within the Disorder cluster are displayed at the top of Graph 3.4. This makes clear the two periods of most rapidly increasing con-cern: between the 1440s–50s and the 1460s–70s, and again between the 1480s–90s and the 1500s–10s. It also shows the existence of level pla-teaus at 18–19 percent both in the 1460s–90s and after 1540, with a peak in the 1500s–30s. The difference between the highest and the lowest level of concern, 29 percent, is about double that seen in the first cluster. Because there is no political or ideological evidence suggesting that concern with issues of order declined after 1540, and because we have no reason to suspect that conduct had in fact become more orderly, the apparent decrease in attention seen here was almost certainly the result of shifting patterns of jurisdiction whereby the church courts and Sessions of the Peace took on much of the responsibility for these problems.[86]

The Poverty cluster

The third group of offences revolved around the social implications of poverty and idleness. Here we are witnessing a punitive aspect of the emotionally fraught and potentially divisive process whereby commu-nities struggled to develop an appropriate set of responses to the diverse kinds of poor people.[87] As Graph 3.8 displays, concern with hedgebreaking, giving hospitality to vagabonds or beggars, living idly or refusing to work if one was poor, and allowing subtenants to live in

[85] Herts. RO 47296.
[86] See Chapter 1, section one above and Chapters 5, section one, and 8, section one below.
[87] See the Introduction, above, and Chapters 4, section two, and 8 below.

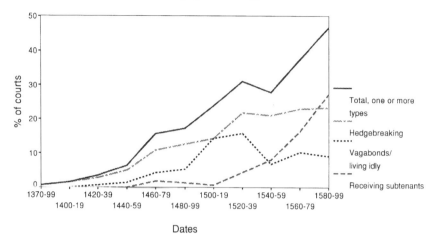

Graph 3.8   Percentage of courts under observation that reported offences in
the Poverty cluster

one's holding emerged around the middle of the fifteenth century and
continued to rise in importance throughout the sixteenth.[88] By the
1580s–90s a startling 46 percent of all courts under observation were
reporting one or more of these problems. In this area local efforts were
reinforced during the Elizabethan period by the increasing attention
directed at vagrants by the JPs, joined eventually by the Justices of
Assize.[89] Moreover, from the 1550s onwards legal action worked together with the decisions of poor relief officials within the parishes,
who were able to withhold assistance from anyone whose conduct
offended community norms; in some settings they could recommend
that an able-bodied idler be sent to a bridewell or house of correction.[90]
Yet while concern with the harmful consequences of poverty was
obviously very high, the language used by local court jurors in making
these presentments was restricted. Like England's more educated
leadership, who found it difficult to generate either thoughtful analyses
of the issues surrounding poverty or effective solutions to the complex
problems, local jurors experimented with forceful measures against
miscreants but seldom tried to articulate the reasons for their concern.[91]

---

[88] Because only evidence from jury presentments is used in this study, there is no
possibility that these issues were raised in the course of private suits whose actual
intent was to establish title to land.   [89] See Chapter 1, section one above.

[90] The same kind of men named to local court juries were likely to be elected as Collectors
(or, after 1598, Overseers) of the Poor for their parish.

[91] See Chapter 8, section one below.

Clearly visible in these records are a growing divergence and mounting tension between two approaches to poverty – between older (more tolerant) and newer (more selective) attitudes. Traditional forms of assistance were obviously being provided to the needy, including travelers and immigrants, right through the sixteenth century. Compassion and aid to the poor were advocated by both the Catholic church and the Protestant Church of England. Providing shelter for the homeless, giving food and clothing to the hungry and naked, and bestowing alms upon the needy were among the familiar "seven works of mercy." Many people had a deeply rooted sense that it was socially and morally right to offer personal assistance to their poor neighbors, even if such people might be regarded by more discriminating critics as lazy and feckless; if a destitute person with young children arrived in the community, surely it was a Christian act to allow them to stay at least temporarily in one's empty back shed.

Yet as early as the 1460s–70s and increasingly across the sixteenth century some jurors were prepared to present and punish their neighbors for committing customary acts of charity. These leaders presumably felt that they had to take action to preserve the stability, good order, and economic well-being of their community against the multiple challenges imposed by the presence of a rising number of poor people, especially when they were outsiders. This approach relied upon a *de facto* distinction between those poor who warranted sympathy and perhaps charitable assistance because they were unable to labor for their own support, and able-bodied idlers who were to be treated more severely. The two approaches were by no means mutually exclusive: many of the communities whose courts were most energetic in reporting those who gave inappropriate charitable assistance and in punishing misbehavior among the poor were equally vigorous in their efforts to assist those needy people regarded as deserving.[92] Further, by the later sixteenth century a particularly perplexing form of poverty was emerging in many communities: able-bodied people who were willing to work but could not find adequate employment to support themselves and their families.

Because customary money fines were useless against those with no resources, jurors tried other forms of punishment that would serve as effective warnings to their shiftless neighbors while discouraging undesirable newcomers from settling in their communities. As part of this

---

[92] McIntosh, "Local Responses to the Poor." The combination of regulation of behavior with individual compassion is illustrated by the willingness of Elizabethan officials in the town of Hadleigh, Suff. to provide assistance to illegitimate children (McIntosh, "Networks of Care").

effort, the courts were much more likely to enact byelaws for this cluster than for either of the previous two. Similarly, eviction was a favored weapon when dealing with the undesirable poor. By the end of Elizabeth's reign, nearly half of all communities that reported any problems in this poverty-related cluster were also evicting people from the community, by far the highest level seen in this study. A more negative approach to the poor was probably reinforced by the government's increasing fear of vagrants and other disruptive poor, publicized in proclamations and statutes from Henry VIII's reign onwards.[93]

Hedgebreaking

Taking wood from hedges for use as fuel, known commonly as hedgebreaking, was an offence of the poor. This problem, which was reported by nearly a quarter of all courts under observation in the latter part of the sixteenth century, has received scant historical attention. When noted at all, it has usually been conflated incorrectly with the throwing down of newly-built hedges as a protest against enclosures.[94] If a community had ample common woodlands that all residents might use, hedgebreaking was generally not an issue. It became a problem when the wooded area was small in comparison to the population and/or when access to the woods was limited to certain groups of people, such as the tenants of arable land. In these restricted communities, people who were merely subtenants of the direct tenants were not allowed to take fuel for cooking and heating from the woods. If they were too poor to buy wood commercially, they often turned to the common hedges that separated fields, roads, and other areas. Taking a limited amount of dead wood from a hedge does it no harm and presumably had been the practice for centuries, but if too much wood is removed, or if green wood is cut, the hedge develops holes through which animals can pass, or it may even die entirely. Presentments for

---

[93] See Chapter 5 below. Vagabonds were mentioned in government statements before the 1520s–30s, but the serious rhetorical campaign began only then.

[94] The standard term used in court records for this offence is *fractio sepes*, the breaking or tearing of hedges. (Occasionally, especially in the west, the word *haia* was used for a hedge.) These usages were carefully distinguished from the extremely rare charge of *projectio sepes*, the throwing or knocking down of (newly planted) hedges associated with enclosure. Presentments included here as hedgebreaking all referred either to common hedges or to an unspecified "hedges of the neighbors/tenants." Charges of breaking the lord's hedges or of taking trees from his woodlands have not been counted, since that might be a reflection of resistance to seigneurial power rather than a problem among the tenants themselves; nor were the rare reports tallied that refer to breaking the hedges of a named person, which usually reflected a personal conflict between those individuals.

hedgebreaking may thus provide an *a priori* indicator of an actual increase in the number of poor people within a given community, producing legitimate worry about the condition of the hedges, but they also probably reflect a subjective feeling among respectable families that there were now so many poor in the area that some kind of action had to be taken. Hedgebreaking was not addressed in Parliamentary legislation during our period, although in 1601 it was included in a savage statutory prohibition of various thefts committed by the poor, listed alongside robbing gardens and orchards and cutting grain growing in the fields.[95]

As Graph 3.8 shows, hedgebreaking was of minor importance until the middle of the fifteenth century, but it then began to mount. By the 1500s–10s 14 percent of courts were reporting this problem, and after a sharp rise to the 1520s–30s concern remained at a sloping plateau of 21–23 percent through the rest of the century. The church courts handled none of the offences in the Poverty cluster, and JPs paid little attention to hedgebreaking, probably because it involved local residents who were subject to the control of their own courts and was regarded as relatively unimportant. Local communities thus bore the brunt of control over hedgebreaking right through the sixteenth century.

In the fifteenth and sixteenth centuries, as in the twentieth, gathering wood from hedges was a task often assigned to children and older women – a physically appropriate way for them to contribute to the household economy.[96] A presentment of hedgebreakers in Cookham, Berks. in 1598 included three sons of named people, four daughters (two with widowed mothers), a male and a female servant, and four married women.[97] Although the local court records do not specify the age of those charged, there are interesting changes in the gender distribution over time. Prior to 1460, the few presentments show wide swings between men/boys, women/girls, or both (see Graph 3.9). During the 1460s–90s, however, the first period of greater concern with this problem, the proportion of courts reporting females climbed to a total of 73 percent (for either women only or both women and men).

---

[95] 43 Eliz., c. 7 (*Stats. Realm*, vol. IV, pp. 971–2). Several measures from the middle of the century had dealt specifically with preservation of the hedges around woodlands or newly enclosed areas but not with hedgebreaking more generally (e.g., 35 Henry VIII, c. 17, and 3 & 4 Edward VI, c. 3, *Stats. Realm*, vol. III, pp. 977–80, and vol. IV, pp. 102–3).

[96] For the taking of deadwood from hedges in Heref. in the early twentieth century, see Haines, "Hop Picking." Even after World War Two, children on Heref. farms were sent out each morning to gather wood from hedges for their mothers' kitchen stoves (personal communication, Mrs. Judith Wells, The Vauld House Farm, Marden, Heref.).

[97] Berks. RO D/ESk M82.

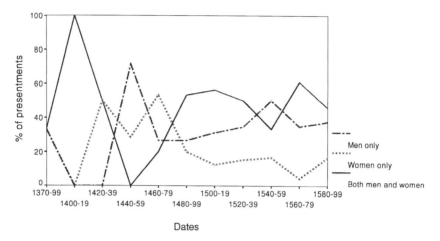

Graph 3.9   Courts that reported hedgebreaking: percentage of presentments
by gender

After 1500 women constituted a smaller and declining fraction of the
total. This suggests that the later fifteenth century may have seen an
unusual number of women among the poor.

The language used to describe hedgebreaking was nearly always
minimal, with such offenders characterized as "a common breaker of
hedges" and their actions said to be "to the harm of the neighbors."
Somewhat more fully, John Cooke of Spilsby cum Eresby, Lincs. was
presented in 1509 because he "breaks the common hedges without
common assent of his neighbors and carries away small wood [*lingin-
cula*]."[98] An order made by the court of the manor of Amberley, West
Sussex in 1561 required that no inhabitant permit his sons or servants
either to lop off branches from any trees on his neighbors' lands or to
pluck (*evellere*) and break any hedges. The manor of Hatfield (Chase) in
West Yorks. presented three men in 1576 because "they do not have
firewood but break hedges of the tenants and carry away the green
wood which they dry."[99] By the Elizabethan period, hedgebreaking
had become explicitly linked with a growing number of subtenants.
Because these poor people, many of them newly arrived in the community, were difficult to punish, jurors directed their orders at the local

[98] Lincs. AO ANC 3/14/67. For below, see West Sussex RO Ep VI/12/6.
[99] West Yorks. Arch. Serv., Leeds, DB 205/1576–7.

residents who took them in. Thus, the court of Wethersfield Hall, Essex ordered in 1561 that no proprietor of a tenement should henceforth permit any subtenant to remain on his holding who is a breaker of hedges, taking wood "furtively for burning."[100] Norton Hall, Suff. ordered in 1574 that "no inhabitant shall receive any person or persons coming from outside the vill to live in any tenement, messuage, or cottage within this vill who is not able to buy sufficient firewood but will break hedges illegally," under the substantial penalty of 20s for each wrongdoer so admitted.

Byelaws seemed particularly suitable as a means of buttressing the courts' ability to deal aggressively with a form of theft in which no single person was wronged, against which Parliament had taken no action, and which had almost certainly been accepted by custom in the past. Although local bodies rarely used their own ordinances when dealing with hedgebreaking prior to 1520, 35–41 percent of the courts reporting this problem passed byelaws in each duodecade thereafter.

In trying to penalize and/or deter hedgebreakers, local officials moved through a variety of techniques. Cash fines were the first method, with the amount of the payment rising from about 1460 onwards. However, as it became increasingly apparent that the very poor people who acquired fuel in this way rarely had money with which to pay fines, some communities turned to eviction or physical punishment. The market center of (Saffron) Walden, Essex illustrates this process. In 1554 the jurors ordered that no one should break hedges under penalty of 12d for the first time, to be paid by the main tenant of the dwelling in which the breaker lived. For the second offence, 2s was to be paid, "and if any one breaks often, he is to be expelled from this domain."[101] These measures were evidently inadequate, for three years later the court issued a new byelaw stating that anyone who breaks hedges "shall be punished by the stocks, viz. shall sit in the stocks for three hours for each time taken, and his landlord to forfeit for each time 12d." The stocks were ordered as a punishment for hedgebreaking in Cookham, Berks. as well: a byelaw of 1582 specified that offenders were to be taken to the place where the action had occurred "and there, by

---

[100] Essex RO D/DFy M18. For below, see Suff. RO, Bury St. Edmunds, 553/65. By 1592 officials in the market center of Henley, Oxon. had become so deeply troubled by hedgebreaking at the hands of "the children of poor people within the said town" that they ordered that any poor child who lived idly or refused to work might be put into gaol until he or she agreed to accept employment making Jersey stockings (Oxon. Archs. MS. D.D. Henley A.III.2/1, no. 10, an "Assembly Book").

[101] Essex RO D/DBy M23. For below, see *ibid.*

and by, in the Sunday or holiday next following, be put in the stocks at morning or evening prayer in some open place."[102] In a few instances imprisonment or whipping were threatened. Eviction was ordered especially for hedgebreakers who had committed other offences as well.[103] The records of the court of Basingstoke, Hants. contain the following (English) entry for 1587: "Alexander Minchen dwelling in one of the tenements which Richard Randole builded in Northbrook street is a great spoiler of hedges, and liveth idly being unmarried, and keepeth Alice Higat in his house, and carrieth about him a saw to cut quick frith [= green wood] and other stuff by night."[104] The bailiffs and constables were therefore told to remove Minchen out of the town before the next court.

Vagabonds and idlers

The next category joins several related offences associated with mobility and labor: giving temporary hospitality to vagabonds or beggars, or being a poor person who lived idly, refusing to work. Within the first element, which constituted the great majority of these presentments, concern focused on vagabonds, people who wandered from place to place and had no regular employment; resident beggars were mentioned less often. The presentments seldom speak of being such a person but aim instead at those who received them into their houses. Closely affiliated were accusations that a person was unwilling to labor: that he or she lived idly, had no income but lived suspiciously, or refused to accept employment. Graph 3.8 shows that these issues rarely troubled local courts around 1400 but rose slowly to a low plateau of 4–5 percent in the 1460s–90s. By the first four decades of the sixteenth century, concern had risen quite sharply to 14–16 percent, declining again from 1540 onwards. This is the only element within the poverty-related cluster in which fewer local courts expressed concern at the end of the sixteenth century than earlier, a variation due almost certainly to the increasing role of JPs in dealing with vagabonds.[105] Sessions offered

[102] Berks. RO D/ESk M75. This example suggests that the stocks could be moved around, as we saw with the tumbrel for women. For more severe punishments, see Droitwich, Worcs. in 1519 and Henley, Oxon. around 1590 (Worcs. RO, Headquarters, County Hall, 261.4/31, BA 1006/#359 [Box 32], and Oxon. Archs. MS. D.D. Henley A.V.5, fol. 55v, an "Assembly Book").

[103] John Mellowes of Ingatestone Hall, Essex was ordered to move out of the vill after being presented in 1538–9 as "badly governed, that is to say in giving opprobrious words to his neighbors and in breaking hedges" (Essex RO D/DP M87).

[104] Baigent and Millard, *A History of Basingstoke*, p. 352.

[105] See Chapter 1, section one above.

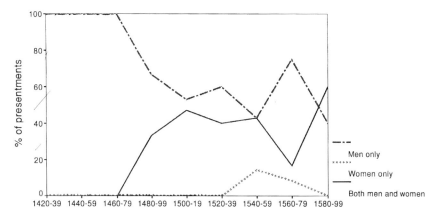

Graph 3.10   Courts that reported vagabonds/living idly: percentage of
presentments by gender

harsher punishments and were better able to deal with people who
moved between communities and hence could readily escape punishment at the hands of any single local court. Although women alone
were seldom charged with being or receiving vagabonds, the proportion of females named together with men rose markedly around 1480,
as Graph 3.10 shows.

   Technically, local courts were not empowered to deal with people
who received vagabonds. It is true that a long series of statutes instructed
constables to apprehend and punish vagabonds and beggars, and these
officers were elected by the leet courts.[106] But the courts themselves
directed their attention at those who *took in* vagabonds, an authority that

---

[106] For more than a century, the operative statute was that passed in 1383 during the
socially repressive mood that followed the Peasants' Revolt. This act authorized
constables and other officials above them to examine any vagabonds and to compel
them to find surety for their good bearing under penalty of being sent to gaol (7
Richard II, c. 5, *Stats. Realm*, vol. II, pp. 32–3). Five years later traveling beggars and
servants were ordered to carry testimonials describing their reasons for being on the
road (12 Richard II, cc. 8 and 3, *Stats. Realm*, vol. II, pp. 55–8). Between 1495–6 and the
end of Elizabeth's reign, Parliament passed eight further statutes about such wan-
derers (11 Henry VII, c. 2, 19 Henry VII, c. 12, 22 Henry VIII, c. 12, 27 Henry VIII, c. 25, 1
Edward VI, c. 3, 14 Eliz., c. 5, 18 Eliz., c. 3, and 39 Eliz., cc. 3, 4, and 17, *Stats. Realm*,
passim). By the statute of 1495 vagabonds were to be set into the stocks by the
constables for three days and nights, while the act of 1530–1 authorized whipping for
them and anyone found begging without a license from the JPs.

no Parliamentary measure assigned to them.[107] The most common term within the generally short and matter-of-fact language used in these presentments stems from the verb *vagare/vagari*, that inherently suspicious form of purposeless movement that appeared in descriptions of nightwalking.[108] Traveling directly from one community to another to take up employment or visit a relative was fine, but wandering aimlessly about was not. Jurors in the market center of Launceston, Corn. referred to vagabonds in 1568 as people who "go idly up and down, contrary to any good order" and "will not keep [with] their masters but run from place to place."[109] Vagabonds were frequently associated with other types of misconduct, especially problems in alehouses/inns and illegal gaming.[110] Officers in Morpeth, Northumb. worried about the influence of vagabonds on susceptible servants: they ordered the bailiffs (in English) in 1523 to keep all vagabonds and beggars out of the town during divine service on holy days, "because it is thought that those that use to go in service time do entice servants, their masters being absent, to imbecile, destroy, and waste their masters' goods."[111] Quite rationally in our eyes, vagabonds were occasionally seen as transmitters of disease. Jurors in Basingstoke, Hants. said in 1521:

We would that all beggars that useth to go about should go and resort to the town or country they were born in, and there to abide and continue; for we think that many of them doth keep and be among sick people of the reigning [= sweating] sickness, and so cometh to this town and putteth the town to great trouble, and it seems that they do affect the town; and it is a great pity that the disease should come by them or any other misfortune, til it please God to send it.[112]

---

[107] In the Assize of Clarendon of 1166, the king had prohibited people from receiving "a wandering or an unknown man" anywhere except in a borough, and then only for one night, but this was overridden in the statute of 1383 (*Translations and Reprints from Original Sources*, vol. I, no. 6, pp. 22–5; 7 Richard II, c. 5, *Stats. Realm*, vol. II, pp. 32–3). The Act of 1530–1 ordered that people who "give any harbor, money, or lodging" to vagabonds or beggars were to be taken before JPs for punishment (22 Henry VIII, c. 12, *Stats. Realm*, vol. III, p. 330).

[108] The term "rogue," used frequently in Parliamentary statutes, turned up in the local records just once, in Cannock and Rugeley, Staffs., where it was given as a synonym for a vagrant person in 1594: Staffs. RO D(W) 1734/2/1/186.

[109] Corn. RO B/LA 298.

[110] See, e.g., Heref. RO AM33/1 (Bishop's Frome, 1475), Devon RO CR 81 (West Budleigh hundred, 1494), Lincs. AO ANC 3/14/66 (Spilsby cum Eresby, 1505), and Berks. RO D/ESk M28 (Cookham, 1508).

[111] Boyle, "Orders for the Town and Borough" (an "Assembly Book"), p. 215. It is interesting that the order assumes that servants did not attend religious services with their masters; servants and children were to be sent to catechizing by their employers or parents.

[112] Baigent and Millard, *A History of Basingstoke*, p. 325. One notes that traveling beggars were not viewed as possible agents of God's intent.

Much of the hostility towards vagabonds stemmed from the fact that they did not labor for their living. Jurors for the vill of Peterborough, Northants. ordered in 1461 that all constables should inquire whether there be "comers and goers and will not work."[113] Any so found were either to be evicted from the town or else "set fast til all men know what goods they have to live by." In Manhood hundred, West Sussex, a man surnamed Chappman whose first name the jurors did not know was presented in 1527 as "a common vagabond who wanders at night and sleeps by day, not exercising any faculty and having nothing by which he is able to live but lives suspiciously."[114]

The main goal when dealing with these transient poor was to keep them moving on and out of the community, rather than letting them put down local roots. As policies created in pursuit of this objective became more stringent over time, they increasingly violated traditional practices of hospitality and charity. As early as 1496 jurors in the manor of Ombersley, Worcs. instructed the constables "to see that outside and suspicious wandering beggars are not permitted to remain here."[115] This rule was clearly inadequate, for six years later they issued a new order: no one "shall henceforth give any hospitality to any poor people unless they are weak or enfeebled [*debil'*], and then for only one night per month." The borough of Droitwich, Worcs. encountered problems with the wandering poor in Henry VIII's reign. The court first ordered in 1516 that vagabonds and beggars might stay only in the almshouse, not in private homes; when that policy proved impractical, the jurors ruled that no one was to harbor or keep such people beyond a day and a night.[116] Whereas local courts usually showed scant interest in Parliamentary legislation, it is interesting that the jurors of Penkridge, Staffs. were aware of the provision in the statute of 1530–1 that beggars must be licensed: order was made in 1555 that no inhabitant "shall henceforth give hospitality to or receive any dishonest person who is called 'vacabondes' nor any begging persons who are called 'beggars' unless they have licence for begging from the Justices of the Peace within the hundred of Cuttleston to ask for alms in the same hundred."[117]

[113] Northants. RO PDC. CR. Bundle D, Roll 32.   [114] West Sussex RO Ep VI/12/2, fol. 95v.

[115] Worcs. RO, St. Helens, 705:56/BA 3910/22/10. For below, see *ibid.*

[116] Worcs. RO, County Hall, 261.4/31, BA 1006/#352 (Box 31) and #409 (Box 32); #409, in which beggars were permitted to ask for assistance only on Wednesdays and Fridays, is undated within Henry's reign but is clearly later than #352. The night-and-a-day rule for beggars was also imposed in Basingstoke, Hants. in 1514, while a limit of a single night was ordered in Seaton Delaval, Northumb. in 1527–8 (Baigent and Millard, *A History of Basingstoke*, p. 316, and Northumb. RO 1 DE/2/4).

[117] Staffs. RO D260/M/E/429/1. One wonders whether the steward of the court brought word of the statute or whether jurors perhaps heard it read at Sessions of the Peace.

Attitudes towards poor local residents who lived idly showed more variation over time. In the fifteenth and early sixteenth centuries those who did not work were usually presented only if they were mistrusted for other reasons. Joan Brene and her daughter Joan of Fowey, Corn. were said in 1456 to "live suspiciously with large expenses but earning nothing through which [they can support themselves]," while in 1502 John Pynne of Hayridge, Devon was not only living with Agnes Scarlott, a woman just presented as "a receiver of vagabonds travelling the country," but compounded his offence by having "no honest means of livelihood."[118] Jurors in the borough of Tiverton, Devon reported James Rowlyng in 1517 because he "lives suspiciously and does not work the land and has no holding where he is able to live honestly." By the 1530s concern was becoming focused upon poor young people who had not taken positions as servants outside their family. Jurors for Great Bradley in the manor of Cookham, Berks. presented four young men in 1539 because "they are unwilling to take themselves to masters for service."[119] In 1554 Widow Cokes of (Saffron) Walden, Essex was reported for keeping at home her two daughters, who were physically able to work. One of the girls was hired as a servant at that very court session, while Widow Cokes was ordered to put the other into appropriate employment by a stated date.

Courts in northern England seem to have been particularly eager during the 1530s and again during the later sixteenth century to get idle young people out of their parental homes, a possible reflection of population pressure unmatched by economic expansion.[120] In 1536 Cecilia Reyd, a widow of Ampleforth, N. Yorks., was ordered to remove her daughters Agnes and Margaret from her tenement and to cease keeping them, while at Eastertime in the same year jurors in Northallerton, N. Yorks. imposed a penalty (in English) on "Tollerton wife, that she avoid [=evict] forth of her house all her daughters and sons saving one afore Pentecost."[121] In 1574 William Barker of Dalston, Cumb. was similarly told to remove from his house and put to service all his children except one within the following two months, while jurors in Doncaster, West Yorks. gave warning in 1573 "that no poor cottagers shall keep within their houses no idle young women or boys who are able to be put to service."

[118] Corn. RO ARB 75/84 and Devon RO CR 124. For below, see Devon RO CR 243.
[119] Berks. RO D/ESk M55. For below, see Essex RO D/DBy M23.
[120] See Chapters 6 and 7 below.
[121] Borthwick Institute, York, CC.P.Ampleforth 12/21 and N. Yorks. County RO, Northallerton, ZBD 1/54/28. For below, see Cumbria RO, Carlisle, DRC/2/68 and Doncaster Archs. Dept. AB.5/1/6.

In dealing with vagabonds and idlers, local ordinances were frequently used: 25–42 percent of all courts that reported such problems in each duodecade between 1460 and the end of the sixteenth century passed byelaws. Eviction was likewise a common form of punishment.

Receiving subtenants

The final offence within this cluster was permitting poor subtenants to live in one's house or tenement. By the 1520s–30s, jurors in some communities were starting to worry about the presence of growing numbers of poor people who held no property of their own, not even a modest cottage, but instead lived in a building owned or rented by another local person. These subtenants, commonly called "inmates" in local records, were viewed with suspicion for several reasons. Because they were often new arrivals who had no regular employment, local leaders saw them as potentially likely to resort to dishonest means to support themselves, including hedgebreaking or more overt theft. If the subtenant was accompanied by children or young people, the expectation of trouble was higher still. Especially alarming from the mid-sixteenth century onwards was the possibility that such people might remain in the community for three years, whereupon they would qualify for local poor relief.

The obvious solution to such problems in the opinion of many local courts was to take all possible measures to get poor subtenants out of the community as soon as possible and to make sure that others of their kind were not allowed to find accommodation. Here Parliament provided partial and belated assistance: a statute of 1589 that prohibited the building of new cottages unless they were accompanied by at least four acres of land included a last-minute provision that no cottage might be inhabited by more than a single family or household, thus barring secondary inmates.[122] Several generations before this, however, local courts had started to tackle the problem. As Graph 3.8 lays out, concern with subtenants was very low through the early sixteenth century. Presentments then mounted to 8 percent in the 1540s–50s before accelerating their pace to reach a peak of 27 percent in the 1580s–90s. Sessions of the Peace paid scant attention to this problem. Since inmates were people attempting to settle in a community, not outsiders traveling through, it was apparently felt that the lesser courts could handle the problem themselves. Because people reported for receiving subtenants were always household heads, women were seldom presented alone for this offence, as shown in Graph 3.11.

---

[122] 31 Eliz., c. 7 (*Stats. Realm*, vol. IV, pp. 804–5).

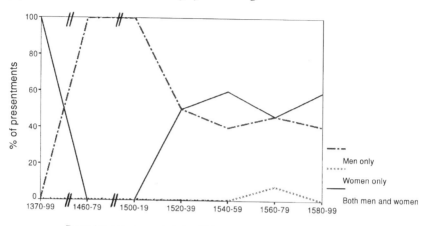

Graph 3.11   Courts that reported receiving subtenants: percentage of
presentments by gender

The reasons for objecting to subtenants became more specific over the course of the sixteenth century. At first, most presentments and bye-laws offered no explanation at all. In Tingewick, Bucks., for example, the jurors passed an ordinance in October, 1520 ordering that all sub-tenants now living within the community should be removed by Christmas.[123] Fourteen years later a new byelaw in Tingewick, ap-proved "by assent of all the tenants," specified that no one should have more than a single tenant in any cottage under penalty of 10s. But with the establishment of *de facto* parish rates for the poor in 1552 and 1563, local courts focused upon the possibility of future financial obliga-tion.[124] In 1564 jurors in Yarcombe, Devon ordered that everyone hol-ding land in the manor should remove "all and every their under tenants and tenants, with their children" or else put in surety for the honest behavior of their subtenants, guaranteeing that they would not become a financial incumbrance upon the community (i.e., apply for poor relief).[125] A fine example of the cooperation and lack of distinction between the leet courts, parish officials, and the nascent system of poor relief is provided by an order made in 1566–7 by jurors in the manor of Old Hall in East Bergholt, Suff., directed at all tenants who allowed "any kind of man, woman, or male or female child" to live in their

---

[123] New College Oxford MS 4140. For below, see *ibid.*
[124] The assessments were labeled "contributions" but could be enforced (McIntosh, "Local Responses to the Poor").
[125] Devon RO CR 1456. For below, see Suff. RO, Ipswich, HA 6:51/4/4.14.

houses. They were told that if "the chief men of the parish of East Bergholt" decided that such a subtenant was "barely able to live" or was likely to become a charge on the parish, the primary tenant was to be warned "by the constables, churchwardens, or collectors for the poor people of East Bergholt" to expel the inmates by a stated day.

Traditional charitable practices that had provided informal relief for the poor were swept aside in many of the later Elizabethan present-ments and orders. William Champion of Downton, Wilts. was fined 5s in 1590 because he "took as a subtenant a certain outsider called William Godfrey with four children, to the grave harm of his neighbors and the inhabitants of the said parish [sic], against the order of the court."[126] Champion was ordered to remove Godfrey and his children from his tenement within the next two months. In the manor of Lidgate, Suff. jurors first reported four people in 1591 for taking in subtenants (including a woman who allowed two men to live in "her backhouse" and a man who had taken in "a certain old woman who is a wanderer [*peregrina*] and is likely to be charged to the poor rate of the vill"), ordering them to evict their inmates; they then passed a generic byelaw prohibiting the inhabitants from receiving any person to live with them as subtenants.[127]

While anxiety about subtenants was widespread in areas of the country experiencing immigration of the poor, we see signs of concern also in the North and West during the late Elizabethan period, even though these regions were probably net exporters of people at the time.[128] In 1583 jurors in Pattingham, Staffs. provided an explicit state-ment (in English) of the communal decisions that had to be made when deciding which newcomers to welcome and which to evict: "There is another pain laid [= penalty imposed in a byelaw] that no man take any 'inmake' into his house but such as neighbors shall like of, but to avoid them within one quarter of a year next after warning given."[129] William Ombler of Burstwick, East Yorks., was presented and ordered in 1595 to pay 10s "because he maintains poor people in one 'le undersettle.'"

More courts used byelaws with respect to subtenants than for any other of the offences examined here. For the full chronological span, 46 percent of all courts reporting problems with subtenants passed bye-laws to strengthen their hands; such ordinances were used by the majority of courts mentioning this problem between 1460 and 1499 and

---

[126] Wilts. RO 490/1171.   [127] Suff. RO, Bury St. Edmunds, E 3/11/1.9.

[128] For reports of inmates in the Honour of Clitheroe, Lancs., in 1592 and in the manor of Cannock and Rugeley, Staffs. in 1594, see Lancs. RO, Preston, DDHCl 3/75 and Staffs. RO D(W) 1734/2/1/186. For emigration, see Chapter 6 below.

[129] Staffs. RO D(W) 1807/160. For below, see Humberside AO, Beverley, DDCC 15/26.

again between 1520 and 1579. Only in the closing decades of the sixteenth century did the use of local ordinances decline, to 33 percent, though the fraction of places reporting the problem continued to rise. This probably resulted primarily from the fact that most communities affected by the problem already had local ordinances in place, but it may have been affected by the statute of 1589. The desperation of jurors in trying to deal with inmates is reflected in the mounting fines they threatened to impose upon those who received subtenants. In an extreme case, jurors in Norton Hall, Suff. ordered in 1589–90 that no person within the vill should henceforth "receive or take into his house to live any man or woman without consent of three or four of the chief pledges at that time," under penalty for each offence of a staggering £5.[130] Equally remarkable is that three-quarters of all courts reporting problems with subtenants in any duodecade employed eviction as a remedy. Compassion had little place here.

The combined pattern for all courts that presented one or more of the offences within this cluster is shown at the top of Graph 3.8. It makes clear the fairly steady increase in concern over time, interrupted only by a slowdown in the 1480s–90s and a temporary decline in the 1540s–50s. The steepest rate of change occurred between the 1440s–50s and the 1460s–70s. A substantial gap of 44 percent separated the lowest and the highest values, far more than seen for either of the previous two clusters.

A special case: gaming

Playing certain games differed from the offences already discussed because although the nature of the social activity was similar to others regulated by the lesser public courts, this one was definitely against the law of the land as laid down in Parliamentary statutes. (Even here, however, responsibility for controlling illegal gaming was never assigned to the local courts.) Gaming therefore provides an opportunity to look more closely at the relation between national legislation and local enforcement. This makes very clear that the leaders of England's smaller communities were only prepared to implement laws about gaming when those leisure-time activities banned by statute constituted a problem within their own particular communities. If local people were playing games in ways that did not appear harmful, jurors simply ignored the legislation. When they did enforce the law, they displayed considerable freedom in deciding which kinds of people and which

---

[130] Suff. RO, Bury St. Edmunds, 553/65.

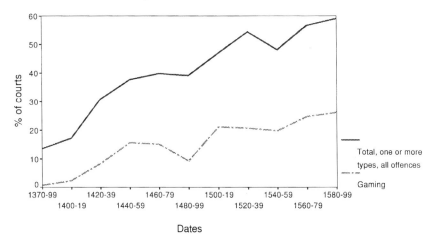

Graph 3.12   Percentage of courts under observation that reported gaming; and total, one or more types of all offences

sorts of games should be reported and how they should be punished. These choices were made in terms of the potential threat such activities posed to good order and a secure economic system within their own community. Not surprisingly, the concerns that underlay local jurors' reactions to gaming were virtually identical to those that led them to report other kinds of social misbehavior.

The percentage of communities that reported gaming, displayed in Graph 3.12, reached an initial plateau in the 1440s–70s, followed by a higher level in the first half of the sixteenth century and a further rise at the end of the century. (This graph shows too the total percentage of places that responded to one or more of the eleven forms of misconduct.) The complex and changing nature of local concern about gaming is suggested by its early appearance, resembling the timing of the Disharmony cluster; it rose together with the Disorder cluster in the second half of the fifteenth century, and the language used in presentments for gaming between the 1460s and 1530s was similar to that employed when reporting violations of good order. Yet reports of gaming continued to increase in frequency during the later sixteenth century, as did problems associated with poverty, even though the difference of 25 percent between the lowest and the highest values for the fraction of communities that reported gaming per duodecade is much less pronounced than for the Poverty cluster. Within Sessions of the Peace, concern with gaming appears to have been very high from 1460 through 1560, dropping somewhat thereafter. This suggests that by the Elizabethan period local leaders felt that they could control their

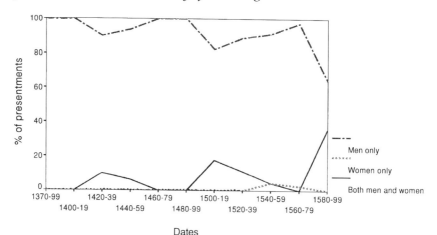

Graph 3.13   Courts that reported gaming: percentage of presentments by gender

own gamers, who were generally resident, and that gaming was not seen by people of higher status as a serious disruption of broader security and stability. As Graph 3.13 lays out, gaming was almost entirely a male activity until the very end of the sixteenth century; when women were presented, they had nearly always been playing dice or cards in a group with men.

Because Parliament did have a role in regulating this form of behavior, we may look briefly at the legislation about gaming. In a series of measures enacted between 1388 and the end of Henry VIII's reign, Parliament proscribed many indoor and outdoor games but in most cases only if they were played by the young and/or poor.[131] The act of 1388 required that all servants and laborers (people who held no land and practiced no craft but were instead dependent upon their wages) have bows and arrows, which they were to use on Sundays and holidays, and that they cease playing tennis and football as well as other games called coits, dice, casting of the stone, cards, hazarding, and kayles.[132] Although this measure expressly linked the prohibition of gaming with the need to practice archery, seen as necessary to the country's military strength, it is likely that Parliament, still shaken by the Peasants' Revolt, was also worried about activities that encouraged the young and poor to gather. Minor revisions of this law were made in

---

[131] Mark Bailey sees a concern with the recreational activities of laborers as a hallmark of the fifteenth century: "Rural Society."

[132] 12 Richard II, c. 6 (*Stats. Realm*, vol. II, p. 57). Quoits involved throwing a disk or ring of stone or metal at a target, while kayles was a kind of ninepins or skittles.

1409–10, including a slightly more specific definition of the social groups precluded from gaming and the unrealistic penalty that offenders should be imprisoned for six days.[133]

These rules remained in place for about seventy years, until one of Edward IV's Parliaments decided to experiment with a very different approach to gaming. The act of 1477–8 applied to everyone, and it no longer prohibited the outdoor games – football, tennis, and bowling.[134] At the same time, it extended the list of indoor activities, ending with an unspecific "and many new imagined games." The intent was obviously to crack down on all kinds of indoor activities, regardless of who played them. The measure also distinguished between people who permitted gaming in their houses, who were to be deterred by the utterly crippling penalty of three years' imprisonment plus a £20 cash fine for each offence, and those who only played games, who faced a punishment of two years' imprisonment and a £10 fine.

This statute was evidently not a success, for its key features were countermanded within twenty years.[135] Legislation of 1495 returned to a narrower social focus, saying that the banned games were off-limits to servants in agriculture and craftwork, apprentices, and laborers, but it again widened the scope of the activities to include tennis and bowls as well as dice, cards, and the other indoor games. Exception was made for the Christmas season, when servants were allowed to play in their master's house or elsewhere if their master was present. Punishments were made much more reasonable: those who played illegal games were to be placed in the stocks for a day, while anyone permitting games in his house could be brought before the JPs and punished with a fine of no less than 6s 8d. The Justices were also empowered to take sureties of alehouse keepers and to close their establishments if they allowed gaming.

[133] 11 Henry IV, c. 4 (*Stats. Realm*, vol. II, p. 163). This lists the prohibited games as "playing at the balls, as well hand-ball as foot-ball, and other games called coits, dice, bowling [defined in another manuscript as 'casting of the stone'], and kayles." Demand for the equipment needed for playing illegal games was large enough by the middle of the fifteenth century to warrant including dice, playing cards, and tennis balls in a statute of 1463 that prohibited pre-made items from being imported into England, in order to protect employment for local craftsmen (3 Edward IV, c. 4, *Stats. Realm*, vol. II, p. 397).

[134] 17 Edward IV, c. 3 (*Stats. Realm*, vol. II, pp. 462–3). It is striking that games of football were not reported even once in all the local records used during the time of their illegality, between 1388 and 1477. The new games mentioned were "closh [an indoors bowling game played with pins], half bowl, hand-in and hand-out, and queckboard [probably chequers or chess]."

[135] 11 Henry VII, c. 2, reissued almost verbatim in 1503–4, 19 Henry VII, c. 12 (*Stats. Realm*, vol. II, pp. 569 and 657). Football was not returned to the list.

Although the statutes of the later fifteenth century made no mention of archery, the connection between it and gaming was still present in the minds of some. In 1541–2, Parliament passed a measure ostensibly introduced by the bowyers, fletchers, stringers, and arrowheadmakers of the realm, who argued that if archery were to be maintained, "diverse and many unlawful games and plays," some of them newly created to bypass earlier statutes, would have to be treated more severely.[136] In this measure, the list of occupations prohibited from gaming was enlarged beyond the now traditional servants, apprentices, and laborers: several large groups including husbandmen and craftsmen were added, as were draughtsmen, journeymen, mariners, fishermen, and watermen. The ten days after Christmas were, however, still excluded, and masters were allowed to license their servants to play with them or any gentlemen if so requested. (The possible need for a gaming partner obviously outweighed any desire for tidy definitions.) After adding some new indoor recreations to the prohibited list, the measure ordered that no one should henceforth keep a house for any illegal games (including an "alley or place of bowling") under penalty of 40s; 6s 8d was to be forfeited by anyone who frequented such establishments, and constables were to conduct weekly or monthly searches of all places where gaming was suspected to occur. This measure remained in effect for the rest of the sixteenth century.

While local court jurors were clearly aware that gaming was outlawed by Parliament, this knowledge ensured neither rigorous enforcement nor careful adherence to the specific terms of the current law. Apart from the years between 1477–8 and 1495, the list of games banned by Parliament was intended to cover virtually all indoor activities and many outdoor sports. It is extremely unlikely that none of these games was ever played by youngsters or poor people in most communities during the fifteenth century. Yet the fraction of courts that reported gaming prior to around 1440 was very low and did not exceed 16 percent until after 1500. This suggests that under many circumstances jurors were prepared to overlook what players were doing. During the sixteenth century, as gaming became a problem in the eyes of respectable local people, the level of presentments rose.

Several factors might persuade fifteenth-century jurors to report their neighbors for indoor gaming. Usually played at night, and hence suspect for that reason in itself, activities like dice, chequers, hazard, and

---

[136] 33 Henry VIII, c. 9 (*Stats. Realm*, vol. III, pp. 837–41). This measure allowed for the licensing of gaming houses, a provision repealed in 1555 (2 & 3 Philip & Mary, c. 9, *Stats. Realm*, vol. IV, p. 285).

tables were opposed in part for economic reasons.[137] Because these games were almost always accompanied by betting, jurors worried that poor men were wasting their resources. A chaplain and three other men were presented in Sherburn in Elmet, West Yorks. in 1444 as "common players at dice within the domain at night, not having the ability to continue such illegal games."[138] It was especially troubling when servants and other young people gamed. Rather than squandering their modest earnings, perhaps even pilfering money or goods to obtain the necessary resources, they should have been at home under the watchful eye of their master or parent preparing for the next day's labor.[139] The numerous presentments from the second half of the fifteenth century of people who had received servants into their houses to play games, or of young people who had themselves played games, are encapsulated in one particularly explicit statement of the presumed connection between gaming and a resistance to labor among the young. Jurors in Fulham, Middx. said in 1475 that John Aleyn of Westend, Thomas Fuller, and John Aleyn, son of Roger Aleyn, "are accustomed commonly to play at dice and other illegal games and to walk about through the whole night and sleep in the day, and they are unwilling to serve or labor when it is required of them."[140] It should be emphasized that concerns about the harmful economic impact of gaming appeared in local courts at least a generation before they were first mentioned by Parliament in the statute of 1477–8. This reminds us that Parliament often responded to new circumstances more slowly than did local bodies.

From around 1440, local courts began to report games of handball, some of which were coming to be known as tennis.[141] Although these records provide no explicit references to where and how such games were played, they seem to have occurred neither inside houses nor in open fields, suggesting that they took place against outside walls or in enclosed outdoor spaces like courtyards. As with indoor games, some jurors were concerned that handball or tennis was accompanied by betting and hence consumed money that should have been used for

---

[137] The indoor games mentioned in fifteenth-century local records include dice, hazard (a game using dice in which the chances were complicated by a number of arbitrary rules), chequers (probably described also as "quekking"), tables (either a game of chance or chequers/chess), cards, closhing, pennyprick (perhaps similar to pennypitch), and "kowtering."   [138] West Yorks. Arch. Serv., Leeds, GC/M3/42.

[139] A royal proclamation of 1511 made explicit the fear that servants might steal from their masters in order to acquire the money with which to game: *Tudor Royal Procls.*, vol. I, pp. 85–93, esp. p. 88. For gaming by children, see Orme, "The Culture of Children."   [140] Guildhall Libr., London MS 10312, Roll 80.

[141] In the fifteenth and sixteenth centuries, tennis did not necessarily involve the use of racquets.

other purposes. In Castle Combe, Wilts. jurors ordered in 1452 that "no tenant shall henceforth play at handball within this domain for any silver."[142] John Cokefield and John Hawne of Horsham St. Faith, Norf. were presented in 1443–4 as "common players at tennis in work days, but they do not have the land nor the rents/income [*redditus*] through which they are able to play at the said game." By the later fifteenth century, tennis was seen as a disruptor of labor, especially that owed by servants to their masters.[143]

During the sixteenth century many presentments for gaming were associated with rising concern about the problems of poverty more generally. Statements about indoor games were now more likely to include an economic emphasis, and in some communities people seem to have been reported only if they played for money.[144] In the great West Yorkshire manor of Wakefield, jurors for the area of Normanton ordered in 1537 that "no man nor woman dwelling within that township or without it shall play at the cards for no silver, day nor night."[145] Ongoing concern with the labor of servants was now joined by attention to gaming by vagabonds.[146] In 1523 jurors in Whittlesford, Cambs. presented Richard Giffery, himself the constable of the vill at the time, because he "keeps his door open at night and receives divers vagabonds playing at 'lez cardes' and other prohibited games against the ordinance and the statute of the lord king."[147] Thomas Griffith, a

---

[142] Brit. Libr. Add. Ch. 18,481. For below, see Norf. RO N.R.S. 19509, 42 C 3.

[143] Officials in the sub-region of Curry within the manor of North Curry, Som. were ordered in 1467 "to report concerning all players at tennis and dice in the vill of Curry ... to the hindrance of the service [owed to] the tenants," while in Cawston, Norf. a man was charged in 1494–5 with allowing tennis to be played at his house, "causing divers servants of the tenants ... to weaken their service to their masters" (Som. RO DD/CC 131903/5 and Norf. RO N.R.S. 6025, 20 E 3).

[144] Jurors in Cookham, Berks. presented three men in 1528 for playing "at games and dice for money on two days," and in 1552 the court of Pattingham, Staffs. imposed a byelaw upon all the inhabitants "that they not play at illegal games for money under penalty for each of 6s 8d" (Berks. RO D/ESk M45, and Staffs. RO D(W) 1807/128). In this period references to playing cards (*cartae pictae*) and various forms of slidegroat or shuffleboard increased; dicing and "tables" remained popular, but there are fewer mentions of other kinds of games.

[145] Yorks. Archaeol. Soc., Leeds, MD225/1/263 and 263A. A transcript of this roll and paper draft was kindly made available to me at the YAS office by Dr. Ann Weikel, who is editing it for publication.

[146] For pointed statements about gaming among servants, see New College Oxford MS 2736 (Colerne, Wilts., 1510), Yorks. Archaeol. Soc., Leeds, MD225/1/263 and 263A (Wakefield, West Yorks., 1537), Devon RO *f.009.4, 64743 (Dartmouth, Devon, 1550), and Ches. RO DVE 2/1 (Kinderton, Ches.).

[147] Cambs. RO, Cambridge, 488/M Whittlesford rolls, 1513–23. For below, see Devon RO CR 1107. The potential for tension among local officials concerning game playing is discussed below.

weaver of Monkleigh, Devon, was reported in 1564 as a vagabond who would not work but plays illegal games.

Because the young, poor, and transient were difficult to punish effectively, sixteenth-century jurors directed their efforts at those who permitted gaming in their establishments, especially keepers of alehouses and inns. Jurors in Horsham St. Faith, Norf. obviously knew about the statutory requirement that operators of public houses prohibit gaming, for they presented Thomas Woodstacke in 1565 as an alehouse keeper who permitted two men to play cards in his house, against the statute.[148] The full and substantial penalty of 40s as specified in the law was then imposed upon Woodstacke. Yet since many of the houses that catered to the poor were run by people of limited means, imposing the statutory fine would put them out of business, which jurors were often reluctant to do.

Unlike tennis, which received little attention from local courts during the sixteenth century, bowling was sometimes presented in Elizabeth's reign.[149] We cannot be sure whether bowling was only now becoming common or whether it was a more traditional sport that jurors had previously been willing to overlook. Although bowling alleys were found in many Elizabethan cities, reports from the lesser courts suggest that rural versions of the sport were concentrated in the southwestern and western parts of England.[150] (We are told in legend that Sir Francis Drake was playing at bowls when he learned of the arrival of the Spanish Armada. The fact that Drake was then in Plymouth makes the story more likely to be true: had he lived in Kent or Yorkshire, he might have been whiling away the time in a different way.) It is also clear that bowling was popular across a wide social range, including leaders of their local communities. The presentments are, however, odd in several respects. Local courts seem either to have misunderstood the statute of 1541–2 or to have deliberately distorted its statement that only young people and those in occupations of lower status were prohibited from bowling (as from all other games): reports often named gentlemen and local officeholders too. Further, relatively few communities mentioned

[148] Norf. RO N.R.S. 19512, 42 C 4.
[149] The small number of presentments concerning tennis or handball after 1500 focused on those who operated commercial courts (e.g., Framlingham, Suff. in 1522 and Hayridge hundred, Devon in 1562: Pembroke College Cambridge MS I1, and Devon RO CR 147). There had been only a few references to bowling during the fifteenth and earlier sixteenth centuries (e.g., a reference to it within a list of other games in Rugeley, Staffs. in 1458–9, a byelaw in Cookham, Berks. from 1513 against bowling under some circumstances, and a presentment from Chesham Higham/Chesham Bury, Bucks. in 1522: Staffs. RO D(W) 1734/2/1/177, Berks. RO D/Esk M32, and Bucks. RO D/BASM 18/193).
[150] For regional variation in other sports, see Underdown, "Regional Cultures?"

bowling more than once within a period of several generations. These anomalies suggest that presentments of bowlers may have been atypical. Perhaps a "new broom" had just arrived in the community, such as a minister with strong convictions that any kind of gaming by any kind of person violated God's mandate for a truly Christian life. Or a disaffected juror or small group of them may have used presentment as a way to get their neighbors into trouble with the law.[151] It is also conceivable that the undermining of social distinctions caused by shared love of bowling may have offended some status-conscious jurors.

Regardless of the reasons for their presentment, there can be no doubt about either the social diversity of bowlers or the popularity of the sport. In 1567 the court roll of Colerne, Wilts. recited at great length the statute of 33 Henry VIII against gaming, noting that five local men – a gentleman and four husbandmen – had nevertheless "played at bowls in the open fields outside the days of Christmas, viz. on 14 June 9 Elizabeth."[152] Similarly, jurors in the manor of Cannock and Rugeley, Staffs. presented six men, three of them gentlemen, for playing bowls in Rugeley in 1583. That bowling was enjoyed even by local officials is made clear by a remarkable presentment from Pattingham, Staffs. in 1600. The jurors reported seven men as bowlers, of whom three were members of the presentment jury at that time and two others were elected constable shortly thereafter.[153] Dramatic confirmation of the popularity of bowling comes from Castle Combe, Wilts. in 1570. A paper sheet listing draft presentments in English begins with a heading, "These have played at bowls or stuball," after which follow seventy-two male names.

Concern with gaming was magnified during the sixteenth century if it occurred during divine service.[154] This was not merely a Puritan or even necessarily a Protestant issue. Between 1527 and 1530 jurors in the manor of Amberley, West Sussex presented a series of people for

---

[151] See Chapter 4, section two below for an example. For below, consider the statutes passed in the later fifteenth century and renewed/expanded thereafter which limited other forms of recreation to people of a certain income or status (e.g., 22 Edward IV, c. 6, *Stats. Realm*, vol. II, p. 474) and tried to ensure that people dressed appropriately for their occupation (e.g., 3 Edward IV, c. 5, and 22 Edward IV, c. 1, *Stats. Realm*, vol. II, pp. 399–402 and 468–70).

[152] New College Oxford MS 2737. For below, see Staffs. RO D(W) 1734/2/1/186.

[153] Staffs. RO D(W) 1807/173. For below, see Wilts. RO 777/1.

[154] Apart from alehouses that remained open during services and gaming, there were few references in these local court records to improper activities on Sundays or holidays: jurors were apparently content to let the ecclesiastical courts deal with this problem. Most of the exceptions came from Devon and Cornwall.

promoting bad rule by permitting coiting in the time of divine service, for allowing bowling and tennis during vespers, and for keeping an alehouse in which games and dice were played on Sundays and other feast days during services.[155] William Nicoll of Liskeard, Corn. was reported in 1537 because he allowed people to play "at painted tables" during services, and five others were presented for playing the game. By the time of a byelaw passed in 1548 in Sutton Coldfield, War., it is possible, though by no means certain, that Protestant views influenced the jurors when they ordered that servants should not be allowed to play at illegal games during divine services.[156] Presentments for allowing or taking part in illegal games during services were made in Monkleigh, Devon in 1567 and 1589 and in the Honour of Clitheroe, Lancs. in 1593. By the end of the century opposition to gaming had extended to the entire day of Sunday in at least a few communities: jurors in Barrow Hall, Suff. said in an English presentment of 1589, "We find that upon the last lord's day Giles Mayne and John Tayler with others were playing at slide thrist in Baler's house."[157]

Gaming provides the only direct evidence in these sources of a conflict between the ongoing appeal of traditional forms of good fellowship and popular culture and the moral or legal values of those members of the community who sought conformity with the statutes.[158] Strikingly, this divergence spanned the sixteenth century rather than being a distinctive feature of the late Elizabethan years, so it was not the result of a specifically Puritan approach. The conflict could take several forms. Because games were so enthusiastically pursued, local people sometimes resisted the efforts of constables to stop their playing. Jurors in Hexton, Herts. reported in 1495 that John Gregory and Thomas Smyth refused to cease their frequent playing of tennis even though the constable, in pursuance of a local byelaw, had expressly prohibited it.[159] In a rougher episode, when the constable of Kirtlington, Oxon. went to John Swetnam's house in 1588 to stop him from organizing games of dice and cards for silver, Swetnam and his players maltreated the officer. More dangerous to good order given the nature of English law enforcement was that some jurors and constables were themselves prepared to ignore orders about gaming or refused to act against players. In 1522 jurors of the manor of Chesham Higham and Chesham

---

[155] West Sussex RO Ep VI/12/2. For below, see Corn. RO B/LIS 103.
[156] Birmingham Central Libr., Archs. Dept., Sutton Coldfield 1. For below, see Devon RO CR 1108 and CR 1110, and Lancs. RO, Preston, DDHCl 3/75.
[157] Suff. RO, Bury St. Edmunds, HA 507/1/18.
[158] Wrightson, "Two Concepts of Order," and Hutton, *The Rise and Fall of Merry England*.
[159] Herts. RO 47289. For below, see Oxon. Archs. Dash I/i/110.

Bury, Bucks. reported that eight men played at "le Bowles" in the presence of two constables, but the latter did not put them into the stocks according to the form of the statute.[160] A juror in Toynton, Lincs. was presented and fined in 1547 because he acknowledged that he saw diverse players at cards but was unwilling to present them in the court by his oath.

Promulgation of local byelaws against gaming offers still more evidence that the lesser public courts operated in their own ways. One might have assumed that the presence of Parliamentary legislation against gaming would carry greater weight than any local measure and hence would have rendered byelaws unnecessary. Yet in most duodecades between 1440 and 1559, 14–29 percent of all courts that reported gaming passed their own ordinances against the problem, with an even higher peak of 45 percent in the 1500s–10s. After 1560 the proportion dropped sharply, to just 7–9 percent for the rest of the century. The complex relationship between national and local law is illustrated by a sequence of byelaws from Great Horwood, Bucks. In 1515 it was ordered "by the consent of the lord and tenants that no tenant or inhabitant within this domain shall play at games or dice except in the time of the nativity of the Lord, under penalty for each default of 20s."[161] This ordinance was more severe than the statute currently in effect because it prohibited everyone from playing such games, not merely servants/apprentices and the poor. Six years later the jurors re-worked their ordinance to read that "no labourer, artificer, or servant" should play any of the proscribed games. This time, however, their measure was less restrictive than the statute, for husbandmen in Great Horwood but not elsewhere were allowed to play.

With characteristic disregard of the more draconian penalties specified in the various pieces of Parliamentary legislation, local jurors punished gaming in almost all cases through a flexible cash fine. The amount of the penalty seems to have been a compromise between the severity of the offence and the practical ability of the offender to pay. During the second half of the sixteenth century, corporal punishment was employed in at least a few places.[162] A real sense of desperation rings through the order made in Hales(owen), War. in 1573: "that Roger Shentall and John Warde nor any other shall henceforth play at dice for money within the town under penalty for each time of imprisonment in

---

[160] Bucks. RO D/BASM 18/193. For below, see Lincs. AO ANC 3/18/74.

[161] New College Oxford MS 3920. For below, see *ibid.*

[162] In 1557, for example, the jurors of Aldwick hundred in West Sussex ordered the constable to place three men presented as common players at illegal games into the stocks for the whole day on the following Sunday (Lambeth Pal. Libr. ED 186).

the stocks for the space of three days, taking for their sustenance during the said time bread and water and nothing else."[163] From the 1460s onwards – once eviction became an option for local courts – more than a third of all places that reported gaming banished offenders from the community.

The evidence presented in this chapter demonstrates that social regulation had a long history in England prior to the well-studied episodes around 1600. Motivated by underlying worries about personal reputation, economic issues, young people, the poor, and outsiders, leaders of a growing proportion of the country's villages and market centers reported misbehavior to their local courts across the fifteenth and sixteenth centuries. For offences involving disharmony, the decrease in local court presentments during the Elizabeth period may have been offset to some extent by more attention within the church courts. Mounting activity within ecclesiastical bodies and Sessions of the Peace probably compensated for the local decline with respect to matters of disorder. Problems with the social consequences of poverty rose right through the end of Elizabeth's reign both locally and in Sessions. We need now to determine whether the attitudes towards wrongdoing described in these lesser court records were limited to that particular legal setting or were found more widely among people of middling and higher status.

---

[163] Birmingham Central Libr., Archs. Dept., Hagley Hall MS 377991, Box 78. The same penalty was ordered for any who permitted people to play in their houses.

4

Social concern in other contexts

While we have obtained a good picture of how and why juries in the lesser public courts responded to social wrongdoing, we do not yet know to what extent their attitudes and actions reflected more widely held responses. Were the concerns of those jurors in some way specific to that context, or have we opened up a window that sheds more general light upon the opinions of respectable local people?[1] How, that is, do the records of the lesser courts fit within a broader social context? To examine these questions, we begin by looking at textual statements and punishments from the three additional types of courts that operated at the lower and intermediate levels of the system of English justice: urban bodies, the church courts, and Sessions of the Peace.[2] These reinforce the argument made in Chapter 1 that the various courts worked in partnership to address wrongdoing, based upon common attitudes about harmony, order, and the problems of poverty. We then turn to two very different kinds of texts: the foundation documents and ordinances of almshouses and hospitals established during the fifteenth and sixteenth centuries, and petitions submitted to the Lord Chancellor of England that contain descriptions of misconduct. The latter are of particular interest due to the specificity of the incidents described and the individuality of the language employed. These sources show that the attitudes and terminology seen in court records were shared by many people, underscoring the point that attempts by legal institutions to limit wrongdoing formed only one component within a wider effort to regulate misbehavior. Nor was acute concern with misconduct by any means limited to ardent Puritans. Because language use is essential

[1] For the ideological context shaped by more educated people, see Chapter 8 below.
[2] See Chapter 1, section one above.

to this analysis, only original texts are considered here, not secondary studies.[3]

Legal settings

The records of other courts provide information about the attitudes of people at two social levels.[4] At the lower rank, our witnesses come from much the same kind of backgrounds as the jurors in the lesser courts. Most men who served on urban juries were little if any wealthier or more literate than their country cousins, and the very same people active in the courts of villages and market centers were likely to appear as lay parish officials before the ecclesiastical courts and as jurymen or constables before Sessions of the Peace. It is therefore unsurprising that the social concerns and phraseology of reports made to these larger and more important courts were very similar to what we have observed in the lesser public bodies. But urban institutions, the church courts, and Sessions were convened by people of higher social, economic, and educational status: more prosperous members of urban centers, professional officials of the church, and JPs selected from among the gentry and leading merchants of the county.[5] Because such men determined the punishments to be imposed upon malefactors, their penalties provide us with information about responses to wrongdoing at a second social layer. This examination suggests that men of higher status were no less troubled by social wrongdoing than were their middling neighbors: to the contrary, the conveners of these courts apparently viewed at least certain kinds of misbehavior with more severity than did less influential residents of the community. Since the continuities in attitudes expressed in reports to all these courts are so pronounced, we will focus upon a few topics of particular interest and upon punishments.

Scolding elicited some explicit statements in the Elizabethan ecclesiastical courts about why this behavior was so disruptive to social harmony, why it undermined the Christian goal of having people live "in charity" with their neighbors.[6] In 1563 Elizabeth Ge[tin] the younger of Brockworth, Gloucs. was said to be a common scold who "is

---

[3] Reference will be made in notes to selected works from among the many fine studies of particular courts or communities.

[4] For a list of the courts examined, with references, see Appendices 1.1–1.3.

[5] For studies of the church courts and Sessions of the Peace, see Chapter 1, section one above.

[6] This was a central concern of both Catholic and Protestant churches, for spiritual as well as social reasons. See Chapter 8, section one below.

able to bring all the whole parish in discord," while Anne Chatterton, a
Shropshire widow, was labeled in 1576 as "a common scold, a disturber
of divine service, a slanderer of her neighbors, a setter of hate between
them"; Ellen Garland of Ivinghoe, Bucks. was described in 1585 as "a
brawler and a busy body, disquieting her neighbors contrary to the
laws of charity."[7] The antagonism which scolds could generate is
illustrated by the experience in 1521 of Agnes Yve, wife of Thomas Yve
als. Clement of rural Bucks. At the church court session at which Agnes
was presented as "a common defamer of her neighbors, calling divers
honest women whores and many other scandalous words and sowing
discord between the said parishioners," forty "honest women of the
parish" came voluntarily to the court to bear witness against her.[8]

As in the lesser courts, the misdeeds of certain types of people
received disproportionate attention. Leisure activities of young people
were watched carefully. The fear that servants would use their masters'
possessions for betting is made clear as early as 1483 in a presentment at
a Nottingham city Sessions, when eight local people, none of them
keepers of public houses, were named for "wickedly receiving into
their houses servants of divers men with their masters' goods, playing
at . . . illegal games . . . to the grave detriment of their masters."[9] Leonard
[Oxonus] was reported to the Hereford city Sessions in 1579 not only
because he allowed illegal card games to be played in his house but
more specifically because he encouraged "the servants and sons of his
neighbors around the age of 14 years to play at the said illegal games."
Jurors at the Sessions held in Hatfield, Herts. in 1589 presented an
unlicensed alehouse keeper from Little Gaddesden who had permitted
"great disorder" in "keeping of men's servants when they should have
been about their masters' affairs and in the nighttime [away] from their
masters' houses."[10]

Some of the major urban centers were troubled by the presence of
unmarried women who were not working for and living under the
supervision of a master.[11] This issue has not come up before, suggesting
that single women in search of employment were likely to move to
cities or towns rather than remaining in smaller communities. Urban

[7] Gloucs. RO GDR 20, p. 28, and Lichfield (Staffs.) Joint RO B/V/1/10, under Deanery of
Newport; Bucks. RO D/A/V 1b, fol. 42v.

[8] Bucks. RO D/A/C 1a, fol. 3r, a curious inversion of oath helpers.

[9] Notts. AO CA 3b. For below, see Heref. RO Hereford City Records, Quarter Sessions,
file for 1579.   [10] Herts. RO HAT/SR 1/176.

[11] For secondary studies of women's roles in larger communities, see the works cited in
Chapter 6, notes 37–8 below, plus, e.g., Barron, "The 'Golden Age' of Women" and
Bennett, "Medieval Women, Modern Women." For urban social regulation more
generally, see, e.g., Beier, "The Social Problems of an Elizabethan Town" and Rosen,
"Winchester in Transition."

leaders seem to have been afraid of the economic competition that self-supporting women offered to men and nervous about their uncontrolled sexuality, though these underlying worries are seldom articulated in the records. Coventry merely ordered in 1495 that "every maid & sole woman being within the age of 40 years that keepeth any house sole by her self, that she take a chamber with a honest person, which shall answer for [her] good demeaning, or else to go to service . . . under pain of imprisonment . . . or else to void the city."[12] Worcester ruled in 1568 that maid servants could only be hired to work in people's residences if they were taken on for the full year and lived with their employer. In 1596 Liverpool jurors said, "Concerning all such young women and others called charr women in this town, as are in no service, whereof diverse of late time have been gotten with child, shall every of them place them selves in some good and honest service, or else be avoided [= banished from the town]."[13]

A few Elizabethan towns described more fully their reasons for concern with independent women. In Southampton, jurors reported in 1579 that "there are in this town diverse young women and maidens which keep themselves out of service and work for themselves in diverse men's houses," but three years later they said more precisely that "within this town there be sundry maid servants that take chambers and so live by themselves masterless and are called by the name of char women, which we think not meet nor sufferable."[14] Similarly, jurors in Manchester first ordered in 1588 that "no single woman, unmarried, shall be at her own hand, to keep house or chamber within the town of Manchester."[15] The following year they progressed to a wonderfully explicit statement of the core reasons for distress: "Whereas great inconvenience is in this town, in that single women being unmarried be at their own hands, and do bake bread and exercise other trades, to the great hurt of the poor inhabitants having wife and children; as also in abusing themselves with young men and others, having not any in control of them, to the great dishonour of God and evil example of others," it was ordered that no single woman should henceforth keep her own house or chamber or sell bread, ale, or any other commodities.

Poverty and its consequences were of grave concern to urban

---

[12] *The Coventry Leet Book*, vol. II, p. 568. For below, see Worcs. RO (St. Helens) Worcester City Records, Frank Pledge, etc., Book 1, fol. 151v.

[13] *Liverpool Town Books*, vol. II, p. 717. The editor says that a char woman was hired by the day to do odd jobs of work, a meaning consistent with the example below from Southampton.

[14] *Court Leet Records [of Southampton]*, vol. I, pt. 2, pp. 186 and 236.

[15] *Continuation of the Court Leet Records of Manchester*, p. 11. For below, see *ibid.*, pp. 17–18.

courts.[16] Throughout the sixteenth century many of the larger communities attempted to counteract the negative economic impact of gaming and drinking upon poor families. Local officials in Coventry were instructed in 1518 to "suffer not poor craftsmen to use bowling there daily and weekly, leaving their business at home that they should live by."[17] In a 1548 order regulating "crock brewers" and other sellers of ale and beer, Gloucester's magistrates noted the "disorder and confusion of the common wealth" that resulted from such houses, explaining that "many poor crafts men and journeymen resort[eth] and sit[teth] all day at this crock ale, not regarding their poor wife and children at home but often times being drunk do fight and brawl and take occasion thereby to play at dice, cards, and other unlawful games, consuming their time in vain."[18] Officials in charge of alehouse inspection in Leicester were instructed in 1569 "to inquire and present the defaults and trespasses of common drunkards that do use to sit tippling at the ale houses all day and all night unthriftily, and their wives and children almost starve at home for lack of good relief and sustentation." Jurors in Southampton in 1579 commented that "divers artificers of this town do now use to haunt taverns and alehouses not only by day but also by night so that many of them spend more than they get, and chiefly in play, and in the meantime their wives and children want both meat and drink."[19] Fear that the poor would claim support from local poor rates, together with a rarely expressed but historically widespread and long-lived sense that poor people breed like rabbits, was made clear in a complaint about subtenants in Southampton from 1582: "This town is marvellously oppressed with undertenants and daily do increase more and more, which for the most part are so poor as daily they lie at men's doors for their relief, [and] increase of children daily groweth among them besides, which in th'end must needs be at the town's charge."[20]

By the end of the sixteenth century many Sessions too were keeping close watch upon poor people, especially those who squandered their scant resources in playing games or drinking. A violent incident in Hoddesdon, Herts. in 1590 began when the constables attempted to arrest two very poor local men who were, as usual, engaged in a card game for money; by their gaming they had "played away all that ever

---

[16] For secondary studies, see the works cited in McIntosh, "Local Responses to the Poor" plus, e.g., Pelling, "Old Age, Poverty, and Disability" and Slack, *Poverty and Policy*.

[17] *The Coventry Leet Book*, vol. III, p. 656.

[18] Gloucs. RO GBR B2/1, fol. 43r–v. For below, see *Records of the Borough of Leicester*, vol. III, p. 128.   [19] *Court Leet Records [of Southampton]*, vol. I, pt. 2, p. 182.

[20] *Ibid.*, p. 236.

they had, to the great impoverishing of their wives and children."[21] Jurors at the Essex Quarter Sessions in the mid-1590s asked that the public house of Joseph Butler of Little Canfield be closed because he kept ill rule and maintained "men's servants and poor labouring men at play, which is a undoing unto the poor men thereabout." In an overt thumbing of the nose at forms of traditional charity, John Clinton and Richard Man of Cottered, Herts. begged money from their neighbors for the relief of their wives and children in 1596 and then lost it all playing illegal games.[22]

The problems that could descend upon both destitute subtenants and those who gave them shelter are poignantly illustrated in a case that came before the Justices of Hatfield, Herts. in 1597. Simon Howe, a laborer of Ardeley, Herts., went away in the fall of 1596, leaving behind his wife and children with no house to live in.[23] Because they "occupied a shed without fire or anything else, except what the inhabitants of Ardeley charitably gave them," a local JP persuaded Philip Cooke als. Putnell to allow them to live in his hayhouse and to have a fire there when the cold weather came. The following midsummer, Cooke asked them to move out as he wanted to use the building to store hay and grain. They were unwilling to do so, because although Simon Howe had now returned to Ardeley, he was living with another woman and refused to provide anything for their maintenance.[24] Cooke, afraid that the lord of the manor would "take advantage of him for maintaining" mistress Howe and her children in the future, asked the JP to require a financial bond of Howe.

The penalties imposed upon social wrongdoers were generally more severe in these courts than in the lesser local bodies. In dealing with sexual offences, the church courts commonly used a mixture of public display and confession, such as standing barefooted and covered only by a white sheet during a church service or in the market, followed by admission of and apology for one's sins to the minister, church-wardens, or full congregation. For people who refused to accept the court's authority, excommunication might be imposed. In an atypical pattern, ecclesiastical officials in Durham used whipping, presumably because the exceptional secular authority held by the Bishop of Durham

---

[21] Herts. RO HAT/SR 2/182. One of the players was described as "an alehouse haunter and often times overtaken with drink will beat his wife, to the great disquiet of his honest neighbors." For below, see Essex RO Q/SR 132/21a.

[22] Herts. RO HAT/SR 8/30. [23] Herts. RO HAT/SR 9/118 for this whole episode.

[24] Because Howe was not working for his living, the JP "presumed he was living by unlawful means"; Howe was also excommunicated by the church courts "for reasons which the Justice passed over because they might offend the chaste ears of his hearers."

extended to his religious courts. At the order of the prior's court John
Duket of (Kirk) Merrington, Durham was whipped six times in front of
the church for adultery in 1435; in 1580 the bishop's court ordered that
John Rowle and Ursula Tuggall of North Bailey, Durham be whipped
and carted "in all open places within the city of Durham."[25]

All Sessions of the Peace were allowed to employ physical punishments. The unmarried parents of a bastard child or people who had
offended local values especially severely might be whipped and/or
placed in a cart and pulled through the town, sometimes accompanied
by "rough music" to attract attention. After the birth of their illegitimate baby, Alice Francke of Steeple Bumpstead, Essex and John
Smeethe of Radwinter were sentenced by the Essex Sessions in 1595 "to
be tied to a cart's tail, and in some open place within the parish be
stripped from the waist upwards and given 10 lashes with a whip fit for
the purpose."[26] In a more complicated case involving a violation of the
protection which a dominant member of the social hierarchy owed to
his dependants, John Milles, a married shoemaker of Rye, East Sussex,
was put in gaol in 1560 by the local JPs because he forced his servant girl
to have sexual intercourse with him: after his incarceration he was "to
be carted with 'basons' about the town." By the later sixteenth century,
punishments for vagabonds or vagrants who came before Sessions
were likewise harsh.[27] Whipping in a public setting was not uncom-
mon, but the most savage punishment authorized by statute for repeat
offenders, branding on the ear, was rarely implemented.[28] Among the
few exceptions were three laborers and an unmarried woman arrested
as vagabonds in Wisbech in 1586 who were to be branded in the right
ear and whipped; William Jennerye, indicted as a vagrant rogue carrying a counterfeit passport in Hatfield, Herts. in 1589, received the same
treatment. In a more menacing threat, John Woodman als. Kynge,
arrested as a vagrant in Rye in 1596, was whipped and then ordered to
leave the town under penalty of losing one of his ears entirely.[29]

25 Durham Univ. Libr., Archs. and Spec. Colls., Prior's Kitchen, DCD Prior's Court of
Durham, fol. 2r; *The Injunctions and Other Ecclesiastical Proceedings of Richard Barnes*,
p. 126.
26 Essex RO Q/SR 132/50. For below, see East Sussex RO Rye 1/2, fol. 43v; for "basons,"
see Chapter 3, note 58 above. Rye and Winchelsea imposed unusually severe punishments during the Elizabethan period, probably because of their association with the
Cinque Ports, which had greater legal powers due to their special military role.
27 For secondary works, see, e.g., Beier, *Masterless Men*.
28 E.g., John Wyght to be whipped and put in the pillory in Faversham, Kent in 1586, and
Robert Fraye and John Morgayne "to be whipped at the cart arse about the town" in
Rye in 1596 (Centre for Kentish Studies Fa/JQs 1, and East Sussex RO 1/6, fol. 61r). For
below, see Cambridge Univ. Libr. Ely Dioc. Recs. E 1/6/8; Herts. RO HAT/SR 1/68.
29 East Sussex RO Rye 1/6, fol. 29r.

Many urban communities ordered vigorous penalties, resembling those imposed by Sessions. Until the mid-sixteenth century, scolds and sexual offenders were punished in separate, if sometimes related ways. In Coventry as early as 1439 it was ordered that William Powet, a local capper, and his paramour should be carried through the town in a cart, "in example of punishment of sin," and that all others found guilty of fornication in the future should receive the same punishment.[30] In 1467 Leicester ordered that both male and female scolds were to be punished "on a cuckstool afore their door ... and then so to be carried forth to the 4 gates of the town." By the Elizabethan period, however, cucking-stools (or thews or tumbrels) were normally used for both female scolds and prostitutes. In 1575 at Archbishop Grindal's visitation of the diocese of York, Jane Haxoppe, wife of Thomas Haxoppe of Bishop-thorpe in the city of York, was presented as a scold. The court ordered that the sheriffs of the city be told to punish her, "viz. to be carried through the city of York tomorrow in the market time upon the thew heretofore used in this behalf."[31] In an unusual statement from 1595, twenty-five men of Lincoln complained to the Bishop of Lincoln's court that Julian Bowker, "a charwoman in gentlemen's kitchens," has frequently made trouble through "the sharpness of her tongue."[32] Because she "has been bold to abuse divers honest men in speeches and words," she was repeatedly presented as a common scold "both to the ecclesiastical court by the churchwardens and swornmen and at the Sessions holden for the City of Lincoln by the constable jury and the leet inquest." As the result of the latter, "the common cuckstool or cart was by commandment of the Mayor (for a terror to her) brought and set before her door." Some evidence suggests that use of the cucking-stool for female offenders may have been decreasing in the later sixteenth century.[33] Southampton's jurors reported in 1576 that their town no longer had a "Cocking stool for the punishment of harlots," although such a chair had previously existed "upon the town ditches."[34]

---

[30] *The Coventry Leet Book*, vol. I, p. 192. For below, see *Records of the Borough of Leicester*, vol. II, p. 291. In other early patterns, scolds in Hereford were ordered, probably in 1486, to stand in a public place with their feet bare and their hair hanging loose, while Gloucester's officials ordered in 1504 that a "which" (= a cage or lock-up) be constructed in the public market place, following the example of London and Bristol, into which prostitutes, male adulterers, and priests found guilty of sexual offences could be placed. (Heref. RO Hereford City Records, Bound Volumes, no. 1, "Customs of Hereford," fol. 16v; Gloucs. RO GBR B2/1, fol. 19r.)
[31] Borthwick Institute, York, V.1575/CB.1, fol. 25r.
[32] Lincs. AO Lincoln Dioc. Recs. Ch.P.1, fol. 14r–v.
[33] This disagrees with descriptions of increasingly harsh punishment of female scolds and sexual offenders during the later sixteenth century: see, e.g., the works cited in the Introduction, note 3, and Chapter 3, note 59 above.

Three years later, when registering the continued absence of a cucking-stool, jurors said that it had previously been used "for the punishment and terror of harlots, scolds, and such malefactors." Presentments in Manchester in 1590 and 1591 noted that the cuckstool was in disrepair, with its water-ditch "taken away and enclosed."[35] Vagrants or particularly severe "evil livers" were commonly punished in the stocks/pillory or by whipping, sometimes at the back of a cart while led through the town. This evidence suggests no disparities between the attitudes of jurors in village and market center courts and what was reported to other bodies; punishments suggest that the men of higher rank who officiated in such courts were if anything more troubled by wrongdoing than were the lesser jurors.

Almshouse regulations and Chancery petitions

Since it is possible that all reports by jurors within local and intermediate-level courts were shaped by the nature of the legal context, we may look also at wrongdoing as discussed in other settings. An interesting vantage-point is provided by the founding charters or later ordinances of residential institutions for the elderly poor. Here we are witnessing one aspect of a more positive reaction to the needy, albeit one that replaced direct personal assistance with a "distanced" form of institutionalized relief.[36] A characteristic charitable act among people of moderate means during the later fifteenth and sixteenth centuries was to establish an almshouse that offered free housing (and usually some kind of a stipend, food, and/or fuel) to elderly poor people. Among the residential institutions created between 1400 and 1600, almshouses progressively replaced the hospitals so popular in the earlier medieval period, which had provided care as well as housing and food for their inhabitants.[37] Almshouses were usually endowed by people of less wealth than the founders of the great hospitals: many of the donors

[34] *Court Leet Records [of Southampton]*, vol. I, pt. 1, p. 141. For below, see *ibid.*, vol. I, pt. 2, p. 174.
[35] *Continuation of the Court Leet Records of Manchester*, pp. 20 and 23. For below, see e.g., *Court Leet Records [of Southampton]*, vol. I, pt. 1, p. 49, *Records of the Borough of Leicester*, vol. III, p. 133, and *The Third Book of Remembrance of Southampton*, vol. III, pp. 22–3.
[36] Heal, *Hospitality*.
[37] Whereas 88 percent of the 112 residential institutions for the poor and sick founded between 1300 and 1399 that gave themselves a title were hospitals, only 45 percent of 103 houses founded between 1400 and 1459 were hospitals, the rest being almshouses. Between 1460 and 1599, just 22 percent of 231 new foundations were hospitals and the rest almshouses (76 percent) or "bridewells" (= workhouses, 2 percent). (McIntosh, "The Foundation of Hospitals and Almshouses.")

were intermediate landholders, local merchants, or craftsmen/traders within the community in which their house was endowed. Although the old folks selected for admission into an almshouse were unlikely to be violent disruptors of the good order of their village or town, the foundation documents and ordinances reveal a familiar set of concerns in stipulating what appropriate conduct entailed. Almshouse dwellers, whose actions could be observed, regulated, and disciplined, were to be models of social behavior as well as of devout religious observance.[38]

Maintaining the harmony and peace of the house, as in our first cluster of local court offences, was high on the list of concerns. (The proximity of institutional living would of course have exacerbated any problems in this area.) The occupants of the almshouses in Saffron Walden, Essex were told at the beginning of the fifteenth century to be "of good and honourable intercourse, not ... quarrelsome nor chiding one another."[39] At God's House in Ewelme, Oxon., founded around 1437, "charity, peace, & rest" were to be preserved among the thirteen poor men: they were to keep themselves "from jangling and chiding" and from "evil slander."[40] Among the grounds for removal from Westende's Almshouses in Wokingham, Berks., established in 1451, were being a scold or "a night stroller." John Isbury, founder of an almshouse in Lambourne, Berks. in 1501, said that "if any of my said poor be ... a brawler amongst his fellows or any the inhabitants of Lamborne, a quarreler or maker of debate," he was to be punished by subtraction of his salary or expulsion from the house.[41] The statutes of Wyggeston Hospital in Leicester from 1574 specify that the twelve men and twelve women living in the house should not be "liars, tale tellers, brawlers, chiders, quarrel pickers, fighters, railers, or slanderers."

Concern with order, control, and governance was likewise visible in the almshouse charters, especially those of the later fifteenth and six-

---

[38] Cf., for a somewhat later period, Foucault, *Discipline and Punish* and *Madness and Civilization*.

[39] Steer, "The Statutes of Saffron Walden Almshouses" (quotation here translated from the Latin text). This house was founded by a group of local merchants.

[40] Univ. of Nottingham Libr. MSS Dept. MS Mi 6/179/18 (a copy made c. 1500). Alice, Duchess of Suffolk and her husband William de la Pole endowed this house; it is one of only two institutions discussed here whose founders were members of the nobility. For below, see Berks. RO D/QWo 35/1/1 (calendar entry), an institution set up by a clerk of this market center.

[41] Berks. RO D/Q1 Q7/15. The house was founded by a local gentleman. For below, see Leics. RO 10 D 34/1419 (1), published in *A Calendar of Charters [... of] the Hospital of William Wyggeston*, pp. 54–83, esp. p. 77. The institution was endowed by William Wigston the younger, a Merchant of the Staple of Calais, himself from Leicester, around 1513.

teenth centuries. The ability to regulate one's own actions was commonly required. The five local poor men received into Roger Reede's
almshouse, founded in Romford, Essex in 1483, were to be "no common
beggars but such as have been of good governance and be fallen in
poverty."[42] At Ewelme, the residents were not to be "incontinent,
commonly drunk, or a glutton, ... a tavern haunter or of any other
suspect or unlawful place."[43] If any of the poor at John Isbury's almshouses in Lambourne were "a drunkard, a haunter & frequenter of
alehouses, inns, or taverns," he would be punished. The orders for
Wyggeston Hospital in Leicester said that the residents were to be "no
drunkards, no haunters of taverns nor alehouses"; they were neither to
commit adultery or fornication (assisted by the rule that men and
women were not allowed to enter each others' rooms) nor to be "dicers,
carders, table players, bowlers, or users of any such unthrifty and
unlawful games."[44] The inhabitants of Long Melford Hospital in Suffolk, founded in the later part of Elizabeth's reign, were similarly
prohibited from playing illegal games, except at Christmas, when they
might play among themselves. Good order was promoted by obedience
to the ordinances and/or the master of the house, stipulated in virtually
all the charters. At Ewelme, for example, if any of the poor men "be
rebel in deed or in word against the correction of the foresaid master,
that then he correct such a rebellious man by subtraction and taking
away of such wages after his discretion"; should the inmate remain
"incorrigible, obstinate & froward," he was to be put out of the house
forever.[45] The poor of Wyggeston Hospital were to "reverence and
obey" the master of their house.

Several other features are familiar as well. Wandering was forbidden.
The poor men of Ewelme were not to leave the precincts of their
almshouse and the church for more than an hour, nor were they to
"walk much about in the said parish, neither without the said parish
without a reasonable cause to be allowed."[46] At John Isbury's almshouses, the poor were not to go "wandering or traveling" unless they

---

[42] Essex RO D/Q 26. This house was established by a local tenant of about 150 acres who
produced and sold wood.
[43] Univ. of Nottingham Libr. MSS Dept. MS Mi 6/179/18. For below, see Berks. RO D/Q1
Q7/15.
[44] Leics. RO 10 D 34/1419 (1). For below, see Suff. RO, Bury St. Edmunds, OC 88 (a house
founded between 1581 and 1598 by Sir William Cordell, knight).
[45] Univ. of Nottingham Libr. MSS Dept. MS Mi 6/179/18. For below, see Leics. RO 10 D
34/1419 (1).
[46] Univ. of Nottingham Libr. MSS Dept. MS Mi 6/179/18. For below, see Berks. RO D/Q1
Q7/15.

had obtained leave. Inhabitants of Wyggeston Hospital might not be away from their own chamber overnight or absent from the hospital for a full day without license of the master.[47] By the sixteenth century, attention was being given to the speech and reputation of the residents. The almshouses founded in Stoke Poges, Bucks. in 1564 were intended for four poor and elderly men, "disposed to serve God in prayer and good conversation," and for two poor women "of good and honest fame"; the twelve poor men aged 55 years or more chosen for Long Melford Hospital were to be not only "of sober and honest life" but also "of good fame."[48] All these statements echo attitudes and language we have heard before: we observe no distinction between what was tolerated among unruly or idle residents and vagrants as presented to local courts and what was accepted among the elderly (and supposedly godly) poor living within charitable almshouses.

For a final set of texts, we turn to the descriptions of social misconduct contained within petitions submitted to the Lord Chancellor alleging an injustice perpetrated against the complainant and requesting intervention by the court of Chancery. Here we are looking not at the court as a legal institution nor at the specific matters of law put forward in the complaints but rather at the narratives of particular social episodes included, sometimes rather peripherally, in these documents. Because this was an equity or prerogative court, the "bills" sent in by those who hoped to persuade the court to address their case did not have to confine their claims to the boundaries and terminology of common law actions. Instead they were written (or dictated) fairly informally by local people who had problems which they claimed the common law could not resolve, using whatever arguments and forms of expression they thought would be most convincing. Although one finds conventional phrases even in these bills, and although we do not know whether the claims made were correct, the social descriptions contained in the petitions corroborate the widespread acceptance of attitudes we first encountered in the lesser public courts.

Complainants to Chancery assumed that social harmony was important and that the court's officials would agree with that view. People who disrupted local peace through causing ill-will between their neigh-

---

[47] Leics. RO 10 D 34/1419 (1). See also the Minute Book of Christ's Hospital, Abingdon, Oxon., 1578–1694, fol. 10r, ordinances from 1558. I am grateful to W. J. H. Liversidge and the Governors for permission to use these records.
[48] Bucks. RO CH 7/G.5 (Edward, Lord Hastings of Loughborough, founded the house); Suff. RO, Bury St. Edmunds, OC 88.

bors or bringing vexatious suits were inherently harmful.[49] Although few of the Chancery petitions between 1370 and 1600 focused expressly on scolding, a case from Plymouth, Devon in the 1530s provides some interesting material. Anthony Beere and his wife Joan complained against James Horswell, the mayor of Plymouth, for attempted extortion from Joan and for her false imprisonment.[50] They said that Horswell maliciously and wrongly charged her with scolding, threatening her with public punishment if she did not pay him 26s 8d. When she refused to give him that sum, he arranged on the next market day to have Joan "openly led through the market place to the water side." After summoning all the important people of the town, he ordered that she be "put on a stool commonly called a 'koken stole' which is a punishment used for common harlots, and from thence caused her to be let fall into the water." This, the only description of dunking encountered in this project, shows that extra ignominy accompanied the cuckingstool due to its use for sexual offenders.

Many petitions confirm people's eagerness to maintain the quality of their name or reputation. In one of an interesting group of cases from Henry VIII's reign, John Wolcott of Exeter claimed around 1520 that when John Rypley and his wife "did hang a ram's horn in a ring of the utter door" of his house, implying that he was being cuckolded, it was "to the defame and hurt of his name and honesty."[51] Robert Wynter, a clerk of South Petherton, Som. who had been accused locally of sexual transgressions in the 1530s, said that this slander hurt his "good name and fame" as well as jeopardizing his employment. The economic consequences of harm to one's reputation were likewise stressed by William Eyre of Salisbury around 1540.[52] Although he had previously been regarded as "of honest conversation," when he was charged with a theft of books from the church of Stockton, Wilts., it not only took from him "the good name and fame" that he had enjoyed "amongst the sad [= sober] and honest subjects" of the king, it also meant that those people "that used to occupy, buy, and sell" with him henceforth refused to deal with him, "so that now he is not able to get his living." In precisely parallel fashion, despite the difference in gender, Agnes Peryham of Devon said around 1540 that because Richard Wyll and his wife Margaret falsely accused her of stealing [feather] beds from a house, she is both "hurt in her good name and fame" and finds that she is "mistrusted at such places as she doth come to work in."[53] This

---

[49] E.g., PRO C 1/329/19 (from 1504–15), C 1/845/38–9 (from 1533–8), C 1/1068/50–51 (from 1538–44), and C 1/1074/57–60 (from 1538–44).   [50] PRO C 1/726/13.
[51] PRO C 1/565/42. For below, see PRO C 1/922/82.   [52] PRO C 1/981/119–20.
[53] PRO C 1/1053/32. For women employed on a daily basis, see section one above.

example reminds us that evidence from the church courts about the almost exclusive importance of their sexual reputations to women must be regarded with some caution: since the ecclesiastical courts dealt with sexual slanders but not with economic issues, the reasons alleged for damage from defamation may have been artificially limited in scope.

A larger body of these bills dealt with problems of disorder and lack of control. The terminology used in describing such problems is strikingly similar to that we have seen elsewhere, including the lack of specificity of many of the allegations. A cluster of such cases comes from London during Henry VIII's reign, the period of highest concern in the local courts too. Suspicion about unruly public houses underlay a petition submitted some time between 1518 and 1529 by Thomas More, keeper of a victualing house, against the mayor, aldermen, and sheriffs of London.[54] More said that he operated a house in London "where concourse of people doth daily resort for meat and drink . . . as well by night as by day at times and hours lawful and convenient." John Bridges, a citizen and alderman of London living within the same ward, because of his malice and ill-will towards More, falsely reported that "persons of evil name and disposition" came to his house and that "dishonest rule" was kept there. More was therefore arrested and placed in London's Compter until he gave bond of £5. In the 1530s Henry Phyllyppes and his wife Elizabeth were ordered out of the parish of St. Benet Fink after a pair of presentments at the Wardmote: Elizabeth was accused of "misliving of her body," and both of them were charged because "there is and hath been much resort of ill disposed and light persons repairing to their house, and there been maintained, aided, and succoured."[55] In parallel fashion Margaret and Richard Rande were expelled from Tower ward in the 1530s because Margaret was said to be "incontinent of her living and not good nor honest of her body." Criticizing the behavior of others in such terms could also lead to trouble. Thomas Bukland of Woodchester, Gloucs. claimed around 1520 that he had recently rebuked Roger Fowler of Stroudwater, a clothier, who "of long time hath been of an evil life in his disposition and conversation."[56] Although Bukland merely "exhorted and moved" Fowler "by good counsel to amend his demeanor," the angry Fowler in retaliation had him arrested on suspicion of felony.

Other petitions were written by people who claimed they had been wrongly arrested as vagrants and were appealing to the Lord Chancellor for trial and release. These are concentrated in the later fifteenth

---

[54] PRO C 1/543/30. The ward is not named in this damaged petition.
[55] PRO C 1/872/49. For below, see PRO C 1/883/7.   [56] PRO C 1/477/30.

century, just as concern with vagabonds was starting to rise in the local courts. In the 1480s, Richard Payne, a tailor of Horndon, Essex, complained from Hertford gaol that he had been improperly arrested as "a misgoverned man and a vagabond."[57] In reality, he claimed, he had "of great amity and love walked with certain special friends of his" from Horndon to Waltham Abbey, "to bring them forward in the way towards our lady of Walsingham." Payne spent the night in Waltham because he wanted to see a man who owed him money for making garments. When he and his customer fell into a heated argument, the bailiff of Waltham Abbey sent him to gaol and would not release him even though people from Horndon have "reported him of honest rule and conversation, and of good name and fame." Other men claimed that they were improperly arrested as vagabonds while on their way to London "to take the king's wages and go with him in his army beyond the sea" (from the later 1470s or early 1480s), while working on the archbishop's construction project at Lambeth (from c. 1490 or the early sixteenth century), or while "on pilgrimage" to the town of New Windsor, Berks. to visit the tomb of King Henry VI (in 1500–1).[58]

   A final issue that appears in Chancery bills especially of the Henrician period was gaming. Because the forms of indoor gaming were illegal, people who felt they had been cheated financially could not bring suit in the common law courts, but they could ask for help from the Lord Chancellor. These texts reinforce the point that gaming was regularly accompanied by betting and indicate that it was regarded as a disreputable recreation. Thus, around 1510 William Povy, a merchant tailor of London, bet and lost "many gages of gold and silver" amounting in sum to £10 while gaming with three other men who, he alleged, used false dice.[59] Because, however, he was embarrassed to have been "keeping company of the said persons at such a lewd pastime or game, dreading the shame of the world and the great displeasure of his friends," he gave bond for payment of the full amount. In the 1530s, Agnes Burton of an unstated place, "being a common hazarder, dicer, and carder whose living hath always been suspected," persuaded Thomas Covell's wife "craftily and under a subtle fashion" to play a card game called "one and thirty."[60] Through her deceitful playing against an inexperienced opponent, Burton first won 10s and then persuaded mistress Covell to take out of her husband's chest "a bag containing £40 sterling and more," with which they continued to play until Burton had won the entire sum contained in the bag. This loss was

---

[57] PRO C 1/61/246.   [58] PRO C 1/66/377, C 1/145/44, and C 1/238/36.
[59] PRO C 1/348/39.   [60] PRO C 1/767/49.

"not only to the blemish and hu[rt] of the good name and fame" of Covell's wife but also to her husband's "great hindrance and impoverishment."

The theme of the defenceless victim of unscrupulous gamers was coupled with concern about the activities of young people in several petitions from the 1530s. Richard Hawkyns als. Fissher, a victualer of Warwick, sent his servant, aged 16 or 17 years, to Newcastle [-under-Lyme] to buy fish, giving him 31s 8d in cash with which to purchase the goods plus five horses for carrying them back.[61] On his way there, the young man stopped at an inn in Stone, Staffs., where the proprietor, "perceiving that the servant of your said beseecher had much money in his purse and that he was but a very young man, enticed him to fall to game and to play with him at the cards." The innkeeper called one of his neighbors to join them, and the trio "sat up all night," at the end of which the servant had lost all his master's money. Aghast at what he had done, the servant fled and was never seen again, and the innkeeper turned loose the horses. Similarly, Laurence Foster, an apprentice to a grocer of London, was sent to Canterbury about his master's business. He traveled in the company of several other people, and they decided to lodge together when they arrived.[62] In the evenings, after they had conducted their business, the group "did use to pass the time at cards and dice" and a game called "faring," in the course of which Foster bet away all the money his master had entrusted to him.

A case involving outdoor sports reinforces the suggestions made above that bowling was enjoyed by many men, at least in the Southwest and West, and that presentments in the local courts may have stemmed from personal motives.[63] George Welsshe of Rockbeare, Devon, complained in the later 1550s that Henry Androwe had reported him and twenty-two other people to the hundred court of East Budleigh for bowling.[64] Androwe's presentment grew out of "a special malice" towards Welsshe and his neighbors, "minding to put them to great costs and charges." The costs were indeed great, for the twenty-three people were together fined £6 13s 4d by the court, an average of about 6s each. In this case Androwe's defence survives as well. He claimed, in a singularly smug tone, that as a tithingman at the court he was sworn on his oath "to make a true presentment of the ill demeanors" of all the king's and queen's subjects; in reporting the bowlers, he acted according to his "bounden duty and as every faithful subject ought to do … for the better preservation of the wealth of the realm and maintenance

---

[61] PRO C 1/824/77–81.   [62] PRO C 1/834/7.   [63] See Chapter 3, section four above.
[64] PRO C 1/1484/42–3, containing the petition and Androwe's response.

of the laws of the same." We note that Androwe made the familiar connection between playing games and loss of economic resources.

We have now considered three of the main questions addressed by this study: what were the mechanisms through which misbehavior was tackled between 1370 and 1600, what was the history of social regulation in the courts of villages and market centers, and what were the attitudes that underlay that response? This chapter has shown that the social and economic concerns that led to worry about misconduct in the lesser courts were shared by jurors and officials of other institutions and by people of middling status functioning in different contexts. In the following chapters we turn to the remaining question, the influences that shaped the amount and types of wrongdoing experienced by local communities and their reaction to it.

PART II

Factors that influenced social regulation

5

Some political considerations

Within any given community, a variety of factors must have affected both the extent and nature of misbehavior and the decisions made by middling-level families about how to respond to it. These influences included legal and political considerations, geographic, demographic, and economic features, and the ideological and religious context within which wrongdoing was defined and addressed. While these factors will be separated for purposes of analysis in the following chapters, we must remember that they were closely interwoven in practice. The artificial nature of the division is perhaps most visible with respect to ideological and religious issues, which played an essential role though they will be considered last. Nor does the exclusion of other considerations from this discussion indicate that they have been dismissed as unimportant. It is likely, for example, that cultural and educational factors affected social regulation, especially during the later sixteenth century when contrasts between local officeholders and the poor widened in many communities.[1] Such issues are not discussed in detail here because the kinds of sources used for this project provided little information about them. Only with respect to the tension seen in responses to poverty and divergent reactions to bowling did we encounter suggestions of cultural differentiation.[2]

Because the influences that affected social regulation operated in different ways, diverse approaches will be used in assessing their probable impact. The legal and political changes that shaped how control was implemented, as discussed in Chapter 1, and the ideological and religious stances to be considered in Chapter 8 presumably had consequences for the country as a whole and therefore are considered in general terms. In other cases, our focus becomes sharper, as when we compare changes in government and political thought at the national

---

[1] See the Introduction, note 11 above.   [2] See Chapter 3, sections three and four above.

and county levels with the pattern of local response to misconduct traced in Chapter 3 (see section one below). Some influences operated at a still more specific level and must therefore be examined within individual communities. For the same 255 places studied in Chapter 3, we will investigate how local political traditions affected their reactions to wrongdoing (see section two below) and how their geographic, demographic, and economic characteristics varied in accordance with their reactions to misbehavior (see Chapters 6 and 7). While only detailed local studies can trace the particular influences and people that drove events within a given community, this discussion provides a framework within which more focused research may be placed and makes suggestions for future investigation.

For all the factors investigated here, we observe marked changes between the fifteenth century and the end of the sixteenth. Prior to around 1500, social regulation resulted overwhelmingly from specific local issues and did not necessarily reflect the concerns of central authorities. Communities that confronted severe problems with wrong-doing and/or responded strongly to it were marked by distinctive locational, demographic, economic, and institutional features. Al-though people's attitudes were of course influenced in a general sense throughout our span by the forms of legal and political control and by the moral teachings of the Christian churches, there is no evidence that social regulation in fifteenth-century villages and market centers was moving in parallel with political developments at a higher level or was affected by new ideas about social issues. By the end of Elizabeth's reign, however, the situation was very different. Worry about miscon-duct was now found in many different sorts of communities, most of them burdened by severe population pressure and acute problems with poverty. The extension of legal and political authority at both national and county levels resulted in closer supervision of many aspects of life at the same time that it diminished the role of the lesser local courts in dealing with social problems in some parts of the country. By the 1580s–90s both the ethical teachings of the Church of England and in some communities a new commitment among zealous Puritans to enforce moral behavior provided a basis for active attention to wrong-doing. Social regulation had thus become a national phenomenon by the end of Elizabeth's reign, with a variety of different influences reinforcing each other.

With respect to political and legal issues, the major changes that marked the fifteenth and sixteenth centuries have already been sum-marized in broad terms.[3] In this chapter we explore two specific ques-

---

[3] See Chapter 1, section one above.

tions. Political events and ideas about government formed part of the
context within which local regulation of wrongdoing took place, but
their effect was by no means consistent over time. We will examine this
relationship by looking at selected periods to see how political factors at
the national and county level compared with the patterns of local
regulation of conduct laid out in Chapter 3 above. This indicates
marked contrasts between the responses of local courts as compared
with national/county patterns prior to c. 1500 but generally similar
movement thereafter. We turn then to the question of whether a tradition of "political" autonomy within individual communities affected
their willingness to tackle social problems. Here the experience of the
particular communities studied in Chapter 3 points to the importance
of quasi self-governmental institutions during the fifteenth century but
not thereafter.

National vs. local responses

The Black Death and the Peasants' Revolt defined a period of potential
political and actual social instability. As the result of those events,
England's leaders and the major landlords became deeply concerned
about the labor and mobility of the poor as well as about unrest and
violence.[4] Their efforts to control the peasantry were not, however,
reflected in increased concern with order and wrongdoing at the local
level. The Statute of Labourers of 1351, based upon an ordinance of
1349, attempted to regulate the conditions of paid employment and to
fix maximum wage rates at their levels prior to the plague; in an effort
to limit the movement of workers, service for a term of one full year was
encouraged. The statute spoke also of able-bodied beggars who "refuse
to labour, giving themselves to Idleness and Vice, and sometime to
Theft and other Abominations," upon whom no pity or alms should be
bestowed "so that thereby they may be compelled to labour for their
necessary Living."[5] The Commons' petitions that followed these
measures similarly expressed considerable hostility towards people
who were unwilling to work.[6] After the uprising of 1381 county officials
and the large landholders punished not only the participants in the

---

[4] It has been suggested more broadly that during the generation after the Black Death the
upper levels of English society, led by Edward III and his advisors, deliberately pulled
together into a more coherent and effective government able to maintain the status quo
in the face of the new demographic and socio-economic conditions (Palmer, *English
Law*).   [5] 23 Edward III, c. 7 (*Stats. Realm*, vol. I, p. 308).

[6] Aers, "*Piers Plowman*: Poverty, Work, and Community," esp. p. 30. As Aers notes,
classifying mobile workers as idle beggars and mendicants was an important rhetorical
weapon within the social and political struggle waged by England's leadership at the
time.

rebellion but also those who only expressed sympathy with the movement, if they were suspect in other ways as well. In an example that displays marked resemblances to the concerns described in Chapter 3, John Shirley of Nottingham was said to be "a vagabond in various counties" during the disturbance, carrying "lies as well as silly and worthless talk from district to district"; while passing on his news at a tavern in Cambridge, he compounded these offences by criticizing John Ball's execution, leading to his own trial and hanging.[7] The revolt heightened Parliament's fear of the wandering poor too: the first use of the term "vagabond" in official legislation came in 1383, when all JPs and sheriffs were given power to punish such people.[8]

Yet there is no evidence that the worry about order, stability, and labor seen at the top level of English government and law in this period was shared by the middling families that provided the leadership of villages and market centers. As we saw in the Introduction and Chapter 3, the amount of concern with wrongdoing in the lesser public courts between 1350 and 1400 was very low, as measured both by the small number of presentments of offenders and by the absence of any rhetoric surrounding such misconduct even when it was reported. Rather than troubling themselves with issues that must have seemed relatively unimportant, local leaders were presumably devoting their attention to the more immediate problems of keeping economic activity going in their community despite the demographic collapse and holding together some sense of social unity. During this half-century, marked in most regions of the country by secondary plague outbursts occurring on average every ten years or so, newcomers were probably welcomed to the community if they were willing to work at all, not harried out as vagabonds. Even the idlers were less of a problem than in more densely populated periods: empty housing was abundant, and because real wages were high those who chose not to seek regular employment could get by with only a limited amount of daily or harvest-time labor.

The next episode of serious unrest derived not from changes in the demographic and economic underpinnings of society but rather from conflicts within the ruling group itself over power at the highest level. The period before and during the Wars of the Roses saw a weakening of political and legal power at both national and county levels, counterbalanced in this case by more aggressive attention to misbehavior within the lesser courts. Although there had frequently been disputes among the magnates, more serious and widespread disagreement over who

---

[7] *The Peasants' Revolt*, pp. xxviii–xxix, as cited in Hanna, "Pilate's Voice/Shirley's Case."
[8] 7 Richard II, c. 5 (*Stats. Realm*, vol. II, p. 32).

should advise and control the king and ultimately over the crown itself took shape during the 1430s, 1440s, and early 1450s; during the following decades this led to occasional battles between the Lancastrian and Yorkist factions. As most of the noble families and some gentry houses were involved in this wrangling, their attention to local matters and their ability to provide stable leadership at the county level were disrupted.[9]

Political theorists and advisors to the crown were deeply worried by these events, accelerating an interesting shift in the definition of royal authority and its ends. Traditional medieval thought concentrated upon the king's role as a bestower of mercy, forgiveness, and reward.[10] Early in Henry VI's reign, however, one sees the beginnings of a new emphasis upon the need for control by the king as maintained through punishment. During the 1420s and 1430s, works in the tradition of such continental forms as the *Speculum Regis* or *Miroir au Prince* together with more original pieces all started to call for forceful governance. Treatises like Hoccleve's *Regement of Princes* and James Yonge's mirror for the Earl of Ormond emphasize that rulers must maintain order and control through use of the royal right to punish offenders.[11] By the third quarter of the century, a variety of works were insisting upon the obligation of the king and his representatives to implement their authority by subduing miscreants: by enforcing the law, they will inspire appropriate fear in their subjects.[12]

Diminished control at the national and county levels during the fifteenth century may well have been a factor in the increasing concern with social regulation seen within the lesser local courts. In particular, it is possible that new attention to forms of misconduct that threatened order and control, appearing as a serious issue in village and market center courts in the 1460s–70s, stemmed in part from a sense among local leaders that since those above them were not carrying out their normal duties, they had better take responsibility themselves for the governance and security of their own communities. (This concern

---

[9] For local unrest, see Hare, "The Wiltshire Risings of 1450," and I. M. W. Harvey, *Jack Cade's Rebellion.*

[10] Much of the following paragraph derives from McCune, "Late Medieval Strategies." I am grateful to Dr. McCune for permitting me to use and cite her work.

[11] *Hoccleve's Works,* pp. 97–113, and *Three Prose Versions,* pp. 127–45, both as cited by McCune, "Late Medieval Strategies." See also "Tractatus de Regimine Principium," in *Four English Political Tracts,* pp. 48–168, written c. 1435–50 for Henry VI.

[12] Even the most innovative thinker of the century, Fortescue, employs in his works of the 1460s and 1470s the now-familiar rubric of forceful governance within which to offer a more sophisticated analysis of the actual nature of control within different types of political structures. See, e.g., Fortescue, *De Laudibus Legum Angliae* and *The Governance of England;* Ferguson, *The Articulate Citizen,* esp. ch. 5.

would have been magnified by the demographic and economic developments described in Chapters 6 and 7 below.) There is also a pronounced similarity between the language about order and control used in local courts and analyses of rule at the level of the monarchy or state. While it is unlikely that village or market center jurors were familiar with political advice manuals through their own reading, such texts may well have expressed ideas that were being discussed more generally in the country by those responsible for maintaining order at whatever level. The rhetoric used in local presentments from the 1460s–70s and the attitudes towards control that underlay their statements may have been further strengthened by the jurors' recognition that they were expanding the jurisdiction of their courts into new areas and hence needed to provide more explicit justification for their actions. By appropriating concepts and terminology from the broader debate, they could thus have attempted to legitimize their decision to act in the absence of formal legal authorization.

Beginning in the later 1470s and extending for the next forty years, Parliament and the crown too began to express concerns and use language about social misconduct that resembles closely what we observed first in the lesser local courts. The statute against gaming of 1477–8, for example, focuses upon the harmful economic consequences of such activity, an issue visible in local presentments at least a generation earlier. After commenting rather perfunctorily upon the fact that gaming is against the laws of the land and offends God when pursued on holy days, the measure says that people play "to their own Impoverishment, and by their ungracious Procurement and encouraging, do bring other to such Games, till they be utterly undone and impoverished of their goods."[13] The revised statute of 1495 specified when and where games might be played and whether the masters of servants were present at the time, thus paralleling the concern with youthful labor visible in the local context three decades before.[14] Because the

---

[13] 17 Edward IV, c. 3 (*Stats. Realm*, vol. II, p. 462–3).

[14] 11 Henry VII, c. 2, heading 5 (*Stats. Realm*, vol. II, p. 569). A royal proclamation of 1511 concerning unlawful games feared that servants would "fall to robberies and oftentimes to robbing of their masters" to support their playing (*Tudor Royal Procls.*, vol. I, pp. 88–9). For other examples of ideas and language similar to that previously encountered in local court records, see two royal proclamations from 1487 concerning the damage done by verbal abuse within political and military contexts (*Tudor Royal Procls.*, vol. I, pp. 12–14), the statute of 1495, which was the first to provide even a minimally thoughtful discussion of the various sorts of poor people, their needs, and the response appropriate to each (11 Henry VII, c. 2, *Stats. Realm*, vol. II, p. 569), and a 1513 proclamation laying out ordinances of war for Calais that speaks of quarreling, brothel-keeping, and gaming (*Tudor Royal Procls.*, vol. I, pp. 113–14).

ideas and terminology seen in statutes and royal proclamations in all cases followed their initial appearance in the courts of village and market centers, we are probably watching a gradual extension of concern from the smaller communities where unfamiliar practical problems were first encountered upwards to higher levels of control that were slower to notice and react to the realities of everyday life.

During the sixteenth century, local concern with wrongdoing seems to have moved in parallel with broader political developments. The 1520s and 1530s form an interesting period for analysis. Not only did they include an initial peak in social regulation in the local courts (54 percent of all places under observation reporting one or more of the offences studied here), they also witnessed England's break from Rome, the dissolution of the monasteries, a serious rebellion, partial reorganization of the central government's bureaucracy, an enormous burst of statutory activity at the Parliamentary level, and the demographic and economic developments considered in Chapter 7 below. There is no indication that the local courts received instructions from above to address misbehavior more aggressively, so it is likely that village and town leaders were moving in tandem with their political betters, influenced like them by worries about order and control.

The impact of the increased institutional stability of government is seen during the years between 1547 and 1558. The most striking feature of this period is that rapid turnover in rulers and armed opposition to some of their policies were not reflected in the form of more reports to local courts concerning social wrongdoing. To the contrary, for each of the three clusters of misconduct described in Chapter 3 we see a drop in the percentage of courts presenting problems in the 1540s–50s as compared with the 1520s–30s. This suggests that even though the central government saw four different monarchs within twelve years – one of them a child – and three armed rebellions, local leaders did not feel that they themselves had to act to preserve stability. This contrast with the period before and during the Wars of the Roses may have derived in part from greater continuity of royal administrative personnel and from the expanded royal bureaucracy; it must also have been affected by the normal operation of Parliament and the central common law courts during the crises of Edward VI's and Mary's reigns. From the perspective of villages and market centers, however, the most important difference was probably that gentry and even some noble families were by the mid-sixteenth century firmly embedded within the intensified system of administrative and legal control now operating within the counties. Leaders of the smaller communities did not feel a need to take unusual steps in their own courts because the families and institutions directly above them continued to enforce local order.

During Elizabeth's reign, increasing powers and further institutionalization of government and law at the national and county levels affected social regulation in several ways. As we have seen, the more effective authority over wrongdoing wielded by the church courts and Sessions of the Peace led many of the lesser public courts in East Anglia, the Southeast, and the lower Midlands to hand over responsibility for certain offences to those bodies.[15] By the end of the sixteenth century control over misconduct was distributed among a variety of different courts rather than being concentrated at the bottom as had been true in the past. At the same time, the expansion of political and legal control that marked the period between 1530 and the end of the century, with more Parliamentary legislation, new roles for the Privy Council, and greatly increased duties for the JPs, all contributed to a widespread if not uniform acceptance among respectable people that it was appropriate for the government to regulate many aspects of life. Rules addressing behavior formed part of this extended range.[16] If we had detailed local studies able to measure the total amount of control over social wrongdoing throughout the period between 1370 and 1600, looking at all the bodies that implemented control within a given community and at the amount of force they could exert, we would almost certainly find that there was more concerted regulation and more effective power behind it at the end of Elizabeth's reign than at any previous time.[17]

"Political" activity at the community level

Though in most respects the types of evidence used for this project do not allow us to examine political issues within individual settings, we can offer some suggestions about the importance of a tradition of strong community activity. It seems logical that a village or market center accustomed to working as a unit to address problems of a public nature would be better prepared to tackle social misbehavior.[18] Because few of

[15] See Chapter 1, section one above.

[16] Kent, "Attitudes of Members of the House of Commons," and Dean and Jones, "Individualising Morality." I am grateful to Drs. Dean and Jones for permission to use and cite their paper.

[17] This conclusion differs from that of Sharpe and Wrightson in emphasizing the gradual increase in authority of county institutions and the regional nature of the patterns: see the Introduction above.

[18] For the importance of such forms of local self-government in shaping the response to poverty in the later medieval and Tudor periods, see McIntosh, "Local Responses to the Poor."

the communities studied here were formally constituted as boroughs, they lacked clearly defined urban institutions expressly charged with acting on behalf of the whole group. Nevertheless, some of the market centers and even a few of the villages had structures that facilitated cooperation around common issues. In some instances a religious fraternity or a craft or merchants' gild came gradually to function as the *de facto* government of a market center.[19] A body of men functioning as trustees could hold property on behalf of the village or town to support charitable purposes, including care of the poor; their attention might readily expand to encompass other public issues as well. Among the most powerful of these bodies were the bridgewardens of communities located at the point where a major road crossed one of the large rivers, whose financial and political expertise could readily be transferred to additional areas of concern. The community might work cooperatively to control its fenlands, or the locally elected churchwardens might move beyond the powers normally assigned to such officers to take on atypical responsibilities in secular areas as well.

Of the 221 villages and market centers examined in Chapter 3, twenty are said in secondary studies to have possessed one or more of these forms of quasi self-government. But those 9 percent were not distributed evenly among the various categories of response to social wrongdoing. We may compare those places that reported no problems at all with misbehavior during a given period (the "no response" communities) with those that expressed an unusually wide range of concern, reporting four or more different kinds of offences within a single duodecade (the "broad response" places).[20] Between 1420 and 1499 not a single one of the "no response" places contained any of the nascent political institutions, whereas a full third of the "broad response" places did. During the first part of the sixteenth century (1500–59) the contrast diminished – 5 percent of the "no response" places had such bodies as compared with 18 percent of the "broad response" ones – and by the Elizabethan period it was gone. At all times, a higher fraction of the communities that reported problems within the Disorder cluster had a tradition of self-government than did those that expressed no concern or mentioned the other clusters of offences.

This evidence suggests that during the fifteenth century, when local

---

[19] For examples from this study, see, Chesterfield, Derby., Saffron Walden, Essex, Basingstoke, Hants., and Loughborouth, Leics. For the patterns below, see, e.g.: for town lands, Clare and Framlingham, Suff.; for bridgewardens, Maidenhead, Berks. (in the manor of Bray), Staines, Middx., Henley, Oxon., and Kingston-upon-Thames, Surrey; for control of fens, Willingham, Cambs.; for churchwardens, Brightwalton, Berks.

[20] See Chapter 6, section one below for a fuller description of these categories.

communities had greater autonomy in handling social wrongdoing, they were more likely to respond aggressively if they were already experienced at confronting other public issues through related institutions. (It is also obvious that the larger and more complex places that encountered practical problems with misbehavior in this period would by their nature have been more likely to have incipient political institutions as well.[21]) By the late sixteenth century local self-government no longer mattered, presumably because attention to misbehavior had spread to a far wider range of communities and because the role of many of the lesser bodies in regulating conduct was more limited as well as more closely supervised by institutions above them. The next two chapters continue to focus upon the places studied in Chapter 3, looking now at their geographic, demographic, and economic features.

[21] See Chapters 6 and 7 below.

6

Social ecology I: "broad response" and "no response" communities

Another set of potential influences upon the amount of social wrong-doing and efforts to control it consists of the geographic, demographic, and economic circumstances of individual communities. To explore the impact of these factors, we will focus on the 255 places (containing 267 courts) whose records were used in Chapter 3, linking up evidence about their responses to misconduct with other sorts of information. Chapters 6 and 7 both present quantitative analyses of such features as the type of community, its regional setting and specific location, the nature of its economy, the size and direction of population movement, the level of total wealth and changes in prosperity over time, and the distribution of resources among its residents. Chapter 6 compares places that reported a broad array of behavioral offences with those that mentioned no problems at all within three chronological periods; Chapter 7 divides the communities into groups based upon the type of offences they presented and then examines their characteristics during four pivotal duodecades. Because each of these approaches involves breaking down the full set of communities into smaller subsets within periods, the number of places within the individual groupings is almost never larger than 100 and more commonly is less than 50. Since these numbers are so small in statistical terms, common sense indicates that mathematical measures of significance and correlation not be presented: I do not want to imply that the figures allow us to assess in a quantitative fashion the precise role played by each of the factors considered. Instead we will compare groups of communities based upon their level and type of concern with misconduct in order to identify patterns, similarities, and contrasts.

These analyses are important in several respects. First, they offer a new approach to what one may call "social ecology," providing an assessment of a series of factors during the period of the late medieval/early modern transition for communities distributed throughout England.[1] Because the methods used are novel, they are described carefully in the opening section of each chapter. Secondly, this investigation reveals significant changes in the role of such factors in helping to shape misconduct and/or a concern with it across the fifteenth and sixteenth centuries. During the later fifteenth century we can identify specific characteristics that accompanied and presumably influenced regulation, several of them linked to the early phases of capitalism. By the end of the sixteenth century, however, attention to misbehavior was found in communities of many different sizes and kinds, located in all sorts of settings. What characterized those with a wide array of concerns or particular problems with the Poverty cluster were population pressure and rising numbers of very poor people.

It must again be stressed that neither the local court evidence upon which this comparison rests nor the new data presented here allow us to distinguish between the factors that led to higher levels of actual wrongdoing and those that caused local leaders to feel they needed to report and punish whatever problems did occur. While the social ecology of a community must have exerted a direct influence upon the amount and type of misbehavior, a variety of other considerations – legal, political, and ideological – played an important part in the jurors' decisions of what issues and people to report publicly and which court to use. Only local studies can determine the relative contribution of each of those factors, untangling specific processes and motives. In approaching its task, this chapter begins by laying out the evidence. The data are presented in tables and maps by topic, with a description of the sources from which the material was taken, the problems in working with them, and the methods of analysis. The information is then integrated by chronological period and some possible explanations offered for the patterns observed.

Method and evidence

We are investigating here the geographic, demographic, and economic characteristics of those communities that expressed concern with a wide range of social problems, comparing them with places that did not mention any misbehavior at all. In defining these categories, I counted the number of types of wrongdoing mentioned by each court during

---

[1] For a sophisticated linkage of social, demographic, and economic developments in a somewhat later period, see Kussmaul, *A General View of the Rural Economy*. The patterns seen here are not obviously related to those she describes.

Table 6.1 *Type of community and court by duodecade: "broad response"*
*places**

N + % of all courts under observation per duodecade	Villages (all manor courts)	Market Centers			Composite manorial estates
		Manor courts	Borough courts	Hundreds	
1400s–10s	1= 1%	0	1	0	0	0
1420s–30s	3= 2%	0	3	0	0	0
1440s–50s	4= 3%	0	3[†]	1	0	0
1460s–70s	13= 8%	2[†]	9	1	0	1
1480s–90s	7= 5%	1	4[††]	1[†]	1	0
1500s–10s	11= 7%	4[††]	3	2	0	2[†]
1520s–30s	22=12%	8[††]	7	3[†]	1	3
1540s–50s	10= 6%	2	4[††]	2	1	1
1560s–70s	12= 7%	4[††]	6[††]	0	1	1
1580s–90s	13= 7%	7	3	2	0	1

* "Broad response" places are those that reported four or more different types of offences within a given duodecade.
† Each symbol represents one court that reported six or more types of offences within that duodecade.

each duodecade under observation. As in Chapter 3, nine combined sorts of misconduct were assessed (scolding, eavesdropping/night-walking, sexual wrongdoing, disorderly alehouses, bad governance, hedgebreaking, sheltering vagabonds/living idly, receiving sub-tenants, and gaming); a presentment of one or more people for a given type of misbehavior or promulgation of a byelaw about it within the courts sampled during a given duodecade counted as a response. For all observations in all duodecades between 1370/80 and 1599, 59 per-cent of the courts reported no problems of any kind, 36 percent reported one to three different kinds of misconduct per duodecade, and 6 per-cent reported four or more distinct forms of wrongdoing. The latter response indicates that a community was troubled by assorted forms of misbehavior, spanning at least two separate clusters.[2]

Of the 255 places in this study, 59 (= 23 percent) reported four or more kinds of misconduct during at least one duodecade between 1370 and 1599, with just a single instance prior to 1420.[3] (Table 6.1 displays

---

[2] See the Introduction above for the clusters.
[3] Of these, 44 places (17 percent of the total) mentioned four or five different types of offences within a single duodecade, while 15 (6 percent of the total) demonstrated exceptionally wide concern with social wrongdoing, reporting six or more different kinds of problems within a single duodecade.

these communities by duodecade and type of community and court, and Appendix 6.1 provides a list of them.) In nearly all duodecades between 1460 and 1599, 5–8 percent of the courts under observation registered concern at this extended level; in the 1520s–30s the figure rose to 12 percent. If these figures reflect even approximately the minimum proportions for other lesser public courts in England, a very large number of local bodies must have been struggling with multiple forms of misconduct at some point during the later fifteenth and six-teenth centuries. The duodecades were then grouped into three longer units for analysis: 1420–99, 1500–59, and 1560–99.[4] If a court reported four or more types of misbehavior during any duodecade within one of those periods, it is classified as a "broad response" community for that period. Those places that expressed no concern with misbehavior in any of the courts sampled throughout the full span of the period under consideration are defined as "no response" communities.

The analysis is affected by the methodology used in working with the court records, as discussed in Chapter 2. Because I decided to sample within duodecades the records of many communities, rather than using all surviving records for a much smaller number of places, I have doubtlessly failed to pick up the full set of offences that in fact con-cerned some communities within some duodecades. If we had com-plete information, the number of "broad response" places would al-most certainly be larger and the number of "no response" communities smaller.[5] Further, I decided not to record the number of people reported for a given offence during each duodecade: that information cannot be interpreted in the absence of accurate demographic data, which could not be obtained in a large-scale study like this. The evidence employed here about the number of different offences reported thus measures the breadth of a community's problems with and/or response to miscon-duct, but it does not assess the intensity with which a place dealt with a particular type of wrongdoing as measured by the number of present-ments for that offence alone. We know also that by the second half of the sixteenth century the role of the lesser public courts in controlling misbehavior was diminishing in some regions, supplanted by the greater authority of the church courts and Sessions of the Peace in addressing certain kinds of offences.[6] The number of communities that fell into the "broad response" category between 1560 and 1599 on the

---

[4] The "broad response" places for 1420–99 include also the one community that met the criteria in the 1400s–10s, but the "no response" group covers only 1420–99.

[5] The distortions are presumably greater for smaller communities and less active courts than for larger, more vigorous bodies that reported many types of offences at every court session: see Chapter 2 above.   [6] See Chapter 1, section one above.

basis of the lesser courts' records is therefore an incomplete measure of the actual level of concern, which was now increasingly shared with other courts.

This study provides additional support for my own earlier sugges-tion that vigorous social regulation in some market centers during the later fifteenth century resembled the patterns visible in many more communities by around 1600.[7] The similarities may be illustrated by the presentments made in just a few of these "broad response" places between 1460 and 1499. At a single View of Frankpledge in 1460, jurors in the manor of Loughborough, Leics., a market center and stopping point on the main road from London to Nottingham and York, pres-ented one widow, two married women, and three unmarried women as scolds; a man for receiving another man and a married woman in adultery; three men for wrongdoing in offering hospitality at night and other illegal times; and eight men and two male servants for playing dice and cards.[8] The suburban London manor of Fulham, Middx. during two general courts in 1474–5 presented a married woman as a scold between her neighbors; a man described as a common procurer who keeps a certain Margaret [blank], a whore, in his house; three unmarried and one married woman as breakers of hedges; and four men for various gaming offences, several linked with nightwalking and a refusal to labor. Acute social concern in the manor, market center, and port of Minehead, Som. during the 1490s was heightened by fear of poor Irish immigrants. In three Legal courts held in 1495–6 jurors reported the tenants of Alice Blake for being scolds as well as badly governed, living as whores; Christine Watte for permitting her tenants to be nightwalkers and keeping bad governance; Cornell Herte for being a common bawd and keeping vagabonds in her house; Juliana Spencer for nourishing suspect persons within her house and serving as a procuress; Katherine Langhwyll and the tenants of Thomas Chepman for keeping bad governance; [Teye Clasath?] for supporting badly governed men and women in his/her house; John Corsye for receiving people who carry away the hedges of the tenants; Thomas Power for maintaining bad governance in his house and receiving vagabonds against the order of the court; John Thye for transporting vagabonds from Ireland against the order of the court; and Thomas Whyte for keeping vagabonds in the town and refusing to carry them back to

---

[7] In "Local Change and Community Control" and *Autonomy and Community*, pp. 250–61.
[8] Huntington Library (San Marino, Calif.) HAM Box 21, #8. For below, see Guildhall Libr., London, MS 10312, Roll 80, courts held c. St. Katherine the Virgin, 14 and 15 Edward IV.

Ireland.[9] For many "broad response" communities, control of social wrongdoing in the later fifteenth century was a serious issue, one that looked very much like the reactions seen more widely by the end of the sixteenth – even though the political/ideological/religious context had by then changed considerably.

Presentation of the data begins with the type of community within which the courts were located. Table 6.1 and the left side of Table 6.2 use the categories of villages, market centers, hundreds, and composite manorial estates[10]; within market centers, they distinguish further between manor courts and borough courts. To make sense of these figures, we must look more closely at the nature of the hundreds and combined manorial estates as compared with individual villages and market centers. Although this project includes many fewer of the extended units, they differed from the separate communities in ways that affect our interpretation of the evidence. As we saw in Chapter 2, hundreds were larger than the individual communities in both geographic area and population, but they rarely included substantial market centers and were fairly homogeneous in economic terms, since they covered adjacent parishes. While a larger population might lead us to expect a greater number of presentments for social problems, several factors argue in the opposite direction: the dispersal of the population among small settlements, and the overwhelmingly rural nature of the hundreds. Most of the composite manorial estates were not only large in terms of their total area and population, they were generally spread among non-contiguous parishes. Some contained diverse forms of economic activity, including market centers and, in certain cases, mining, ironmaking, and metalworking operations. The total population under their control might thus be substantial and the range of economic life potentially great. One would expect, therefore, a heightened response to social misbehavior as recorded in the court rolls of many of the composite estates, stemming from their large population and in some cases from their varied economic context.

During the fifteenth century, there was a sharp contrast between the responses of the two types of courts held in market centers, with the manor courts much more active than the borough ones. After 1500, however, the patterns became more similar. Since market centers with manor courts were on average somewhat smaller in population but spanned a larger geographical area than did those with borough courts (see Table 2.1), some of the variations probably stem from underlying

---

[9] Som. RO DD/L P28/15.
[10] For the definition of these units, see the Notes to Appendix 2.1.

Table 6.2 *Type of community/court and region of the country: "broad response" and "no response" places**

Percentage of courts in each chronological grouping that fell into each category (= row percentages)

	N	Type of community and court					Region of the country			
		Village	Market center		Hundred	Composite manorial estate	North/ Northwest	West/ Southwest	Midlands/ East Central	East Anglia/ Southeast
			Manor	Borough						
1420–1499										
0 offences reported	112	68%	12%	3%	11%	7%	13%	23%	37%	28%
4+ types of offences	19	11%	68%	11%	5%	5%	5%	26%	16%	53%
1500–1559										
0 offences reported	96	66%	20%	3%	9%	2%	9%	20%	41%	30%
4+ types of offences	33	30%	39%	15%	6%	9%	27%	18%	21%	33%
1560–1599										
0 offences reported	60	57%	15%	10%	13%	5%	8%	22%	33%	37%
4+ types of offences	21	38%	38%	10%	5%	10%	19%	48%	10%	24%

*Includes for each period all courts that reported no social offences of any kind throughout the span plus those that reported 4 or more different types of offences within any duodecade. The "broad response" group for 1420–99 includes the one "broad response" place from the 1400s–10s. For definition of regions, see Map 2.1 and note 10 to Ch. 6.

demographic and economic issues. In addition, boroughs may have possessed other forms of legal/political control over wrongdoing that limited the use of these lesser courts for such purposes. Yet if we compare the six market centers for which we have records of both manor and borough courts, we find that the two kinds of courts displayed roughly similar responses, with the same types of misconduct turning up in both courts over time but in a haphazard way. There seems to have been no systematic decision within a given place to allow one court to handle all problems with certain forms of wrongdoing: instead attention moved between the courts or was shared by them in an apparently flexible fashion, on the basis of particular factors invisible to us. Because residents of market centers seem to have drawn no generic distinctions between the various public courts available within their communities, we shall henceforth follow their example by treating the market centers as a group, regardless of the type of court.

The question of regional variation is investigated on the right side of Table 6.2.[11] Although interesting contrasts emerge between regions, we need to confront the possibility that some of this difference is artificial, deriving from the uneven distribution of surviving records and hence of the types of courts studied within the four areas. (See Map 2.1, which shows the location and type of all the courts within the four regional groupings utilized here.) Appendix 6.2 shows the observed number of communities by type within each region as compared with what the value would have been if the distribution had been consistent across all four regions. It shows that in the North/Northwest, the deficiency in the number of courts in market centers (which were more likely to be concerned with misconduct) was more than outweighed by the preponderance of composite manorial estates, which were apt to respond very strongly, and by a shortage of hundred courts, which were in general less troubled by social problems. Hence one would *a priori* expect to see an elevated level of concern in the North/Northwest. The West/Southwest was likewise predisposed to social regulation, though to a lesser degree: it had a relative shortage of villages, which were less likely to respond, and a slight weighting of market centers. The Midlands/East Central region should have been slightly less inclined to report social

[11] The North/Northwest includes Ches., Cumb., Durham, Lancs., Northumb., Westml., Yorks. East Riding, Yorks. North Riding, and Yorks. West Riding. The South/Southwest includes Corn., Devon, Dorset, Gloucs., Heref., Shrops., Som., Staffs., Wilts., and Worcs. The Midlands/East Central includes Beds., Bucks., Derby., Hunts., Leics., Lincs., Northants., Notts., Oxon., Rutl., and War. East Anglia/Southeast includes Berks., Cambs., Essex, Hants., Herts., Kent, Middx., Norf., Suff., Surrey, and Sussex (East and West). These crude categories were sufficient for the purposes of this analysis. For a more thoughtful division of England into fourteen "cultural provinces," see Phythian-Adams' introduction to *Societies, Cultures and Kinship* and Figs. 1.1–1.4.

issues because it had more than the normal fraction of villages and somewhat fewer market centers. East Anglia/Southeast was within 5 percent of the expected value in all respects, with differences that should have canceled each other out.

But the skewing introduced by the uneven distribution of our types of records is not entirely invalid, for the distribution of local public courts was in reality uneven too. Manor courts located within villages were more common in the lower Midlands and East Central region, East Anglia, and the Southeast than they were in the North, Northwest, West, and Southwest; hundred courts still functioning during our period were almost certainly more numerous in the Southwest, South, and Derbyshire/Nottinghamshire than in other regions; and great composite manorial estates were without doubt more prevalent in the North and Northwest than elsewhere. Hence our evidence probably provides a reasonably accurate reflection of the layout of courts on the ground.

Another factor that might have influenced local juries when dealing with misconduct was the lord of the manor, acting in his seigneurial role. We saw in Chapter 1 that the steward of the court, appointed by the lord, played little role in dealing with public issues other than to read the charge (which was often interpreted loosely by jurors anyway), but it is possible that an energetic individual or monastic lord, especially if resident within the community, might have influenced local attitudes towards wrongdoing. The top part of Table 6.3 examines the lords of the manorial units included within the "broad response" and "no response" groups during the fifteenth century as compared with their lord in 1460, while the lower part compares such courts in the later sixteenth century with their lord in 1580.[12]

The relationship between a community's particular location and economic situation and its recorded response to misconduct can be investigated with the assistance of computer-based mapping.[13] This analysis is limited to the 221 villages and market centers whose location

[12] The boroughs and hundreds have not been included here, as it is impossible to determine in many cases how much actual control was exercised by their nominal lords; since most composite manorial estates were held by episcopal institutions or lay noble lords, they have been excluded so as not to bias the distribution. Information is taken from the *VCH* volumes and other county and local secondary studies.

[13] I used MapInfo software, to which could be transferred data files generated in SPSS to produce maps of the places under observation during a particular period, with symbols indicating the category into which each community fell. These data maps could then be combined with other computer-based maps taken from the Digital Chart of the World (produced from satellite images) or digitized from maps in historical atlases; my data maps could also be turned into transparencies to be compared with maps available only in printed form. I am grateful to Bill Thoen of GISnet BBS in Boulder, Colorado for his assistance.

Table 6.3 *Lord of the manor: "broad response" and "no response" places (manor courts only)*

		Lord of the manor in 1460[†]						
1420–1499	N	Monastic (%)	Episcopal (%)	Lay: noble (%)	Lay: non-noble (%)	Duchy of Lancaster (%)	Crown (%)	Other (%)[*]
0 offences reported	76	32	12	26	11	7	3	11
4+ types of offences	14	7	36	14	7	7	14	14

		Lord of the manor in 1580[†]					
1560–1599	N	Episcopal (%)	Lay: noble (%)	Lay: non-noble (%)	Duchy of Lancaster (%)	Crown (%)	Other (%)[*]
0 offences reported	38	16	18	42	3	11	11
4+ types of offences	11	–	18	64	–	9	9

[†] All numbers are row percentages.
[*] "Other" includes Oxford and Cambridge colleges, hospitals, and divided lordships.

can be specified. The first three columns of Table 6.4 display proximity to major routes of transportation or London: location on a long-distance road, on a main river or along the coast, and lying within 25 km (= 15.6 miles) of the capital.[14] In assessing the importance of industrial activity, I decided not to rely on the very crude regional maps that are currently available for the sixteenth and seventeenth centuries. Instead I consulted a wide variety of secondary studies and only counted a community as having some kind of industrial presence if I found a specific reference to it during the period under study.[15] I may therefore have under-measured the amount of industrial activity but have probably not over-counted its presence – though the amount of manufacturing in some communities may have been limited. I looked also at the impact of elevation, measured in units of 76.2 m (= 250 ft), but since this assessment revealed few interesting contrasts, the results will be mentioned only where relevant.[16]

One would expect that the forms of land use practiced within a given local area might have had some impact on wrongdoing and/or the response to it, due to the divergent demographic, economic, and social

---

[14] For roads, I looked at whether a community was a major stopping point on a main long-distance road (termed a "stage stop" in later sixteenth-century travel guides for merchants), was on such a road but was not a stage stop, or was on a secondary long-distance road. No systematic variations were seen between these sub-categories, so they are combined on Table 6.4. Information about roads came from Edwards and Hindle, "The Transportation System," Figs. 2 and 3, and from Map 1 (prepared by Michael Frearson) in Spufford (ed.), *The World of Rural Dissenters*, pp. 38–9. "Stage stops" were identified through Frearson's "The English Corantos of the 1620s," Appendix 1, "Richard Grafton's London Highways, 1571–1611." (I am grateful to Dr. Frearson for permission to use and cite this material.) For rivers, I used the categories of being a port on a major navigable river, being on such a river but not a port, or being on a secondary navigable river. Little variation was seen between the various river categories, so they were combined on this table together with coastal communities. For rivers I used Langdon, "Inland Water Transport," Fig. 1, and Edwards and Hindle, "The Transportation System," Fig. 2, as compared with the Digital Chart of the World. In defining distances from London, I used London Bridge as an arbitrary center point.

[15] I divided industrial activity into woolen cloth manufacture, mining/metal working, and other (of which the largest component was leather working). Cloth manufacture was in all cases more common than the other two, but no systematic contrasts or changes were observed so the figures have been combined here. To gather information about industrial activity, I looked at standard economic histories, at county histories published between the eighteenth century and the present, and at all detailed local studies of these 221 communities available at the British Library. I am extremely grateful to the archivists of England's county record offices, to whom I wrote for advice on what county and local works are regarded as the most reliable.

[16] On the computer-based map produced from the Digital Chart of the World against which I compared these 221 places, contour lines were displayed at 250-ft intervals. For the impact of elevation, see Chapter 7, section two below.

Table 6.4 Locational and economic factors: "broad response" and "no response" places (villages and market centers only)*

| | N | On long-distance road (%) | On navigable river or the coast (%) | Within 25 km of London (%) | Industrial activity (%) | Broad agrarian categories | | |
						Mixed farming (arable) (%)	Pasture Open (%)	Pasture Wood (%)
1420–1499								
0 offences reported	92	23	11	1	10	58	18	24
4+ types of offences	17	51	40	17	44	44	25	33
1500–1559								
0 offences reported	85	24	18	5	5	56	26	20
4+ types of offences	28	61	25	11	64	38	27	38
1560–1599								
0 offences reported	49	34	21	2	11	57	15	28
4+ types of offences	21	34	23	0	39	22	44	28

*For definitions and sources, see text.

patterns that accompanied different agrarian regimes.[17] David Underdown has proposed a contrast between "chalk" and "cheese" regions of the Southwest in the seventeenth century – between areas devoted primarily to crop raising and those that combined animal rearing and industrial bye-employment.[18] The economic and social conditions of these regions, he argued, led to differing attitudes towards such matters as social wrongdoing, popular culture, and religion, contributing in turn to dissimilar reactions during the English Civil War. Other historians have added to Underdown's two categories a range of additional features thought to accompany "fielden vs. forest" communities.[19] The resulting picture suggests that acute problems with disorder and poverty in the pastoral and cloth-making areas stemming in part from weak manorial control contributed to cultural differentiation between respectable local leaders and those unable to support themselves, culminating in regulation of conduct; these regions were also more likely to contain a strong Puritan presence. By contrast, older forms of behavior and traditional popular pastimes remained acceptable to a wide range of people within the more vertically integrated communities located on the arable downlands, areas that remained more conservative in religious terms as well.

Because it seemed unlikely that the essentially dichotomous "fielden vs. forest" model would in itself prove sufficiently complex to be of value when analyzing responses to wrongdoing throughout England over a longer span of time, two other approaches were developed. Each is based upon classifications and maps of farming types suggested by more specialized agricultural historians. (Only a few of the secondary studies of places included in this project provided detailed information on agricultural practices, forcing me to rely on general maps.) I wanted first to look at broad patterns of land use. Since there is no published map of agrarian regions that covers the fifteenth and sixteenth centuries, I used Joan Thirsk's map for the period 1500–1640, dividing the 221 communities among the twelve farming types shown there and then grouping them into the three main categories she suggests: mixed farming (primarily arable), open pasture,

---

[17] This study does not deal with several important agricultural factors about which the sources used provided no information, such as inheritance customs, enclosing, and engrossing.

[18] Underdown, "The Chalk and the Cheese," "The Taming of the Scold," and *Revel, Riot, and Rebellion*; critiques are offered by Morrill, "The Ecology of Allegiance" (and see Underdown's response: "A Reply to John Morrill") and by Davie, "Chalk and Cheese?" For a thoughtful testing of this general thesis, see Stoyle, *Loyalty and Locality*.

[19] The literature is conveniently summarized in Davie, "Chalk and Cheese?"

and wood pasture.[20] The results are shown on the right side of Table 6.4. In presenting a more detailed breakdown of agrarian patterns, the system of eight types suggested by Alan Everitt and accepted by Thirsk seemed more readily comprehensible than Thirsk's original twelve regions.[21] I was also influenced by Neil Davie's arguments in favor of a continuum of systems.[22] I therefore laid out Everitt's eight categories along a rough spectrum extending from the most heavily arable to the most fully pastoral forms of land use, on the basis of practices common before 1600 (e.g., fenlands were placed nearer the pastoral end of the range since there was relatively little draining and conversion of those areas into arable prior to the end of Elizabeth's reign). Appendix 6.3 describes the eight agrarian types more fully and displays the distribution of "broad response" and "no response" places within that continuum.

Although in the most general sense this study supports the suggestion that regions devoted to arable farming displayed fewer problems with and/or concern about social wrongdoing than did pastoral regions, the analysis reveals no continuing contrasts between particular agrarian types across the fifteenth and sixteenth centuries.[23] It thus offers a correction to any simple model of causation based upon land-use regimes, suggesting that insofar as the social ecology of a community affected regulation of misconduct, it was not types of soil and farming practices that shaped regulation but rather a changing balance among other factors, many of which were only loosely associated with agricultural patterns.

In exploring the demographic and economic characteristics of the places included in this project, I used the records of several national taxes, the only ones within 50–75 years of our period that are sufficient-

[20] I compared my computer-based maps arranged by period and type of concern against Map 2 of Thirsk's *Agricultural Regions*, p. 29. Because that map's rendering of the coastline of England is quite severely skewed, it was in some cases difficult to match it precisely with my own computer-based data maps. Kerridge's map of "English farming countries" in the sixteenth and seventeenth centuries contains a larger number of regions than could be assessed in this study (frontispiece to *The Agricultural Revolution*).

[21] Everitt, "Country, County and Town," and Thirsk, *Agricultural Regions*, pp. 37–9.

[22] In "Chalk and Cheese?"

[23] It may be that any investigation based upon a relatively small number of arbitrarily defined categories, even if laid out as elements within a spectrum, is inherently flawed because it obscures the individual variations that distinguished one community from even its near neighbors within a given region. If that is the case, we will have to abandon all groupings in favor of Davie's proposal (in "Chalk and Cheese?") for a "pointilliste" approach, which will render general comparisons impossible.

ly detailed and complete to provide useful comparative data.[24] For measures of population, I noted three sets of information about those communities for which records survive: the number of people assessed per place in the Poll Taxes of 1377–81; the number of people assessed in the 1524/5 Lay Subsidies; and the number of households assessed in the Hearth Taxes of the 1660s and 1670s. As indicators of wealth, I likewise utilized the records of three taxes wherever available: the total amount of tax assessed per place in the 1334 Lay Subsidy; the total amount of tax assessed per place and information about the distribution of payments within the community from the 1524/5 Subsidies; and the total number of hearths per place and their distribution between households from the Hearth Taxes.[25] Because taxes were levied on parishes rather than by lordship, I was not able to get data about the composite manorial estates; nor was the coverage as good for hundreds after 1334 as for individual communities. The rest of this discussion is therefore limited to the 221 villages and market centers.

A series of methodological problems must be addressed when working with the tax records. Some involve the nature of the sources and, once recognized, can be compensated for. For example, most of the 1334 tax payments were based on an assessment of one-fifteenth of full value but some were assessed at one-tenth; the Poll Tax of 1377 provides a more complete listing of people than do those of 1379 and 1381; and the boundaries of some of the market centers expanded over time into the surrounding rural parishes, potentially distorting evidence about population and wealth. Other documentary problems could not be corrected here, such as the possibility that the 1524/5 Subsidies provide more accurate information for urban communities than for rural ones. Nor can we assume with any of the taxes that the assessments necessarily provide a full and reliable reflection of actual population and wealth

---

[24] Alan Dyer demonstrated that these taxes could be used to compare communities in his study of England's urban areas, *Decline and Growth*.

[25] See Appendix 6.4 for a fuller discussion of these sources and the number of records used by type. The documents are all at the PRO, class E 179; they are listed under county, hundred, and date in various volumes of the List and Index Society's publications. For 1334 I used *The Lay Subsidy of 1334*; for the others I used the original documents, plus a few printed volumes for individual areas and years. I am grateful to Richard M. Smith for permission to check my numbers against his computer-based listings of the Poll Taxes. My use of the 1524/5 Subsidy returns was greatly facilitated by the revised Appendix of Sheail's "The Regional Distribution of Wealth," as deposited at the library of the Cambridge Group for the History of Population and Social Structure. In working on Herts. I was generously allowed access to an early version of the new listing of E 179 records being prepared at the PRO under the supervision of Dr. David Crook.

(though that problem was to some extent bypassed by comparisons within this set of communities). The techniques used in working with the tax records are described in Appendix 6.4, which also summarizes how many individual records of each type were consulted. Because median figures are presented for the tax values, the variations contained within the "broad response" and "no response" groupings are muted; I used medians instead of means to minimize the distortions introduced by a few unusually large or wealthy communities. Lastly, though the tax data make it possible to view at least rough shifts in population and wealth over time, our ability to measure change precisely is limited by the long gaps between the records used. For population, nearly 150 years separate the first and second assessments, with another 140–150 years between the 1524/5 Subsidies and the Hearth Taxes. The situation is worse for indicators of wealth, with 190 years between the first two assessments – not only a very long period but one that included the great outbreak of plague in 1348–9 and its economic repercussions. These unfortunately long chronological intervals mean, for example, that although we may be able to determine that a given community was smaller in population or less wealthy in 1524/5 than it had been in the fourteenth century, we cannot tell when within that span the decline had occurred.

The demographic and economic material has been analyzed in two different ways. Table 6.5 presents some measures of population and wealth in *relative* terms within these communities. All values for population or wealth from a given tax assessment were rank ordered within the full group, and the ranks were then converted to percentiles. Henceforth I could compare the median percentile ranking of one subset of communities with others and see how the percentile rankings of the groups changed between the various taxes. Use of relative measurements solves the problem of non-equivalent measures between the two taxes (e.g., income vs. hearths) and obviates the need to convert the numbers of taxpayers and levels of assessed wealth into estimates of total population and total wealth – a complex and often unreliable exercise. The first set of columns in Table 6.5 provides some measures of relative population over time: for the earlier centuries, the percentile ranking of the "broad response" and "no response" places in the 1377–81 Poll Taxes and the 1524/5 Subsidies, with an indicator of the percentage change in ranking over that span; for the sixteenth century the same information plus the percentile ranking of the number of households in the Hearth Taxes, with an indicator of the percentage change between 1524/5 and the 1660s–70s. The second group of figures speaks to the

Table 6.5 Some measures of relative population and wealth: "broad response" and "no response" places (villages and market centers only)*

	Measures of relative population					Measures of the relative wealth of the community				
	Size in 1377/81, ranking as %	Change in ranking, 1377/81–1524/5 (%)	Size in 1524/5, ranking as %	Change in ranking, 1524/5–Hearth Tax (%)	Size in Hearth Tax, ranking as %	Wealth in 1334, ranking as %	Change in ranking, 1334–1524/5 (%)	Wealth in 1524/5, ranking as %	Change in Wealth in ranking, 1524/5–Hearth Tax (%)	Wealth in Hearth Tax, ranking as %
1420–1499										
0 offences reported	46	−15	31	+6	37	43	0	43	−9	34
4+ types of offences	78	−1	77	+6	83	65	+2	67	+17	84
1500–1559										
0 offences reported	48	−7	41	0	41	45	0	45	−7	38
4+ types of offences	62	−7	55	+15	70	51	+3	54	+16	70
1560–1599										
0 offences reported	54	−9	45	−12	33	46	−1	45	−7	38
4+ types of offences	32	+20	52	+4	56	51	0	51	+2	53

* See App. 6.4 for explanation of sources and methods, with the N for which information was available. For the total N of each group, see Table 6.4. All figures are medians.

total wealth of the communities, presenting the percentile rankings in 1334, 1524/5, and the Hearth Taxes.

Table 6.6 uses a different approach, providing rough measures of *absolute* size, wealth, and the extent of poverty within these villages and market centers. To understand the demographic situation of the later sixteenth century, we need to know something about the actual amount of population rise between the 1520s and the 1660s–70s, as opposed to merely the relative measure, since the latter obscures the growth occurring in virtually all communities by the end of Elizabeth's reign. (Any estimate of absolute values is of course affected by the methodological problems described above and hence is only approximate.) The first set of columns looks at the number of taxpayers or household heads in these two assessments, together with the change in percentage over time. The second group of columns displays some measures of the distribution of wealth within communities, of how resources were divided among their inhabitants: the median tax paid per capita in 1524/5, and the median number of hearths per house in the 1660s–70s. These reflect the standard of living of people at the middle of their community's spectrum of individual wealth. The right-most columns show the fraction of the population in these two taxes who were assessed at objectively low levels of personal wealth, using definitions of the very poor provided by other studies: for the 1524/5 Subsidies, those assessed on an annual income of less than 40s; and for the Hearth Taxes, the percentage of households recorded as having just one hearth or exempted from the tax entirely due to poverty.[26] The change in percentage of the very poor between the two taxes is also displayed.

Integration and discussion of the data

We may now pull together the characteristics of the "broad response" communities within each of the three chronological periods, comparing them with the "no response" places and proposing explanations of the patterns seen within each period. Between 1420 and 1499 (see Map 6.1), marked contrasts separate the two groupings, suggesting that specific geographic, demographic, and economic factors were of considerable importance in shaping misbehavior and/or the response to it. The nineteen "broad response" communities were overwhelmingly market centers (79 percent as opposed to just 15 percent of the "no response" places); of the market communities, those with manor courts responded

---

[26] See, e.g., Skipp, *Crisis and Development*, pp. 78–9, and Wrightson and Levine, *Poverty and Piety*, pp. 31–5.

Table 6.6 *Some measures of absolute size, wealth, and extent of poverty: "broad response" and "no response" places (villages and market centers only)**

	No. of taxpayers or households			Distribution of wealth within the community		Extent of poverty: % of very poor taxpayers or household heads		
	In 1524/5 Hearth Tax	% change, 1524/5- Hearth Tax	In Hearth Tax	Median tax per capita, 1524/5 (in shillings)	Median no. of hearths per house in Hearth Tax	In 1524/5 Hearth Tax	% change, 1524/5- Hearth Tax	In Hearth Tax
1420–1499								
0 offences reported	44			14.6		37		
4+ types of offences	131			15.3		29		
1500–1559								
0 offences reported	47	+62	76	15.4	1.67	33	+17	50
4+ types of offences	61	+156	156	16.3	1.89	31	+13	44
1560–1599								
0 offences reported	48	+29	62	14.5	1.56	38	+15	53
4+ types of offences	56	+98	111	13.6	1.44	20	+32	52

*See Appendix 6.4 for explanation of sources and methods, with the N for which information was available. For the total N of each group, see Table 6.4. All figures are medians except for the central two columns, which are means of the medians.

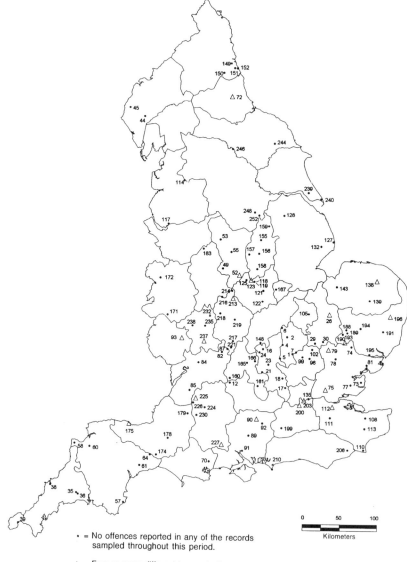

• = No offences reported in any of the records
sampled throughout this period.

△ = Four or more different types of offences reported
in one or more duodecades within this period.

Map 6.1   "Broad response" and "no response" communities, 1420–99

See App. 2.1 for identification numbers by place.

both earlier and much more strongly than those with borough courts. A disproportionate number of the "broad response" communities lay in East Anglia and the Southeast. The lords of the "broad response" manors were likely to be bishops or the crown, as compared with a weighting of "no response" manors in the hands of monastic or lay noble lords. This suggests that active regulation was associated with a distant and impersonal rather than a resident lord, an observation consistent with the evidence presented in Chapter 5 about the prevalence of forms of local self-government in these communities. Nine-tenths of the broadly concerned courts lay on major roads, rivers, or the coast, and one-sixth were within 25 km of London. More than two-fifths of them had industrial activity, as compared to only one-tenth of the "no response" communities. They were less likely to practice mixed farming than the "no response" places, and of those that did, most were located on the wolds and downland rather than in arable vales. A concentration in areas of forest or wood pasture is also visible.

The demographic and economic indicators show that during the fifteenth century communities that reported a wide range of social problems were much larger in population than those that showed no concern. On the surface they remained approximately level in relative population between 1377–81 and 1524, but here we may be misled by the long interval between the assessment points: it seems likely from local studies that some of these places, especially the thriving market centers, had suffered major demographic loss prior to 1460 but were beginning to experience renewed population growth through immigration during the later decades of the fifteenth century.[27] The "broad response" communities were also much wealthier than the "no response" places. Although there was little change in their relative prosperity between 1334 and 1524/5, more marked growth was to follow, and this may already have started in some settings by the later fifteenth century. In 1524/5 the median tax paid per capita in these places was to be a little above that of the "no response" communities, and they were to have a lower proportion of very poor people.

Heightened attention to social wrongdoing during the fifteenth century seems to have been a temporary phenomenon in most cases. Of the "broad response" places between 1420 and 1499, the majority (68 percent) responded at this level in only a single duodecade, while another 21 percent reported four or more offences in two consecutive duodecades, perhaps reflecting merely a divergence between the boundaries of our twenty-year sampling periods and the span of in-

---

[27] McIntosh, "Local Change and Community Control."

creased concern within those communities. Only two places remained in the "broad response" category for three duodecades.[28]

In proposing possible explanations for these observations we will draw upon some of the underlying demographic, economic, and social changes that marked the period of transition from medieval to early modern patterns. Because the number of "broad response" communities was small, this discussion must remain suggestive rather than conclusive. Our discussion focuses upon the decades between 1460 and 1499, when sixteen of the nineteen "broad response" places were active. The presence of strangers was probably a feature of nearly all the communities that regulated misbehavior most actively – those located on major routes of transportation and the market centers. In both settings transient visitors would have been common: travelers moving along a road or river and perhaps stopping for a meal or overnight accommodation, people coming from surrounding areas to use the market, and merchants from larger places buying rural produce. The officers of such communities were therefore confronted with the problems inherently associated with outsiders: any wrongdoing on their part might be particularly unsettling because their background was unknown, and it was hard to punish people who had no local roots and were free to move out of the area at will.

These generally large and wealthy communities almost certainly contained many immigrants as well, people who planned to remain there at least for the time being. This was not a result of population growth in the country as a whole (to the contrary, there are indications of generally high mortality in the later fifteenth century) but rather of the specific circumstances of these communities.[29] We know that during the later sixteenth and early seventeenth centuries, market centers usually had much higher mortality rates than did rural communities, with especially elevated levels of infant deaths.[30] Because these features were presumably due to diseases carried by people coming into the town as well as to problems with sanitation and water-borne illnesses, they probably characterized the "broad response" places in the later fifteenth century too. Since the birth rate was unlikely to match the death rate under those conditions, immigration was required for the community just to maintain a level population, and many of the "broad

---

[28] These were the market community and early cloth making center of Castle Combe, Wilts. and the regional market center of (Saffron) Walden, Essex, a major producer of dried saffron from crocuses.

[29] Hatcher, "Mortality in the Fifteenth Century," and Barbara Harvey, *Living and Dying in England*, ch. 4.

[30] Wrigley and Schofield, *Population History*, pp. 48 and 165–6, and Schofield and Wrigley, "Infant and Child Mortality."

response" places may have been growing in this period. Although some of the new arrivals probably came from the surrounding area and hence may have been from families already known to the community, the presence of even familiar newcomers was likely to strain established social patterns.[31] Those communities that were getting larger would have felt the pressures of more densely packed housing and competition for goods and employment. Some of the market centers in the later fifteenth century may also have been attracting craftsmen/traders and capital that would previously have been associated with the cities and larger towns. Expansion of the market communities, free from urban and guild control as well as from the burdensome and expensive obligations of citizenship, would thus constitute the obverse of the much discussed "late medieval urban decline."[32] Because most of the "broad response" communities were prospering economically, it is unlikely that they experienced with any severity the phenomenon seen in some of the cities between 1460 and 1530: regulation of social conduct resulting from the dangerous combination of economic decline plus continued immigration of poor people whose hopes of finding employment were thwarted.[33]

Local court rolls from many market centers in the later fifteenth and early sixteenth centuries document heightened concern with the behavior of two particular groups – young people and women. Although some adolescents received training for their adult responsibilities entirely within their own families, many young males and some females left home to live with and work for another master as a temporary, "life-cycle" servant.[34] They remained with one or several masters in a series of one-year contracts, helping with agriculture, craftwork, trade,

[31] Other studies show that late medieval/early modern mobility was likely to occur in the first instance from rural communities to somewhat larger centers within c. 32–40 km (20–25 miles) of the person's original home; if a longer-distance move occurred at all, it generally happened later. See, e.g., Butcher, "The Origins of Romney Freemen," Patten, "Patterns of Migration," and Goldberg, *Women, Work, and Life Cycle*, esp. ch. 6.

[32] McIntosh, "Local Change and Community Control."

[33] See, e.g., Goldberg, *Women, Work, and Life Cycle* and Phythian-Adams, *Desolation of a City*. Of the twenty-one urban communities whose records were used in Chapters 1 and 4 above, all of which expressed concern with social misconduct, twelve declined in economic and/or demographic terms during the fifteenth century (Alan Dyer, *Decline and Growth*, Appendix 5, and Goldberg, *Women, Work, and Life Cycle*).

[34] For medieval servants, see Goldberg, "Female Labour, Service and Marriage," "Marriage, Migration, Servanthood and Life-Cycle," and *Women, Work, and Life Cycle*, and Hanawalt, *Growing Up in Medieval London* and "'The Childe of Bristowe.'" Sixteenth-century servants are discussed in Kussmaul, *Servants in Husbandry*, McIntosh, "Servants and the Household Unit," and Ben-Amos, *Adolescence and Youth*. Relatively few parents could afford to pay the fee required for a formal apprenticeship, but service provided similar kinds of occupational training.

and/or domestic tasks, until they were financially able to marry and set up their own household, usually some time in their mid-twenties. Whereas adolescent servants had apparently been far more numerous in the cities than in rural areas during the later fourteenth century, preliminary evidence suggests that during the later fifteenth century their presence was increasing in market communities as well.[35] A rising number of servants within a community was likely to trigger concern with their conduct since they were by definition young, unmarried, and at least temporarily poor.[36] Nor did all masters keep a close eye on what their youthful employees did during their free time. Even in settings where service was not expanding, concern could have stemmed from the presence of adolescents unable to find positions.

Although we know little about the demographic and economic situation of women in England's smaller towns between 1460 and 1540, several different scenarios might have contributed to the elevated concern with female wrongdoing. The preponderance of women seen in many English cities during the fifteenth and sixteenth centuries, stemming from uneven gender immigration and employment opportunities, may have extended to some of the larger market centers as well.[37] This imbalance threatened customary marriage patterns and may have raised fears about unregulated female sexuality as well as the economic competition single women offered to male artisans and laborers. In some regions this period probably saw considerable female involvement in the extra-domestic economy. The rapid expansion of woolen cloth manufacture after the mid-fifteenth century provided new employment for some women, as did the increase in dairying, and it appears that women were unusually active in the craft and trading worlds of certain market communities.[38] Since women were expected to

---

[35] McIntosh, "Local Change and Community Control."

[36] They were paid wages in addition to board, room, and training, but their master kept their pay until the end of the period of service. For below, see Griffiths, *Youth and Authority*, Mitterauer, "Servants and Youth" and his *Sozialgeschichte der Jugend*; for deeper fears of servants, see Dolan, *Dangerous Familiars*, ch. 2. Von Friedeburg's definition of young people as one of three models of deviance is not persuasive, as he gives no social reasons for concern with this age and emphasizes pre-marital sexual activity as one of the key forms of misconduct for this group, a tautology given the relatively late age of marriage (*Sündenzucht und sozialer Wandel*, pp. 144–5). His other two models are people who through their own actions disrupted "good neighborliness" and those who fell into a stereotyped category that warranted suspicion, such as vagrants (pp. 146–8).

[37] See, e.g., Goldberg, *Women, Work, and Life Cycle* and Phythian-Adams, *Desolation of a City*. For the issues below, see Chapter 4, section one above.

[38] McIntosh, "Local Change and Community Control," *Autonomy and Community*, and *A Community Transformed*. For female employment more generally, see the works cited in

form part of household units primarily supported by men, it could be socially disturbing when they had their own independent sources of income.

More direct economic influences are suggested by the presence of manufacturing in nearly a half of the "broad response" places in the fifteenth century and by a cluster located in areas of forest/wood pasture. The early stages of industrialization would have led to a rising number of wage laborers, some of them probably immigrants. New forms of craftwork or industry, based often upon part-time production (or "bye-employment") by skilled or semi-skilled workers, were beginning to appear in some of the wood pasture areas.[39] This development, which was to become more pronounced in the sixteenth century, contributed to net migration of the poor into wooded areas: the varied natural resources, lack of tight social and economic structure, and availability of some paid employment made it possible for a family without arable land to eke out an existence. For artisans and traders in many regions, the scale of production and degree of specialization seem to have increased around 1460, features that spread more widely during the following century. This enlarged the demand for servants/apprentices and wage laborers and gradually eliminated from competition most of the smaller male craftspeople and shopkeepers and nearly all the female ones. (In this case, the appearance of new economic forms would have diminished rather than improved the opportunities for employment among women.) The disproportionate number of "broad response" communities in East Anglia and the Southeast, with several located within 25 km of London, may have been influenced by the beginnings of agrarian capitalism in that area. During the later fifteenth century, land within easy reach of London was increasingly held in very large units by people able to devote abundant capital to focused production of foodstuffs for the city's consumer market.[40] Such farming relied upon a substantial wage-labor force and brought considerable profits to the leading landholders, some of whom were urban merchants rather than members of the gentry or nobility.

These economic changes, characteristic of the transition to early capitalism, probably contributed to social regulation in several ways.

Chapter 4, note 11 above, plus, e.g., Goldberg, *Women, Work, and Life Cycle* and his introduction to *Women in England* (but cf. Bailey, "Demographic Decline"); for the sixteenth century, see Cahn, *Industry of Devotion*.

[39] This development was commonly described as "proto-industrialization" by earlier economists: e.g., Kriedte, Medick, and Schlumbohm, *Industrialization Before Industrialization*. See also Zell, *Industry in the Countryside*.

[40] McIntosh, "Local Change and Community Control."

Most of them increased the number of people dependent upon their wages, lacking land or artisanal skills. An unfamiliar number of poor workers within a given community was likely to have raised concern about their conduct among respectable families, whether warranted or not. Further, by expanding the range between poorest and richest, the new economic patterns must often have led to disruption of traditional social practices.[41] Cultural differentiation was accentuated when employers attempted to discipline and control the social activities of their workers. (We saw that local court presentments speak to a concern with issues of labor in the later fifteenth century, including the need for a disciplined, regulated work force.) Yet in 1524/5 the "broad response" communities of the fifteenth century were to display a comfortable standard of living and contain few seriously poor people. Economic growth was therefore apparently sufficient to absorb the new populations without an increase in poverty. This may help to explain why few of these places seem to have remained actively concerned about social regulation for more than a single generation within this period.

Moving now to the period between 1500 and 1559 (see Map 6.2), we note that the thirty-three "broad response" communities were more likely to be villages than had been true in the fifteenth century, with a decline in the proportion of market centers. The earlier concentration in East Anglia/the Southeast had diminished, with a rise in the importance of the North/Northwest. More "broad response" places were situated on main roads but fewer adjoined a main river or were close to London than was true before. An industrial presence had become even more significant, with a striking 64 percent containing some kind of manufacturing or mining activity. Changes had also occurred in agrarian patterns. A smaller percentage were located within mixed farming areas, with most of the increase lying in the broad cluster of wood pasture regions. The emphasis on wolds and downland had disappeared; more now lay in the arable vales.

"Broad response" places continued to be relatively larger and more prosperous than those showing no concern with social issues, though the contrast was far less pronounced than prior to 1500. These communities were going to grow markedly in both population and wealth between 1524/5 and the Hearth Taxes of the 1660s–70s, with a remarkable increase of 156 percent in median absolute size. A higher standard of living among the "broad response" places than among the "no response" ones is indicated by higher payments in 1524/5 and a larger number of hearths in the Hearth Tax. The fraction of very poor people

<hr>

[41] See, e.g., Macfarlane, *Witchcraft*.

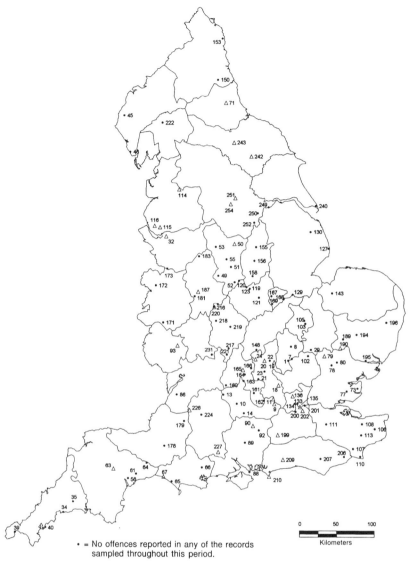

• = No offences reported in any of the records
    sampled throughout this period.

△ = Four or more different types of offences reported
    in one or more duodecades within this period.

Map 6.2   "Broad response" and "no response" communities, 1500–59

See App. 2.1 for identification numbers by place.

in 1524/5 was at an intermediate level, but by the 1660s–70s it was to be lower than for any other group studied. Of the "broad response" places, 82 percent had not reported such varied concern at any time during the fifteenth century.

These observations suggest that the new economic and social patterns that had increased wrongdoing and/or raised concern with it during the later fifteenth century were spreading into a wider range of communities. Some of the specific locational features that had previously characterized "broad response" places were less pronounced, though more than half of the communities were still market centers and three-fifths lay on major roads. Now, however, we see increasing evidence of industrial activity and the opportunities for bye-employment found in areas of wood pasture. Social regulation during the first half of the sixteenth century thus appears to have resulted from the continuation and expansion of the patterns observed in the decades before 1500.

By the period between 1560 and 1599 (see Map 6.3), the twenty-one "broad response" places as identified from the lesser court evidence form an unknown fraction of all those communities that were in fact actively concerned with misbehavior. The fraction of "broad response" places that were market centers had continued to decline in favor of more villages, and although the North/Northwest still had more than its share of communities engaged in vigorous social regulation, it was now outmatched by the West and Southwest. The nature of the lord of the manor made little difference, apart from a slight weighting among manors held by lay non-noble lords. The "broad response" communities were virtually indistinguishable from the "no response" ones in terms of proximity to a major transportation route or to London. In a big decline from the previous period, only 39 percent of them had some kind of industrial activity; fewer were now located in areas of wood pasture, with a percentage similar to that of the "no response" communities. The fraction situated in mixed farming areas had dropped even further (limited to the wolds and downland or the Norfolk heath), while a surprising 44 percent were located in regions of open pasture.

In demographic and economic terms, the "broad response" places in the later sixteenth century had been slightly above average in relative population in 1524/5 and were to grow over the following century and a half, unlike the very large relative decrease in size of the "no response" communities. In absolute terms the "broad response" places nearly doubled between the 1520s and the Hearth Taxes, but their relative wealth grew only slightly over the sixteenth and seventeenth centuries. On a per capita basis, they had a lower standard of living

Map 6.3   "Broad response" and "no response" communities, 1560–99

See App. 2.1 for identification numbers by place.

than the "no response" communities in both measures. Perhaps most important, the percentage of their residents who were very poor was unusually low in 1524/5 (the smallest fraction of any group in this study) but rose in absolute terms by 32 percent between then and the 1660s–70s, by far the highest rate of increase seen here. Of these places 73 percent had not displayed equivalently diverse regulation at any time during the fifteenth and earlier sixteenth centuries.

This evidence suggests that particular local attributes are of relatively little value in explaining local court responses to wrongdoing by the later sixteenth century. Many of the "broad response" places were now small rural communities, where there is no reason to expect any substantial net immigration; industrial activity was found in a minority of them, with a smaller fraction than before lying in wood pasture areas. Nor did specific locational features distinguish the "broad response" communities from the "no response" ones, apart from a new cluster in the West/Southwest and the very strong representation in regions of open pasture.

In this period our attention is directed instead at indications of population rise joined no longer by equivalent economic growth but rather by clear indications of mounting poverty. (This is reminiscent of the concern with social issues around 1300, a period of even higher population density and greater economic hardship.[42]) By the 1580s–90s, many of the "broad response" communities were evidently confronting a serious increase in the number of very poor inhabitants, a rise stemming primarily from natural population growth (i.e., the birth rate exceeded the death rate). For England as a whole, the cumulative impact of demographic growth that had probably started some time around 1520 was now being felt throughout the country. Wrigley and Schofield estimate that the total population of the country rose from 2,774,000 in 1541 to 4,020,000 in 1599, an increase of 45 percent over fifty-eight years, and rapid growth occurred in nearly all communities.[43] The consequences of natural demographic rise would have been felt initially in the form of a mounting number of children and adolescents, followed a decade or two later by insufficient land or employment to support young adults. If the economy of the area was unable to expand, or if geographic/ecological factors limited the number of people who could be supported on that type of land (as with higher elevations in the North and Southwest), the community was forced either to export its excess population or to face a decrease in its standard

---

[42] See the Introduction, section three above.
[43] Wrigley and Schofield, *Population History*, esp. Table A3.3.

of living and possible mortality crises.[44] Although some of the regions undergoing rapid economic change by the later Elizabethan period could provide expanded employment or eventually developed new forms of land use that enabled them to support a larger population, many regions contained a rising fraction of very poor people who scraped together a minimal economic existence only through a combination of licit and illicit activities.[45]

The consequences of worsening poverty for social regulation are obvious. In addition to the overt kinds of poverty-related wrongdoing described in Chapter 3, we know from local studies that a growing number of poor people was likely to cause anxiety about harmony and order as well.[46] By the end of the sixteenth century the needy could not simply be ignored as outsiders or expelled from the community: many of them were local people whose families had in the past been self-supporting but who could no longer manage on their own. It is therefore not surprising that active efforts to control misbehavior were so often accompanied by equally active institutional efforts to provide assistance to the worthy poor.[47] Nor was a larger number of poor people a temporary phenomenon resulting from specific economic changes, as had been true in most communities during the later fifteenth and early sixteenth centuries. Although the specific problems of the 1590s raised the level of acute poverty to new heights, many communities faced the prospect of ongoing, endemic need even in normal years.

We have seen that in all three periods vigorous social regulation as documented in the local courts was likely to be fairly short-lived: few communities remained in the "broad response" category for more than a single duodecade or two consecutive ones, though they might become active again several generations later. The kinds of evidence utilized in this study do not allow us to differentiate between several possible reasons for this observation. It may be that we are seeing only part of the full story: as new problems emerged within particular communities they were first tackled through aggressive regulation by the local courts, whereas in subsequent generations similar offenders were pros-

---

[44] Certain areas in the Lake District, for example, suffered from famine during the bad harvests of the late 1580s and 1590s: Appleby, *Famine*.

[45] Skipp, *Crisis and Development*.

[46] E.g., Wrightson and Levine, *Poverty and Piety*, and von Friedeburg, *Sündenzucht und sozialer Wandel*.

[47] McIntosh, "Local Responses to the Poor" and her evidence on where and why residential institutions for the poor were established during the fifteenth and sixteenth centuries ("The Foundation of Hospitals and Almshouses").

ecuted in the intermediate-level courts, in hopes of more effective control. It may also be, however, that in at least some cases the lesser court data accurately portray an initial surge in problems and concern followed by a decline in regulation. Prior to the late sixteenth century, most of the demographic, economic, and social developments dis-cussed above must have caused the greatest dislocations when they first appeared within a given community. A larger number of new-comers, wage laborers, young people, independent women, or the destitute poor would have seemed especially upsetting if that place had previously contained many fewer residents like these. As the propor-tion of such people rose, respectable families at some point presumably became alarmed, crossing an emotional threshold that led to energetic regulation of misconduct. With the passage of time, however, officials may have begun to relax their efforts. Perhaps the actual amount of misbehavior had indeed subsided (outsiders, for example, may have begun to adapt to local mores), but it seems more probable that the leadership group gradually concluded that the dominant social and economic patterns of the community could continue, that their own political/legal authority was not impaired, and that the community did not dissolve into sinful chaos even if the standard of behavior among marginal groups was not so high as their own. They may also have decided that earlier efforts had not achieved any real improvement in conduct: time and effort had been expended to little avail.[48] This new mood would last unless a further set of demographic/economic, politi-cal, or ideological/religious changes triggered another round of con-cern at some later time.

Analysis of the "broad response" communities and comparison with the "no response" places have thus suggested that the social ecology of a given area played a considerable role in shaping the amount of misconduct and/or the reaction to it, although the reasons for concern changed over the course of the fifteenth and sixteenth centuries. Be-tween 1420 and 1499 the specific kinds of locational, demographic, and economic features that characterized the "broad response" places pointed to immigration and the impact of the early stages of capitalism; the large populations seen in the places that regulated diverse forms of misconduct were apparently matched by comparable economic growth, obviating long-term problems with poverty. In the first part of the sixteenth century, those factors probably remained important, though the contrasts between "broad response" and "no response"

---

[48] Generational factors may have played a part too. As the local officials who had been determined to move aggressively against offenders retired from power, their suc-cessors may well have displayed a more pragmatic and relaxed attitude.

communities were less marked: active regulation was spreading to a more diverse array of places. By the later sixteenth century, however, the situation was very different. Instead of specific reasons for concern, we observe the paramount importance of natural population rise and worsening poverty.

7

Social ecology II: analysis by type of offences reported

The geographic, demographic, and economic characteristics of the 255 smaller communities may also be examined when the places are grouped on the basis of the particular types of offences they reported over time. Variations between these groupings during the fifteenth century suggest that prior to around 1500 the "social ecology" of a community exerted some influence upon the particular forms of wrongdoing it encountered or that its leaders decided to report to their courts. In the early sixteenth century, however, the differences between groupings are blurred, so explanations are harder to propose. At the end of Elizabeth's reign we can again identify some distinctive characteristics of the communities that reported the various offences, most importantly evidence of a high and probably rising proportion of needy residents among those that mentioned problems associated with poverty. Since the data reveal fewer definite patterns than were visible in the previous chapter when comparing the "broad response" and "no response" communities, the explanations offered here should be regarded as more tentative, constituting possibilities to be explored in detailed local studies.

Method and evidence

Although our approach will in many respects be similar to that employed in Chapter 6, a strategy had to be devised for coping with the greater complexity of the data when they are subdivided by the type of offences reported. In theory one might trace the geographic, demographic, and economic characteristics of each subset of communities during each of the eleven duodecades examined here. An illustration of

170

this exercise is given in Appendix 7.1a–i, graphs that show how the type of community varied chronologically among those places that reported each of the nine combined offences. (The small number of cases for hundreds and composite manorial estates in many duodecades magnifies any changes in percentage distribution, resulting in apparently dramatic shifts over time.) Because, however, analysis in such depth hampers the identification of broader patterns, detail has been reduced in two ways in the tables that accompany this chapter. First, the offences are grouped into the three clusters employed in Chapter 3. The Disharmony cluster includes scolding and eavesdropping/nightwalking; the Disorder cluster includes sexual misbehavior, unruly alehouses, and loosely defined charges such as being "badly governed"; and the Poverty cluster includes hedgebreaking, sheltering vagabonds/living idly, and receiving inmates. (Gaming is excluded from this analysis.) Secondly, attention is limited to four pivotal duodecades. Between them these duodecades cover the first period of sharply rising concern with each of the three clusters of offences as well as the periods of highest concern: for the Disharmony cluster, the 1420s–30s initially and the 1520s–30s as the peak; for the Disorder cluster, the 1460s–70s initially and the 1520s–30s as the peak; and for the Poverty cluster, the 1460s–70s initially and the 1580s–90s as the peak (see Appendix 3.1).

Grouping offences into clusters, though useful for bringing the data into manageable form, carries with it several consequences which together lessen the contrasts. Analyzing wrongdoing by clusters assumes that there is indeed some similarity between the particular offences contained within each cluster. Because the clusters were defined largely on the basis of how local people described the offences in their presentments, the kinds of social thinking that underlay their specific concerns, the groupings contain types of misconduct that may be quite different in practical form. Further, a given sort of wrongdoing, although assigned to one cluster, might contain secondary features of another.[1] Hence the boundaries separating clusters are not impermeable. Another factor that weakens the distinctiveness of the clusters is that some communities reported problems within more than one cluster during a given duodecade and hence appear in several groupings. Until 1460, no more than 9 percent of the courts under observation in each duodecade reported offences in two or three clusters, but the level then rose to a peak of 27 percent in the 1520s–30s before dropping back somewhat for the rest of the century. (See Maps 7.1–7.4 below, with symbols indica-

---

[1] See Chapter 3, note 3 above.

ting the clusters of offences reported.) These considerations help to
explain why we do not find such clear contrasts between groups as
were visible in Chapter 6 when comparing "broad response" with "no
response" communities.

Because the tables presenting this evidence contain the same kinds of
information as were described in Chapter 6, using the same layout, they
have been placed in Appendices rather than in the text. The discussion
in the previous chapter of sources, methods, and problems in using the
data applies here too. Appendix 7.2 shows the type of community and
court for the four selected duodecades and types of offences while
Appendix 7.3 displays the region of the country. (These include all 255
communities, with their 267 courts, whereas the subsequent figures
examine just the 221 villages and market centers.) Appendix 7.4 presents locational and economic factors, and Appendix 7.5a–b separates
the groupings along the continuum of agrarian regions. Appendix 7.6
displays measures of relative population and wealth; Appendix 7.7
gives measures of absolute size, wealth, and extent of poverty.[2] For the
1420s–30s (see Map 7.1), Appendices 7.3–7.6 display information only
about communities that reported no offences and those that reported
the Disharmony cluster, for the number of places that presented the
Disorder and Poverty clusters (just eight and five communities respect-
ively) is too small to warrant analysis.

Integration and discussion of the data

The evidence presented in the appended tables can be integrated and
discussed within each of the selected duodecades. The proposed explanations rely upon the same underlying changes that were introduced in
Chapter 6. Analysis concentrates upon the 1460s–70s, the 1520s–30s,
and the 1580s–90s, where information is fullest; the Disharmony cluster
from the 1420s–30s will be considered as a parallel to the 1460s–70s.

Beginning our analysis of the 1460s–70s (see Map 7.2) with those
communities that reported problems in the Disharmony cluster, we
note that more than half were located in market centers, as compared
with a heavier concentration in villages and hundreds for those places
that did not report any offences to their local courts at all. The regional
distribution of communities in the Disharmony cluster was similar to
that of the inactive places, with a slightly higher fraction in the

[2] See Appendix 6.4 for further information about the sources and methods used here.
Because the analysis of type of response by lord of the manor revealed little of interest, it
is not presented in this chapter.

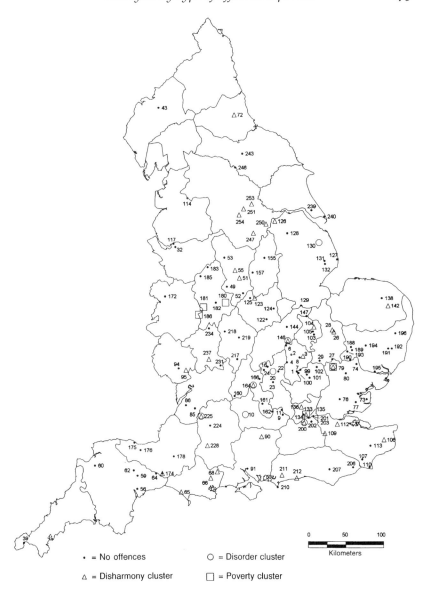

Map 7.1 Communities under observation in the 1420s–30s, showing type of response to wrongdoing

See App. 2.1 for identification numbers by place.

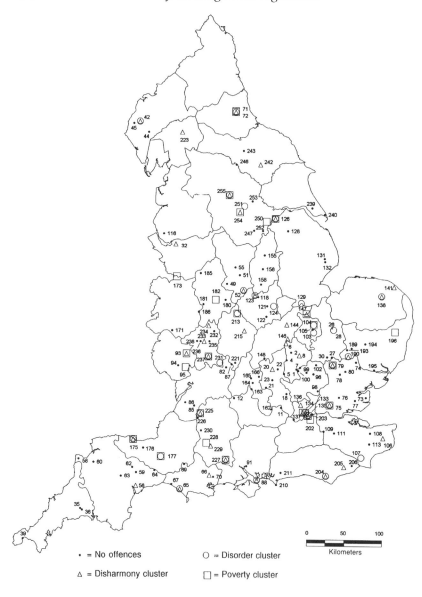

Map 7.2   Communities under observation in the 1460s–70s, showing type of
response to wrongdoing

See App. 2.1 for identification numbers by place.

North/Northwest and somewhat fewer in the Midlands/East Central area. Seventy percent of the places in the Disharmony cluster lay on major roads, rivers, or the coast, and 13 percent were close to London. Somewhat over a third of these communities contained industrial activity, and nearly a third were located in wood pasture. Places not troubled by social issues were situated more commonly in areas of mixed farming. Communities in the Disharmony cluster had many more inhabitants than those that did not report any problems with social misconduct, and they were growing relative to the others in our sample. They had been of about average relative wealth in 1334 and were to remain so in 1524/5, indicating little economic expansion. They were considerably less wealthy as communities than their population would have suggested and were to have intermediate levels of per capita payments and a sizeable fraction of very poor people in 1524/5. Their features resemble those of the communities that reported problems in the Disharmony cluster during the 1420s–30s.[3]

　　This evidence suggests that many communities in the Disharmony cluster in the 1460s–70s may have been encountering unfamiliar social problems as a result of rising population density due to immigration into market centers and places on transportation routes. If new arrivals and established families were being forced into closer contact in housing, commerce, and employment, harmonious social interactions may well have been jeopardized. The spread of quarreling, malicious gossip, and invasions of privacy could thus all have been magnified as popula-

---

[3] The Disharmony cluster in the 1420s–30s included higher fractions in market centers and hundreds than did the communities that did not mention any offences as well as a concentration in the North/Northwest, especially in the West Riding of Yorks. Fewer lay in the Midlands/East Central area. (See Map 7.1.) Locational factors were very important: nearly half of the places that reported problems in the Disharmony cluster were located on major roads, with another quarter on main rivers or the coast; about a tenth lay within 25 km of London. Industrial activity was starting in some of the Disharmony cluster communities: 37 percent were the site of some kind of manufacturing, three times the level of those that did not report any problems. In terms of agrarian regions, the Disharmony cluster places resembled those that did not report any social wrongdoing in that just over half practiced mixed farming; a somewhat higher fraction of the Disharmony cluster communities, however, were located in areas of open pasture, at the expense of wood pasture. The demographic and economic tables indicate that these places were larger than average within this sample and growing: they had been more populous in the later fourteenth century than communities which did not present any social issues, and by the 1520s they would be a great deal larger. They appear to have been increasing in relative prosperity too: they had been just below average in 1334 but were much wealthier in relative terms by the 1520s, though we cannot tell when this transition occurred.

tion levels increased.[4] Those people reported to the courts might be either new arrivals or more deeply-rooted residents responding to a presence that seemed to invade their accustomed space. Under such conditions, social harmony was threatened even if the newcomers did not violate local standards of conduct with respect to order/disorder and did not cause any of the problems associated with poverty. It is interesting that the punishments imposed upon offenders within this cluster were usually small money fines, almost never eviction. This suggests that those guilty of such forms of misconduct were regarded as members of the community, even if some/many of them were newcomers; they were not unwelcome residents whose departure from the community could be hastened by banishment.

Offences within the Disorder cluster were first reported in substantial numbers during the 1460s–70s. Seventy percent of these places were located in market centers, the highest fraction seen in any group in any period, but their regional distribution was close to that of the communities that did not express any social concerns within the local courts. Places in the Disorder cluster differed in some interesting locational respects both from those that mentioned no problems and from the Disharmony cluster communities. Nearly three-quarters of them lay on major roads, rivers, or the coast. Some kind of industrial activity – primarily the production of woolen cloth – was practiced in 45 percent of them. Their distribution between the three agrarian regions was quite different from that of the other groupings: fewer than a third of them lay in areas of mixed farming, with a quarter in wood pasture regions and the exceptionally high figure of 45 percent in open pasture. The more detailed agrarian breakdown shows an unusual concentration in the fenlands, which offered a variety of secondary employments. In demographic and economic terms, Disorder cluster places were definitely large – the most populous of any of the groups in 1377–81 and remaining big in the 1520s, though their relative position declined a little across the intervening years. They appear also to have been increasing in total wealth, moving from below average prosperity in 1334 to better than average status in 1524/5. They had been considerably less wealthy than their level of population would have suggested in the fourteenth century, and although this contrast had decreased to

---

[4] That astute observer of twentieth-century English village life, Agatha Christie, makes much the same point when describing the impact of a new housing estate upon the (fictitious) village of St. Mary Mead: as one of the immigrants comments, "There's something about a new estate like this that makes people look sideways at their neighbours. Because we're all new, I suppose. The amount of backbiting and tale-telling and writing to the council and one thing and another round here beats me!" (*The Mirror Crack'd*, pp. 147–8).

some extent by 1524/5, they were to have very low per capita payments in 1524/5 and the highest proportion of poor people seen in any of the groups.

It thus seems possible that many of the places reporting problems within the Disorder cluster were experiencing a different kind of growth than were communities reporting the Disharmony cluster. This version was probably tied more directly to the transition to capitalism, especially industrial activity, bringing with it poor wage laborers and other kinds of people whose presence was likely to trigger social regulation. Although these were generally large communities, the net rise in wealth that occurred prior to 1524/5 was not distributed evenly among their residents, and many of them faced substantial problems with poverty. Some of the communities that did not have an industrial presence were market centers on main roads and rivers, places that may have been attracting adolescent servants and women seeking employment during this period. All these changes probably caused respectable families to fear that order was imperiled: the standards of behavior of the newcomers may indeed have differed from those of established families. The possibility that many of these Disorder cluster offenders were not regarded as full members of the community is supported by the frequency with which eviction was used as a punishment against them.[5]

Communities that reported problems in the Poverty cluster during the 1460s–70s were to show no signs of objectively severe problems with poverty as of the 1520s. Fewer than a quarter of them were located in villages, and a comparatively low percentage lay in the Midlands/East Central region, with higher concentrations in the West/Southwest and North/Northwest. Two-thirds of these places were located on a long-distance road, navigable river, or the coast, and a quarter lay within 25 km of London. Just over two-fifths had some form of industrial activity, mainly woolen cloth manufacture and the production of leather goods. An unusually low fraction (29 percent) practiced mixed farming, with the rest spread fairly evenly between areas of wood and open pasture; clusters are seen in the wolds and downland, fenlands, and forests/wood pasture. These communities were somewhat above average in relative population, though smaller than places in the Disharmony and Disorder clusters, and were growing slightly in relative terms between 1377–81 and 1524/5. Their net wealth was average and stable. By 1524/5 they were to have very high per capita tax payments and the smallest fraction of very poor inhabitants seen in any of the groups analyzed here in any period.

[5] See Chapter 3, section two above.

These observations are consistent with the possibility that during the later fifteenth century concern with the problems of poverty was a temporary phenomenon resulting mainly from a rising number of people dependent upon their wages. Industrial activity and the concentration in wood pasture areas may imply a rising number of immigrant laborers, some engaged in proto-industrial production. The quarter of the Poverty cluster places that were close to London may likewise have felt strains as a result of the shift to larger-scale, specialized agriculture in its vicinity. The higher fraction of women among those reported for hedgebreaking in this period suggests that the early stages of the economic transition may have affected them with particular severity. But since the figures from 1524/5 indicate that these communities were not overburdened by the poor, it is likely that over the course of the intervening two generations economic growth proved sufficient to absorb the incoming labor force.

During the 1520s–30s (see Map 7.3), contrasts in the social ecology of communities when grouped by cluster are less sharp than in the later fifteenth century. Although this duodecade saw the highest fraction of presentments for offences in the Disharmony and Disorder clusters of any of the duodecades, the communities reporting these problems were diverse, covering a range of different patterns rather than being clearly distinguished from each other and from the places that did not mention any misbehavior to the courts. While this lack of separation stems in part from the methodological problems described above, it appears also to reflect the spread of new economic and demographic patterns into a wider range of places, no longer focused within specific kinds of communities as was the case before 1500. Further, the early sixteenth century witnessed the appearance of some additional developments that henceforth were to affect communities throughout the country. Increasing poverty and vagrancy, of concern to both Cardinal Wolsey and Thomas More, probably derived from inflation, the beginnings of natural population growth, and a severe drop in real wages.[6] (Even in the 1520s–30s the latter were only about 70 percent of their level between 1500 and 1509, and they were to drop much further thereafter.)

Among communities in the Disharmony cluster, the concentration in market centers during the 1520s–30s had declined somewhat, with a rise in the fraction of villages. A slightly higher fraction now lay in the Midlands/East Central region and fewer in the West/Southwest.

[6] Although Wolsey and More assigned much of the blame to enclosure, recent research suggests that it was generally not a cause of the symptoms they observed (*The Domesday of Inclosures*, and More, *Utopia*, esp. p. 24; Blanchard, "Population Change, Enclosure" and Christopher Dyer, "Deserted Medieval Villages." Real wages, below, were calculated from Wrigley and Schofield, *Population History*, Table A9.2.

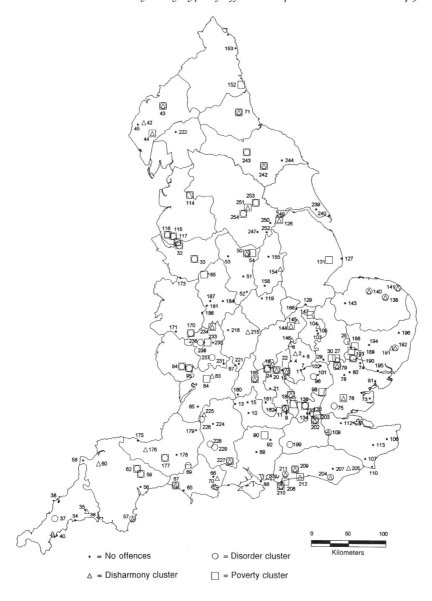

= No offences   ○ = Disorder cluster

△ = Disharmony cluster   □ = Poverty cluster

Kilometers

Map 7.3   Communities under observation in the 1520s–30s, showing type of
response to wrongdoing

See App. 2.1 for identification numbers by place.

Places in the Disharmony cluster were somewhat less likely than before to be situated on a main road, river, or the coast, and proximity to London was also less important. But the fraction of places with known industrial activity had risen slightly to 43 percent, and concentration in areas of wood pasture was at 35 percent, the highest level seen for any cluster in any period. In contrast to the pattern of the later fifteenth century, communities in the Disharmony cluster were of only average relative size; as before, they were of average total wealth. Over the following century and a half they were to grow in absolute size but less than the other types of places. Further, they had extremely low per capita payments in 1524/5 and the highest fraction of very poor people of any of the groups. No obvious explanations leap out of these data.

Of the communities that reported offences within the Disorder cluster in the 1520s–30s, just under half lay in market centers, a substantial decline from the previous period though still higher than the other groupings, and there was a high concentration in the West/Southwest coupled with a marked shortage of places in the Midlands/East Central region. Location on a major road was more common than in the late fifteenth century but being on a river or the coast was much less so. Industrial activity was documented in 49 percent of these communities. There had been a big shift in favor of mixed farming and wood pasture instead of open pasture, suggesting that even arable, nucleated villages with open fields were beginning to confront problems with order or at least to use their local courts in addressing such issues. Communities in the Disorder cluster were still larger in relative terms than the other clusters, though the difference had declined; they were to grow quite sharply in absolute terms between the 1520s and the 1660s–70s. They were also very slightly wealthier in a relative sense than the others, having been increasing in prosperity during the previous period and going to rise further over the next 140–150 years. In contrast to the preceding period, they made very high per capita tax payments and had an intermediate fraction of poor people in both the 1520s and the Hearth Taxes. While those places with industrial activity may have been troubled about disorder for much the same reasons as were their predecessors, our analysis provides no clear reasons for concern in the remaining communities.

Among places in the Poverty cluster during the 1520s–30s, fewer were located in market centers than had been true before, and they now included a strong weighting in the North/Northwest. About three-quarters of the Poverty cluster communities lay on main roads, rivers, or the coast, an increase since the later fifteenth century, but they were much less likely to be near London. A large fraction of all these communities (57 percent) had industrial activity, a great rise since the previous period and one of the highest proportions seen for any group at any time. More of these places lay in areas of mixed farming and wood pasture, with a corresponding drop in the fraction in open pasture areas. Poverty cluster communities were just above average in relative size, but they would grow at an extremely high rate in absolute terms over the next century and a half, more than doubling during that period. Although they were in the middle rank of relative prosperity in 1524/5, their position would improve by the Hearth Taxes. Their per capita payments in the 1520s were of an intermediate level, suggesting that economic growth in that period was still keeping up with the arrival of many poor newcomers. By the 1660s–70s, however, these places would have declined substantially in per capita wealth and seen a huge rise in the proportion of very poor people: nearly three-fifths of their residents were by then poor, an increase of 20 percent since the 1520s. While it is clear that by the 1520s–30s problems and/or concern with poverty were spreading to a more diverse set of places, probably associated in many cases with the expansion of manufacturing activity, the individual standard of living seems to have remained comfortable, presumably thanks to growth of the local economies.

If we move now to the 1580s–90s (see Map 7.4), when concern with the Disharmony and Disorder clusters had declined within the lesser public courts and only attention to the Poverty cluster continued to rise, we still see some specific locational and economic characteristics among the first two groupings. Those places concerned with the Poverty cluster, however, displayed widely assorted features apart from their shared evidence of high and rising levels of the very poor. In assessing this evidence, we must remember that since other courts in some regions were now handling many of the problems that had previously been addressed solely or primarily at the bottom level, the evidence from the lesser local courts illuminates only part of the total picture.[7]

Among the small number of communities that reported problems in the Disharmony cluster in the 1580s–90s (just 23 out of 176 places under observation in this period), the distribution among villages and market centers differed little from that of the places that reported no social problems, but fewer were found among the hundreds and more among the composite manorial estates. A exceptional 61 percent of these communities lay in the North/Northwest and only a tiny fraction in East Anglia/the Southeast, raising the possibility that by the late sixteenth

---

[7] See Chapter 1, section one above.

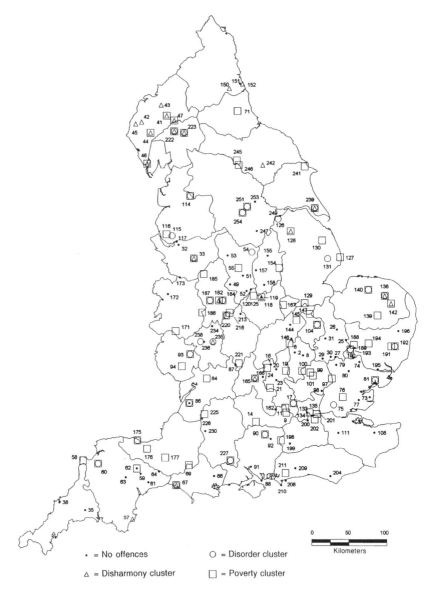

    • = No offences   ○ = Disorder cluster

    △ = Disharmony cluster   □ = Poverty cluster

Map 7.4   Communities under observation in the 1580s–90s, showing type of
response to wrongdoing

See App. 2.1 for identification numbers by place.

century concern with scolding – by now the overwhelming component of this cluster – had become focused in regional terms.[8] (It is also likely that the church courts had assumed a greater share of the responsibility for verbal problems in southeastern England by this period.) Location on transportation routes was no longer important, and only about a third of the Disharmony cluster places had industrial activity, down noticeably from the early sixteenth century. When compared to earlier periods, there had been a large drop in the fraction of Disharmony cluster communities located in areas of wood pasture, balanced by marked rises in regions of mixed farming or open pasture. Particularly interesting is the increased fraction now located in the arable and pastoral vales. Places in the Disharmony cluster were no longer larger than average within our sample, and their relative size remained almost flat between 1524/5 and the Hearth Taxes. They were also much poorer than before: the communities concerned with the Disharmony cluster in the 1580s–90s had been much less prosperous than any of the other groups in the 1520s and remained at an unusually low level into the 1660s–70s. They had by far the lowest level of per capita payments of any of the groups in both 1524/5 and the Hearth Taxes, and the proportion of very poor people increased by an unusual 24 percent in absolute terms over that interval. (Notice the far smaller rise in the fraction of poor in those places that reported no misbehavior at all.) Many communities that presented disruptions of local harmony in their local courts at the end of the sixteenth century – more than three-fifths of them located in the North/Northwest – were thus fairly small and very poor. It may well be that these communities were confronting unfamiliar levels of population density, as before threatening tranquil dealings between neighbors, though now pressure presumably resulted mainly from natural population growth.[9]

Of the slightly larger number of places that reported the Disorder cluster's offences, nearly half were market centers, the same level as in

---

[8] Of thirteen courts in Cumb., Northumb., and Westml. under observation during the 1580s–90s, eleven reported scolding. The language of the presentments suggests deep concern with people's personal reputation (see Chapter 3, section one above). This regional concentration was linked to an unusually high fraction of Disharmony cluster communities in the 1580s–90s that lay at higher elevations: 26 percent at between 76 and 152 m (= 250–499 ft), and a startling 26 percent higher than 152 m (= 500 ft). The set of Disharmony places in West Yorks. in the 1420s–30s forms an intriguing parallel (see note 3 above).

[9] Yet even in the North and Northwest, which were net exporters of people to southeastern England in the late sixteenth century, there must also have been some intraregional migration away from the more fragile rural ecologies into market centers, larger towns, and industrial areas, especially in the wake of bad harvests.

the previous period and higher than for the other groupings. More were situated in the Midlands/East Central area than before and fewer in East Anglia/the Southeast. Location on routes of travel and proximity to London no longer varied significantly between the various types of response, but communities in the Disorder cluster were extremely highly industrialized (58 percent of the total, the highest recorded for any period and well above the other clusters at that time). Barely more than a quarter of these places practiced mixed farming and only a fifth were in wood pasture, as opposed to an exceptional fraction of 54 percent in areas of open pasture. None at all lay in the arable vales; others were located on the fells and moorland or in the fenland, marshland, or pastoral vales, including some dairying regions. Places that reported offences within the Disorder cluster in this duodecade had been the largest of any group in 1524/5 but would grow only very slightly in relative terms by the Hearth Taxes, despite an absolute increase in population of 90 percent. They had likewise been much more prosperous than the other groups in 1524/5 and would hold that relative lead into the 1660s–70s. These communities had enjoyed extremely high per capita payments and very few poor people in 1524/5, but by the Hearth Taxes they would have much lower per capita wealth and an intermediate fraction of the poor. Perceived threats to good order at the end of the sixteenth century may thus have been an issue for the leaders of two different kinds of communities, both of which were probably encountering a drop in their standard of living. The first were places involved in industrial production, where a large fraction of poor workers may have heightened concern with control and governance in this period as they had before. The location of many of the other places, in fells/moorland, coastal areas, or the pastoral vales, is consistent with the suggestion that natural demographic rise was causing pressure on their varied but limited resources – unaccustomed population density that would be relieved through immigration or, in the worst cases, increased mortality rates before the 1660s–70s.

Communities concerned with the problems of poverty and labor in the 1580s–90s were not only extremely numerous, totaling 47 percent of all places under observation, they were also found in all regions and types of settings. The distribution by type of community now differed little from that of places that did not express any concern with social wrongdoing; their geographical distribution was intermediate among the groupings. Neither location on a major transportation route nor proximity to London distinguished these communities, and the fraction with industrial activity had declined very sharply. The movement towards mixed farming first visible in the 1520s–30s had continued, with fewer in wood pasture. The communities reporting poverty-related offences in the 1580s–90s had been of average size and wealth in 1524/5. They were slightly larger in relative terms by the Hearth Taxes, having grown in population at the high absolute rate of 91 percent, but they remained stable in relative prosperity. Of great significance, whereas they had an intermediate level of per capita wealth in 1524/5 and would remain in that position in the 1660s–70s, they also had an unusually high percentage of very poor dwellers in both assessments, reaching the exceptional level of 59 percent (the highest of any group) in the Hearth Taxes. It therefore seems likely that by the 1580s–90s what distinguished the communities that reported problems with poverty were not any specific locational or economic features but rather an unusually large fraction of the poor: many of them had already been burdened with needy people in the early sixteenth century and may have been experiencing an overwhelming rise in the number of the acutely poor by the end of the century. This forms a pronounced contrast with Poverty cluster places in the later fifteenth and earlier sixteenth centuries but accords with the pattern visible among the "broad response" communities at the end of Elizabeth's reign.

This analysis suggests that the impact of a community's social ecology upon the types of wrongdoing that it confronted and reported to its local court changed markedly across the fifteenth and sixteenth centuries. For the 1460s–70s, the kinds of geographic, demographic, and economic factors investigated here provide some interesting if not entirely clear-cut distinctions between places that responded to the various clusters of offences, allowing us to offer some plausible suggestions about the changes that may have underlain those concerns; similar patterns are observed during the 1420s–30s for communities that had already started reporting problems in the Disharmony cluster. During the 1520s–30s the differentiation between clusters is weak, due in part to consequences of the methodology but also probably to the movement of the new economic and demographic patterns that affected social regulation into a more diverse range of communities. During the final two decades of the sixteenth century, some specific locational or economic factors may well have remained important for the first two clusters, though by now few local courts reported such problems. The Poverty cluster, despite being reported by all kinds of communities, was for the first time characterized by signs of a high and rising fraction of poor people. The relatively limited evidence of differentiating features between the clusters during the sixteenth century emphasizes the need to incorporate into our analysis the kinds of legal and political factors discussed in Chapters 1 and 5 above and the ideological and religious influences to be considered in Chapter 8.

Ideological/religious influences

Though it has been convenient to separate our discussion of influences upon social regulation into thematic units, beliefs about the nature of society and what promoted its well-being and about moral behavior obviously provided the foundation for many of the patterns described in the first half of this study and interacted with many of the factors described in Chapters 5 through 7. In considering the ideological/religious context of control over misbehavior, this chapter provides only a brief discussion of a few selected topics: detailed analysis would require a book in its own right.[1] Each section explores some aspect of the central question of how social and religious attitudes may have affected the course of local regulation between 1370 and 1600. It is of course impossible to identify ideological or religious factors with any assurance in the absence of personal documents that indicate how individual people's responses to wrongdoing were influenced by their ethical beliefs and by new approaches they encountered through sermons or lectures, plays, conversation, or reading. Instead we will note parallels between educated thought and local responses as a sign that local jurors were acting in accordance with the wider climate of values; we will look also for evidence that new ideas about society or the particular forms of misbehavior were introduced shortly before similar changes are observed in the lesser courts' responses, opening up the possibility of a more direct and immediate impact.

The chapter begins at a general level, tracing ideas about harmony, order, and poverty, the fundamental social concerns that lay at the root of local attention to wrongdoing. Here we find correspondences be-

---

[1] Martin Ingram is considering ideological as well as legal issues in his current work: see, e.g., his "'Scolding Women Cucked or Washed',"part of a larger forthcoming study.

tween the attitudes of more educated authors and the reactions of jurors in village and market center courts but no indication that changes in the ideological setting were contributors to the specific patterns that we observed locally. Our focus then narrows to the fifteenth century, where we can look at whether written statements about the precise categories of misconduct contain novel ideas or increased energy that could have shaped the observed pattern of changing local court presentments. This investigation suggests that although religious and moral texts placed growing emphasis on backbiting, idleness, and gaming, fifteenth-century jurors were not exposed to any significant new teachings about misbehavior. After around 1500 attitudes towards wrongdoing can only be understood as part of the broader debate over what constituted a true Christian society. Our attention therefore shifts to the various religious/intellectual movements of that ideologically complex century, noting their conceptions of social morality and their willingness and ability to implement those ideas in practice. In this area we find stronger connections to the patterns of local control. The chapter concludes with a reassessment of the contested role of Puritanism at the end of the sixteenth century, an analysis that highlights the harm done to the core social values by aggressive regulation.

The fundamental social concerns

In the widest sense, the ideological context of control over wrongdoing was formed by attitudes towards the three concerns that lay beneath the particular violations examined here – harmony, order, and the problems of poverty. In addressing issues of harmony and order the leaders of villages and market centers were clearly operating within a framework articulated and defended by educated people in written form, though there is no evidence of changing values that might have contributed to the differing levels of enforcement seen in the local courts over time. With respect to poverty, however, intellectual, moral, and political leaders were themselves struggling with many of the same problems that confronted local people in practical terms; thus they offered little guidance on how to conceptualize or approach these difficult issues. We will look at the main emphases within these discussions and at the interesting tensions between them not as immediate causes of changing social regulation but as part of the general ideological setting within which it occurred. The analysis emphasizes the shared nature of values and language between upper and lower levels of society and authority, precisely because the common ideology served the functional needs of people operating in a range of settings.[2]

During the fifteenth and much of the sixteenth centuries, the importance of harmonious and peaceful relations within the community was a powerful and widely held feeling. This ideological stance was consistent with the pattern of enforcement seen in local court records, which shows fairly consistent concern with the forms of wrongdoing contained within the Disharmony cluster between the 1420s–30s and the 1520s–30s.[3] Social harmony, sometimes described as "living in charity with one's neighbors," was defended in spiritual, social, and political terms. In the 1420s the old-fashioned moralist John Audelay said that people should not cause debate or discord with their neighbors, because if a person is "euer out of charyte;/ To al payne ent domysday he schal go."[4] In a more secular vein, the mother in the poem "How the Good Wijf Taughte Hir Doughtir," written in the mid-fourteenth century but still being copied in the fifteenth, stresses to her daughter the importance of being on friendly terms with one's neighbors. If she is financially able, the younger woman should welcome them "with mete, drinke, & honest chere" for the utterly pragmatic reason that in the future she may need help from "thi neighboris that dwelle thee biside."[5] At the furthest end of the spectrum, an undated political poem, "Advice to the Several Estates," exhorts the English people to "set all yovr myndes to norysshe amyte;/ for vnto a royalme the syngvler defence/ restyth en love, concorde, and vnete."[6]

A need to remain on good terms with one's neighbors was heightened by the spiritual requirement that the laity be "in ful charyte with frynd and with foo" when going to confession before receiving

---

[2] Less visible here is the role of power in defining and spreading an ideology, as suggested by the theory of hegemonic discourse. (The latter has been explored from very different philosophical vantage-points by Marxists, Foucault, and feminist theorists: e.g., Jameson, *The Political Unconscious*, Foucault, *The Archaeology of Knowledge* and his "Truth and Power," and Macdonell, *Theories of Discourse*.) As will be considered below, practical concerns about social issues could also rise upwards in legal/political terms, triggering attention at the more formal ideological level.

[3] See Chapter 3, section one above.   [4] *Poems of John Audelay*, pp. 46–7 and 117.

[5] In *Early English Meals and Manners*, esp. pp. 44–5. For the sake of goodwill, the mother advises that if any discord should arise between her neighbors, the daughter should "make it no worse, meende it if thou may" (*ibid.*, p. 44). For the revised dating of this work, see the introduction to *The Good Wife Taught Her Daughter*; for its ideological context, see Riddy, "Mother Knows Best."

[6] "Advice to the Several Estates, II," in *Historical Poems of the XIVth and XVth Centuries*, pp. 233–5.

communion.[7] This traditional idea was defended during the fifteenth century in such popular works as the *Lay-Folks Mass Book* and John Mirk's collection of homilies known as the *Festial*.[8] The post-1558 Church of England continued the rule, prohibiting the laity from receiving communion if they were not "in love and charity with their neighbors"; enforcement is noted in church court records until the mid-1580s but becomes rare thereafter.[9] The Elizabethan laity also heard homilies read by their parish minister each year in favor of Christian love and charity and against contention, strife, and debate, attitudes which may have started to sound a little old-fashioned as the sixteenth century drew to a close.[10]

Many groups attempted to institutionalize or ritualize harmonious and amicable social interactions. Urban economic guilds and the pre-Reformation parish fraternities exhorted their members to live together in peace and love and commonly forbade them to go to law against each other, at least until the heads of the organization had attempted to resolve any disputes.[11] Civic bodies worked to restore good relations in other ways too. In York, the mayor and aldermen persuaded two couples who had been quarreling with each other in 1543 to agree to use

[7] *Poems of John Audelay*, p. 38. The author of a Worcester Chapter sermon written between c. 1389 and 1404 instructed lay people coming to confession that "the schalt ben e charite with thyn emcristen," and a religious poem of around the 1420s said that people should not receive the communion while "in synne and stryf." (*Three Middle English Sermons*, p. 60; "Of the Sacrament of the Altar," in *Twenty-Six Political and Other Poems*, pt. 1, p. 105.)

[8] *The Lay-Folks Mass Book*, pp. 46–9; *Mirk's Festial*, p. 168. *The Lay-Folks Mass Book* said that the requirement of being at peace with others when receiving the communion is represented by the kissing of the Pax (pp. 48–9). The kiss of peace was part of lay symbolism too: the poem "Love God, and Drede" says that "Yif a man do a-nother mys,/ Neighbores shuld hem auyse,/ The trespasour amende and kys,/ Do bothe parties euene assise" (in *Twenty-Six Political and Other Poems*, pt. 1, p. 6).

[9] E.g., Notts. AO DDTS 14/26/1, pp. 10–11 (a Newark man who claimed in 1565 that he had not received communion because he was "out of charity" with two others who had misused him); Borthwick Institute, York, V.1575/CB.1, fols. 47v (a minister accused in 1575 of allowing a man to receive communion with whom he was out of charity) and 81v (a layman charged that same year with not receiving communion who said he was "not then in charity but he did receive the Sunday then next following"); and Berks. RO D/A 2 e 1, fol. 2v (three laymen who defended their absence from Easter communion in 1583 "for that as they say they were not in perfect love and charity").

[10] *Certaine Sermons or Homilies*, vol. I, pp. 40–5 and 89–98.

[11] E.g., Tyne and Wear Archs. Serv., Newcastle GU/Sk/1/2, orders of the Skinners and Glovers Guild, 1437, and Lichfield (Staffs.) Joint RO D77/4/4/1, a 1554 copy of the earlier byelaws of the Corvisers Company; *English Gilds*. See also McRee, "Religious Gilds and Regulation of Behavior" and Brigden, "Religion and Social Obligation."

"them selves with gentle words, one to an other after, as honest neighbors should do."[12] Should either couple break the agreement by returning to their wrangling, they were to forfeit 40s for each offence to the common chamber of the city. Symbolic representations of harmony were displayed in rituals of reconciliation. Examples of the latter abound in the mid-sixteenth-century records of (the) Devizes, Wilts. In 1560, for instance, a controversy between two of the citizens was brought before the mayor to be resolved. After the two had been "thoroughly made friends" again in public, each freely forgave the other for "all matters that be or ever hath been between them from the beginning of the world unto this day."[13] The men then took each other by the hand and agreed there would be "no more recital thereof," whereupon they "went to the Harte and drank together."

It is striking, however, that attention to social harmony in moral/social texts and in the records of voluntary or civic communities seems to have declined during the course of Elizabeth's reign, following by a generation the drop in concern with the Disharmony cluster in local courts. By 1600 amicable relations between neighbors and group members no longer appeared so critical. The shift is reflected, for example, in the decreasing use of arbitration for settling local disputes. Arbitrators, widely employed both in informal conflict resolution and in medieval and early sixteenth-century courts, normally awarded something to both parties, enough to save face and allow the parties to return to friendship.[14] Trial juries, by contrast, usually gave all-or-nothing decisions which only perpetuated the ill-will, and this mechanism became more common locally in the second half of the sixteenth century.

The second goal that underlay worry about wrongdoing was the maintenance of order and control. This topic was increasingly emphasized in written works from the middle of the fifteenth century right through the end of the sixteenth. Hence it paralleled practical enforcement of good order, which rose from the 1460s–70s through the 1520s–30s in the lesser courts, with authority increasingly transferred to Sessions of the Peace and probably the church courts thereafter.[15] Nor is it coincidental that heightened concern with order both in the textual

---

[12] *York Civic Records*, vol. IV, p. 94.   [13] Wilts. RO G20/1/11, fol. 5r.

[14] This point is discussed, with references, in McIntosh, *Autonomy and Community*, ch. 5, and *A Community Transformed*, ch. 5. For other examples of town-backed arbitration, see York in 1477 (*The York House Books*, pp. 132–3), Hereford in 1519 (Heref. RO Hereford City Records, Tourn, 1499–1537), and Northleach, Gloucs. in 1550–1, which named six official arbitrators for the year (Gloucs. RO D 398/1, fol. 109r).

[15] See Chapter 1, section one and Chapter 3, section two above.

world and in local communities during the later sixteenth century accompanied declining attention to local harmony: there was an inherent tension between a desire to maintain good relationships throughout the community and the need to prevent or punish disorder and disobedience. The ideology of order has been discussed by others, so we will only address two meanings of the term as it pertained to local settings in the fifteenth and sixteenth centuries: preserving a structured and deferential social order, and preventing unrest or disorder.[16]

Images of a hierarchical social order, central to contemporary perceptions of how individuals related to each other and to communities, assumed a society in which everyone had an accepted if loosely defined place in terms of such features as socio-economic status, age, position in the household, gender, and geographical base. Most English people had internalized this concept so thoroughly that little formal justification was needed.[17] Belief in social hierarchy affected the ideological context of social regulation because each of the groups we have noted as potential triggers of social regulation (young people, outsiders, the poor, and unusually independent women) undermined this conventional picture. Young people fit into an orderly pattern if they were subordinate to household heads, either their own parents or their masters or mistresses. These authorities were to train them in proper habits of work and to oversee their leisure time, especially their sexuality. Should young people free themselves from that control, through their physical mobility or lack of supervision, they upset the social order. Outsiders, strangers, and vagrants were by definition misfits within a geographically based social structure. If they moved into a new community to take up land, assume regular employment, or marry, they were generally accepted and assimilated. But deeply troubling were those strangers who did not appear likely to settle – those who showed no desire to put down roots and who were responsible to no obvious master, employer, or senior family member. Poor people filled an accepted stratum within a pyramidal notion of the social order, provided they had a fixed location and were prepared to act out the roles seen as appropriate to their station. Problems arose when the poor left their homes or refused to display suitable obedience and deference in social, economic, religious, or political situations. The fact that a disproportionate number of poor households were headed by widows

---

[16] Wrightson has provided several thoughtful discussions of the way order was perceived in the later sixteenth, seventeenth, and/or eighteenth centuries: "Two Concepts of Order," "Social Order," and *English Society*, ch. 6. For order within a wider political and legal setting, see, e.g., Elton, *Policy and Police*, Fletcher, *Tudor Rebellions*, and Sharpe, *Crime in Early Modern England*.   [17] Tillyard, *The Elizabethan World Picture*.

introduced a dislocation of familiar gender roles as well. This accentuated the discomfort felt by traditional members of society when a considerable number of women lived independently or had their own sources of income.

A second aspect of the wider concern with order was associated with a desire to prevent challenges to authority or actual violence. The authors of later fifteenth- and sixteenth-century moral and social texts, like those of political treatises, emphasized that it was the duty of people in power to enforce stability and security; for the members of a Christian society, obedience to their superiors and to the laws and traditions of the community and nation was a religious as well as a civic obligation. Among the most forceful articulations of the importance of a law-abiding and disciplined social and political structure were the late Elizabethan homilies against disobedience and willful rebellion.[18] The emphasis upon order in ideological sources must thus have reinforced whatever concerns local leaders had for other reasons.

As we turn to the issues associated with poverty, we find a more complicated picture. The broader ideological situation mirrors what we saw in the local courts, where concern with problems in the Poverty cluster rose fairly steadily across the fifteenth and sixteenth centuries amidst signs of a growing contrast between customary tolerance of the poor and newer (and often harsher) responses based upon a distinction between the kinds of poverty.[19] Although educated analysis of these matters lagged far behind local efforts to address practical problems, we see a similar opposition between traditional Christian teachings about charity and more selective ideas about who warranted relief.

The most conspicuous feature of the discussion of poverty among educated authors in the fifteenth century was how little of it there was, even during the decades after 1460 when serious problems were beginning to appear in villages and market centers.[20] This lag between changes in behavior as demanded by new developments in the socioeconomic environment and a revised cultural statement that explains and justifies the changing responses illustrates the incompatibility that

---

[18] *Certaine Sermons or Homilies*, vol. II, pp. 275–319.

[19] See Chapter 3, section three above.

[20] This observation disagrees with historical studies that describe severe practical problems with poor people and intense concern with and antagonism to them throughout the later fourteenth and fifteenth centuries (e.g., Rubin, *Charity and Community*, heavily influenced by Mollat, *The Poor in the Middle Ages*, and Mollat, ed., *Études sur l'Histoire de la Pauvreté*). Such portrayals err, I think, by failing to discriminate with sufficient care between rhetoric and reality, between continental and English texts, and between attitudes of the second half of the fourteenth century and the rather different situation of the fifteenth century. Cf. Rubin's later essay, "The Poor."

David Aers has noted between "received cultural categories and the demands posed by present practical realities."[21] Explaining how inherited modes of action, assumptions, and values (often termed *habitus*) incorporate change has indeed been a challenge for many theorists of "practice."[22]

Among the generally brief and rather superficial textual references to the fifteenth-century poor, traditional and positive definitions of poverty were still present. Images of the poor as filling a special spiritual and social role (God's poor) appear in didactic moral works and occasionally in other contexts, especially during the earlier decades of the fifteenth century and among more conservative authors and regions of the country.[23] We also find restatements of customary ideas about the importance of charity to relieve the poor and needy, principally the seven works of mercy.[24] In Lollard writings too the Christian obligation to help the poor was a powerful theme.[25] Some fifteenth-century texts, however, accepted a crude differentiation between the acceptable and the unworthy poor. Whereas the deserving poor, people who were unable to labor for their own support, qualified for charitable assistance, the idle poor who were capable of working but chose not to do so were to be ignored or punished. When the able-bodied poor left home to wander, they were labeled in terms that echo Parliamentary legisla-

---

[21] Aers, "Introduction," in his *Community, Gender, and Individual Identity*, p. 4, commenting on Bakhtin. Aers notes that "the 'praxis' of medieval people ... involves practical reference which put their cultural systems at risk in changing historical circumstances" (*ibid.*, p. 6). For such lags, defined often in terms of Louis Althusser's concept of the relative autonomy of various domains, see, e.g., Williams, *Marxism and Literature*.

[22] E.g., Bourdieu, *Outline of a Theory of Practice*. For critiques of Bourdieu's concept of *habitus* focusing upon its inability to explain how changes are introduced, see Harker, Mahar, and Wilkes, eds., *Introduction to the Work of Bourdieu*, esp. ch. 9, and de Certeau's comments on Bourdieu and Foucault in *The Practice of Everyday Life*, esp. ch. 4.

[23] *Mum and the Sothsegger*, for example, says when talking about support for the church and clergy that God's part of the church's wealth should be given to God's men, namely the poor (pp. 46–7); it was written at the turn of the fifteenth century.

[24] In the 1420s both the old priest John Audelay and a poem, "Loue That God Loueth," repeat the familiar emphasis on the acts of mercy, a theme forcibly represented in the scenes of the Last Judgment in some of the cycle plays (*Poems of John Audelay*, p. 7, and *Twenty-Six Political and Other Poems*, pt. 1, pp. 73–5). The seven works of mercy may have lingered with particular power in the North: see Cullum, "Hospitals and Charitable Provision." They were also represented visually in a number of fifteenth-century wall-paintings in parish churches (Caiger-Smith, *English Medieval Mural Paintings*, pp. 53–5).

[25] See, e.g., *Selections from English Wycliffite Writings*, *English Wycliffite Sermons*, vol. I, and *Lollard Sermons*. This provides additional interest to Bowers's suggestion of a link between the *Piers Plowman* tradition and Lollardy in the fifteenth century: "Piers Plowman and the Police."

tion of the middle and later fourteenth century.[26] But no attempt was made to analyze with care the nature and causes of poverty. Fifteenth-century authors did not pursue or develop Langland's painfully honest efforts in *Piers Plowman* to wrestle with the actual manifestations of poverty and the reasons for these problems.[27] What limited interest we can discern prior to c. 1520 focused upon the rich and their relation to the poor, particularly the emotionally charged issue of how wealthy people could use charitable acts to help achieve salvation.[28]

It was not until the 1520s and 1530s that a more thoughtful and nuanced approach to the problems of poverty began to emerge. Like the distinctions made by jurors in villages and market centers, this analysis attempted to define the various sorts of poverty and develop an appropriate response to each.[29] By the later sixteenth century, theorists – like local officials – were forced to confront not only the deserving poor and able-bodied people who refused to labor but also a third form of need that was becoming progressively more common: people who were capable of working and willing to do so but could not find employment. Although Parliament proposed a series of legislative solutions from the Henrician period onwards, the most creative experimentation occurred within the cities and larger towns, which tried out various means of assisting the worthy poor while punishing idlers and/or forcing them to labor. Of particular importance was the use of taxes or required "contributions" levied against wealthier members of the community to support the qualifying poor, an approach authorized more generally by Parliamentary legislation of 1552 and 1563.[30] At the very end of the

---

[26] For the emergence in the later fourteenth century of the stereotype of the mobile, physically capable beggar, see Aers, "*Piers Plowman*: Poverty, Work, and Community," p. 37, and Chapter 5, section one above.

[27] While *Piers Plowman* remained part of fifteenth-century culture, the work seems to have evoked no particular interest among its scribes and readers in Langland's descriptions of the non-clerical poor. See Uhart, "The Early Reception of Piers Plowman," and Scase, "*Piers Plowman*" *and the New Anti-Clericalism*, both of which document interest in *clerical* poverty. I am grateful to Dr. Uhart for permission to consult her thesis and to John M. Bowers for loaning his copy of it to me. For editions and secondary studies of *Piers Plowman*, see note 92 to McIntosh, "Finding Language for Misconduct."

[28] For a fuller discussion, see McIntosh, "Finding Language for Misconduct," pp. 108–9.

[29] The history of this discussion has already been described. See, e.g., Slack, *Poverty and Policy*, Rudd, "The Involuntarily Poor" (a copy of which was kindly provided to me by Dr. Rudd), Fideler, "Poverty, Policy and Providence," "Poverty in Tudor Ethical and Political Discourses," and "'The Poor' in Early Elizabethan Thought and Policy," and McIntosh, "Local Responses to the Poor." I am grateful to Dr. Fideler for permission to use and cite his papers.

[30] See Slack, *Poverty and Policy*, and McIntosh, "Local Responses to the Poor." The 1552 statute stipulated that any who refused to pay were to be taken before the bishops,

sixteenth century the now more sophisticated social/intellectual analysis of poverty was coupled with the lessons learned from local experiments in the famous Elizabethan Poor Laws, a set of statutes that required all parishes in England to support their own deserving poor through compulsory taxes while placing those who refused to work into county houses of correction; poor people unable to find employment were to be given supplies with which to work.[31] Yet even though charitable relief was becoming institutionalized, with a strong feeling on the part of most officials at the national, county, and urban levels that aid should be administered either through govermental units (including the parish) or through formal bodies like residential almshouses, the older virtues of simple Christian charity were not entirely abandoned: both the early Elizabethan homily on "Christian love and charity" and the later one on "alms deeds and mercifulness toward the poor and needy" present a strong case for personal assistance, with little apparent concern about the merits of the recipients.[32] While the reactions of local court jurors were obviously embedded within this general reticulum of ideas, their efforts to address social issues were not simple reflections of the dominant ideology.

Fifteenth-century ideas about social wrongdoing

To assess whether educated thought had immediate and detectable impact upon social regulation at the local level, we turn to the fifteenth century. A variety of texts about the particular types of wrongdoing examined in this study may be compared with the changing patterns visible in local courts to see whether there is evidence of specific influence. That century is well suited to such an analysis for several reasons. Because the Catholic church provided a stable and shared moral foundation for most English people, any changes in attitudes towards the individual forms of misbehavior stand out more clearly, while the pronounced changes in levels and types of concern with social problems as reported to local courts provide a good basis for comparison.[33] Although fifteenth-century moral texts have received little scholarly attention, they are of interest in their own right as well as providing in most cases the intellectual/emotional basis for better

reinforced in 1563 by the JPs: 5 & 6 Edward VI, c. 2, and 5 Eliz., c. 3 (*Stats. Realm*, vol. IV, pp. 131–2 and 411–12).

[31] 39 Eliz., cc. 3–5, modified somewhat in 43 Eliz., c. 2 (*Stats. Realm*, vol. IV, pp. 896–903 and 962–6).

[32] *Certaine Sermons or Homilies*, vol. I, pp. 40–5, and vol. II, pp. 154–66.

[33] As will be discussed below, Lollards did not differ from the established church with respect to moral values.

known sixteenth-century responses. Several overlapping types of texts are considered here: didactic treatises or poems written for a lay audience by educated clerics, more secular poems or stories offering advice on how to lead a proper life, and popular plays and poems which provided moral edification as well as entertainment. This comparison places the responses of local jurors firmly within the general context provided by the moral and social teachings of clerical and other writers, but it provides no indication of more concrete impact upon the changing patterns of regulation seen in the courts.

Fifteenth-century moral discussion was highly conservative, in many cases even static.[34] Although this may well have been a period in which the clergy were making a more strenuous effort to educate the laity about general Christian ethics, through active translation of continental texts, new versions of earlier didactic works, and expanded use of such forms as the exemplum, ideas about moral behavior show little sign of change.[35] The much-copied *Jacob's Well*, for example, prepared probably in the 1440s, was the newest addition to the series of redactions of the thirteenth-century French work *Somme le Roi* and resembled its predecessors fairly closely in terms of content.[36] While local people may thus have been more fully aware of the details of Christian morality than their predecessors had been, the ethical environment within which they functioned was traditional, unlikely to bring about altered patterns of actual social conduct or even to respond quickly to new concerns emerging within villages and market centers. Nor is there reason to think that the fifteenth-century clergy was calling for more aggressive legal regulation of misbehavior.

Texts about the specific types of misconduct included in the Disharmony cluster display considerable attention to scolding, especially backbiting, but do not explain why concern with such offences rose after 1420 in the lesser courts. Scolding, routinely condemned in moral tracts across the later fourteenth and fifteenth centuries, was often portrayed as an outgrowth of gossiping; the latter, while not an offence in itself, was discouraged as conducive to idleness as well as to more harmful speech. The argumentative or quarrelsome aspect of scolding received some attention in moral works, but backbiting was given a

---

[34] For a general discussion of this literature, see Bloomfield, *The Seven Deadly Sins*.
[35] I am grateful to Larry Scanlon for discussing with me the efforts to improve moral awareness and for letting me see in advance several chapters from his book, *Narrative, Authority and Power*.
[36] See, e.g., *Dan Michel's Ayenbite of Inwyt*, *The Book of Vices and Virtues*, and *Jacob's Well*. The latter offers more complex categorization and a few new images through which to analyze human sinfulness.

more thoughtful analysis, in terms that suggest that this problem was regarded as more prevalent than it had been previously. *Jacob's Well* presents a detailed discussion of ten "sins of the tongue," under the heading of gluttony.[37] Backbiting is described as "whan thou spekyst euyll be-hynde a man, & turnyst all that thou mayst the gode dedys of an-other man to the werste." The sowing of discord, which the author classifies as a deadly sin, was "whanne thou makyst hem enemyes that were freendys, & makyst stryif & debate wyth talys & lesynges [= false-hoods] berynge aboute." Especially interesting is the common equation of backbiting with envy. Near the beginning of the fifteenth century, the author of a sermon delivered to the Worcester Chapter launched a long attack on backbiting, which he suggested was associated with circum-stances in which some people were getting richer while others lagged behind.[38] This surely characterizes the kinds of communities concerned with scolding in the early fifteenth century.[39] The relationship appears in dramatic and poetic works as well. The early fifteenth-century play *The Castle of Perseverance* shows Envy ordering Backbiting (or Detrac-tion) to attack any of Mankind's neighbors who are thriving, killing them "wythowtyn knyve"; he is told to "Speke thi neybour mekyl schame,/ Pot on hem sum fals fame,/ Loke thou vndo hys nobyl name/ Wyth me, that am Envye."[40] Backbiting might also disrupt the stability of the broader community. The extended poem "The Assembly of Gods" links scolds, malicious murmurers, feigners of tales, seekers of debate, and maintainers of quarrels with "makers of clamours" and traitors among the host of commons led by the character Idleness, suggesting that there were dangers to the state as well as to society from misuse of the tongue.[41]

Although women were certainly perceived as inherently talkative – unable to control their tongues and devoted to gossip with their peers – it is not clear to what extent the particular types of harmful speech comprised within the term "scolding" were identified with women in fifteenth-century analyses.[42] The author of the Worcester sermon, like most other moralists, was careful to argue that backbiting was common to both sexes: he speaks always of "this man or this womman," and his most vivid example refers to a man.[43] Though the mother in "How the

---

[37] *Jacob's Well*, pp. 147–55; for below, see *ibid.*, p. 83 and pp. 99 and 83.
[38] *Three Middle English Sermons*, pp. 35–40.   [39] See Chapter 7, note 3 above.
[40] In *The Macro Plays*, pp. 1–111, esp. p. 36.
[41] Previously attributed to Lydgate, the work was probably written around 1420.
[42] Cf., e.g., Hallissy, *Clean Maids, True Wives*, esp. ch. 6, Poos, "Sex, Lies, and the Church Courts," and Karras, *Common Women*, esp. pp. 138–40.
[43] *Three Middle English Sermons*, e.g., pp. 35 and 39–40.

Good Wijf Taughte Hir Doughtir" does indeed advise her daughter to be of good tongue, "How the Wise Man Taught His Son" (from c. 1430) places some weight on this point too.[44] The father warns, "thin owne tunge may be thi foo," especially in carrying tales; a word you say today may return to make trouble in the future. In the very rare cases when the image of bridling the tongue was used, it was not applied particularly to women.[45] This limited gender specificity contrasts with the predominance of women among those actually reported for the offence in fifteenth-century local courts (though less so in the later sixteenth century) and with the almost exclusively female images of scolding produced in ideological statements after c. 1580.

Neither eavesdropping nor nightwalking received much attention from the clerical authors of didactic works, and they appeared only occasionally in other kinds of texts. As in the court records, they were usually portrayed as types of behavior suspect largely through association. Roaming around at night was connected sometimes with lingering at a tavern, sometimes with eavesdropping. "The Wise Man" tells his son not to stay out too late or to sit drinking, because "of late walking cometh debate."[46] In "The Assembly of Gods," eavesdroppers are paired with "stalkers by nyght" in the company that follows Idleness, and a moral poem laid out as the inverse of all true virtue advises its reader to "Rechelesly the gouerne,/ Day and nyght; walke late/ At cokes hostry and tauerne."[47]

Discussion of the forms of misconduct within the Disorder cluster likewise changed relatively little across the fifteenth century. While spiritual condemnation of fornication and adultery was maintained in all texts, we find no indication of intensified disapprobation around 1460, as was seen in local courts. Alehouses and taverns had likewise been regarded with traditional suspicion by moralists of many hues. By the later fourteenth century they were associated with overindulgence in food and drink as well as with linguistic abuses.[48] Though there may have been a new emphasis upon alehouses as centers of waste and loss

---

[44] *Early English Meals and Manners*, pp. 37 and 48–53, esp. p. 49 for below.

[45] In an attack on evil tongues ("fals detraccioun, lesyng & dysclaunder/ Hath slay mor peple than dud kyng Alysunder"), an undated poem commented, "Oft yll reportis engenderyth sorw[e and c]are;/ Were-for in spekyng at no tyme [is] he ydill/ That can hys tong at all tyme wysly bridill" ("See Much, Say Little," in *Religious Lyrics of the XVth Century*, pp. 279–80).   [46] In *Early English Meals and Manners*, p. 50.

[47] "The Assembly of Gods," p. 21; "To Lyf Bodyly, Is Perylous," in *Twenty-Six Political and Other Poems*, pt. 1, pp. 25–7 (written perhaps around the start of the fifteenth century).

[48] For heightened opposition to alehouses in this period, part of a class-based set of worries centered on peasant misconduct, see Hanna, "Pilate's Voice/Shirley's Case" and his "Brewing Trouble."

of economic substance in the early fifteenth century, criticisms from later in the century do not castigate them especially as centers of disorder.[49] The cluster of vague terms like being badly governed or ruled, living suspiciously, or of evil reputation do not appear in these moral or literary texts, suggesting that they served a specifically legal purpose.

The Poverty cluster's offences received mixed attention in didactic and literary sources. Whereas the issues directly related to poverty are seldom mentioned (hedgebreaking and subtenants do not appear at all, and beggars and vagabonds were accorded scant notice), idleness was actively and sometimes thoughtfully discussed.[50] In keeping with the customary moral position on sloth, poetic or dramatic representations from the earlier decades of the fifteenth century focus upon the spiritual harm caused by idleness or suggest that it is harmful in both spiritual and practical terms. Lydgate, for example, characterizes Idleness as having a shield which displays a barren tree: by encouraging many vices and voluptuous desires as well as lack of thrift, Idleness "in vertu maketh a man ful bare."[51] *The Castle of Perseverance* likewise figures Idleness's ability simultaneously to pull a man into hellfire and to put him into poverty on this earth. Until around 1460, though refusal to work was seen as conducive to nearly all the other forms of misconduct we have examined, the character Idleness was occasionally allowed to express the traditional social virtues of good fellowship with which he was associated.[52] Later in the century, however, most works talk only about pragmatic issues, especially the link between idleness and poverty. The poetic "Advice to the Several Estates" notes that "where slovth hath place, there welth es faynt and small."[53] George Ashby advocated stimulating the cloth industry in order to keep the common people out of idleness and put the poor into work.

The final type of wrongdoing, gaming, was similarly the subject of vigorous objection, both moral and practical, during the fifteenth century. In this case the conceptual attack may possibly have influenced the local response, which rose steadily across the century. *Jacob's Well*, with its customary thoroughness, identifies nine distinct kinds of sin

---

[49] For the former, see, e.g., "La Male Regle de T. Hoccleue," in *Selections from Hoccleve*, pp. 12–23. Ralph Hanna, who kindly suggested the previous reference, agrees that attitudes towards alehouses remained relatively static across the fifteenth century (personal communication).   [50] For a general account, see Wenzel, *The Sin of Sloth*.

[51] *Lydgate's Reson and Sensuallyte*, vol. I, pp. 181–2, written at the beginning of the century. For below, see *The Macro Plays*, p. 51.

[52] As in "Occupation and Idleness," from around the mid-century: *Non-Cycle Plays*, pp. 192–208.

[53] In *Historical Poems of the XIVth and XVth Centuries*, p. 233. For below, see "Active Policy of a Prince," in *George Ashby's Poems*, p. 29, written in the 1460s.

connected with playing games.[54] Here, as in many other sources, game playing was associated with the idea of betting – the lure of money that led men to risk whatever resources they might have. The poem "Money, Money!" includes both indoor and outdoor games among the settings in which "money hathe euer the floure."[55] When a virtuous Bristol apprentice asks his master for financial assistance after having spent his inheritance to rescue his father's soul, his master accuses him of having "played atte dice,/ or at som other games nyce,/ and lost vp sone tht thu had."[56] Other authors emphasized the association between game playing and idleness. Lydgate, for example, in *Reson and Sensuallyte*, portrays Venus's son Deduit (or Pleasure) as the god of games, who himself specializes in dice, tables, and chess; "The Assembly of Gods" lists players of cards and such games as hazard and closhing as among the followers of Idleness.[57] The location of dicing and the other indoor games – frequently in alehouses – was likewise to their discredit.[58] The negative associations of dicing may have been increased by the scene in the mystery plays that shows dice being used to divide up Jesus' clothing after the crucifixion. More vivid still for the laity of at least a few parishes were visual reminders of the spiritual damage of gaming. Stained-glass images or wall paintings in their churches showed the fate of dice players in Hell or represented Christ surrounded by a group of implements, representing the concept that sins committed in our daily lives wound Him; among the objects that cause Him to suffer are dice and cards.[59] Fifteenth-century texts thus display heightened concern with backbiting, idleness, and gaming but few new ideas even about these problems. There is no reason to conclude that changing attitudes among educated people had a concrete impact upon social regulation as documented within local courts.

Conceptions of a Christian society in the sixteenth century

Because analysis of wrongdoing after c. 1520 was to a large extent subsumed into discussion of the nature and goals of a Christian society

---

[54] *Jacob's Well*, pp. 134–5.
[55] In *Historical Poems of the XIVth and XVth Centuries*, pp. 134–7, written in the late fourteenth or early fifteenth century.
[56] "Childe of Bristow," p. 22, and see Hanawalt, "'The Childe of Bristowe'."
[57] *Lydgate's Reson and Sensuallyte*, vol. I, pp. 63–4; "The Assembly of Gods," p. 21.
[58] "The Wise Man," for example, warns his son to beware of dice, which in his mind were connected with taverns (in *Early English Meals and Manners*, p. 50). For below, see, e.g., *The Chester Mystery Cycle*, vol. I, pp. 306–9.
[59] Marks, *Stained Glass*, p. 80, and Caiger-Smith, *English Medieval Mural Paintings*, pp. 55–8 and Plate 20.

and the actions of its members, we will turn to two aspects of that debate: the social and moral ideals of the religious and intellectual movements that competed with Catholic views during this rapidly changing period, and the extent to which supporters of these movements were eager and able to implement their vision in practical terms. While the arguments used against particular forms of misconduct remained generally conservative, wider notions of the Christian community developed in new ways.[60] In this century we find stronger correlations between the ideological context and responses to misbehavior within local communities.

The Lollard movement had never articulated a distinctive position concerning appropriate and godly behavior among the laity. Whereas Wycliffite authors were deeply concerned about the righteousness of the clergy, they appear to have offered no innovative ideas about lay social conduct.[61] Within their local communities, however, Lollards may have made a more concerted effort to practice and enforce those types of behavior they saw as fitting for a Christian society than did orthodox Catholics.[62] It is also possible that their presence and interests elevated concern with wrongdoing among their Catholic neighbors.[63] As Map 7.3 displays, there was a fascinating concentration of presentments for social misconduct in villages and market centers in Buckinghamshire and the adjacent region of Berkshire during the 1520s–30s, areas with a strong Lollard presence. Yet attention to wrongdoing does not seem to have stemmed directly from the participation of Lollards on the juries, for during this same period jurors in some of those communities were going far beyond their legal charge by reporting to their manorial courts people who held Wycliffite beliefs.[64]

Some of the most idealistic efforts to define or create a more just and charitable society in many parts of sixteenth-century Europe were

[60] See, e.g., Todd, *Christian Humanism*, which presents a strong case for considerable continuity across the sixteenth century but assumes what she describes as "a radical departure from medieval values" without providing evidence to support this claim (p. 120). [61] See, e.g., the references cited in note 25 above.

[62] Jeremy Goldberg thinks that Coventry's ordinances of 1492 may have been shaped by the Lollard sentiments or sympathies of members of the city council (personal communication).

[63] For social regulation and Lollardy in the Berks. manors of Cookham and Bray, around Maidenhead, during the later fifteenth and early sixteenth centuries, see Mattingly, "Cookham, Bray and Isleworth Hundreds."

[64] E.g., jurors in the manor court of Chesham Higham and Chesham Bury, Bucks. presented several fellow residents for holding Lollard views between 1532 and 1535, and a few people were burned for heresy (Bucks. RO D/BASM 18/202–7). See also Spufford, ed., *The World of Rural Dissenters*, esp. ch. 7.

made by men deeply influenced by the ideas of Christian humanism.[65] Many humanists tried deliberately to gain positions of power within the government of their country or city-state in order to put their radical social goals into practice, often with a particular emphasis upon the problems of poverty. The "commonwealth" ideas proposed during Edward VI's reign by Protestant humanists linked to the royal council emphasized the king's and Parliament's duty to pursue social and economic equity as well as spiritual truth. This combination of a clear image of what society should be like and an emphasis on control and guidance from more powerful members of the commonwealth echoes some of the statements made in local courts from the 1460s onwards by jurors reporting offences in the Disorder cluster.

Yet within smaller communities, the contribution of such men was generally far more muted, perhaps because they lacked the authority to impose their own opinions upon their more conservative fellows. This is illustrated by the 1549 ordinances of the newly incorporated market town of Saffron Walden, Essex, one of the communities analyzed in Chapters 3, 6, and 7. The orders were written almost certainly by Sir Thomas Smith, the treasurer of the new civic body as well as an advisor to Edward VI and a noted humanist author.[66] Although we see some humanistic uses of language, the ordinances make clear that older social values were being appropriated and modified, not discarded. The statement begins by stressing the importance of harmony and cooperation. All members of the corporation were encouraged to be "knit and conjoined as it were in one knot of mutual love and correspondent hearty good wills, that the prosperity and flourishing wealth of the one may be the joy, hearty desire and comfort of the other, and the hindrance, displeasure and decaying of the one may be an equal grief and sorrow to the other."[67] The ordinances speak also of order. The social hierarchy will be promoted by "every man ... using himself and doing according as his estate requireth and so duly and uprightly walking in his vocation and calling"; all ordinary people were enjoined

---

[65] The goal of moral reformation was the creation of a godly society (see Todd, *Christian Humanism*, esp. ch. 2). For humanists' concern with poverty, see, e.g., More's *Utopia* and Vives's "De Subventione Pauperum" (in *Some Early Tracts on Poor Relief*, pp. 1–31). For attempts to shape policy in England, see Elton, "An Early Tudor Poor Law," Guy, *The Public Career of Sir Thomas More*, pp. 151–6 (on Christopher St. German), and Slack, "Social Policy and the Constraints of Government." For Augsburg, Nuremburg, and Ypres, see Ashley, *An Introduction to English Economic History and Theory*, vol. II, pp. 340–7, and *Some Early Tracts on Poor Relief*, pp. 32–79; for Lyon, see Davis, "Poor Relief, Humanism, and Heresy."

[66] Dewar, *Sir Thomas Smith*, and Smith's *De Republica Anglorum*.

[67] Essex RO T/A 104/1, for this and all subsequent references to the ordinances.

to be "obedient, loving and assistant unto their heads in all due and lawful their proceedings and affairs, with all hearty favor, obeisance and good will." Attention is given to the poor, but in a curiously old-fashioned way, one that shows none of the normal humanist commitment to tackling the root causes of destitution. The ordinances merely stipulate that because "we see by daily experience that many a man either by God's hand and provision, by sickness and impotency, by fire, robbing, or by some other unfortunate losses and casual means cometh sometime to extreme poverty and necessity, though peradventure whilst he was able to shift for himself and in his most prosperity he would little have thought to have had any such need," all the common councilors were to contribute money each quarter to be used towards the relief of those struck by unexpected misfortune.

The framers of an official Protestant ideology and church within the English context during Edward VI's reign and the early years of Elizabeth's were acutely aware of the need to demonstrate that their faith and social vision could be put into practice, creating a more truly Christian community than was found under the Roman church. In reading the works of "the Fathers and early writers of the reformed English Church" as published by the Parker Society, for example, one is struck by their eagerness to demonstrate in concrete terms what a (Protestant) society should be like, in both spiritual and behavioral ways.[68] In the short term, however, the bishops were unable to implement many of their social goals. The need to institutionalize their new church, the bitter disputes over divergent beliefs within it, and the struggle against continuing Catholic/traditional ideology among some of the lesser clergy and the laity was too great: the church's leaders lacked the energy and the resources to tackle social wrongdoing in an aggressive manner as well.[69]

As the Elizabethan church assumed its mature form, it worked hard to educate the laity about how to lead a moral life in the world. This took the direct form of homilies (and in some parishes sermons) on such subjects as whoredom and adultery, gluttony and drunkenness, and idleness and was reinforced by the church's control over many forms of

---

[68] E.g., Becon, *The Catechism* and his *Prayers and Other Pieces*, Sandys, *The Sermons*, and Woolton, *The Christian Manual*. An influential continental parallel, Martin Bucer's *De Regno Christi*, provides a particularly effective illustration of this point (in *Melanchthon and Bucer*), a comparison suggested by Margo Todd.

[69] Wenig, "The Ecclesiastical Vision and Pastoral Achievements of the Progressive Bishops." For the response of the Scottish Presbyterian movement to precisely these shortcomings, see Margo Todd's forthcoming study.

education and communication, both oral and written.[70] As the result of such efforts church-going members of the generations maturing after c. 1560 – a group that presumably included the great majority of local court jurors – may well have internalized Christian ethics more fully than had been true in the past, or at least been more fully persuaded that each individual bore the responsibility for implementing those moral precepts. The church courts, relying heavily upon the reports furnished by lay officials from the parishes, enforced these standards. A moral stance based upon the church's teachings could join with practical concerns about order and the poor during the years around 1600 to trigger and justify social regulation even in communities untouched by Puritanism, as Ingram has argued.[71]

It was, however, among some of the most committed Puritan ministers and lay people that we find a rather different vision of social morality. In a genuinely Christian community, they argued, all residents should be required to honor God's wishes concerning behavior, obedience, and idleness; by doing so, they would manifest His glory. While their understanding of ideal conduct might differ little from mainstream members of the Church of England, opposition to wrongdoing was placed within a more highly charged social and religious context. More important was the determination of many ardent Puritans to implement their ideal. The number of deeply motivated reformers within a community might be small, but their conviction and self-assurance and in some cases their personal charisma often persuaded others to cooperate with their views about social issues. Their influence was commonly increased by a powerful rhetoric, in speech and in print, while their practical ability to enforce proper conduct was enhanced by their willingness to use physical punishment against miscreants, an attitude probably affected by their thorough familiarity with the Old Testament.[72]

Whereas the impact of Puritan attitudes towards social behavior was felt most strongly after 1580, the new intensity had started to appear within certain local communities several decades earlier. For an example of moral reprobation that could have flowed from the lips of the most militant seventeenth-century Puritan, consider this order from the town book of (Kingston upon) Hull in 1563 – one in which righteous indignation threatens to overcome clarity:

For as much as in every well ordered common wealth most principally is sought out the heinous offenders and insensible persons which be delighted in drunkeness, excess, riot, whoredom, wantonness, lightness, idleness, and

---

[70] *Certaine Sermons and Homilies*, vol. I, pp. 78–89, and vol. II, pp. 94–101, 249–55, and 154–66.   [71] See the Introduction, above.
[72] This point was kindly suggested to me by John Craig.

scolding, with such like, that they by reasonable and politic laws and ordinances may be corrected, made sensible, and brought to good order, we
therefore, the said Mayor, Aldermen, and Burgesses, knowing nothing more
convenient, needful, or requisite than to redress, supplant, or pluck up these
great infections and enormities ... , do with one assent ... ordain that ... no
manner of person or persons within this town or any the liberties of the same be
so hardy to commit any whoredom, fornication, or adultery nor use or exercise
him self in excessive drinking, riot, dispending his or their time in idleness,
wantonness, lightness, scolding, or maliciously blaspheming the name of God,
to the great provocation or kindling of God's wrath against this town, upon
pain that every one offending contrary to the tenor and effect of this ordinance
... be punished and made an example to all others, whether it be by cart,
tumbrel, cookstool, the stocks, pillory, or otherwise by imprisonment.[73]

While we cannot be certain who was responsible for this order, it is
presumably no coincidence that the town corporation had recently
persuaded Melchior Smith, a zealous reformed preacher, to come from
Boston to take the living of Hull's Holy Trinity church.[74]

Though many lay leaders and their moderate clerical brethren in
Hull and other English communities would probably have found the
tone of this order somewhat excessive, they may have been willing to
cooperate with the social goals of fervent Puritan leaders precisely
because they confronted directly the practical problems troubling local
villages and towns. The entire package of rigorous Calvinist theology
and social ideology went beyond what most people were willing to
accept, but they were frequently prepared to work with dedicated
Puritan ministers and fellow citizens in tackling social problems that
everyone agreed had to be addressed.[75] When, however, these ideologically-driven leaders moved away, died, or became discouraged about
moral reform, the level of enthusiasm left among the others was often
revealed to be far lower. This reinforced the well-established pattern
whereby efforts at social reform were quietly dropped within a few
decades after their inception.

In seeking to understand the factors that contributed to a concern
with social regulation, we must therefore recognize zealous Puritans as

[73] Kingston upon Hull City RO BRB 2, fol. 49. Fear of God's wrath because of social
misconduct was not limited to Puritans or even to Protestants, however. As early as
1383 the City of London had justified a crack-down on fornication and adultery in
similar terms, deciding to "purge their City from such filthiness, lest through God's
vengeance, either the pestilence or sword should happen to them, or that the earth
should swallow them" (Stow, *A Survey of London*, vol. I, pp. 189–90).

[74] *VCH York, East Riding*, vol. I, p. 95. I am grateful to Conrad Russell for telling me of
Smith's appointment.

[75] See, e.g., Elizabethan Norwich: McClendon, "Religious Change and the Magisterial
Ethos" and "Religion and the Politics of Order." I appreciate Dr. McClendon's permission to use and cite these studies.

dynamic – if not essential – players. Puritan reformers did not enter the scene until a century after the patterns of active social regulation were becoming established, and even in the later sixteenth and seventeenth centuries they appeared on stage only in certain settings. (Additional local studies are needed to determine what fraction of those places concerned with social regulation around 1600 were motivated by Puritan goals.) When committed Puritans took part, however, supervision of misconduct was implemented with a degree of fervor and confidence rarely found in communities motivated solely by practical factors and/or general Christian ethics. While late Elizabethan and early Stuart communities would certainly have controlled behavior if the Puritan movement had never developed, some of them would have done so with less conviction and energy. This assessment accords with Wrightson's emphasis upon the importance of Puritan leaders to social reform in certain settings.[76]

The social costs of aggressive regulation

But a peculiar irony must be noted. Strenuous and often intrusive local campaigns to curtail misbehavior in the decades around 1600, led in nearly all cases by Puritans, were disruptive of precisely those values that had previously lain at the core of the social thinking of local communities: harmony, order, and some accommodation to the needs of the poor were all shattered at least temporarily by aggressive social regulation. In the past when local jurors had addressed misconduct, they knew that the central goals enjoyed considerable support within the community. In the later fifteenth century, for instance, most established families probably agreed that the kinds of offences reported were indeed threats to local well-being. Many of the miscreants were outsiders, often adolescents/young adults or landless laborers who could readily be defined as "other," distanced from the more permanent residents. If wrongdoers failed to conform to local standards, they could readily be evicted from the community.

Circumstances had changed in several respects by the end of Elizabeth's reign and even more so by the early seventeenth century. Many of the vigorous assaults upon social misbehavior initiated by Puritans included a broader range of issues than were addressed during the fifteenth and most of the sixteenth centuries. This occurred in part through defining new kinds of activities as wrong – placing outside the

---

[76] E.g., in his "Postscript" to the revised edition of Wrightson and Levine, *Poverty and Piety*.

pale of legitimate conduct behaviors that had been acceptable before. Commonly included were aspects of popular culture, like seasonal festivals or dancing, and leisure activities on Sundays, like drinking or engaging in sports.[77] In some settings the campaign also expanded the boundaries of sexual misconduct, so that pregnant brides and their husbands were now prosecuted for pre-marital sexual activity which before had been tolerated so long as the couple was betrothed when they began sexual relations and were officially married before the baby was born. Further, in most places a far higher fraction of those reported for misbehavior around 1600 were residents than had been true in the fifteenth and earlier sixteenth centuries. These people, some of whom were deeply rooted in the community, were now being treated as "other" due to their conduct and often their poverty as well. Local studies suggest that zealous Puritan reformers were prepared to be far more inquisitive and interfering than their predecessors, even when their activity was keenly resented: earning the hostility of one's neighbors on God's behalf was for them a badge of spiritual honor. As Wrightson has commented, Puritans were ultimately defined by their willingness to engage in conflict with others: they were not just godly people but godly activists.[78]

All these changes weakened or destroyed at least in the short term the very social values that had previously supported and justified regulation of conduct. Local harmony was acutely threatened by attempts on the part of some members of the community to reform the leisure-time activities of their fellows and to stigmatize customary practices like sexual activity after betrothal. In such settings we find examples of Wrightson's "two concepts of order," with local officials caught between the instructions handed to them by highly motivated leaders above them and widespread acceptance of many of these forms of popular culture beneath them. In some cases the non-godly but previously integrated members of the community whose actions were now under moral/religious fire launched their own counter-attacks. Since they commonly lacked access to political and legal power, they used traditional but highly effective forms of social warfare such as witty and scurrilous satires against their opponents, spread through being read aloud in alehouses or posted in public places.[79] Yet in the

---

[77] Disputes over these activities came to a head with the royal issuance of the Book of Sports in 1617–18, becoming even more virulent with its successor of 1633.

[78] In his "Postscript" to the revised edition of Wrightson and Levine, *Poverty and Piety*, p. 206.

[79] E.g., Underdown, *Fire from Heaven*, esp. pp. 147–66, and Richard Dean Smith, "Social Reform in an Urban Context."

eyes of those propelled by a sense of Puritan morality, a temporary loss in local harmony was a small price to pay for the improvement in the community's adherence to godly norms. Order too might be sacrificed for the higher moral and religious good. The disruptions caused by an energetic campaign of social correction could certainly jar the stability of the community, leading to verbal or even physical attacks upon those spearheading the effort and to abuse of the courts through which it was implemented. Finally, because aggressive efforts to correct wrongdoing frequently included a strong emphasis upon the misconduct of the local poor, they added new rancor to the split that had been developing across the later fifteenth and sixteenth centuries with respect to poverty and how it should be handled. Although many Puritans were themselves generous contributors to institutionalized forms of relief and improvement for the poor, whether parish systems or private charitable foundations, they were often uneasy about aid given from one individual to another and felt that no support should be awarded to idlers or sinners, on both spiritual and practical grounds. Yet they commonly lived alongside people who still felt a Christian obligation to assist the needy on a personal basis even if the latter were shiftless and morally weak.

These observations confirm the choice of 1600 as a terminus for this study. The evidence presented here establishes without doubt that concern about social misbehavior during the closing years of Elizabeth's reign was a later stage in a long history. Even without Puritans, there would certainly have been considerable attention to wrongdoing at the end of the sixteenth century, due to the demographic and economic pressures of those decades, enhanced political and legal power at the national and county levels, and lay acceptance of the moral teachings of the Church of England. Yet it is also indisputable that by 1600 some communities with an activist Puritan presence were operating on a rather different basis. In these settings, Puritan beliefs provided a religiously defined vision of society together with a powerful incentive to act – a determination to enforce godly behavior even if such reform undercut the social goals that had previously justified attempts to limit wrongdoing.

Conclusion: social regulation and the transition from medieval to early modern England

To resolve the historiographic debates summarized in the Introduction, this study has explored four central questions concerning social regulation in England between 1370 and 1600. It began by describing the mechanisms through which misconduct could be addressed, looking at the role of informal and formal institutions and situating the courts within a wider setting for the resolution of conflicts. This analysis traced changes over time in the distribution of responsibility between local courts and those operating at an intermediate level (the church courts and county Sessions of the Peace), identified the essential part played by the thousands of public courts held within England's villages, market centers, and hundreds, and highlighted the personal agency of the jurors who dominated those institutions. Marked contrasts between the levels of activity of sixteenth-century local courts in accordance with their geographic location were also revealed. Secondly, the project has established in a quantified fashion the history of social regulation as handled by the lesser public courts. By analyzing eleven types of misconduct, it documented a general increase in concern with wrongdoing across the fifteenth and sixteenth centuries while revealing significant chronological variations in the specific sorts of offences that caused anxiety, in the gender of those reported, and in the procedures and punishments employed. A third question focused upon the attitudes that shaped local responses to misbehavior. Here we saw a set of core values held widely throughout society: preserving harmonious and tranquil relationships within a commuity; enforcing good order, control, and discipline; and developing some kind of appropriate response to the various kinds of poor people. Beneath those concerns lay a series of more focused social and economic issues, including the importance of maintaining one's personal credit or good

reputation, controlling the labor force, and supervising especially closely the actions of those groups of people whose presence was thought to
imperil community well-being (young people, outsiders, the poor, and
in some periods and settings independently employed or unmarried
women).

Lastly, this book has investigated the factors that influenced a community's problems with and reactions to misbehavior. Here too major
contrasts were seen over time. During the fifteenth century, those
places concerned with wrongdoing displayed distinctive geographic,
demographic, and economic characteristics and often had a tradition of
local "political" activity. By the end of the sixteenth century, however,
social regulation had spread to a far more diverse array of places,
among which only population pressure and rising numbers of poor
people appear as common features. Around 1600 other factors were
playing a more significant part: the expansion of government at the
county and national levels, a modified ideological formulation by the
educated elite concerning government and society, and the effective-
ness of the Church of England in communicating its moral teachings
and persuading the laity to accept responsibility for them. In some
communities these considerations were joined by the determination of
ardent Puritans to impose godly behavior upon all residents. (Further
local studies are needed to establish what fraction of those places
concerned about wrongdoing in the decades around 1600 were motivated solely by a mixture of practical and general ethical concerns and
which were moved by Puritan goals as well.) This study has emphasized the social costs that accompanied aggressive control over wrongdoing. By insisting upon righteous conduct and condemning behaviors
that had traditionally been regarded as acceptable, zealous Puritans
destroyed the consensus that had previously supported and justified
regulation.

Though it can no longer be argued that Puritanism was responsible
for social regulation in early modern England, is it possible that a very
different relationship linked Puritanism and concern with misconduct?
We have seen that most of the communities that reported a broad array
of behavioral offences during the later fifteenth century possessed some
common features, such as being a market center, located on a major
transportation route, and/or having some kind of manufacturing activity, especially production of woolen cloth. For those few places actively
troubled by social wrongdoing between 1460 and 1500 whose religious
history I have been able to trace in detail, most were receptive to early
Protestant views between c. 1530 and 1560 and contained a vigorous

Puritan presence by the end of the sixteenth century.[1] The kinds of practical characteristics that accentuated concern with wrongdoing prior to 1500 made those communities especially likely to hear about new religious ideas and may well have predisposed them to be open to such beliefs.[2] It thus seems clear that recent efforts to reassess the nature and impact of Puritanism could profitably be extended to include a return to the debate initiated by Marx, Weber, and Tawney over the relation between economic patterns, religious ideology, and social responses.[3] In particular, we need to look again at the contexts within which Puritanism flourished, and why, and to explore the consequences of energetic Puritan efforts to implement their vision of a godly Christian community.

Previous assumptions about the history and causes of social regulation illustrate the narrowed vision caused by the system of periodization within which nearly all scholars working in the twentieth century were educated, one that blinds us to many of the key features of the transition from medieval to early modern patterns.[4] As the result of positivist conceptions of history during the middle and later nineteenth century, European history and culture came to be divided into a set progression of periods, defined in terms of some mixture of ideas and institutions and separated by clear chronological boundaries. Since academic disciplines were themselves becoming institutionalized in the later nineteenth century, each one adopting rather self-conscious

---

[1] I had hoped to pursue this issue through secondary studies of the 255 places examined in Chapters 3, 6, and 7, but very few provided full enough information about the community's religious history between 1520 and 1600 to make the study possible. Careful analysis of the wills, churchwardens' accounts, and other local records on which this assessment rests must therefore be left to others.

[2] This idea parallels Spufford's emphasis on the ease of communication between areas of rural industry (in *The World of Rural Dissenters*, ch. 1) and Morrill's suggestion that the concentration of Puritanism in clothing regions may have stemmed in part from their location on routes of trade and their contact with London, as well as from "the intrinsic appeal of Puritan discipline and biblicism within the context of cloth working" (in "The Ecology of Allegiance," p. 462).

[3] See, e.g., Lake, "Calvinism and the English Church" and *Anglicans and Puritans?*, Todd, ed., *Reformation to Revolution*, Durston and Eales, eds., *The Culture of English Puritanism*, and Lamont, *Puritanism and Historical Controversy*. For the earlier debate, see the Introduction, section one above.

[4] The term "early modern" has been deliberately used in this study and the work of many other scholars in the 1990s because it avoids the unduly narrow concentration upon certain topics and limited groups of people suggested by the term "Renaissance and Reformation" as well as the privileging of political events at the level of the monarchy suggested by "Tudor/Stuart."

forms of precise scholarship, contemporary beliefs about the relevance of periodization and the particular eras chosen became embedded within the structure of universities in Europe and its current and former colonies. Because we were trained to accept a major break in English life and culture with the accession of Henry Tudor to the throne – the end of the Middle Ages and beginning of the Renaissance and Reformation period – many scholars lack a clear understanding of the transition that occurred between the plague of 1348–9 and the seventeenth century. For those medievalists who received little instruction concerning the era after 1485, it is tempting to assume that because the quality of the records declines after the mid-fourteenth century, they may legitimately concentrate attention on the pre-plague period; it is only recently that the fifteenth century has started to attract its share of scholarly attention. Some early modernists, minimally educated about the medieval past, continue to accept a simplistic and often inaccurate picture of the fifteenth century as a time of decline and weakness, a conveniently dismal background against which the achievements of the Tudor period stand out in vivid color.

Inherited notions of historical periodization have thus obscured the many areas of continuity as well as the nature of the changes that marked the medieval to early modern transition. The account of social regulation provided here forms one strand within a more general explanation of that process. To summarize my own formulation, the earliest and most fundamental set of transformations occurred between 1348–9 and c. 1460 in the demographic, economic, and social infrastructure. An exogenous factor, the initial outbreak of plague, provided a sharp jolt to the demographic underpinnings of society; its successors contributed to a low and probably gradually declining population until somewhere around 1520. These circumstances in turn initiated rapid economic and social change. Between c. 1460 and 1560, new patterns began to appear in the superstructure – in government, law, and ideas, most of them given their particular form by further economic and social dislocations. Dramatic alterations in religion and culture, shaped to a large extent by new beliefs introduced from the continent, were relatively late arrivals within this process. The more stable Elizabethan era saw the working through and resolution of many of the tensions that resulted from these changes, including the formulation of a revised, Protestant English ideology. Yet by 1603 the transition was still not complete. Ongoing demographic pressure and rapid economic change created unfamiliar practical problems at the same time that some people, especially rigorous Puritans and dedicated Arminians, refused to accommodate themselves to the moderate compromise. The political, social, and ideological upheavals of the mid- and later seventeenth century may therefore be regarded as the final stages of the medieval to early modern transition. It is hoped that the present study has untangled at least one set of threads within the complex weave of continuity and change that form the rich fabric of the transitional period.

Appendices

Appendix 1.1
Urban records used to trace responses to misbehavior, 1370–1599

Method

Evidence was sampled from two of the six communities classified here as cities and from nineteen of the thirty-two towns, between 1370 and 1599 (see the Notes below for the criteria used to define these categories and the records used to assign communities to them). The dates indicate the earliest and latest records examined for this project. The documents consulted were of two different types: (1) "Assembly Books," including any kind of minute book, notes of meetings of mayor and aldermen, town orders/ordinances, or other events/decisions at assemblies of local officials that document concern with social behavior (except for financial accounts); and (2) the regular proceedings of public courts, equivalent to the records used in Chapter 3 for the courts of villages and market centers. Since the policies and orders recorded in the "Assembly Books" were not necessarily enforced by the courts, the patterns described on the basis of this evidence may suggest earlier and/or more pronounced concern than is seen in the lesser public courts or the intermediate-level bodies.

Urban records used*

Abbreviations used in references:

A[O] = Archive(s) [Office]
RO   = Record Office

1. Berks., Reading, 1431–1598, town. Borough (Corporation) Diary, Berks. RO R/AC 1/1/1.
2. Devon, (Great) Totnes, 1389–1525, town. Manor court rolls, Devon RO 1579 A/9/9–12, 17, 22–23, 25–26, and 29.
3. Essex, Colchester, 1372–9 and 1580–9, town. *Court Rolls of the Borough of*

Colchester, vol. 3, 1372–9, ed. I. H. Jeayes (Colchester, 1941); borough court rolls, 1580–9, Essex RO Colchester Borough Court Rolls 144–154. I am grateful to Richard Dean Smith for the later information and references.

4. Gloucs., Bristol, 1374–1599, city. *The Great Red Book of Bristol*, ed. E. W. W. Veale, Text, pt. 1, Bristol Rec. Soc., vol. 4 (Bristol, 1933); *The Ordinances of Bristol, 1506–98*, ed. Maureen Stanford, Bristol Rec. Soc. Publs., vol. 41 (Gloucester, 1990).

5. Gloucs., Gloucester, 1486–1599, town. "Red Book" (Memoranda) of Borough, Gloucs. RO GBR B2/1.

6. Hants., Southampton, 1514–99, town. *Court Leet Records*, vol. 1, pt. 1, 1550–77, and pt. 2, 1578–1602, ed. F. J. C. Hearnshaw and D. M. Hearnshaw, Southampton Rec. Soc. Publs., vols. 1 and 2 (Southampton, 1905–6); and *The Third Book of Remembrance of Southampton, 1514–1602*, vols. 1–4, Southampton Rec. Soc., vol. 32 (Southampton, 1932–79).

7. Hants., Winchester, 1552–99, town. First Book of Ordinances, Hants. RO W/B1/1.

8. Heref., Hereford, 1441–1597, town. Heref. RO Hereford City Records, Bound Volumes, no. I (Customs of Hereford), and Tourns, 1499–1537 and 1541–58; "Hereford City Records," Hist. MSS Comm., 13th Rept., App., Pt. 4 (London, 1892).

9. Kent, Maidstone, 1382–1522 and 1561–99, town. Manor court rolls, Lambeth Pal. Libr., London, ED 619–20, 632–633, 635–636, 638–839, 649, 651, and 655, and borough records in *Records of Maidstone, Being Selections from Documents in the Possession of the Corporation*, ed. K. S. Martin (Maidstone, 1926).

10. Leics., Leicester, 1370–1599, town. *Records of the Borough of Leicester*, ed. Mary Bateson. Vol. 2, 1327–1509 (London, 1901), and vol. 3, 1509–1603 (Cambridge, 1905).

11. Lincs., Lincoln, 1511–99, town. City Minute Books, Lincs. AO L1/1/1/1–3, and "The Manuscripts of the Corporation of Lincoln," Hist. MSS Comm., 14th Rept., App., pt. 8 (London, 1895).

12. Norf., Great Yarmouth, 1390–1592, town. Borough court rolls, Norf. RO Y/C4/103–105, 131, 133, 151, 153, 176, 178, 195, 197, 234–235, 257, 259, 286, and 288.

13. Notts., Nottingham, 1370–1599, town. *Records of the Borough of Nottingham*, vols. 1–4 (London, 1882–9).

14. Shrops., Shrewsbury, 1389–1592, town. Great Court rolls, Shrops. RO 3365/798–9, 802, 856, 862, 911, 955, 1018, 1022, 1055–6, 1112, and 1116.

15. Suff., Bury St. Edmunds, 1570–5, town. Town Book, Suff. RO, Bury St. Edmunds, C 2/1.

16. War., Coventry, 1420–1555, town. *The Coventry Leet Book or Mayor's Register*, 4 vols., ed. Mary D. Harris (EETS, Orig. Ser. vols. 134–5, 138, and 146 (London, 1907–1913).

17. Wilts., Salisbury, 1387–1599, town. General Entry Books, Wilts. RO G23/1/1–3.

18. Worcs., Worcester, 1532–99, town. Worcs. RO, St. Helens, Worcester City Records, Frank Pledge, Council of Marches, and Army Musters Books 1 and 2.

19. Yorks., York, 1461–1591, city. *The York House Books, 1461–1490*, ed. Lorraine C. Attreed (Stroud, 1991); *York Civic Records*, vols. 2–8, ed. Angelo Raine, Yorks. Archaeol. Soc. Rec. Ser., vols. 103, 106, 108, 110, 112, 115, and 119

(1940/1–1952/3); and *York Civic Records*, vol. 9, ed. Deborah Sutton, Yorks. Archaeol. Soc. Rec. Ser., vol. 138 (1976/8).
20. East Yorks., Beverley, 1382–1599, town. *Beverley Town Documents*, ed. Arthur F. Leach, Selden Soc., vol. 14 (London, 1900); *Beverley Borough Records, 1575–1821*, ed. J. Dennett, Yorks. Archaeol. Soc. Rec. Ser., vol. 84 (Wakefield, 1933); and *Report on the Manuscripts of the Corporation of Beverley*, Hist. MSS Comm. (London, 1900).
21. East Yorks., (Kingston upon) Hull, 1445–1599, town. Bench Books (Minutes of Meetings of Mayor and Aldermen), Kingston upon Hull City RO BRB 1–2.

Notes

Type of community. Communities have been classified as Cities or Towns according to the criteria listed below.

City = 6 places (of which 2 are studied here) that were the leading communities in terms of wealth and/or population as listed on the majority of the following records: the Subsidy of 1334, the Poll Tax of 1377, the Subsidy of 1524/5, and the Hearth Tax of 1662. Apart from London, most of these cities had taxable wealths of £1,200–1,900 in 1334 and £400–750 in 1524/5; the range of their total estimated population was 6,000–14,000 in 1377 and 6,000–9,000 in 1524/5. (Information drawn from Appendices 1–4 of Alan Dyer, *Decline and Growth in English Towns*.) Includes *Bristol, Exeter, London, Newcastle (upon Tyne), Norwich, and *York. Asterisks mark places analyzed here.

Town = the 32 next wealthiest or most populous places (of which 19 are studied here). These were included among the top 20 places for wealth and/or population on any one of the individual tax records listed above, or were among the top 25 places on two or more of the records. Most of these towns had taxable wealths of £400–1,000 in 1334 and £100–300 in 1524/5; the range of their total estimated population was 3,000–5,600 in 1377 and 3,000–5,000 in 1524/5. Includes *Beverley, Boston, *Bury St. Edmunds, Cambridge, Canterbury, Chester, *Colchester, *Coventry, *Gloucester, *Great Yarmouth, *Hereford, *(Kingston upon) Hull, Ipswich, Lavenham, *Leicester, *Lincoln, Lynn, *Maidstone, Newbury, *Nottingham, Oxford, Plymouth, Portsmouth, *Reading, Rochester, *Salisbury, *Shrewsbury, *Southampton, St. Albans, *Totnes, *Winchester, and *Worcester. Asterisks mark places analyzed here.

Appendix 1.2
Church court records used to trace responses to misbehavior, 1435–1599

Method

The records of twenty-eight church courts between 1435 and 1599 were sampled. Within the documents consulted, I noted only public business, not private suits between parties, during selected one-year intervals by decade. The dates are those of the specific records examined for this project. Because the number of records used is small prior to around 1560, the earlier patterns described on the basis of this evidence must be regarded as tentative.

Church court records used

Abbreviations used in references:

A[O] = Archive(s) [Office]
RO   = Record Office

1. (Berks.) Archdeaconry of Berkshire. Visitation Book, 1560–2, Berks. RO D/A 2 e 5; Act Book, 1583, Berks. RO D/A 2 e 1.
2. (Bucks.) Archdeaconry of Buckingham. Visitation Book, 1489–95, Bucks. RO D/A/V 1a and *The Courts of the Archdeaconry of Buckingham, 1483–1523,* ed. E. M. Ivey, Bucks. Rec. Soc., vol. 19 (1975); Act Book, 1521, Bucks. RO D/A/C 1a and *The Courts of the Archdeaconry of Buckingham, 1483–1523;* Visitation Book, Detecta, 1584–6, Bucks. RO D/A/V 1b.
3. (Ches.) Diocese of Chester. Archbishop's Visitation, Act Book, 1578–9, Borthwick Institute, York, V.1578–9/CB.2, and Comperta and Detecta, Borthwick Institute V.1578–9/C.B.3; Visitation Correction Book, 1581–2, Ches. RO EDV 1/6d. See also: (Yorks. and Ches.) Dioceses of York and Chester.
4. (Ches. and Lancs.) Court of High Commission. Proceedings, 1543, Ches. RO EDA 12/1; 1562–5, Ches. RO EDA 12/2.
5. (Dorset) Wimborne Minster Parish, Peculiar Court. Visitation Presentments, 1591–7, Dorset RO PE/WM CP 2/10.

6. (Durham) Diocese of Durham. Detecta, Comperta, and Injunctions, 1578–80, *Injunctions and Other Ecclesiastical Proceedings of Richard Barnes, Bishop of Durham, from 1575 to 1587*. Publs. of the Surtees Soc., vol. 22 (1850).

7. (Durham) Prior of Durham, Court of Durham. Court Books, 1435–9 and 1496–8, Durham Univ. Libr., Archs. and Spec. Colls., The Prior's Kitchen, DCD Prior's Court of Durham.

8. (Essex) Archdeaconry of Essex, cases pertaining to parishes of Havering-atte-Bower, Hornchurch, and Romford. Act Books, 1563–99, Essex RO D/AEA 2–29, *passim*.

9. (Gloucs.) Diocese of Gloucester. Visitation Book, 1548, Gloucs. RO GDR 4; Presentments, 1563, Gloucs. RO GDR 20.

10. (Hants.) Diocese of Winchester. Visitation Book, 1517–18, Hants. RO 21M65/B1/1; Act Book, 1586–7, Hants. RO 21M65/C1/23/1; Act Book, 1593–4, Hants. RO 21M65/C1/25.

11. (Heref.) Diocese of Hereford. Act Books, 1442–3 and 1468–9, Heref. RO Diocese of Hereford Court Books, Acts of Office, Books 2 and 8.

12. (Kent) Archdiocese of Canterbury. Visitation of Kent, 1511–12, *Kentish Visitations of Archbishop William Warham and His Deputies, 1511–12*, ed. K. L. Wood-Legh, Kent Archaeol. Soc., Kent Rec., vol. 24 (1984).

 – (Lancs.) See: (Ches. and Lancs.) Court of High Commission.

13. (Leics.) Archdeaconry of Leicester. Act Books, 1561–2, Leics. RO 1 D41/13/3; 1593–4, Leics. RO 1 D 41/13/19.

14. (Lincs.) Diocese of Lincoln. Court Book, 1446–9, Lincs. AO Lincoln Diocesan Records Cj.O; Visitation Books, 1473, Lincs. AO Lincoln Diocesan Records Vj.4; Visitation Books, 1517–20, Lincs. AO Vj.7; *Visitations in the Diocese of Lincoln, 1517–1531*, vols. 1–2, ed. A. Hamilton Thompson, Publs. of the Lincoln Rec. Soc., vols. 33 and 37 (1940 and 1947); Presentments, c. 1583 and 1595, Lincs. AO Lincoln Diocesan Records Ch.P. 1.

15. (Notts.) Archdeaconry of Nottingham. Register (transcript), 1565–70, Notts. AO DDTS 14/26/1; Register (transcript), 1574–8, Notts. AO DDTS 14/26/2; Presentment Bills, 1587 and 1589, Nottingham Univ. Libr., MSS Department PB 292/1587 and 1589; Register (transcript), 1595–7, Notts. AO DDTS 14/26/6.

16. (Oxon.) Archdeaconry of Oxford. Act Book, 1584, *The Archdeacon's Court: Liber Actorum, 1584*, ed. E. R. Brinkworth, 2 vols., Oxon. Rec. Soc., vols. 22 and 23 (1942).

17. (Shrops. and Staffs.) Archdeaconries of Salop. and Stafford. Libri Clerici from Visitations, with Comperta, 1559/60 and 1576, Lichfield Joint RO B/V/1/3 and 10.

18. (Som.) Diocese of Bath and Wells. Comperta Book, 1547, Som. RO D/D/Ca 17; Visitation Book, 1552, Som. RO D/D/Ca 20; Visitation Comperta, 1557, Som. RO D/D/Ca 27; Visitation Comperta, 1568, Som. RO D/D/Ca 40; Visitation Presentments, c. 1594, Som. RO D/D/Ca 98.

19. (Staffs.) Archdeaconry of Stafford. Libri Clerici from Visitations, with Comperta, 1558, 1566–75, 1584, and c. 1580–90, Lichfield Joint RO B/V/1/2, 6, 17, and 22. See also: (Shrops. and Staffs.) Archdeaconries of Salop. and Stafford.

20. (Suff.) Deanery of South Elmham. Court Book, 1525–40, Suff. RO, Ipswich, IC/AA2/6A.

21. (Surrey) Archdeaconry of Surrey. Visitation and Act Book, 1567–70, Hants. RO 21M65/B1/9.
22. (Wilts.) Archdeaconry of Wiltshire. Detecta Book, 1586–99, Wilts. RO D3/7.
23. (Wilts.) Diocese of Salisbury. Visitation Detecta Book, 1550 and 1553, Wilts. RO D1/43/1; Metropolitan Visitation Detecta Book, 1584, Wilts. RO D1/43/5.
24. (Yorks.) Archdiocese of York, Archbishop's Court of York. Cause Papers, 1555 or 1556, 1566–7, 1595, and 1597, Borthwick Institute, York, CP.G 2038, CP.G 1276, CP.G 1305; CP.G 2579, and CP.G 2944.
25. (Yorks.) Court of High Commission. Act Book, 1562–5, Borthwick Institute, York, HC.AB.1; Cause Papers, 1566, Borthwick Institute HC.CP 1566/1; Act Book, 1572–4, Borthwick Institute HC.AB.7; Act Book, 1580–85, Borthwick Institute HC.AB.10; Cause Papers, 1590, 1594, and 1596–7, Borthwick Institute HC.CP. 1590/15, HC.CP. 1594/2–3; HC.CP. 1596/7, and HC.CP. 1597/3; Act Book, 1591–6, Borthwick Institute HC.AB.12.
26. (Yorks.) Dean and Chapter of York, Court. Cause Papers, 1553 and 1556, Borthwick Institute, York, D/C.CP 1553/1–2 and D/C.CP 1556/1.
27. (Yorks.) Diocese of York. Visitation Book, 1575, Borthwick Institute, York, V.1575/CB.1.
28. (Yorks. and Ches.) Dioceses of York and Chester. Archbishop's Visitation, Detecta, 1595–6, Borthwick Institute, York, V.1595–6/CB.3.

Appendix 1.3
Sessions of the Peace records used to trace responses to misbehavior, 1351–1599

Method

The records of twenty-eight Sessions of the Peace between 1351 and 1599 were sampled here, using the same method as described in Appendix 1.2 and with the same warning applying. The dates are those of the records examined for this project.

Sessions records used

Abbreviations used in references:
$$A[O] = Archive(s)\ [Office]$$
$$RO\ \ \ = Record\ Office$$

1. Cambs., Wisbech. Borough Sessions of Peace held by the Bishop of Ely's Justices, 1574 and 1586; Cambridge Univ. Libr. Ely Dioc. Rec. E 1/5/2 and E 1/6/8.
2. Ches., County Palatine. Quarter Sessions, 1559–99. *Quarter Sessions Records with Other Records of the Justices of the Peace for the County Palatine of Chester, 1559–1760*, ed. J. H. E. Bennett and J. C. Dewhurst, Rec. Soc. of Lancs. and Cheshire, vol. 94 (1940).
3. Dorset, Lyme Regis. Borough Quarter Sessions, 1578–98. Dorset RO DC/LRA4/1.
4. Essex, Colchester. Borough Sessions, 1580–9, Essex RO Colchester Borough Court Rolls 144–154, *passim*. I am grateful to Richard Dean Smith for this information and references.
5. Essex, county. Quarter Sessions, 1556–96, *passim*. Essex RO Q/SR 1–135, *passim*.
6. Hants., county. Quarter Sessions, 1559–77. Hants. RO Q3/1.
7. Heref., Hereford. City Quarter Sessions, 1475–1557 and 1579–99. (Worcs. and) Heref. RO Hereford City Records, Quarter Sessions, 1475–1535, 1535–57, and 1579–1605.
8. Herts., Hatfield. Borough Sessions, 1589–98. Herts. RO HAT/SR 1–10.

9. Kent, county. Quarter Sessions papers and indictments, 1594–8. Centre for Kentish Studies QM/SB 21–287, QM/SI 1593–1597, and QM/SO 1, *passim*.
10. Kent, Faversham. Borough Quarter Sessions, 1571 and 1586. Centre for Kentish Studies Fa/JQs 1 and 24.
11. Lancs., county. Quarter Sessions, 1590–9. *Lancashire Quarter Sessions Records*, vol. 1, 1590–1606, ed. James Tait, The Chetham Soc., New Ser., vol. 77, Manchester, 1917.
12. Lincs., county. Sessions of the Peace, 1360–75 and 1381–98. *Records of Some Sessions of the Peace in Lincolnshire, 1360–1375*, ed. Rosamond Sillem, Publs. of the Lincoln Rec. Soc., vol. 30 (Hereford, 1936), and *Records of Some Sessions of the Peace in Lincolnshire, 1381–96*, ed. Elisabeth G. Kimball, Publs. of the Lincoln Rec. Soc., vol. 49 (Hereford, 1955).
13. Lincs., Lincoln. City Sessions of the Peace, 1351–4. *Records of Some Sessions of the Peace in the City of Lincoln, 1351–4*, ed. Elisabeth G. Kimball, Lincoln Rec. Soc., vol. 65 (Lincoln, 1971).
14. Middx., county. Sessions, 1549–65, *passim*, and 1590–1. Greater London RO MJ/SR 5/1–126/23, *passim*, and 295.
15. Notts., Newark (-upon-Trent). Borough Quarter and Petty Sessions, 1579–88. Newark Museum D6.75/H1 and H16.
16. Notts., Nottingham. Borough Quarter Sessions, 1467–1575, *passim*. Notts. AO CA 1b–49, *passim*.
17. Shrops., Shrewsbury. Borough Quarter Sessions, 1594. Shrops. RO3365/2209.
18. Som., county. Quarter Sessions indictments, 1571 and 1593–5. Som. RO Q/SI 1–2.
19. Staffs., county. Quarter Sessions, 1581–97. Staffs. RO Q/SR 7–53, *passim*, and *The Staffordshire Quarter Sessions Rolls*, vols. 1–3, 1581–9, 1590–3, and 1594–7, ed. S. A. H. Burne, The William Salt Archaeol. Soc., 1931–3.
20. Suff., Ipswich. Borough Sessions of the Peace, 1458–1535. Suff. RO, Ipswich, C 8/1/5–29 and C 8/4/1.
21. Suff., Sudbury. Borough Sessions of the Peace, 1580–6. Suff. RO, Bury St. Edmunds, EE 501 C 141 B/1 and C 142 C/2.
22. Sussex, county. Quarter Sessions, 1594. East Sussex RO QR/E 1–2.
23. Sussex, Rye Hundred. Sessions of the Peace, 1546–96, *passim*. East Sussex RO Rye 1/1–6, *passim*.
24. Wilts., county. Quarter Sessions, 1563–92. Wilts. RO A1/150/1, and *Wiltshire County Records: Minutes of Proceedings in Sessions, 1563 and 1574 to 1592*, ed. H. C. Johnson, Wilts. Archaeol. and Natl. Hist. Soc., Recs. Branch, vol. 4 (Devizes, 1949).
25. Wilts., Salisbury. City Quarter Sessions, 1540. Wilts. RO A3/110/1.
26. Yorks., county. Sessions of the Peace, 1361–4. *Yorkshire Sessions of the Peace, 1361–1364*, ed. Bertha H. Putnam, Yorks. Archaeol. Soc., Rec. Ser., vol. 100 (1939).
27. Yorks., West Riding. Sessions Rolls, 1598–9. *West Riding Sessions Rolls, 1597/8–1602*, ed. John Lister, Yorks. Archaeol. and Topograph. Assoc., Rec. Ser., vol. 3 (1888).
28. Yorks., York. City (and Ainsty) Quarter Sessions, 1559–70 and 1590–9. York City A. F2 and F6.

Appendix 2.1
Records of the lesser public courts used in Chapters 3, 6, and 7

Sequence of information on this list: identification number of the place (for use with maps), name of county, name of place or institution (e.g., the manor or Honour) for which court was held, type of court, range of dates of records used, number of twenty-year periods for which records were analyzed, type of community in which court was located; document references. If records from two types of courts were analyzed for a given place, full information is provided for each type. For further explanation, see the Notes at the end.

Abbreviations used in references:

> A[O] = Archive(s) [Office]
> PRO = Public Record Office, London
> RO = Record Office

1. Beds., Barton (in the Clay), manor, 1377–1537, 7 prds., village; PRO SC 2/179/41, 43, 52, 56, 61, 66–67, 70, 74, and 89.
2. Beds., Biddenham Newnham, manor, 1415–1596, 10 prds., village; Beds. RO TW 713–726.
3. Beds., Blunham, manor, 1414–1573, 6 prds., village; Beds. RO L 26/51–55, 57, and 60.
4. Beds., Cranfield, manor, 1377–1537, 8 prds., village; PRO SC 2/179/41, 43, 52, 56, 61, 67, 70, 74, 82, and 89.
5. Beds., Leighton (Buzzard), manor, 1393–1558, 4 prds., market center; Beds. RO KK 619, 622–623, 625, and 627.
6. Beds., Podington, manor, 1383–1598, 7 prds., village; Beds. RO OR 798–804 and 808.
7. Beds., Shitlington (= Shillington), manor, 1377–1537, 8 prds., village; PRO SC 2/179/41, 52, 56, 61, 66, 70, 74, 80, and 89.
8. Beds., Willington, manor, 1394–1594, 9 prds., village; Beds. RO Russell Box 212, Bundle 12.
9. Berks., Bray, manor, 1374–1599, 8 prds., market center; Berks. RO D/EG M17–M18, M30, M35–M36, M41, M43, M48, M55, M62, and M68–M72.

10. Berks., Bright Waltham (= Brightwalton), manor, 1386–1529, 6 prds., village; PRO SC 2/153/70, 72–73, and 76–77.
11. Berks., Cookham, manor, 1389–1598, 10 prds., market center; Berks. RO D/ESk M2, M6–M8, M11, M13, M15, M20, M24–M55, M58, M61, and M64–M82.
12. Berks., (Great) Faringdon, manor, 1461–1576, 2 prds., market center; Berks. RO D/EE1 M85–M86 and M97.
13. Berks., Shrivenham Salop, manor (and hundred), 1528–97, 3 prds., village; Berks. RO D/EE1 M32, M34, M36, M52, and M68.
14. Berks., Thatcham, manor, 1408–1597, 3 prds., village; Berks. RO D/EHy M1–M2 and D/ENm1 M63.
15. Berks., West Hanney, manor, 1400–1554, 6 prds., village; New College Oxford MSS 4180 and 4060–4062.
16. Bucks., Akeley cum Stockholt, manor, 1383–1583, 7 prds., village; New College Oxford MSS 4084–87.
17. Bucks., Chalfont St. Peter, manor, 1480–1598, 5 prds., village; Bucks. RO D/BASM/15/9 and 12–13, and PRO DL 30/80/1107.
18. Bucks., Chesham Higham and Chesham Bury, manor, 1444–1578, 6 prds., village; Bucks. RO D/BASM/18/140, 153, 160, 184, 191, 193, 195, 199, 202–203, 205, 207, 212, and 216.
19. Bucks., Great Brickhill, manor, 1490–1596, 5 prds., market center; Bucks. RO D/BASM/10/1–4.
20. Bucks., Great Horwood, manor, 1383–1582, 10 prds., market center; New College Oxford MSS 3915–3917 and 3919–3922.
21. Bucks., Long Crendon, manor, 1473–1595, 6 prds., village; Bucks. RO D/BASM Manorial, Long Crendon, C/6 6/48, 8/48, 9/48, and 10/48.
22. Bucks., Newton Longville, manor, 1422–1558, 7 prds., village; New College Oxford MSS 3877–3881.
23. Bucks., Quarrendon, manor, 1396–1591, 9 prds., village; Oxon. Archs. Dil X/a/1–2, 4, 6, and 8–15.
24. Bucks., Tingewick, manor, 1382–1586, 10 prds., village; New College Oxford MSS 4133–4142.
25. Cambs., Chippenham, manor, 1381–1597, 9 prds., village; Cambs. RO, Cambridge, R55/7/1a–1b and 1d–1g.
26. Cambs., Ely Barton, manor, 1422–1599, 7 prds., market center; Cambridge Univ. Libr. E.D.R. C/6/1, 6, 11, 17–19, and 26–27.
27. Cambs., Great Abington, manor, 1386–1597, 9 prds., village; Cambs. RO, Cambridge, 619/M2–M3, M6–M9, and M11.
28. Cambs., Downham, in Little Downham, manor, 1384–1579, 7 prds., village; Cambridge Univ. Libr. E.D.R. C/11/1–3.
29. Cambs., Topcliffes, in Meldreth, manor, 1390–1599, 9 prds., village; Greater London RO H.1./ST/E79/2, 6, 8–9, 20, 22, and 24–25.
30. Cambs., Whittlesford, manor, 1391–1592, 7 prds., village; Cambs. RO, Cambridge, 488/M Whittlesford court rolls.
31. Cambs., Willingham, manor, 1380–1596, 8 prds., village; Cambs. RO, Cambridge, L1/177–181.
32. Ches., Halton, Honour and Fee of, composite manorial estate, 1384–1594, 9 prds., various places; PRO DL 30/2/33, 4/55, 5/64, 5/71, 6/82, 8/103, 10/124, and 13/146.
33. Ches., Kinderton, Barony (and halmote) of, composite manorial estate,

1534–92, 4 prds., various places; Ches. RO DVE 2/1.

34. Corn., Fowey, manor, 1415–1539, 4 prds., market center; Corn. RO ARB 75/84.

35. Corn., Liskeard: manor, 1414–1592, 7 prds., market center, PRO SC 2/160/27, 30, 32–33, and 35–36; borough, 1392–1586, 7 prds., market center, Corn. RO B/LIS 90–96, 99, and 101–105.

36. Corn., Menheniot, manor, 1472–1528, 4 prds., village; Devon RO CR163–179.

37. Corn., Mitchell, manor, 1443–1546, 5 prds., village; Courtney Libr., Royal Inst. of Corn., Truro, HH/14A/1–2, 6–9, 12–13, 15–16, 27–29, and 32.

38. Corn., Padstow, manor, 1457–1581, 6 prds., market center; Corn. RO PB/4/11–12, 20–21, 27–28, 30–31, 34, 36–45, and 49–51.

39. Corn., Penwith, hundred, 1410–1572, 6 prds., various places; Corn. RO ARB 80/198–201, and PRO SC 2/161/76–79.

40. Corn., Tregear, in Gerrans, manor, 1419–1536, 3 prds., village; Devon RO CR 395–398.

41. Cumb., Castle Sowerby, manor, 1370–1598, 2 prds., village; PRO SC2/165/5–6.

42. Cumb., Cockermouth, borough (or honour), 1472–1597, 6 prds., market center plus other places; Cumbria RO, Carlisle, D/Lec 299/1/1/1–3, 7–9, 25– 29, and book for 1567–9.

43. Cumb., Dalston, manor, 1423–1595, 7 prds., village; Cumbria RO, Carlisle, DRC/2/60–66 and 68–69.

44. Cumb., Derwentfells, Lordship of, composite manorial estate, 1472–1597, 6 prds., various places; Cumbria RO, Carlisle, D/Lec/299/1/1/1–3, 7–9, 25–30, and book for 1567–9.

45. Cumb., Five Towns, Lordship of the, composite manorial estate, 1472–1597, 6 prds., various places; Cumbria RO, Carlisle, D/Lec/299/1/1/1–3, 7–9, 25–29, and book for 1567–9.

46. Cumb., Millom, Seignory of, composite manorial estate, 1511–96, 5 prds., various places; Cumbria RO, Carlisle, D/Lons/W8/1–2, 4, and 8.

47. Cumb., Penrith, manor, 1370–1599, 2 prds., market center; PRO SC 2/165/19 and SC 2/227/79.

48. Cumb., Whitbeck, near Silecroft, manor, 1540–62, 2 prds., village; PRO DL 30/80/1084–1085 and 1087.

49. Derby., Appletree, hundred, 1387–1592, 8 prds., various places; PRO DL 30/46/533, 47/551, 48/568, 48/570, 48/578, 49/584, 50/607, 50/615, 51/625, and 52/644.

50. Derby., Chesterfield, borough, 1396–1582, 5 prds., market center; Notts. AO DDP 59/2–7, and PRO SC 2/165/26–27.

51. Derby., Duffield, manor, 1386–1592, 9 prds., village; PRO DL 30/33/321, 34/332, 34/340, 34/346, 34/351, 35/364, 36/368, 37/377, and 37/392.

52. Derby., Melbourne, manor, 1373–1599, 9 prds., market center; Derby. RO D 3809/1 (reference thanks to Maureen Jurkowski), Huntington Libr., San Marino, Calif., USA, HAM Box 62, #13–16, and PRO DL 30/45/518, 48/576, 49/586, and 52/651.

53. Derby., Peveril, Honour of, composite manorial estate, 1427–1588, 6 prds., various places; Nottingham Univ. Libr., Dept. of MSS, Mi MP 1, 5, 13, 15, 20, and 23(a), and PRO SC 2/165/33–34.

54. Derby., Scarsdale, hundred, 1519–82, 3 prds., various places; Notts. AO

DDP 59/2–7.

55. Derby., Wirksworth, wapentake (=hundred), 1387–1592, 8 prds., various places; PRO DL 30/46/533, 47/551, 48/568, 48/571, 48/578, 49/584, 50/607, 50/615, 51/625, and 52/644.

56. Devon, Bishop's Clyst, in Clyst St. Mary, manor, 1407–1567, 7 prds., village; Devon RO CR 20069–20071, 20073–20074, 20076–20077, and 20083–20085A.

57. Devon, Dartmouth, borough, 1484–1592, 6 prds., market center; Devon RO *f.009.4, 64741–64743 and 64746.

58. Devon, Hartland: manor, 1469–1582, 4 prds., market center, Corn. RO ARB 90/435 and 437–440; hundred, 1494–1574, 5 prds., various places, Corn. RO ARB 90/428–432.

59. Devon, Hayridge, hundred, 1434–1596, 8 prds., various places; Devon RO CR 115–127, 139–141, 147–148, and 155–156.

60. Devon, Monkleigh, manor, 1409–1591, 9 prds., village; Devon RO CR 1093–1104, 1106–1108, and 1110–1111.

61. Devon, Ottery St. Mary, manor, 1390–1587, 6 prds., market center; Devon RO CR 1288.

62. Devon, Tiverton: borough, 1451–1595, 8 prds., market center, Devon RO CR 227, 234–237, 243, 248–250, 256, 262–263, and 270–271; hundred, 1434–1597, 7 prds., various places, Devon RO CR 339–341, 347–348, 359–360, 372–373, 376–377, and 386–387.

63. Devon, West Budleigh, hundred, 1454–1592, 5 prds., various places; Devon RO CR 77–81, 84, and 86–89.

64. Devon, Yarcombe, manor, 1393–1583, 7 prds., village; Devon RO CR 1438, 1441, 1447, 1453, 1456, and 1458–59, and PRO SC 2/168/58, 61, and 64.

65. Dorset, Abbotsbury, manor, 1424–1578, 7 prds., market center; Dorset RO D/FSI Boxes 2–4.

66. Dorset, Badbury, hundred, 1391–1598, 8 prds., various places; Dorset RO D/BKL CF 1/1/1–2, 32, 34, 43, 49, 63, 68, 73, and 76.

67. Dorset, Bridport, borough, 1386–1594, 9 prds., market center; Dorset RO DC/BTB C33, C39, C54, C62, C72, C75, C77, C82, E2, and E5.

68. Dorset, Knowlton, hundred, 1396–1567, 6 prds., various places; Nottingham Univ. Libr., Dept. of MSS, Mi 5/164/1, 3, 8–9, 12, 14, 20, 26, 28–31, and 33–34.

69. Dorset, Sherborne, hundred, 1406–1594, 7 prds., various places; Dorset RO Old Museum ref. KG 1, 5, 9, 16, 19, 24, and 27.

70. Dorset, Wimborne Minster, borough, 1396–1563, 5 prds., market center; Dorset RO D/BKL CF 1/1/73, D/BKL CJ 1/3, 9, and 11, and Old Museum ref. 1044 and 5331, and PRO DL 30/57/715.

71. Durham, Durham, Bishop of, Halmote Court, composite manorial estate, 1388–1596, 10 prds., various places; Durham Univ. Libr., Archs. and Spec. Colls., 5 The College, HC/I/1, 9, 21, 34, and 42, and PRO DURH 3/13–16 and 19.

72. Durham, Durham, Dean and Chapter of, Halmote Court, composite manorial estate, 1388–1507, 6 prds., various places; Durham Univ. Libr., Archs. and Spec. Colls., Prior's Kitchen, DCD Halmote Ct.

73. Essex, Bacons, in Dengie, manor, 1381–1599, 9 prds., village; Essex RO D/DP M1191–1192, M1194–1197, and M1201.

74. Essex, Borley (Hall), manor, 1371–1599, 9 prds., village; Essex RO D/DWg M1–M5 and M7.
75. Essex, Havering (-atte-Bower), manor, 1382–1599, 11 prds., market center; Essex RO D/DU 102/1–93, and PRO SC 2/172/25–40 and SC 2/173/1–4.
76. Essex, Ingatestone Hall, manor, 1392–1595, 9 prds., village; Essex RO D/DP M27, M32, M37, M43, M51, M69, M86–87, M97–98, and M100.
77. Essex, North Fambridge, manor, 1381–1596, 7 prds., village; Essex RO D/DMj M2 and M14.
78. Essex, Priors Hall, in Lindsell, manor, 1463–1568, 6 prds., village; New College Oxford MSS 3658–3663.
79. Essex, Walden (=Saffron Walden), manor, 1384–1589, 9 prds., market center; Essex RO D/DBy M1–M2, M4–M5, M8–M11, M20–21, M23, and M25.
80. Essex, Wethersfield Hall, manor, 1390–1583, 9 prds., village; Essex RO D/DFy M1, M6–M8, M10, M12, M15, M18, and M20.
81. Essex, Wivenhoe, manor, 1394–1596, 8 prds., village; Essex RO D/DBm M100 and M102–105, and PRO SC 2/174/34 and 36.
82. Gloucs., Bourton-on-the-Hill (with Moreton-in-Marsh in some years), manor, 1376–1545, 5 prds., village; Westminster Abbey Libr., London, W.A.M. 8358–8360, 8362, and 8371–8373.
83. Gloucs., Cheltenham, hundred, 1407–1529, 2 prds., various places; PRO SC 2/175/26–27.
84. Gloucs., Churchdown, Barony of (and manor), composite manorial estate, 1440–1598, 6 prds., various places; Gloucs. RO D 621/M 1–6.
85. Gloucs., Hawkesbury, manor, 1393–1529, 6 prds., village; PRO SC 2/175/46, 48, 52, 56, and 59.
(See also No. 221, Sutton-under-Brailes, administratively in Gloucs. during the period under study.)
86. Gloucs., Thornbury: manor, 1386–1585, 9 prds., market center, Staffs. RO D641/1/4C/5–7 and 9–11b, D641/2/E/3/1, and D(W) 1721/1/7; borough, 1377–1585, 8 prds., market center, Staffs. RO D641/1/4E/4–10 and D641/2/E/3/1.
87. Gloucs., Todenham, manor, 1460–1596, 5 prds., village; Gloucs. RO D 1099/M1–4 and 23.
88. Hants., Alverstoke, manor, 1378–1583, 7 prds., village; Hants. RO Eccles I 80/10, 81/9 and 13, 82/5, 83/9, 86/8, and 90/6.
89. Hants., Avington, manor, 1382–1576, 5 prds., village; Huntington Libr., San Marino, Calif., USA, STBM Box 1, #2–3 and #8–9, Box 2, #1–2, and STTM Box 18, #9.
90. Hants., Basingstoke, borough, 1390–1592, 8 prds., market center; Hants. RO 148M71/2/I/88, and Francis J. Baigent and J. E. Millard, *A History of the Ancient Town and Manor of Basingstoke in the County of Southampton* (Basingstoke, 1889).
91. Hants., Bitterne, manor, 1387–1596, 7 prds., village; Hants. RO Eccles I 74/10, 75/15 and 29, 76/18, 77/12, 31–32, and 34, 78/4 and 18, and 90/6.
92. Hants., Hoddington, manor, 1395–1594, 8 prds., village; PRO SC 2/201/18–23.
93. Heref., Bishop's Frome, manor, 1475–1595, 5 prds., village; Heref. RO AA59/603727–603728 and AM33/1–7.

94. Heref., Holme Lacy, manor, 1386–1595, 9 prds., village; Heref. RO AF72/2, 16–17, 19, 22–25, 28–29, 31, and 34–37.
95. Heref., Much Marcle, manor, 1417–1571, 8 prds., village; Heref. RO G37/I/11–12 and J20/1–2.
96. Herts., Ardeley, manor, 1475–1595, 5 prds., village; Guildhall Libr., London, MS 25,301/1–2.
97. Herts., (Bishop's) Stortford, manor, 1405–1585, 5 prds., market center; Guildhall Libr., London, MS 10,312/93–96 and 182–183, and PRO SC 2/178/65.
98. Herts., Broxbourne, manor, 1382–1593, 8 prds., village; Herts. RO B14–17, 20, 26, 28A, and 30–32.
99. Herts., Great and Little Wymondley, manor, 1395–1599, 10 prds., village; Herts. RO 57496–57497, 57499–57500, 57502–57504, and 57514–57518.
100. Herts., Hexton, manor, 1380–1598, 10 prds., village; Herts. RO 40706, 40709, 47283–47331, 47341–47354, 47365–47368, and Acc 2510 (book of copies).
101. Herts., Stevenage, manor, 1384–1585, 8 prds., market center; Guildhall Libr., London, MS 10,312/93–96 and 181, and PRO SC 2/178/53, 57, 59, and 61–62.
102. Herts., Therfield, manor, 1377–1537, 7 prds., village; British Libr., London, Add. Ch. 34831, 39771, and 39774, and PRO SC 2/179/41, 43, 52, 56, 70, 80, and 89.
103. Hunts., Broughton, manor, 1377–1537, 7 prds., village; PRO SC 2/179/41, 43, 52, 55, 57, 66–67, 70, 82, and 89.
104. Hunts., Ramsey, borough, 1379–1591, 10 prds., market center; British Libr., London, Add. Roll 34368, 34376, 34388, 34394, 34400, 34402, 34405, 39625–39626, 39634–39635, 39637–39638, 39641, 39643, 39645–39646, 39650, 39653A, 39654, 39658, 39665, and 39704; PRO SC 2/179/47 and 59. This information was kindly provided by Edwin DeWindt and includes all surviving rolls, 1370–1599.
105. Hunts., Wistow, manor, 1377–1537, 6 prds., village; British Libr., London, Add. Ch. 34823, and PRO SC 2/179/41, 43, 52, 55, 70, 80, 82, and 89.
106. Kent, Adisham, manor, 1395–1573, 8 prds., village; Canterbury Cath. A. U15/9/21–22, 9/28–29, 9/40, 9/52, 10/2, 10/9, and 34/9 and DCc/CR 70.
107. Kent, Appledore, manor, 1382–1555, 8 prds., market center; Canterbury Cath. A. U15/10/13–14, 10/19, 10/30–31, 10/35, 10/43–45, 10/49J, 34/6, and 34/11–12.
108. Kent, Boughton under Blean: manor, 1549–88, 3 prds., village, Lambeth Pal. Libr., London, ED 1791, 1796–1797, 1808, and 1812–1813; hundred, 1448–1564, 4 prds., various places, Lambeth Pal. Libr., London, ED 272–275, 277–278, 466, and 1796.
109. Kent, Codsheath, hundred, 1388–1557, 8 prds., various places; Lambeth Pal. Libr., London, ED 339–344, 804–805, 808, 825–826, 828–829, and 967.
110. Kent, Denge (= Dunge) Marsh, near Lydd, manor, 1403–1536, 4 prds., village; PRO SC 2/180/58, 60–61, and 65.
111. Kent, Ightham, manor, 1461–1586, 6 prds., village; Nottingham Univ. Libr., Dept. of MSS, Mi 5/163/10–24.
112. Kent, Toltintrough, hundred, 1396–1557, 6 prds., various places; Lambeth Pal. Libr., London, ED 233, 343–344, 763–764, 768–769, 773–774, 776, and 967.

113. Kent, Wye, hundred, 1370–1534, 7 prds., various places; PRO SC 2/182/20, 26, 30, 37, 46, 48, and 63.
114. Lancs., Clitheroe, Honour of, composite manorial estate, 1377–1598, 8 prds., various places; Lancs. RO DDHCl 3/75 and 80, and *The Court Rolls of the Honor of Clitheroe in the County of Lancaster*, ed. William Farrer, vol. 1 (Manchester, 1897), and vols. 2–3 (Edinburgh, 1912–13).
115. Lancs., Prescot, manor, 1510–83, 5 prds., market center; *A Selection from the Prescot Court Leet and Other Records, 1447–1600*, ed. F. A. Bailey, Rec. Soc. of Lancs. and Ches., vol. 89 (n.p., 1937).
116. Lancs., West Derby, manor, 1452–1595, 7 prds., village; Liverpool RO 920 SAL 1/1–3, 9–10, 44, 46, 65, 74–75, 103, and 105.
117. Lancs., Widnes, Lordship and Fee of, composite manorial estate, 1384–1594, 7 prds., various places; PRO DL 30/2/33, 3/44, 4/60, 5/64, 8/103, 10/124, and 13/146.
118. Leics., Barrow upon Soar, manor, 1460–1590, 5 prds., village; Huntington Libr., San Marino, Calif., USA, HAM Box 45, #12–13, Leics. RO DE 169/3–5, 9, 17–18, 85, 87, and 91, and PRO SC 2/183/100.
119. Leics., Beaumanor, near Barrow upon Soar, manor, 1481–1597, 4 prds., village; Leics. RO DG 9/1849–57, 1884, and 1889–90.
120. Leics., Castle Donington, manor, 1457–1591, 7 prds., market center; Huntington Libr., San Marino, Calif., USA, HAM Box 8, #2 and #7–8, and PRO DL 30/80/1090, 1093, and 1098.
121. Leics., Hungarton, manor, 1378–1501, 6 prds., village; PRO SC 2/183/74–75 and 100.
122. Leics., Kibworth Harcourt, manor, 1370–1594, 7 prds., village; Merton College Oxford MSS 6407, 6413–6414, 6424, 6432, 6439, 6442c, 6442f–g, 6444, and 6446–6447.
123. Leics., Loughborough, manor, 1397–1574, 9 prds., market center; Huntington Libr., San Marino, Calif., USA, HAM Box 20, #2 and #5–8, Box 21, #3, #6, and #8, Box 22, #4–5, Box 23, #3–5, Box 24, #5, and Box 25, #2.
124. Leics., Owston, manor, 1386–1482, 6 prds., village; PRO SC 2/183/75 and 87–90.
125. Leics., Shepshed, manor, 1385–1592, 7 prds., village; British Libr., London, Add. Ch. 26842–26845.
126. Lincs., Crowle, manor, 1385–1592, 10 prds., village; Lincs. AO Crowle Manorial I/38–40, 50, 52–53, 64–66, 86–87, 119–120, 156, 194–195, 215, 247, and 259–260.
127. Lincs., Ingoldmells, manor, 1387–1596, 8 prds., village; Lincs. AO M.M.8/22–23, 30–32, 33a–34, 38–40, 44–45, 51–52, and 55, and PRO DL 30/94/1285.
128. Lincs., Kirton Lindsey, manor/soke, 1384–1592, 7 prds., market center plus other places; Lincs. AO K.R./345–346, 348–352, 418, 425, 431, 473–476, 492, 497, 499, 501, 517–518, and 532.
129. Lincs., Langtoft and Baston, manor, 1418–1596, 9 prds., village; Lincs. AO 6.Ancaster 1/55, 57, 67, 72, 85–86, 112, and 125, and 3/1–2 and 14.
130. Lincs., Louth, manor, 1392–1595, 7 prds., market center; Lincs. AO Goulding Papers 4B 5/1.
131. Lincs., Spilsby cum Eresby, manor, 1370–1589, 9 prds., market center; Lincs. AO ANC 3/14/40–42, 44, 47–48, 50–52, 54–55, 66–67, 71–73, 86–87, and 92.

132. Lincs., Toynton, manor, 1386–1596, 9 prds., village; Lincs. AO ANC 3/18/39–41, 51–52, 54–56, 66–67, 71–76, 86–87, and 93–94.
133. Middx., Acton, manor, 1384–1585, 8 prds., village within 15 km of London Bridge; Guildhall Libr., London, MS 10,312/91–96, and PRO SC 2/188/65, 69, and 72, and SC 2/189/2, 17, and 19.
134. Middx., Ealing, manor, 1384–1585, 8 prds., village within 15 km of London Bridge; Guildhall Libr., London, MS 10,312/91–96, and PRO SC 2/188/65, 69, and 72 and SC 2/189/2, 17, and 19.
135. Middx., Fulham, manor, 1384–1585, 8 prds., village within 15 km of London Bridge; Guildhall Libr., London, MS 10,312/55, 80, and 91–96, and PRO SC 2/188/65, 69, and 72 and SC 2/189/2, 17, and 19.
136. Middx., Harrow, manor, 1399–1558, 7 prds., village; Greater London RO Acc.76/2413–2414, 2416, 2418, and 2420–2423.
137. Middx., Staines (with Yeoveney), manor, 1382–1569, 5 prds., market center; Westminster Abbey Libr., London, W.A.M. 16954, 16958–16959, 16961–16965, and 16969–16970.
138. Norf., Cawston, manor, 1370–1586, 8 prds., market center; Norf. RO MS 3652 (16 E 1), N.R.S. 2562 (12 A 2), 2563 (12 A 1), 2567 (12 A 3), 2570 (12 A 4), 2571 (12 A 5), 6024 (20 E 2), and 6025 (20 E 3).
139. Norf., Deopham, manor, 1381–1596, 3 prds., village; Canterbury Cath. A. U15/13/65–68.
140. Norf., Fakenham (Lancaster), manor, 1485–1599, 5 prds., market center; Norf. RO N.R.S. 20466 (35 X 2), 20743 (41 D 4), 20744 (41 D 4), and 20745 (41 D 4).
141. Norf., Gimingham, manor, 1405–1529, 5 prds., village; PRO DL 30/103/1413, 1415–1416, 1419, and 1421–1422.
142. Norf., Horsham St. Faith, manor, 1383–1593, 8 prds., village; Norf. RO N.R.S. 19246 (33 F 4), 19507 (42 C 2), 19509 (42 C 3), 19511 (42 C 3), 19512 (42 C 4), and 19513 (42 C 4).
143. Norf., West Winch, manor, 1380–1559, 5 prds., village; Cambridge Univ. Libr. Ch(H) Working Papers Rolls 92 and 94–97.
144. Northants., Brigstock, manor, 1424–1596, 6 prds., village; Northants. RO Buccleugh MSS, manor court rolls, and PRO SC 2/194/72.
145. Northants., Glapthorn, manor, 1391–1597, 5 prds., village; Northants. RO Bru.I.v.1, 3, 9a–b, 14, 20, 29, 31, 51–52, 61, 65, and 83.
146. Northants., Higham Ferrers, borough (and duchy), 1384–1596, 11 prds., market center; Northants. RO Higham Ferrers court rolls, and PRO DL 30/105/1497 and 1498A.
147. Northants., Peterborough, Dean and Chapter of, composite manorial estate, 1373–1590, 10 prds., various places; Northants. RO PDC. CR. Bundles A-G and I.
148. Northants., Silverstone, manor, 1390–1542, 5 prds., village; Westminster Abbey Libr., London, W.A.M. 27769–27770, 27772–27773, 27776–27778, and 27780.
149. Northumb., Bedlington, manor (Bishop of Durham's Halmote Court), 1380–1562, 3 prds., village; PRO DURH 3/13, 19, 24, and 135.
150. Northumb., Black Callerton, manor, 1490–1593, 5 prds., village; Northumb. RO 1 DE/2/1–3 and 6 and 2795/1.
151. Northumb., Hartley, manor, 1486–1592, 5 prds., village; Northumb. RO 1 DE/2/3 and 6 and 2795/1–2.

152. Northumb., Seaton Delaval, manor, 1494–1592, 6 prds., village; Northumb. RO 1 DE/2/3–4 and 2795/1.
153. Northumb., Stamford, manor, 1512–45, 3 prds., village; PRO DL 30/107/1540.
154. Notts., Newark (-on-Trent), wapentake (=hundred), 1535–95, 3 prds., various places; PRO SC 2/196/12, 14, and 23.
155. Notts., Ollerton, manor (and wapentake=hundred), 1425–1593, 6 prds., village plus other places; PRO DL 30/107/1542–1543, 1546, 1557–1558, 1568–1569, and 1586–1587.
156. Notts., Oxton, manor, 1447–1509, 4 prds., village; PRO SC 2/227/98–100 and 130–131.
157. Notts., Peveril, Honour of, composite manorial estate, 1427–1589, 5 prds., various places; Nottingham Univ. Libr., Dept. of MSS, MP 1, 5, 13, 15, 20, and 23(a), and PRO SC 2/196/88–89.
158. Notts., Plumtree, manor (and wapentake=hundred), 1404–1593, 7 prds., village plus other places; PRO DL 30/107/1541, 1544–1546, 1557–1558, 1568–1569, and 1586–1587.
159. Notts., Wheatley (=North Wheatley), manor, 1483–1556, 4 prds., village; PRO DL 30/131/2003–2004 and 2010.
160. Oxon., Clanfield, manor, 1392–1555, 5 prds., village; PRO SC 2/212/18 and WARD 2/34/121/1–2 and 7–8.
161. Oxon., Ewelme, hundred, 1412–1544, 5 prds., various places; PRO SC 2/212/1, 4, 12, 18–19, and 21.
162. Oxon., Henley (-on-Thames), borough, 1433–1594, 6 prds., market center; Oxon. Archs. D.D. Henley B.IV.5–6, 9, 12–15, and 39/1–2.
163. Oxon., Holywell, near Oxford, manor, 1377–1504, 5 prds., village; Merton College Oxford MSS 4537b, 4549, 4554, 4555b, and 4558.
164. Oxon., Islip, manor, 1374–1546, 6 prds., village; Westminster Abbey Libr., London, W.A.M. 14863–14864, 14882–14883, 14911–14912, 14935, 14949–14952, and 14964.
165. Oxon., Kirtlington, manor, 1470–1599, 6 prds., village; Oxon. Archs. Dash I/i/1–7, 16, 22–25, 27, 44, 46, 48, 52–53, 59, 61, 66–68, 83, 90, 101, 104, 106, 110, 116, and 132–137, and PRO DL 30/108/1594.
166. Oxon., Launton, manor, 1373–1596, 7 prds., village; Westminster Abbey Libr., London, W.A.M. 15436–15437, 15465–15466, 15494–15495, 15515, 15524–15525, 15527–15528, 15544–15545, and 15573–15574.
167. Rutl., Oakham (with Barleythorp), manor, 1410–1598, 5 prds., market center; Westminster Abbey Libr., London, W.A.M. 20363–20366, 20372–20374, 20374*, and 20376–20377.
168. Rutl., Tinwell, manor, 1414–1537, 2 prds., village; Northants. RO PDC. CR. B/20 and E/60–62.
169. Rutl., Uppingham, manor, 1510–68, 3 prds., market center; PRO SC 2/197/88–90.
170. Shrops., Cleobury (Mortimer), borough (and liberty), 1515–51, 3 prds., market center; PRO SC 2/197/101–103.
171. Shrops., (Great) Bromfield, manor, 1389–1591, 7 prds., village; Shrops. RO 20/1/10, 31, 41, 47, 51, 55, and 62.
(See also No. 234, Hales(owen), administratively in Shrops. during the period under study.)
172. Shrops., Ruyton (Patria=Ruyton XI Towns), manor, 1382–1586, 6 prds.,

village; PRO SC 2/197/127, 129, 133–135, 137, 139, and 142.
173. Shrops., Whitchurch, manor, 1440–1598, 7 prds., market center; Shrops. RO 212/Boxes 20/1 and 11, 22/4, 23/17, 24/2 and 7, and 35.
174. Som., Chard: borough, 1421–44, 2 prds., market center, Lambeth Pal. Libr., London, ED 333, 1186, and 1188; hundred, 1379–1444, 4 prds., various places, Lambeth Pal. Libr., London, ED 329, 332–333, 1186, and 1188.
175. Som., Minehead, manor, 1380–1589, 9 prds., market center; Som. RO DD/L P26/4, 6, and 8, P27/10–11, P28/13–16, and P29/25, 29, 32, and 40.
176. Som., Nettlecombe, manor, 1387–1594, 9 prds., village; Som. RO DD/WO 41/11, 17, 19–22, 24–25, and 27–28.
177. Som., North Curry, manor, 1385–1597, 6 prds., market center; Som. RO DD/CC 131903/2 and 5, 131913/7, 131920/10, 131921/13, 131922/2–3, and 131925a/7 and 12.
178. Som., Somerton: borough, 1413–1572, 4 prds., market center, Huntington Libr., San Marino, Calif., USA, HAM Box 69, #9–12, and PRO SC 2/200/32 and 35; hundred, 1376–1574, 4 prds., various places, Huntington Libr., San Marino, Calif., USA, HAM Box 69, #6–7, #10–11, and #14, and PRO SC 2/200/33–34.
179. Som., Wellow: manor, 1372–1539, 5 prds., village, PRO SC 2/200/45, 47–48, and 51; hundred, 1403–1515, 3 prds., various places, PRO SC 2/200/46–47 and 50.
180. Staffs., Alrewas, manor, 1388–1549, 7 prds., village; Staffs. RO D(W) O/3/84, 99–100, 114–115, 127, 134, 137, and 142.
181. Staffs., Brewood, manor, 1387–1566, 8 prds., market center; Staffs. RO D590/433/10, 13–14, 16–17, 19, 21, and 23–25.
182. Staffs., Cannock and Rugeley, manor, 1413–1594, 9 prds., market center; Staffs. RO D(W) 1734/2/1/176–178, 180, 182, 184, and 186.
183. Staffs., Horton, manor, 1405–1586, 8 prds., village; Staffs. RO D(W) 1490/2, 6, 11, and 14.
184. Staffs., Longdon, manor, 1512–90, 4 prds., village; Staffs. RO D(W) 1734/2/1/605, 625, 640, and 655.
185. Staffs., Newcastle-under-Lyme, manor, 1387–1595, 8 prds., market center; PRO DL 30/230/9–10, 231/13–14, 232/8–9, 233/13, 234/1, 235/6–7, 236/16–17, and 237/9–10, 22, and 24.
186. Staffs., Pattingham, manor, 1387–1583, 9 prds., village; Staffs. RO D(W) 1807/34, 48–49, 59–60, 72, 86, 103, 119, 128, and 160.
187. Staffs., Penkridge, manor, 1398–1591, 5 prds., market center; Staffs. RO D260/M/E/429/1–2.
188. Suff., Barrow Hall (with Feltons), manor, 1370–1593, 6 prds., village; Suff. RO, Bury St. Edmunds, HA 507/13–18.
189. Suff., Chevington, manor, 1388–1585, 10 prds., village; Suff. RO, Bury St. Edmunds, E3/15.3/1.25–1.27, 1.34(a), 1.35–1.36, 1.39, and 1.41–1.44.
190. Suff., Clare, borough, 1388–1589, 10 prds., market center; PRO DL 30/116/1797, 116/1801, 117/1823, 118/1826, 118/1835, and 119/1842, SC 2/203/64, 66–67, and 70–72, and SC 2/213/66 and 69–73.
191. Suff., Earl Soham, manor, 1394–1595, 8 prds., village; Suff. RO, Ipswich, V5/18/1.3–1.8 and 1.11.
192. Suff., Framlingham, manor, 1370–1594, 8 prds., market center; Pembroke College Cambridge MSS A2, B, D1, E1–2, F–G, H1, I1, K1, and L1.
193. Suff., Lidgate, manor, 1392–1593, 9 prds., village; Suff. RO, Bury St.

Edmunds, E3/11/1.1–1.7 and 1.9.

194. Suff., Norton Hall, manor, 1380–1595, 9 prds., village; Suff. RO, Bury St. Edmunds, 553/57, 59–63, and 65.

195. Suff., Old Hall, in East Bergholt, manor, 1390–1597, 8 prds., village; Suff. RO, Ipswich, HA 6:51/4/4.7–4.11, 4.14, and 4.16–4.17.

196. Suff., South Elmham, manor, 1381–1589, 11 prds., village; Suff. RO, Ipswich, HA 12/C2/19–20, 25–26, 28–34, and 36.

197. Surrey, Carshalton, manor, 1393–1482, 4 prds., village; *Court Rolls of the Manor of Carshalton, from the Reign of Edward III to That of Henry VII*, ed. D. L. Powell, Surrey Rec. Soc., vol. 2 (London, 1916).

198. Surrey, Farnham, manor, 1501–98, 4 prds., market center; Hants. RO Eccles I 79/28 and 37–38, 86/3 and 5, 90/6, and 144/4.

199. Surrey, Godalming, manor (and hundred), 1382–1596, 7 prds., market center plus other places; Surrey RO, Guildford, LM 204, 207, 209, 211–212, 215, and 219–220.

200. Surrey, Kingston (-upon-Thames), manor, 1434–1598, 6 prds., market center; Surrey RO, Kingston-upon-Thames, KF 1/1/1 and 5–13.

201. Surrey, Lambeth, manor, 1385–1592, 6 prds., village within 15 km of London Bridge; Lambeth Pal. Libr., London, ED 1901, 1903-4, 1906, and 2022.

202. Surrey, Tooting Bec (=Upper Tooting), in Wandsworth, manor, 1394–1586, 9 prds., village within 15 km of London Bridge; Greater London RO M95/BEC/1–3, 5, 9–10, 14, 16, 18, and 20.

203. Surrey, Vauxhall, manor, 1374–1524, 7 prds., village within 15 km of London Bridge; PRO SC 2/205/13, 15–19, and 21.

204. Sussex (E.), Alciston, manor, 1383–1599, 7 prds., village; East Sussex RO SAS G18/30, 46–49, 55–57, 60–61, 63, and 77, and G45/14.

205. Sussex (E.), Battle (Abbey), manor, 1405–1536, 6 prds., market center; Huntington Libr., San Marino, Calif., USA, BA 550–551, 562, 620–621, 631–632, 640–641, 751, 756–758, 871, 876, and 881.

206. Sussex (E.), Gostrow, hundred, 1380–1516, 5 prds., various places; PRO SC 2/205/59 and 63 and SC 2/206/1 and 3–4.

207. Sussex (E.), Shiplake, hundred, 1372–1577, 7 prds., various places; British Libr., London, Add. Ch. 32420–32423, 32459–32460, 32488, 32508, 32511–32513, 32531–32533, and 32539–32540.

208. Sussex (W.), Aldwick (formerly called Pagham), hundred, 1454–1589, 6 prds., various places; Lambeth Pal. Libr., London, ED 143, 145–146, 154–155, 179–180, and 186, and West Sussex RO Acc 2481, Box 18, and Add MS 26846.

209. Sussex (W.), Amberley, manor, 1370–1585, 7 prds., village; West Sussex RO Ep VI/12/1–2 and 6–7, and VI/19A/1.

210. Sussex (W.), Manhood, hundred, 1400–1585, 8 prds., various places; West Sussex RO Ep VI/12/1–2 and 6–7 and Ep VI/38A/1.

211. Sussex (W.), Tangmere, manor, 1437–1595, 6 prds., village; Lambeth Pal. Libr., London, ED 186, 995, 997–998, 1005–1006, and 1031–1032, and West Sussex RO Goodwood MS E 143.

212. Sussex (W.), West Tarring, manor, 1426–1547, 5 prds., market center; Lambeth Pal. Libr., London, ED 452, 1043–1044, 1045A, 1046, and 1052.

213. War., Atherstone, manor, 1387–1585, 5 prds., market center; War. RO MR 13/1/6, 13, 27, 30, 34–37, and 42.

214. War., Austrey, manor, 1376–1596, 5 prds., village; PRO DL 30/109/1630, 110/1648, 111/1669–1670, and 113/1717A.
215. War., Brandon, manor, 1466–1596, 6 prds., village; Nottingham Univ. Libr., Dept. of MSS, Mi M 128/1–4, 6–16, 17/1, and 18.
216. War., Middleton, manor, 1455–1590, 4 prds., village; Nottingham Univ. Libr., Dept. of MSS, Mi M 131/42, 72 a and b, 74, 78, 85, 99, 101, 107, 113, 126, 129, and 133.
217. War., Oxhill, manor, 1394–1551, 4 prds., village; PRO SC 2/207/59, 61–62, and 84.
218. War., Solihull, borough, 1408–1541, 5 prds., market center; British Libr., London, Add. Ch. 17758–17760, 17763–17765, and 17767.
219. War., Stoneleigh, manor, 1389–1561, 5 prds., village; PRO SC 2/207/77–81.
220. War., Sutton Coldfield: manor, 1493–1519, 2 prds., market center, Nottingham Univ. Libr., Dept. of MSS, Mi M 134/16–21, and PRO DL 30/127/1901A; borough, 1547–90, 2 prds., market center, Birmingham Cent. Libr., Archs. Dept., Sutton Coldfield 1.
221. War., Sutton-under-Brailes, manor, 1460–1596, 5 prds., village; Gloucs. RO D 1099/M 1–4 and 23. Administratively in Gloucs. during the period under study.
222. Westml., Bampton Cundale and Knipe, manor, 1536–97, 4 prds., village; Cumbria RO, Carlisle, D/Lons/L5/2/2/1–2, 5–6, 12–13, 18, 28–29, and 31.
223. Westml., Maulds Meaburn, in Crosby Ravensworth, manor, 1479–1597, 5 prds., village; Cumbria RO, Carlisle, D/Lons/L MM 4–5.
224. Wilts., Bromham, manor, 1398–1534, 5 prds., village; PRO SC 2/208/18, 22, 24–25, and 27.
225. Wilts., Castle Combe, manor, 1372–1596, 10 prds., market center; British Libr., London, Add. Ch. 18478–18479 and 18481, Wilts. RO 777/1, and G. Poulett Scrope, *History of the Manor and Ancient Barony of Castle Combe, in the County of Wilts.* (London, 1852).
226. Wilts., Colerne, manor, 1461–1588, 6 prds., village; New College Oxford MSS 2735–2737 and 2750.
227. Wilts., Downton: manor, 1464–1591, 6 prds., market center, Wilts. RO 490/1169 and 1171, 492/9, and 893/1; borough, 1464–1592, 7 prds., market center, Wilts. RO 490/1171; 492/9, and 893/1–4.
228. Wilts., Heytesbury, hundred, 1380–1535, 6 prds., various places; PRO SC 2/208/52, 61–62, 65, and 77–78.
229. Wilts., Stockton, manor, 1475–1566, 5 prds., village; Wilts. RO 906/SC 14, 18–19, and 24.
230. Wilts., Trowbridge, manor, 1382–1599, 5 prds., market center; Wilts. RO 192/19/K-P, and PRO DL 30/127/1911–1911A.
231. Worcs., Broadway, manor, 1382–1538, 7 prds., market center; PRO SC 2/210/25–27, 29–30, 32, and 94.
232. Worcs., Bromsgrove and King's Norton, manor, 1464–1571, 4 prds., market center; Worcs. RO (St. Helens) 850: Bromsgrove, St. John Baptist/BA 821/51–52 and 57–61, and *The Court Rolls of the Manor of Bromsgrove and King's Norton, 1494–1504*, ed. A. F. C. Baber, Worcs. Hist. Soc. (Kineton, 1963).
233. Worcs., Droitwich, borough, c. 1440–c. 1535, 5 prds., market center; Worcs. RO (Headquarters, County Hall) 261.4/31 BA 1006/247, 291, 298, 309, 318, 342, 350, 352, 356, 359, and 409.

234. Worcs., Hales(owen): manor, 1536–90, 3 prds., market center, Birmingham Cent. Libr., Archs. Dept., Hagley Hall MSS 346749, 377991, and 377993; borough (and hundred), 1391–1590, 8 prds., market center, Birmingham Cent. Libr., Archs. Dept., Hagley Hall MSS 346645, 346672, 346693, 346711, 346736, 346745, 346753, 377991, and 377993. Administratively in Shrops. during the period under study.

235. Worcs., Hanbury, manor, 1466–1596, 7 prds., village; Worcs. RO (St. Helens) 705:7/BA 7335/64 (iv)/5–7 and 10, 65 (i)/7–9, 65 (iii)/2–3 and 5, and 66 (ii)/1–4.

236. Worcs., Ombersley, manor, 1464–1592, 6 prds., village; Worcs. RO (St. Helens) 705:56/BA 3910/20 (v–vi), 22 (ix–x), 27 (xiv–xvi), 30 (xvi and xxv), and 40 (xi).

237. Worcs., Pershore, manor, 1390–1538, 7 prds., market center; PRO SC 2/210/72–75, 78–79, and 94.

238. Worcs., Shrawley, manor, 1463–1594, 7 prds., village; Worcs. RO (St. Helens) 705:7/BA 7335/50/1–4, 10–11, 15, 18–20, 22, 24, 26, and 44–45 and 705:66/BA 4221/7 (ii).

239. East Yorks., Burstwick, manor, 1381–1595, 10 prds., village; Humberside AO, Beverley, DDCC 15/2, 4–5, 7, 10, 16, 18, and 21–26.

240. East Yorks., Easington, in Holderness, manor, 1433–1538, 5 prds., village; Staffs. RO D641/1/4X/12, 20–22, and 24.

241. East Yorks., Hunmanby, manor, 1501–87, 4 prds., village; Humberside AO, Beverley, DDHU 10/1/3–4, 8, 12–14, 27, 37, and 39–40.

242. N. Yorks., Ampleforth, manor, 1440–1597, 6 prds., village; Borthwick Inst., York, CC.P.Ampleforth 12/2, 5–7, 10–14, 16, 18– 22, 28, 30–31, 35–38, and 53–54, and N. Yorks. County RO, Northallerton, ZDV(F), manorial records, Ampleforth.

243. N. Yorks., Northallerton: manor, 1407–1536, 6 prds., market center, N. Yorks. County RO, Northallerton, ZBD 1/50/6 and 22, 51/4–5, 9, 14, 16, 19, and 30, 53/10 and 12–13, and 54/28; borough, 1407–1537, 6 prds., market center, N. Yorks. County RO, Northallerton, ZBD 1/50/6 and 22, 51/4–5, 9, 14, 16, 19, and 30, 53/10 and 12–13, and 54/28.

244. N. Yorks., Pickering, Liberty of, composite manorial estate, 1442–1522, 3 prds., various places; PRO DL 30/128/1931 and 1940–1941.

245. N. Yorks., Snape and Well, manor, 1380–1596, 4 prds., village; N. Yorks. County RO, Northallerton, ZAL 1/1/4–8, 22, 27, 34–36, and 56–60.

246. N. Yorks., Tanfield, manor, 1435–1594, 6 prds., village; N. Yorks. County RO, Northallerton, ZJX 3/1/39–41, 59–62, 68–69, 117, 119, and 133.

247. West Yorks., Conisbrough, manor, 1383–1588, 9 prds., village; Doncaster A. Dept. DD.Yar C1/24, 30, 32, 45–46, 71–72, 107–108, 120, 123, and 132–134.

248. West Yorks., Doncaster, manor (and lordship), 1454–1577, 6 prds., market center plus other places; Doncaster A. Dept. AB.5/1/1–3, 6, and 13.

249. West Yorks., Eastoft, in Adlingfleet, manor, 1527–81, 4 prds., village; Humberside AO, Beverley, DDBE 7/3–4.

250. West Yorks., Hatfield (Chase), manor, 1387–1578, 7 prds., village; West Yorks. A. Service, Leeds, DB 205/35–36, 49–50, 1456–7, 1478–9, 1509–10, 1532–3, 1576–7, and 1577–8.

251. West Yorks., Methley, manor, 1372–1590, 11 prds., village; Hubert S. Darbyshire and George D. Lumb, *The History of Methley*, Publs. of the Thoresby Soc., vol. 35 (Leeds, 1937).

252. West Yorks., Rossington and Hexthorpe, manor, 1468–1534, 4 prds., vill-age; Doncaster A. Dept. AB.5/5/1.
253. West Yorks., Sherburn in Elmet, manor, 1386–1589, 9 prds., market center; West Yorks. A. Service, Leeds, GC/M3/9–10, 32–33, 42, 44, 59–60, 86–88, 112–113, 123–124, 127, and 130.
254. West Yorks., Wakefield, manor, 1389–1598, 9 prds., market center plus other places; Yorks. Archaeol. Soc., Leeds, MD225/1/115, 152/1–2, 173, 194, 223, 263–263A, 264, 285, 302, and 323.
255. West Yorks., Yeadon, manor, 1381–1473, 4 prds., village; *A Transcript of the Court Rolls of Yeadon, 1361–1476*, ed. G. R. Price (Draughton, 1984).

Notes

Type of court. The headings and sequence used are: manor; borough; hundred; or composite manorial estate (for clusters of manors held by a given lay or religious body for which a common set of courts was held). The nature of the court is derived from the rolls themselves.

Dates. For each entry, the dates indicate the earliest and the latest records used.

Number of periods analyzed. The number of periods indicates for how many of the designated periods evidence from this community and court has been analyzed. The first period covers 1370–99, with twenty-year periods thereafter to 1599. Negative evidence (i.e., that records survive for a given period and were examined but show no concern with the types of social regulation under study) has been utilized for this project as well as positive evidence.

Type of community. This study includes only villages and those market centers which are estimated to have contained fewer than 3,000 people on the basis of the Poll Tax of 1377 and/or the Subsidies of 1524/5. Their taxable wealth was generally under £300 in the Subsidy of 1334 and under £100 in the Subsidies of 1524/5. (Guidelines developed from Appendices 1–4 of Alan Dyer, *Decline and Growth in English Towns*.) For England's six cities and thirty-two larger towns, see notes to Appendix 1.1.

Communities have been classified as follows:

Market centers = places included on Everitt's list of market towns in the sixteenth and early seventeenth centuries ("The Marketing of Agri-cultural Produce," esp. pp. 468–75), plus three places said in local studies to have had an active market in the fifteenth century that had died out by Everitt's period (Great Horwood, Bucks., Melbourne, Derby., and Broadway, Worcs.).

Villages = places with no market. Six villages located within 15 km of London Bridge have been noted as such on the list and were counted as market centers for the analyses in this study.

Estates held by a cathedral priory/chapter. Lands held by a cathedral priory before the Reformation and by a Dean and Chapter thereafter are listed only under the latter.

References. The references list all records used for each place and court. For manuscripts, the name (and, if needed for clarity, location) of the re-cord/archive office and the document call numbers are given; for printed works, publication information is included.

Appendix 3.1

Percentage of all courts under observation that reported social wrongdoing, by type of offence and duodecade*

	1370–99 N=148	1400–19 N=128	1420–39 N=143	1440–59 N=141	1460–79 N=166	1480–99 N=151	1500–19 N=147	1520–39 N=184	1540–59 N=162	1560–79 N=166	1580–99 N=176
Disharmony cluster											
Scolding	9.5%	11.7%	18.9%	20.6%	19.3%	12.6%	16.3%	22.8%	10.5%	15.1%	10.8%
Eavesdropping/nightwalking	3.4%	6.2%	9.1%	9.2%	8.4%	8.6%	5.4%	5.4%	3.7%	1.2%	2.3%
Total, one or more offences	12.2%	14.8%	24.5%	24.8%	24.7%	17.2%	19.7%	25.5%	11.7%	15.7%	13.1%
Disorder cluster											
Sexual misconduct	0.7%	2.3%	4.2%	3.5%	9.6%	7.3%	12.2%	9.2%	5.6%	6.6%	5.7%
Rowdy alehouses	0.7%	0.8%	1.4%	2.8%	5.4%	6.6%	9.5%	7.6%	7.4%	9.0%	8.5%
Badly governed	0.0%	1.6%	2.1%	7.8%	11.4%	14.6%	16.3%	21.2%	11.7%	10.8%	10.2%
Total, one or more offences	0.7%	3.1%	5.6%	8.5%	18.1%	18.5%	27.9%	29.9%	19.1%	18.7%	18.2%
Poverty cluster											
Hedgebreaking	0.7%	1.6%	2.8%	5.0%	10.8%	12.6%	14.3%	21.7%	21.0%	22.9%	23.3%
Vagabonds/living idly	0.0%	0.0%	0.7%	1.4%	4.2%	5.3%	14.3%	15.8%	6.8%	10.2%	9.1%
Receiving subtenants	0.0%	0.0%	0.0%	0.0%	1.8%	1.3%	0.7%	4.3%	8.0%	16.3%	27.3%
Total, one or more offences	0.7%	1.6%	3.5%	6.4%	15.7%	17.2%	23.8%	31.0%	27.8%	37.3%	46.6%
Gaming	0.7%	2.3%	8.4%	15.6%	15.1%	9.3%	21.1%	20.7%	19.8%	24.7%	26.1%
Grand total, one or more offences	13.5%	17.2%	30.8%	37.6%	39.8%	39.1%	46.9%	54.3%	48.1%	56.6%	59.1%

*For references, see Appendix 2.1.

Appendix 3.2
Market centers whose "Assembly Books" were used in Chapter 3*

Abbreviations used in references:

A[O] = Archive(s) [Office]
RO = Record Office

1. Berks., Abingdon, 1557 and 1591–9. Borough (Corporation) Minute Book, Berks. RO T/F 41.
2. Berks., Wallingford, 1507–99. Minutes of the Borough (Corporation), Berks. RO W/AC 1/1/1.
3. Bucks., Aylesbury, c. 1590. "Ordinance for the Government of the Town," Birmingham Central Libr., A. Dept., Hampton MS 1793.
4. Bucks., High Wycombe, 1398–1599. *The First Ledger Book of High Wycombe [1475–1734]*, ed. R. W. Greaves, Bucks. Rec. Soc., vol. 11 (Welwyn Garden City, 1956).
5. Cambs., Wisbech, 1566–99. Assembly and Order Book, Wisbech and Fenlands Museum, Wisbech Corporation Records, 1566–99.
6. Ches., Middlewich, 1537–99. Borough Court Books, Ches. RO DVE 2/8–9.
7. Corn., Launceston, 1566–90. Borough Courts, Corn. RO B/LA 291–292 and 298–302.
8. Durham, Crossgate, within town of Durham, 1498–1528. Durham Univ. Libr., Archs. and Spec. Colls., The Prior's Kitchen, DCD Borough of Crossgate, Court Books, 1498–1524 and 1524–8.
9. Essex, Saffron Walden, 1549–91. Ordinances and Statutes of the Corporation, Essex RO T/A 104/1.
10. Gloucs., Northleach, 1548–99. Court Book, Gloucs. RO D 398/1.
11. Kent, Faversham, 1436–1583. Borough Wardmote Minutes, Centre for Kentish Studies Fa/AC 1 (Microfilm FA/Z33).
12. Lancs., Liverpool, 1540/1–98. *Liverpool Town Books: Proceedings of Assemblies, Common Councils, Portmoot Courts, etc.*, ed. Jesse A. Twemlow. Vol. 1, 1550–1571 (Liverpool, 1918); vol. 2, 1571–1603 (Liverpool, 1935).
13. Lancs., Manchester, 1552–99. *A Volume of Court Leet Records of the Manor of Manchester in the Sixteenth Century*, ed. John Harland, The Chetham Soc., Old Ser., vol. 63 (1864); and *Continuation of the Court Leet Records of the Manor of Manchester, A.D. 1586–1602*, ed. John Harland, The Chetham Soc., Old Ser., vol. 65 (1865).

14. Lincs., Grimsby, 1518–90. Court Leet Books (orders only), S. Humberside RO, Grimsby, 1/106 and 108.
15. Northants., Northampton, 1547–99. First Assembly Books, Northants. RO Northampton Borough Records 3/1.
16. Northumb., Berwick-upon-Tweed, 1568–99. Court Book, Berwick-upon-Tweed RO C.1/1.
17. Northumb., Morpeth, 1523. J. R. Boyle, Appendix, "Orders for the Town and Borough of Morpeth, 1523," *Archaeologia Aeliana*, n.s. 13 (1889), 209–16.
18. Notts., Newark (-upon-Trent), 1550–99. First Minute Book, Newark Museum, D6.75/HT 8.
19. Oxon., Banbury, 1554–99. *Banbury Corporation Records: Tudor and Stuart*, ed. J. S. W. Gibson and E. R. C. Brinkworth, The Banbury Hist. Soc., vol. 15 (Oxford, 1977).
20. Oxon., Henley (-on-Thames), 1395–1599. *Henley Borough Records: Assembly Books i–iv, 1395–1543*, ed. P. M. Briers, Oxon. Rec. Soc. (Banbury, 1960); and Oxon. Archs. MSS D.D. Henley A.III.2/1 and A.V.1–5.
21. Oxon., Witney, 1538–99. *Calendar of the Court Books of the Borough of Witney, 1538–1610*, ed. James L. Bolton and Marjorie M. Maslen, Oxon. Rec. Soc., vol. 14 (Gloucester, 1985).
22. Shrops., Ludlow, 1590–99. Borough (Corporation) Minute Book, Shrops. RO 356/2/1, Box 2.
23. Suff., Sudbury, 1562–81. Town Book, Suff. RO, Bury St. Edmunds, EE 501 C 141/B/1.
24. Surrey, Guildford, 1514–99. *Guildford Borough Records, 1514–1546*, ed. Enid M. Dance, The Surrey Rec. Soc., vol. 24 (Frome, 1958); and Surrey RO, Guildford, BR/OC/1/20.
25. Sussex (E.), Lewes, 1542–99. *The Town Book of Lewes, 1542–1701*, ed. L. F. Salzman, Sussex Rec. Soc., vol. 48 (Lewes, 1945–6).
26. Sussex (E.), Winchelsea, 1527–97. Court Books, East Sussex RO Winchelsea 51–54.
27. War., Stratford-upon-Avon, 1553–98. *Minutes and Accounts of the Corporation of Stratford-upon-Avon and Other Records*, vols. 1–5, ed. Richard Savage, E. I. Fripp, and Levi Fox, Dugdale Soc. Publs., vols. 1 (Oxford, 1921), 3 (London, 1924), 5 (London, 1926), 10 (London, 1929), and 35 (Hertford, 1990).
28. Wilts., Chippenham, 1597–9. Borough of Chippenham A., Minute Book of the Bailiffs and Burgesses, 39 Eliz.–1684.
29. Wilts., Devizes, 1556–99. Borough Court Books, Wilts. RO G20/1/10–17.
30. Wilts., Marlborough, 1514–98. General Entry Books, Wilts. RO G22/1/13–19 and 39.
31. Wilts., Wilton, 1454–99. General Entry Books, Wilts. RO G25/1/21.

---

*Notes

Market Centers = places not classified as a City or Town (see the note to App. 1.1) but included in Everitt's list of market towns in the sixteenth and seventeenth centuries ("The Marketing of Agricultural Produce," esp. 468–75). Nearly all these places had taxable wealths of under £300 in 1334 and under £100 in 1524/5; they had fewer than 3,000 people in 1377 and/or 1524/5. Includes a total of c. 715 places, of which 32 places are analyzed here.

Assembly Books include any kind of minute book, notes of meetings of mayor and aldermen, town orders/ordinances, or other reports of events/decisions at assemblies of local officials that document regulation of social behavior (except for financial accounts). They do not include records that document the regular proceedings of local public courts, which are listed in Appendix 2.1.

Dates. For each entry, the dates indicate the earliest and the latest record used.

Appendix 6.1
List of "broad response" places

Listed here are the identification number (for use with maps), county, place name, type of court, and duodecades of "broad response" for all courts that reported four or more different types of offences in one or more duodecades. For fuller information and references, see Appendix 2.1.

9. Berks., Bray, manor, 4–5 types of offences, 1500s–10s.
11. Berks., Cookham, manor, 4–5 types of offences each in 1500s–10s and 1520s–30s.
17. Bucks., Chalfont St. Peter, manor, 4–5 types of offences, 1580s–90s.
18. Bucks., Chesham Higham and Chesham Bury, manor, 4–5 types of offences, 1520s–30s.
19. Bucks., Great Brickhill, manor, 4–5 types of offences each in 1520s–30s and 1540s–50s.
20. Bucks., Great Horwood, manor, 4–5 types of offences, 1520s–30s.
24. Bucks., Tingewick, manor, 4–5 types of offences, 1520s–30s.
26. Cambs., Ely Barton, manor, 4–5 types of offences, 1440s–50s.
32. Ches., Halton, Honour and Fee of, composite manorial estate, 4–5 types of offences, 1520s–30s.
33. Ches., Kinderton, Barony (and halmote) of, composite manorial estate, 4–5 types of offences, 1560s–70s.
38. Corn., Padstow, manor, 6 or more types of offences, 1560s–70s.
50. Derby., Chesterfield, borough, 4–5 types of offences, 1520s–30s.
52. Derby., Melbourne, manor, 4–5 types of offences, 1460s–70s.
60. Devon, Monkleigh, manor, 6 or more types of offences, 1560s–70s; 4–5 types, 1580s–90s.
63. Devon, West Budleigh, hundred, 4–5 types of offences, 1540s–50s.
67. Dorset, Bridport, borough, 6 or more types of offences, 1520s–30s; 4–5 types, 1580s–90s.
68. Dorset, Knowlton, hundred, 4–5 types of offences, 1560s–70s.
71. Durham, Durham, Bishop of, Halmote Court, composite manorial estate, 4–5 types of offences each in 1500s–10s, 1520s–30s, and 1540s–50s.

72. Durham, Durham, Dean and Chapter of, Halmote Court, composite manorial estate, 4–5 types of offences, 1460s–70s; 6 or more types, 1500s–10s.
75. Essex, Havering (-atte-Bower), manor, 4–5 types of offences, 1460s–70s; 6 or more types, 1480s–90s.
79. Essex, Walden (= Saffron Walden), manor, 4–5 types of offences each in 1420s–30s, 1460s–70s, and 1480s–90s; 6 or more types, 1540s–50s.
81. Essex, Wivenhoe, manor, 4–5 types of offences each in 1560s–70s and 1580s–90s.
86. Gloucs., Thornbury, manor, 4–5 types of offences, 1580s–90s.
90. Hants., Basingstoke, borough, 4–5 types of offences each in 1440s–50s, 1540s–50s, and 1580s–90s.
93. Heref., Bishop's Frome, manor, 4–5 types of offences each in 1460s–70s and 1540s–50s.
112. Kent, Toltintrough, hundred, 4–5 types of offences, 1480s–90s.
114. Lancs., Clitheroe, Honour of, composite manorial estate, 4–5 types of offences each in 1520s–30s and 1580s–90s.
115. Lancs., Prescot, manor, 4–5 types of offences, 1520s–30s; 6 or more types, 1540s–50s; 4–5 types, 1560s–70s.
116. Lancs., West Derby, manor, 4–5 types of offences, 1520s–30s.
123. Leics., Loughborough, manor, 4–5 types of offences, 1460s–70s.
135. Middx., Fulham, manor, 6 or more types of offences each in 1460s–70s and 1500s–10s.
136. Middx., Harrow, manor, 4–5 types of offences, 1520s–30s.
138. Norf., Cawston, manor, 4–5 types of offences each in 1480s–90s and 1560s–70s.
142. Norf., Horsham St. Faith, manor, 6 or more types of offences, 1560s–70s.
165. Oxon., Kirtlington, manor, 6 or more types of offences each in 1500s–10s, 1520s–30s, and 1580s–90s.
173. Shrops., Whitchurch, manor, 6 or more types of offences, 1560s–70s.
175. Som., Minehead, manor, 4–5 types of offences, 1460s–70s; 6 or more types, 1480s–90s.
182. Staffs., Cannock and Rugeley, manor, 4–5 types of offences each in 1400s–10s, 1560s–70s, and 1580s–90s.
187. Staffs., Penkridge, manor, 4–5 types of offences each in 1540s–50s and 1580s–90s.
190. Suff., Clare, borough, 4–5 types of offences, 1460s–70s; 6 or more types, 1480s–90s; 4–5 types, 1520s–30s.
193. Suff., Lidgate, manor, 4–5 types of offences, 1580s–90s.
196. Suff., South Elmham, manor, 4–5 types of offences, 1480s–90s.
199. Surrey, Godalming, manor (and hundred), 4–5 types of offences, 1520s–30s.
200. Surrey, Kingston (-upon-Thames), manor, 4–5 types of offences, 1420s–30s.
202. Surrey, Tooting Bec (= Upper Tooting), in Wandsworth, manor, 4–5 types of offences, 1520s–30s.
209. Sussex (W.), Amberley, manor, 6 or more types of offences, 1520s–30s.
210. Sussex (W.), Manhood, hundred, 4–5 types of offences, 1520s–30s.
213. War., Atherstone, manor, 4–5 types of offences, 1460s–70s.
220. War., Sutton Coldfield, borough, 4–5 types of offences, 1540s–50s.

223. Westml., Maulds Meaburn, in Crosby Ravensworth, manor, 4–5 types of offences each in 1560s–70s and 1580s–90s.
225. Wilts., Castle Combe, manor, 4–5 types of offences each in 1420s–30s, 1440s–50s, 1460s–70s, and 1560s–70s.
226. Wilts., Colerne, manor, 4–5 types of offences, 1500s–10s.
227. Wilts., Downton: manor, 4–5 types of offences each in 1460s–70s and 1520s–30s; borough, 4–5 types of offences, 1500s–10s.
235. Worcs., Hanbury, manor, 4–5 types of offences, 1580s–90s.
237. Worcs., Pershore, manor, 6 or more types of offences, 1440s–50s; 4–5 types, 1460s–70s.
242. N. Yorks., Ampleforth, manor, 4–5 types of offences each in 1520s–30s and 1540s–50s.
243. N. Yorks., Northallerton: manor, 4–5 types of offences, 1500s–10s; borough, 4–5 types of offences, 1500s–10s.
251. West Yorks., Methley, manor, 4–5 types of offences, 1500s–10s.
254. West Yorks., Wakefield, manor, 4–5 types of cases, 1520s–30s.

Appendix 6.2
Region of the country by type of community: observed numbers vs. an even distribution*

	North/Northwest		West/Southwest		Midlands/East Central		East Anglia/Southeast		Total
	Observed	Even distrib.	Observed	Even distrib.	Observed	Even distrib.	Observed	Even distrib.	
Villages	123=52%	125=53%	164=36%	238=53%	295=64%	246=53%	325=58%	298=53%	907=53%
Market centers	49=21%	78=33%	210=47%	149=33%	121=26%	153=33%	186=33%	186=33%	566=33%
Hundreds	0	20= 9%	70=16%	39= 9%	27= 6%	40= 9%	51= 9%	49= 9%	148= 9%
Composite manorial estates	64=27%	13= 5%	6= 1%	24= 5%	21= 5%	25= 5%	0	30= 5%	91= 5%

*Covers the full period, 1370–1599. For definition of regions, see Map 2.1 and note 11 to Ch. 6.

Appendix 6.3
Eight continuum-based agrarian regions: (a) definition and arrangement of regions, and (b) data for the "broad response" and "no response" places (villages and market centers only)

(a) Definition and arrangement of regions

Primarily grain production:
1. Wolds and downland (light soils, high-quality grain but with sheep required for manure = "sheep-corn" system, common fields)

Mainly arable with some animals:
2. Arable vales (heavier clay soils, generally common fields but in the sixteenth century some enclosure and some convertible agriculture, compact village communities)

Divergent patterns:
3. Heathlands (sandy, gravelly soil, in some cases used as arable with sheep for manure and compaction, esp. Norfolk; in others covered by forest)

Generally pastoral but some arable :
4. Pastoral vales (rearing and fattening of cattle and dairying, poor quality soils, much land enclosed prior to the sixteenth century, some villages but dispersed settlement also common)

Mainly animals but varying amounts of arable in some cases:
5. Fenland (extensive grazing grounds, variable proportions of pasture to arable, stock breeding and fattening, dairying, plus fishing and fowling)
6. Marshland (intensive animal fattening and dairying along eastern and southeastern coasts)

Primarily animal raising:

7. Forests and wood pasture (heavy, clay soils, rough grazing, animal raising often supplemented by industrial activity, especially cloth manufacture, mining, and the working of wood, metals, and hides, as well as by other forms of bye-employment, smaller and dispersed settlements)

8. Fells and moorland (thin, acid soils, wet, cold climate, ample common, dispersed settlements, pastoral activity commonly joined to industrial bye-employment, especially mining and quarrying, found in northern England, north Cornwall, and parts of Devon)

The relation between Thirsk's twelve-category system and the eight types in this continuum model is as follows. Under Mixed Farming in the former: downland, wolds, and breckland became #1 above, wolds and downland, with the exception of the Norfolk heath, which went into #3 with the forest heath included in the former system under Wood Pasture; clay vales became #2, arable vales; and marshland went into #6 with some areas defined as Open Pasture in the former system. Under Wood Pasture in the former: all went into #7, forests and wood pasture, except the forest heaths, which went into #3. Under Open Pasture in the former: fells and moorland became #8; rearing and fattening areas became #4, pastoral vales; areas of fattening of sheep and some cattle went into #6, marshland; fenlands became #5; and dairying went into #4, pastoral vales. See Thirsk, *Agricultural Regions*, Map 2 and pp. 37–9, and Everitt, "Country, County and Town."

Appendix 6.3 (continued)

(b) "Broad response" and "no response" places (villages and market centers only)*

| | Primarily arable | | | | | | | Primarily pastoral | |
	Wolds and downland	Arable vales	Heathlands (divergent patterns)	Pastoral vales	Fenland	Marshland	Forests and wood pasture	Fells and moorland
1420–1499								
0 offences reported	15%	38%	3%	6%	4%	7%	20%	7%
4+ types of offences	28%	11%	6%	11%	6%	0	33%	6%
1500–1559								
0 offences reported	12%	34%	4%	10%	6%	10%	17%	7%
4+ types of offences	15%	22%	7%	11%	4%	0	30%	11%
1560–1599								
0 offences reported	21%	32%	4%	6%	4%	4%	23%	4%
4+ types of offences	11%	0	17%	28%	0	6%	22%	17%

*For categories and sources, see Appendix 6.3a and text; for N of each group, see Table 6.3. All numbers are row percentages.

Appendix 6.4
Information about the tax records used in Tables 6.5–6.6 and Appendices 7.6–7.7

The sources used and their location. See note 25 to Chapter 6.

Nature of the places analyzed. These charts refer only to villages and market centers.

1334 Lay Subsidy. Assessments at a one-tenth value were multiplied by 0.667 to convert them to the same base as the one-fifteenth assessments. Information on the total amount of tax was obtained for 206 places = 93 percent.

Poll Taxes of 1377–1381. Whenever possible listings from 1377 were used, as they are the most complete. For those communities for which the earlier list was not available, I used returns from 1379 or 1381. Richard M. Smith told me that the latter underrecord names by c. 15–30 percent as compared with 1377, so I multiplied values from those records by 1.225. Information on number of taxpayers was obtained for 81 places for 1377 and for 10 places for 1379 or 1381, together = 41 percent.

1524/5 Subsidies. I used values from 1524 whenever possible and did not attempt to correct for possible distortions between urban and rural areas. Information on the total amount of tax was obtained for 179 places = 81 percent, on the number of taxpayers for 169 places = 76 percent, and on the distribution of payments within the community for 157 = 71 percent.

Hearth Taxes. Whenever possible records produced between 1664 and 1674 were used, to achieve the greatest consistency of information; if necessary I used lists from 1662. Information on the total number of hearths and households was obtained for 184 places = 83 percent and on the distribution of hearths per household for 175 places = 79 percent.

Expanding boundaries of market centers. Although the parish boundaries of rural communities did not change over time, some of the market communities that grew within this period gradually took over parts of adjacent parishes, often formerly described as "foreign" neighborhoods. I therefore compared in the various tax records for such places the parishes included/excluded so as to determine what corrections needed to be made.

Method of preparing measures of relative population and wealth. For each category of information, I rank listed the places for which I had information and converted those into percentile rankings for easier comparison. I then produced a median percentile for each group of places as defined by their response to wrongdoing in the various duodecades.

Method of preparing measures of absolute size, wealth, and extent of poverty. The number of taxpayers in 1524/5 and households in the Hearth Taxes are straightforward; medians are displayed. In computing median tax/capita and median number of hearths/house, I noted the median value while working with the records and display the mean of the median in these figures. To identify the percentage of very poor people or household heads I employed the widely used criteria of those assessed on land/goods/income of less than 40s for 1524/5 and of those assessed on only one hearth or excused due to poverty in the Hearth Taxes.

Number of villages and market centers for which tax-based information was obtained within the selected periods and sub-groupings analyzed

1420–99.   "No response": 37–84 (N = 92); "Broad response": 8–17 (N = 17).

1500–59.   "No response": 35–76 (N = 85); "Broad response": 12–27 (N = 28).

1560–99.   "No response": 17–45 (N = 49); "Broad response": 9–20 (N = 21).

1420s–30s. No response: 33–79 (N = 82); Disharmony Cluster: 13–26 (N = 28).

1460s–70s. No response: 39–82 (N = 86); Disharmony Cluster: 16–35 (N = 37); Disorder Cluster: 14–28 (N = 29); Poverty Cluster: 14–22 (N = 22).

1520s–30s. No response: 31–68 (N = 74); Disharmony Cluster: 15–39 (N = 41); Disorder Cluster: 19–44 (N = 45); Poverty Cluster: 23–43 (N = 45).

1580s–90s. No response: 43–53 (N = 60); Disharmony Cluster: 10–16 (N = 19); Disorder Cluster: 24–6 (N = 29); Poverty Cluster: 54–62 (N = 72).

Appendices

Number and type of tax records used for the 221 villages and market centers

1334	1377	1379 or 1381	1524/5 (total only or full listing)	Hearth Taxes (total only or full listing)		No. of places
X	X	—	X	X		64
X	—	X	X	X		7
					Total, 4 sets	71
X	X	—	X	—		8
X	—	X	—	X		2
X	X	—	—	X		5
X	—	—	X	X		80
					Total, 3 sets	95
X	X	—	—	—		3
X	—	X	—	—		1
X	—	—	X	—		13
X	—	—	—	X		18
—	—	—	X	X		5
—	X	—	—	X		1
					Total, 2 sets	41
X	—	—	—	—		5
—	—	—	X	—		1
—	—	—	—	X		5
					Total, 1 set	11
—	—	—	—	—		
					Total, no information	3

Appendix 7.1a
Percentage of courts under observation that reported scolding, by type of community

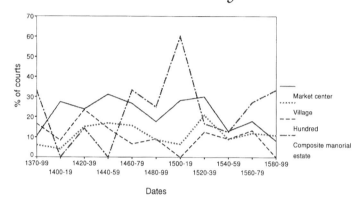

Appendix 7.1b
Percentage of courts under observation that reported eavesdropping/nightwalking, by type of community

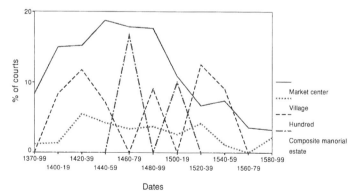

Appendix 7.1c
Percentage of courts under observation that reported sexual misconduct, by type of community

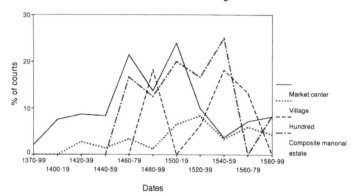

Appendix 7.1d
Percentage of courts under observation that reported disorderly alehouses, by type of community

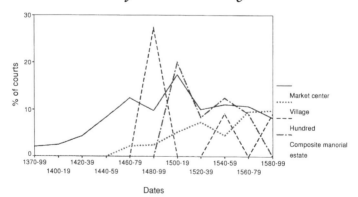

Appendix 7.1e
Percentage of courts under observation that reported being badly governed, by type of community

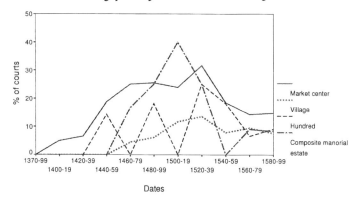

Appendix 7.1f
Percentage of courts under observation that reported hedgebreaking, by type of community

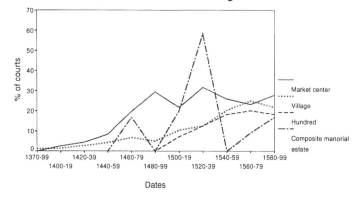

Appendix 7.1g
Percentage of courts under observation that reported vagabonds/living idly, by type of community

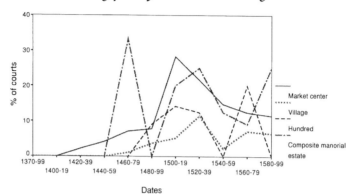

Appendix 7.1h
Percentage of courts under observation that reported receiving subtenants, by type of community

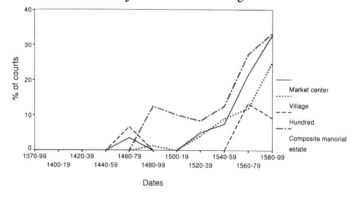

Appendix 7.1i
Percentage of courts under observation that reported gaming, by type of community

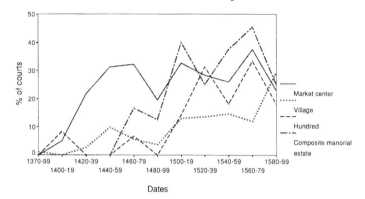

Appendix 7.2
Type of community by type of response to wrongdoing, selected duodecades*

		Distribution of courts in each cluster by type of community (row percentages)			
	N	Villages	Market centers	Hundreds	Composite manorial estates
1420s–30s					
No offences reported	99	57%	26%	11%	6%
Disharmony cluster	35	37%	43%	17%	3%
Disorder cluster	8	25%	75%	0	0
Poverty cluster	5	40%	60%	0	0
Total no. of courts under observation[†]	143				
1460s–70s					
No offences reported	100	65%	21%	12%	2%
Disharmony cluster	41	39%	51%	2%	7%
Disorder cluster	30	27%	70%	0	3%
Poverty cluster	26	23%	62%	4%	12%
Total no. of courts under observation[†]	166				
1520s–30s					
No offences reported	84	68%	20%	8%	4%
Disharmony cluster	47	45%	43%	9%	4%
Disorder cluster	55	35%	47%	9%	9%
Poverty cluster	57	37%	42%	7%	14%
Total no. of courts under observation[†]	184				
1580s–90s					
No offences reported	71	54%	31%	10%	6%
Disharmony cluster	23	52%	30%	0	17%
Disorder cluster	32	44%	47%	3%	6%
Poverty cluster	82	49%	39%	4%	9%
Total no. of courts under observation[†]	176				

*Includes all 267 counts.

[†] Because some courts reported offences in more than one cluster, the numbers for the individual clusters add to more than the total N.

Appendix 7.3
Region of the country by type of response to wrongdoing, selected duodecades[*]

	North/ Northwest	West/ Southwest	Midlands/ East Central	East Anglia/ Southeast
	Distribution of courts in each cluster by region (row percentages)			
1420s–30s				
No offences reported	9%	21%	34%	35%
Disharmony cluster	17%	23%	23%	37%
1460s–70s				
No offences reported	11%	30%	29%	30%
Disharmony cluster	17%	27%	24%	32%
Disorder cluster	13%	27%	27%	33%
Poverty cluster	19%	39%	15%	27%
1520s–30s				
No offences reported	12%	27%	26%	35%
Disharmony cluster	13%	21%	32%	34%
Disorder cluster	24%	31%	13%	33%
Poverty cluster	28%	21%	21%	30%
1580s–90s				
No offences reported	9%	24%	27%	41%
Disharmony cluster	61%	17%	13%	9%
Disorder cluster	25%	31%	22%	22%
Poverty cluster	20%	26%	26%	29%

[*] Includes all 267 courts; for N of each group, see Appendix 7.2. For definition of regions, see Map 2.1 and note 11 to Ch. 6.

Appendix 7.4

Locational and economic factors by type of response to wrongdoing, selected duodecades (villages and market centers only)*

	N	On long-distance road	On navigable river or the coast	Within 25 km of London	Industrial activity	Broad agrarian categories Mixed farming (arable)	Pasture Open	Wood
1420s–30s								
No offences reported	82	25%	19%	6%	13%	51%	20%	28%
Disharmony cluster	28	48%	25%	11%	37%	52%	30%	22%
1460s–70s								
No offences reported	86	28%	20%	1%	21%	57%	21%	22%
Disharmony cluster	37	41%	29%	13%	38%	46%	26%	31%
Disorder cluster	29	31%	41%	10%	45%	31%	45%	24%
Poverty cluster	22	43%	24%	24%	43%	29%	38%	33%
1520s–30s								
No offences reported	74	22%	22%	4%	4%	45%	34%	22%
Disharmony cluster	41	38%	25%	3%	43%	48%	18%	35%
Disorder cluster	45	49%	18%	7%	49%	49%	21%	30%
Poverty cluster	45	50%	23%	7%	57%	45%	25%	30%
1580s–90s								
No offences reported	60	34%	18%	5%	18%	45%	21%	34%
Disharmony cluster	19	38%	21%	0	32%	58%	32%	11%
Disorder cluster	29	35%	24%	4%	58%	27%	54%	19%
Poverty cluster	72	35%	16%	4%	32%	51%	28%	22%

* For definitions and sources, see text.

Appendix 7.5
Eight continuum-based agrarian regions by type of response to wrongdoing, selected duodecades (villages and market centers only)*

	Primarily arable →						Primarily pastoral →	
	Wolds and downland	Arable vales	Heathlands (divergent patterns)	Pastoral vales	Fenland	Marshland	Forests and wood pasture	Fells and moorland
1420s–30s								
No offences reported	10%	32%	3%	9%	5%	10%	27%	5%
Disharmony cluster	25%	21%	4%	0	18%	0	21%	11%
1460s–70s								
No offences reported	14%	37%	5%	7%	6%	6%	17%	7%
Disharmony cluster	18%	23%	5%	5%	8%	0	30%	13%
Disorder cluster	14%	14%	3%	7%	21%	3%	24%	14%
Poverty cluster	19%	10%	0	10%	19%	0	33%	10%
1520s–30s								
No offences reported	12%	27%	3%	12%	9%	8%	19%	9%
Disharmony cluster	15%	25%	10%	0	5%	0	33%	13%
Disorder cluster	16%	23%	14%	7%	5%	0	26%	9%
Poverty cluster	16%	25%	9%	9%	7%	2%	23%	9%
1580s–90s								
No offences reported	14%	25%	4%	9%	5%	4%	32%	7%
Disharmony cluster	11%	32%	11%	11%	0	5%	11%	21%
Disorder cluster	12%	0	12%	19%	12%	8%	15%	23%
Poverty cluster	12%	28%	12%	9%	4%	4%	17%	14%

*For categories and sources, see Appendix 6.3a and text; for N of each group, see Appendix 7.4. All numbers are row percentages.

Appendix 7.6

Some measures of relative population and wealth by type of response to wrongdoing, selected duodecades (villages and market centers only)*

	Measures of relative population					Measures of the relative wealth of the community				
	Size in 1377/81, ranking as %	Change in ranking by size, 1377/81-1524/5	Size in 1524/5, ranking as %	Change in ranking, 1524/5-Hearth Tax	Size in Hearth Tax, ranking as %	Wealth in 1334, ranking as %	Change in ranking by wealth, 1334-1524/5	Wealth in 1524/5, ranking as %	Change in ranking, 1524/5-Hearth Tax	Wealth in Hearth Tax, ranking as %
1420–30s										
No offences reported	48	−5%	43			44	−4%	40		
Disharmony cluster	54	13%	67			47	+14%	61		
1460s–70s										
No offences reported	37	+4%	41			42	−1%	41		
Disharmony cluster	59	+6%	6%			48	+1%	49		
Disorder cluster	69	−4%	65			44	+10%	54		
Poverty cluster	56	+5%	61			50	+1%	51		

1520s–30s										
No offences reported	41	0	41	0	41	42	0	42	−1%	41
Disharmony cluster	46	+5%	51	2%	49	46	+3%	49	+1%	50
Disorder cluster	53	+2%	55	+3%	58	47	+5%	52	+9%	61
Poverty cluster	44	+8%	52	+4%	56	48	+2%	50	+8%	58
1580s–90s										
No offences reported	45	−3%	42		46			46	0	46
Disharmony cluster	45	+1%	46		46			37	0	37
Disorder cluster	55	+2%	57		47			57	−1%	56
Poverty cluster	51	+3%	54		48			51	0	51

*See Appendix 6.4 for a discussion of sources and methods, with the N for which information of each type was available. For the total N of each group, see Appendix 7.4. All figures are medians.

Appendix 7.7

Some measures of absolute size, wealth, and extent of poverty by type of response to wrongdoing, selected duodecades (villages and market centers only)*

	No. of taxpayers or households			Distribution of wealth within the community		Extent of poverty: % of very poor people or household heads		
	In 1524/5	% change, 1524/5– H. tax	In Hearth tax	Median tax/cap., 1524/5 (in shillings)	Median no. of hearths/house in H. tax	In 1524/5	% change, 1524/5– H. tax	In Hearth tax
1460s–70s								
No offences reported	44			15.8		36%		
Disharmony cluster	79			14.5		38%		
Disorder cluster	79			13.5		39%		
Poverty cluster	72			15.7		29%		
1520s–30s								
No offences reported	44	+66%	73	14.8	1.72	35%	+12%	47%
Disharmony cluster	54	+59%	86	11.8	1.69	41%	+10%	51%
Disorder cluster	60	+87%	112	15.5	1.64	38%	+10%	48%
Poverty cluster	54	+104%	110	13.9	1.60	38%	+20%	58%
1580s–90s								
No offences reported	47	+55%	73	13.4	1.63	39%	+13%	52%
Disharmony cluster	49	+63%	80	12.0	1.38	34%	+24%	58%
Disorder cluster	59	+90%	112	15.9	1.40	30%	+22%	52%
Poverty cluster	54	+91%	103	14.0	1.50	38%	+21%	59%

*See Appendix 6.4 for explanation of sources and methods, with the N for which information of each type is available. For the total N of each group, see Table 7.4. All figures are medians except for the central two columns, which are means of the medians. The 1420s–30s are excluded because they are so far removed from 1524/5.

Bibliography

A. Primary sources

This list includes only works cited in the notes. For additional sources, see Appendices 1.1, 1.2, 1.3, 2.1, and 3.2.

Adames, Jonas. *The Order of Keeping a Courte Leet and Court Baron*. [London], 1593. STC #100.

Ashby, George. *George Ashby's Poems*. Ed. Mary Bateson. EETS Extra Ser. No. 76. London, 1899.

Becon, Thomas. *The Catechism of Thomas Becon*. Ed. John Ayre. Parker Soc., vol.3. Cambridge, 1844.

    Prayers and Other Pieces of Thomas Becon. Ed. John Ayre. Parker Soc., vol. 4. Cambridge, 1844.

The Book of Vices and Virtues. Ed. W. N. Francis. EETS Orig. Ser. No. 217. London, 1942.

Boyle, J. R., ed. "Orders for the Town and Borough of Morpeth, 1523." *Archaeologia Aeliana*, n.s. 13 (1889): 209–16.

A Calendar of Charters and Other Documents Belonging to the Hospital of William Wyggeston at Leicester. Ed. A. H. Thompson. Leicester, 1933.

Calendars of the Assize Records for Essex, Herts., Kent, Surrey, and Sussex, Elizabeth I. Ed. J. S. Cockburn. London, 1975–80.

Certaine Sermons or Homilies Appointed to Be Read in Churches in the Time of Queen Elizabeth I. Ed. Mary E. Rickey and Thomas B. Stroup. Gainesville, Fla., 1968.

The Chester Mystery Cycle. Ed. R. M. Lumiansky and David Mills. EETS Supp. Ser. No. 3. London, 1974.

Clark, Elaine, ed. "The Court Rolls of Horsham St. Faith: A Translation, 1265–1292." Typescript.

Continuation of the Court Leet Records of the Manor of Manchester, A.D. 1586–1602. Ed. John Harland. Chetham Soc., vol. 65. Manchester, 1865.

Court Leet Records [of Southampton]. Vol. I, pts. 1 (1550–77) and 2 (1578–1602). Ed. F. J. C. Hearnshaw and D. M. Hearnshaw. Southampton Rec. Soc. Publs. Southampton, 1905–6.

The Court Rolls of the Honor of Clitheroe in the County of Lancaster. 3 vols. Ed. William Farrer. Edinburgh, 1912–13.

Court Rolls of the Manor of Wakefield. Vol. II, ed. W. P. Baildon, and vol. III, ed. J. Lister. Yorks. Archaeol. Soc. Leeds, 1906 and 1917.

The Coventry Leet Book or Mayor's Register. 4 vols. Ed. Mary D. Harris. Coventry, 1907–13.

Dan Michel's Ayenbite of Inwyt. Ed. Richard Morris. EETS Orig. Ser. No. 23. London, 1866.

The Domesday of Inclosures, 1517–1518. 2 vols. Ed. I. S. Leadam. London, 1971; orig. publ. 1897.

Early English Meals and Manners: The Babees Book, Etc. Ed. F. J. Furnivall. EETS Orig. Ser. No. 32. London, 1868.

English Gilds: The Original Ordinances. Ed. Toulmin Smith and Lucy Toulmin Smith. EETS Orig. Ser. No. 40. London, 1870.

English Wycliffite Sermons, vol. I. Ed. Anne Hudson. Oxford, 1983.

Fortescue, John, Sir. *De Laudibus Legum Angliae.* Ed. A. Amos. Cambridge, 1825. *The Governance of England.* Ed. Charles Plummer. Oxford, 1985.

Four English Political Tracts of the Later Middle Ages. Ed. Jean-Philippe Genet. Camden Soc. Fourth Ser., vol. 18. London, 1977.

Goldberg, P. J. P., ed. *Women in England, c. 1275–1525: Documentary Sources.* Manchester, 1995.

The Good Wife Taught Her Daughter, The Good Wyfe Wold a Pylgremage, The Thewis of Gud Women. Ed. Tauno F. Mustanoja. Helsinki, 1948.

Historical Poems of the XIVth and XVth Centuries. Ed. R. H. Robbins. New York, 1959.

Hoccleve's Works. Ed. F. J. Furnivall. EETS Extra Ser. No. 72. London, 1897.

"How the Good Wijf Taughte Hir Doughtir." In *Early English Meals and Manners: The Babees Book, Etc.,* ed. F. J. Furnivall. EETS Orig. Ser. No. 32. London, 1868.

The Injunctions and Other Ecclesiastical Proceedings of Richard Barnes, Bishop of Durham, from 1575 to 1587. Surtees Soc., vol. 22. Durham, 1850.

Jacob's Well: An English Treatise on the Cleansing of Man's Conscience, part 1. Ed. Arthur Brandeis. EETS Orig. Ser. No. 115. London, 1900.

Kent at Law, 1602: The County Jurisdiction: Assizes and Sessions of the Peace. Ed. Louis A. Knafla. London, 1994.

Langland, William. *Will's Visions of Piers Plowman and Do-Well: Piers Plowman, The A Version.* Rev. edn., ed. George Kane. London, 1988.

The Lay-Folks Mass Book. Ed. Thomas F. Simmons. EETS Orig. Ser. No. 71. London, 1879.

The Lay Subsidy of 1334. Ed. Robin E. Glasscock. London, 1975.

Liverpool Town Books: Proceedings of Assemblies, Common Councils, Portmoot Courts, etc. Ed. Jesse A. Twemlow. Vol. I, 1550–71, Liverpool, 1918; vol. II, 1571–1603, Liverpool, 1935.

Lollard Sermons. Ed. Gloria Cigman. EETS Orig. Ser. No. 294. London, 1989.

[Lydgate, John]. "The Assembly of Gods." Ed. Oscar L. Triggs. EETS Extra Ser. No. 69. London, 1896.

Lydgate's Reson and Sensuallyte, vol. I. Ed. Ernst Sieper. EETS Extra Ser. No. 84. London, 1901.

The Macro Plays: The Castle of Perseverance, Wisdom, Mankind. Ed. Mark Eccles. EETS Orig. Ser. No. 262. London, 1969.

Melanchthon and Bucer. Ed. Wilhelm Pauck. Library of Christian Classics, vol. 19. Philadelphia, 1969.

Mirk's Festial: A Collection of Homilies, pt. 1. Ed. Theodor Erbe. EETS Extra Ser. No. 96. London, 1905.

Modus tenend[i] cur[iam] baron[is] cum visu[m] franem [sic] plegii. [London], 1510. STC #7706.

Modus tenendi curiam baronis, cum visum franci plegii. [London], 1536. STC #7713.

More, Thomas. *Utopia*. Ed. Edward Surtz. New Haven, Conn., 1964.

Mum and the Sothsegger. Ed. Mabel Day and Robert Steele. EETS Orig. Ser. No. 199. London, 1936.

Non-Cycle Plays and the Winchester Dialogues. Ed. Norman Davis. Leeds, 1979.

The Peasants' Revolt of 1381. Ed. R. B. Dobson. London, 1983.

The Poems of John Audelay. Ed. Ella K. Whiting. EETS Orig. Ser. No. 184. London, 1931.

Records of the Borough of Leicester. Ed. Mary Bateson. Vol. II, 1327–1509, London, 1901; vol. III, 1509–1603, Cambridge, 1905.

Religious Lyrics of the XVth Century. Ed. Carleton Brown. Oxford, 1939.

Sandys, Edwin. *The Sermons . . . and Some Miscellaneous Pieces*. Ed. John Ayre. Parker Soc., vol. 41. Cambridge, 1841.

Select Cases on Defamation to 1600. Ed. R. H. Helmholz. Selden Soc., vol. 101. London, 1985.

Select Pleas in Manorial and Other Seignorial Courts, vol. II. Ed. F. W. Maitland. Selden Soc., London, 1889.

Selections from English Wycliffite Writings. Ed. Anne Hudson. Cambridge, 1978.

Selections from Hoccleve. Ed. M. C. Seymour. Oxford, 1981.

Smith, Thomas. *De Republica Anglorum*. Ed. Mary Dewar. Cambridge, 1982.

Some Early Tracts on Poor Relief. Ed. F. R. Salter. London, 1926.

The Statutes of the Realm. 12 vols. London, 1810–28.

Steer, Francis W. "The Statutes of Saffron Walden Almshouses." *Trans. Essex Archaeol. Soc.*, n.s. 25 (1955–60): 160–221.

Stow, John. *A Survey of London*. Ed. Charles L. Kingsford. Oxford, 1908.

The Third Book of Remembrance of Southampton, 1514–1602, vol. III, 1573–1589. Ed. A. L. Merson. Southampton Rec. Ser., vol. 8. Southampton, 1965.

Three Middle English Sermons from the Worcester Chapter Manuscript F.10. Ed. D. M. Grisdale. Leeds School of English Language Texts and Monographs, no. 5. Leeds, 1939.

Three Prose Versions of the Secreta Secretorum. Ed. Robert Steele. EETS Extra Ser. No. 74. London, 1898.

"Tractatus de Regimine Principium." In *Four English Political Tracts of the Late Middle Ages*, ed. Jean Philippe Genet. Camden Soc. Fourth Ser., no. 18. London, 1977.

Translations and Reprints from Original Sources of European History, vol. 1, no. 6. Ed. Edward P. Cheyney. Philadelphia, 1897.

Tudor Royal Proclamations. 2 vols. Ed. P. L. Hughes and J. F. Larkin. New Haven, Conn., 1964–9.

Twenty-Six Political and Other Poems, part 1. Ed. J. Kail. EETS Orig. Ser. No. 124. London, 1904.

Vives, Juan Luis. "De Subventione Pauperum." In *Some Early Tracts on Poor Relief*, ed. F. R. Salter. London, 1926.

William Lambarde and Local Government. Ed. Conyers Read. Ithaca, N.Y., 1962.

Woolton, John. *The Christian Manual*. Parker Soc., vol. 49. Cambridge, 1851.
York Civic Records, vol. IV. Ed. Angelo Raine. Yorks. Archaeol. Soc. Rec. Ser., vol. 108. Wakefield, 1945.
The York House Books, 1461–1490. Ed. Lorraine C. Attreed. Stroud, 1991.

B. Secondary Studies

Adair, Richard. *Courtship, Illegitimacy and Marriage in Early Modern England*. Manchester, 1996.
Aers, David. *Community, Gender, and Individual Identity*. London, 1988.
    "*Piers Plowman*: Poverty, Work, and Community." In *Community, Gender, and Individual Identity*, ed. David Aers, 20–72. London, 1988.
Amussen, Susan D. *An Ordered Society: Gender and Class in Early Modern England*. New York, 1988.
Ankarloo, Bengt, and Gustav Henningsen, eds. *Early Modern European Witchcraft: Centres and Peripheries*. Oxford, 1993.
Appleby, A. B. *Famine in Tudor and Stuart England*. Liverpool, 1978.
Ashley, W. J. *An Introduction to English Economic History and Theory*, vol. II. 4th edn., London, 1906.
Ault, W. O. *The Self-Directing Activities of Village Communities in Medieval England*. Boston, Mass., 1952.
    "Some Early Village By-laws." *English Historical Review* 45 (1930): 208–31.
    "Village Assemblies in Medieval England." In *Album Helen M. Cam*. Studies Presented to the International Commission for the History of Representative and Parliamentary Institutions, vol. 23. Louvain, 1960.
Baigent, Francis J., and J. E. Millard. *A History of the Ancient Town and Manor of Basingstoke in the County of Southampton*. 2 vols. Basingstoke, 1889.
Bailey, Mark. "Demographic Decline in Late Medieval England." *Economic History Review*, 2nd ser. 49 (1996): 1–19.
    "Rural Society." In *Fifteenth-Century Attitudes*, ed. Rosemary Horrox, 150–68. Cambridge, 1994.
Bakhtin, Mikhail. *Rabelais and His World*. Trans. Helene Iswolsky. Bloomington, 1984.
Barron, Caroline M. "The 'Golden Age' of Women in Medieval London." *Reading Medieval Studies* 15 (1989): 35–58.
Barry, Jonathan, and Christopher Brooks, eds. *The Middling Sort of People: Culture, Society and Politics in England, 1550–1800*. New York, 1994.
Beckerman, John S. "The Articles of Presentment of a Court Leet and Court Baron, in English, c. 1400." *Bulletin of the Institute of Historical Research* 48 (1974): 230–4.
    "Customary Law in English Manorial Courts in the Thirteenth and Fourteenth Centuries." University of London Ph.D. thesis, 1972.
    "Procedural Innovation and Institutional Change in Medieval English Manorial Courts." *Law and History Review* 10 (1992): 197–252.
Beier, A. L. *Masterless Men: The Vagrancy Problem in England, 1560–1640*. London, 1985.
    "The Social Problems of an Elizabethan Country Town: Warwick, 1580–90." In *Country Towns in Pre-Industrial England*, ed. Peter Clark, 46–85. Leicester, 1981.

Ben-Amos, Ilana K. *Adolescence and Youth in Early Modern England*. New Haven, Conn., 1994.

Bennett, Judith M. "Medieval Women, Modern Women: Across the Great Divide." In *Culture and History, 1350–1600*, ed. David Aers, 147–75. London, 1992.

 Women in the Medieval English Countryside. Oxford, 1987.

Blanchard, I. S. W. "Population Change, Enclosure, and the Early Tudor Economy." *Economic History Review*, 2nd ser. 23 (1970): 427–45.

Bloomfield, Morton. *The Seven Deadly Sins: An Introduction to the History of a Religious Concept with Special Reference to Medieval English Literature*. East Lansing, Mich., 1952.

Boose, Lynda E. "Scolding Brides and Bridling Scolds: Taming the Woman's Unruly Member." *Shakespeare Quarterly* 42 (1991): 179–213.

Bourdieu, Pierre. *Outline of a Theory of Practice*. Trans. Richard Nice. Cambridge, 1977.

Bowers, John M. "Piers Plowman and the Police: Notes Toward a History of the Wycliffite Langland." In *The Yearbook of Langland Studies*, vol. 6 (1992), 1–50.

Brewer, John. *The Sinews of Power*. Cambridge, Mass., 1990.

Brigden, Susan E. "Religion and Social Obligation in Early Sixteenth-Century London." *Past and Present* 103 (1984): 67–112.

Britton, Edward. *The Community of the Vill*. Toronto, 1977.

Brooks, C. W. *Pettyfoggers and Vipers of the Commonwealth: The "Lower Branch" of the Legal Profession in Early Modern England*. Cambridge, 1986.

Burgess, Clive, and Beat Kümin. "Penitential Bequests and Parish Regimes in Late Medieval England." *Journal of Ecclesiastical History* 44 (1993): 610–30.

Burke, Peter. *Popular Culture in Early Modern Europe*. New York, 1978.

Butcher, A. F. "The Origins of Romney Freemen, 1433–1523." *Economic History Review*, 2nd ser. 27 (1974): 16–27.

Cahn, Susan. *Industry of Devotion: The Transformation of Women's Work in England, 1500–1660*. New York, 1987.

Caiger-Smith, A. *English Medieval Mural Paintings*. Oxford, 1963.

Cam, Helen M. "The Community of the Vill." In *Medieval Studies Presented to Rose Graham*, ed. V. Ruffer and A. J. Taylor, 1–14. Oxford, 1950.

Christie, Agatha. *The Mirror Crack'd*. (Orig. British title, *The Mirror Crack'd from Side to Side*). New York, 1962.

Clark, Elaine. "The Custody of Children in English Manor Courts." *Law and History Review* 3 (1985): 333–48.

 "Debt Litigation in a Late Medieval English Vill." In *Pathways to Medieval Peasants*, ed. J. A. Raftis, 247–79. Toronto, 1981.

 "Some Aspects of Social Security in Medieval England." *Journal of Family History* 7 (1982): 307–20.

Clark, Peter. *The English Alehouse*. London, 1983.

 English Provincial Society from the Reformation to the Revolution. Rutherford, N.J., 1977.

Cressy, David. "Gender Trouble and Cross-Dressing in Early Modern England." *Journal of British Studies* 35 (1996): 438–65.

 Literacy and the Social Order: Reading and Writing in Tudor and Stuart England. Cambridge, 1980.

Crowley, D. A. "Frankpledge and Leet Jurisdiction in Later-Medieval Essex." University of Sheffield Ph.D. thesis, 1971.

Cullum, P. H. "Hospitals and Charitable Provision in Medieval Yorkshire, 936–1547." University of York D.Phil. thesis, 1989.

Darbyshire, Hubert S., and George D. Lumb. *The History of Methley*. Publications of the Thoresby Society. Leeds, 1937.

Davie, Neil. "Chalk and Cheese? 'Fielden' and 'Forest' Communities in Early Modern England." *Journal of Historical Sociology* 4 (1991): 1–31.

Davis, Natalie Zemon. "Poor Relief, Humanism, and Heresy: The Case of Lyon." In her *Society and Culture in Early Modern France*, 17–64. London, 1975.

Dawson, John P. *A History of Lay Judges*. Cambridge, Mass., 1960.

de Bruyn, Lucy. *Woman and the Devil in Sixteenth Century Literature*. Tisbury, Wilts., 1979.

de Certeau, Michel. *The Practice of Everyday Life*. Trans. S. F. Rendall. Berkeley, Calif., 1984.

Deal, Laura Kay. "Whores and Witches: The Language of Female Misbehavior in Early Modern England, 1560–1650." University of Colorado Ph.D. thesis, 1996.

Dean, David M., and N. L. Jones. "Individualising Morality in Early Modern England: Parliament and the Regulation of Personal Morality." Unpublished paper presented at the North American Conference on British Studies, Montreal, Oct. 1993.

Deering, Charles. *Nottinghamia vetus et nova*. Nottingham, 1751.

Dewar, Mary. *Sir Thomas Smith, a Tudor Intellectual in Office*. London, 1964.

DeWindt, Anne. "Peasant Power Structures in Fourteenth-Century King's Ripton." *Mediaeval Studies* 38 (1976): 236–67.

DeWindt, E. B. *Land and People in Holywell-cum-Needingworth*. Toronto, 1972.

Dolan, Frances E. *Dangerous Familiars: Representations of Domestic Crime in England, 1550–1700*. Ithaca, N.Y., 1994.

Donahue, Charles, Jr., ed. *The Records of the Medieval Ecclesiastical Courts*. Part II, England. Berlin, 1994.

Duffy, Eamon. *The Stripping of the Altars*. New Haven, Conn., 1992.

Durston, Christopher, and Jacqueline Eales, eds. *The Culture of English Puritanism, 1560–1700*. New York, 1996.

Dyer, Alan D. *Decline and Growth in English Towns, 1400–1640*. Basingstoke, 1991.

Dyer, Christopher. "Deserted Medieval Villages in the West Midlands." *Economic History Review*, 2nd ser. 35 (1982): 19–34.

Edwards, James F., and Brian P. Hindle. "The Transportation System of Medieval England and Wales." *Journal of Historical Geography* 17 (1991): 123–34.

Elton, G. R. "An Early Tudor Poor Law." *Economic History Review*, 2nd ser. 6 (1953): 55–67.

Policy and Police. Cambridge, 1972.

Everitt, Alan. "Country, County and Town: Patterns of Regional Evolution in England." *Trans. of the Royal Historical Soc.*, 5th ser. 29 (1979): 79–108.

"The Marketing of Agricultural Produce." In *The Agrarian History of England and Wales*, vol. IV, (1500–1640), ed. Joan Thirsk, 466–592. Cambridge, 1967.

Ferguson, Arthur. *The Articulate Citizen and the English Renaissance*. Durham, N.C., 1965.

Fideler, Paul A. "'The Poor' in Early Elizabethan Thought and Policy." Unpublished paper presented at the Midwest Conference on British Studies/Sixteenth Century Studies Conference, Toronto, Oct. 1994.

"Poverty in Tudor Ethical and Political Discourses." Unpublished paper presented at the North American Conference on British Studies, Vancouver, Oct. 1994.

"Poverty, Policy and Providence." In *Political Thought and the Tudor Commonwealth: Deep Structure, Discourse and Disguise*, ed. Paul A. Fideler and T. F. Mayer, 194–222. London, 1992.

Fletcher, Anthony. *Gender, Sex and Subordination in England, 1500–1800*. New Haven, Conn., 1995.

Tudor Rebellions. Seminar Studies in History. London, 1968.

Foucault, Michel. *The Archaeology of Knowledge*. Trans. A. M. Sheridan Smith. New York, 1972.

Discipline and Punish: The Birth of the Prison. Trans. Alan Sheridan. New York, 1977.

Madness and Civilization: A History of Insanity in the Age of Reason. Trans. Richard Howard. London, 1965.

"Truth and Power." In *Power/Knowledge: Selected Interviews and Other Writings, 1972–1977*, ed. and trans. Colin Gordon. New York, 1980.

Frearson, Michael. "The English Corantos of the 1620s." University of Cambridge Ph.D. thesis, 1994.

Goheen, R. B. "Peasant Politics? Village Community and the Crown in Fifteenth-Century England." *American Historical Review* 96 (1991): 42–62.

Goldberg, P. J. P. "Female Labour, Service and Marriage in the Late Medieval Urban North." *Northern History* 12 (1986): 18–38.

"Marriage, Migration, Servanthood and Life-Cycle in Yorkshire Towns of the Later Middle Ages." *Continuity and Change* 1 (1986): 141–69.

Women, Work, and Life Cycle in a Medieval Economy. Oxford, 1992.

Gowing, Laura. *Domestic Dangers: Women, Words, and Sex in Early Modern London*. Oxford, 1996.

"Gender and the Language of Insult in Early Modern London." *History Workshop Journal* 35 (1993): 1–21.

"Language, Power and the Law: Women's Slander Litigation in Early Modern London." In *Women, Crime and the Courts in Early Modern England*, ed. Jenny Kermode and Garthine Walker, 26–47. London, 1994.

Gregory, Annabel. "Slander Accusations and Social Control in Late 16th and Early 17th Century England, with Particular Reference to Rye (Sussex), 1590–1615." University of Sussex Ph.D. thesis, 1984.

Griffiths, Paul. *Youth and Authority: Formative Experiences in England, 1560–1640*. Oxford, 1996.

Guy, J. A. *The Public Career of Sir Thomas More*. New Haven, Conn., 1980.

Haigh, C. A. "Slander and the Church Courts in the Sixteenth Century." *Trans. of the Lancs. and Ches. Antiq. Soc.*, vol. 78, 1–13. Manchester, 1975.

Haines, Alec. "Hop Picking." In *Leominster's 20th Century Characters and Its Poacher*, 11–15. Leominster, 1988.

Hallissy, Margaret. *Clean Maids, True Wives, Steadfast Widows: Chaucer's Women and Medieval Codes of Conduct*. Westport, Conn., 1993.

Hanawalt, Barbara A. "'The Childe of Bristowe' and the Making of Middle-Class Adolescence." In *Bodies and Disciplines*, ed. Barbara A. Hanawalt and David Wallace, 155–78. Minneapolis, 1996.

Growing Up in Medieval London. New York, 1993.

Hanawalt, Barbara A., and Ben R. McRee. "The Guilds of *Homo Prudens* in Late Medieval England." *Continuity and Change* 7 (1992): 163–79.
Hanna, Ralph, III. "Brewing Trouble: On Literature and History – and Alewives." In *Bodies and Disciplines*, ed. Barbara A. Hanawalt and David Wallace, 1–18. Minneapolis, 1996.
  "Pilate's Voice/Shirley's Case." *South Atlantic Quarterly* 91 (1992): 793–812.
Hare, J. N. "The Wiltshire Risings of 1450." *Southern History* 4 (1982): 13–31.
Harker, Richard, C. Mahar, and C. Wilkes, eds. *An Introduction to the Work of Pierre Bourdieu*. New York, 1990.
Harvey, Barbara. *Living and Dying in England, 1100–1540*. Oxford, 1993.
Harvey, I. M. W. *Jack Cade's Rebellion of 1450*. Oxford, 1991.
Harvey, P. D. A., ed. *The Peasant Land Market in Medieval England*. Oxford, 1984.
Hatcher, John. "Mortality in the Fifteenth Century: Some New Evidence." *Economic History Review*, 2nd ser. 39 (1986): 19–38.
Heal, Felicity. *Hospitality in Early Modern England*. Oxford, 1990.
Hearnshaw, F. J. C. *Leet Jurisdiction in England*. Southampton, 1908.
Herrup, Cynthia. *The Common Peace*. Cambridge, 1987.
Hill, Christopher. *Change and Continuity in Seventeenth-Century England*. Cambridge, Mass., 1975.
  Society and Puritanism in Pre-Revolutionary England. London, 1964.
Hilton, R. H. "Small Town Society in England Before the Black Death." *Past and Present* 105 (1984): 53–78.
Hindle, Steve. "The Shaming of Margaret Knowsley: Gossip, Gender and the Experience of Authority in Early Modern England." *Continuity and Change* 9 (1994): 391–420.
Hoffman, Philip T. *Church and Community in the Diocese of Lyon, 1500–1789*. New Haven, Conn., 1984.
Holmes, Clive. "Women: Witnesses and Witches." *Past and Present* 140 (1993): 45–78.
Homans, G. C. *English Villagers of the Thirteenth Century*. Cambridge, Mass., 1942.
Houlbrooke, Ralph A. *Church Courts and the People During the English Reformation, 1520–1570*. Oxford, 1979.
Hsia, R. Po-chia. *Social Discipline in the Reformation: Central Europe, 1550–1750*. London, 1989.
Hunt, William. *The Puritan Moment: The Coming of Revolution in an English County*. Cambridge, Mass., 1983.
Hutton, Ronald. *The Rise and Fall of Merry England: The Ritual Year, 1400–1700*. Oxford, 1994.
Ingram, Martin. *Church Courts, Sex and Marriage in England, 1570–1640*. Cambridge, 1987.
  "From Reformation to Toleration: Popular Religious Cultures in England, 1540–1690." In *Popular Culture in England, c. 1500–1850*, ed. Tim Harris, 95–123. New York, 1995.
  "Reformation of Manners in Early Modern England." In *The Experience of Authority in Early Modern England*, ed. Paul Griffiths, Adam Fox, and Steve Hindle, 47–88. Basingstoke, 1996.
  "Religion, Communities and Moral Discipline in Late Sixteenth- and Early Seventeenth-Century England." In *Religion and Society in Early Modern Europe, 1500–1800*, ed. Kaspar von Greyerz, 177–93. London, 1984.

"Ridings, Rough Music and the 'Reform of Popular Culture' in Early Modern England." *Past and Present* 105 (1984): 79–113.

" 'Scolding Women Cucked or Washed': A Crisis in Gender Relations in Early Modern England?" In *Women, Crime and the Courts in Early Modern England*, ed. Jenny Kermode and Garthine Walker, 48–80. London, 1994.

Innes, Joanna. "Prisons for the Poor: English Bridewells, 1555–1800." In *Labour, Law, and Crime*, ed. Francis Snyder and Douglas Hay, 42–122. London, 1987.

Jameson, Fredric. *The Political Unconscious: Narrative as a Socially Symbolic Act.* Ithaca, N.Y., 1981.

Karras, Ruth Mazo. *Common Women: Prostitution and Sexuality in Medieval England.* New York, 1996.

Kelly's County Guides. Various places, various dates.

Kent, Joan R. "Attitudes of Members of the House of Commons to the Regulation of 'Personal Conduct' in Late Elizabethan and Early Stuart England." *Bulletin of the Institute of Historical Research* 46 (1973): 41–71.

The English Village Constable. Oxford, 1986.

Kerridge, Eric. *The Agricultural Revolution.* New York, 1968.

Konig, David Thomas. *Law and Society in Puritan Massachusetts: Essex County, 1629–1692.* Chapel Hill, N.C., 1979.

Kriedte, P., H. Medick, and J. Schlumbohm. *Industrialization Before Industrialization.* Cambridge, 1981.

Kümin, Beat A. *The Shaping of a Community: The Rise and Reformation of the English Parish, c. 1400–1560.* Brookfield, Vt., 1996.

Kussmaul, Ann. *A General View of the Rural Economy of England, 1538–1840.* Cambridge, 1990.

Servants in Husbandry in Early Modern England. Cambridge, 1981.

Lake, Peter. *Anglicans and Puritans? Presbyterianism and English Conformist Thought from Whitgift to Hooker.* London, 1988.

"Calvinism and the English Church, 1570–1635." *Past and Present* 114 (1987): 32–76.

Lamont, William M. *Puritanism and Historical Controversy.* London, 1996.

Langdon, John. "Inland Water Transport in Medieval England." *Journal of Historical Geography* 19 (1993): 1–11.

Lenman, Bruce, and Geoffrey Parker. "The State, the Community and the Criminal Law in Early Modern Europe." In *Crime and the Law: The Social History of Crime in Western Europe Since 1500*, ed. V. A. C. Gatrell, Bruce Lenman, and Geoffrey Parker, 11–48. London, 1980.

Levine, David, and Keith Wrightson. *The Making of an Industrial Society: Whickham, 1560–1765.* Oxford, 1991.

Macdonell, Diane. *Theories of Discourse: An Introduction.* Oxford, 1986.

Macfarlane, Alan. *Witchcraft in Tudor and Stuart England.* London, 1970.

Marchant, Ronald A. *The Puritans and the Church Courts in the Diocese of York, 1560–1642.* London, 1960.

Marcombe, David. *English Small Town Life: Retford, 1520–1642.* Nottingham, 1993.

Marks, Richard. *Stained Glass in England During the Middle Ages.* Toronto, 1993.

Marx, Karl. *Das Kapital.* Hamburg, 1867.

Mattingly, Joanna M. "Cookham, Bray and Isleworth Hundreds: A Study in Changing Local Relations in the Middle Thames Valley, 1422–1558." University of London Ph.D. thesis, 1993.

Mayhew, Graham. *Tudor Rye*. Brighton, 1987.

McClendon, Muriel C. "Religion and the Politics of Order in Sixteenth-Century Norwich." Unpublished paper presented at the North American Conference on British Studies, Montreal, Oct. 1993.

"Religious Change and the Magisterial Ethos in Elizabethan Norwich." Unpublished paper presented at the Sixteenth Century Studies Conference, Atlanta, Oct. 1992.

McCune, Pat. "Late Medieval Strategies of Retribution and Reconciliation." Unpublished paper presented at the American Historical Association, Dec. 1991.

McIntosh, Marjorie K. *Autonomy and Community: The Royal Manor of Havering, 1200–1500*. Cambridge, 1986.

A Community Transformed: The Manor and Liberty of Havering, 1500–1620. Cambridge, 1991.

"Finding Language for Misconduct: Jurors in Fifteenth-Century Local Courts." In *Bodies and Disciplines*, ed. Barbara A. Hanawalt and David Wallace, 87–122. Minneapolis, 1996.

"The Foundation of Hospitals and Almshouses in Medieval and Tudor England." Unpublished paper presented at the Wellcome Unit for the History of Medicine, Oxford University, October 1990.

"Local Change and Community Control in England, 1465–1500." *Huntington Library Quarterly* 49 (1986): 219–42.

"Local Responses to the Poor in Late Medieval and Tudor England." *Continuity and Change* 3 (1988): 209–45.

"Money Lending on the Periphery of London, 1300–1600." *Albion* 20 (1988): 557–71.

"Networks of Care in Elizabethan English Towns." In *The Locus of Care: Families, Communities and Institutions in History*, ed. Peregrine Horden and Richard Smith. Forthcoming in 1997.

"Servants and the Household Unit in an Elizabethan English Community." *Journal of Family History* 9 (1984): 3–23.

"Social Change and Tudor Manorial Leets." In *The Law and Social Change*, ed. J. A. Guy and H. G. Beale, 73–85. London, 1984.

McRee, Ben R. "Religious Gilds and Regulation of Behavior in Late Medieval Towns." In *People, Politics and Community in the Later Middle Ages*, ed. Joel Rosenthal and Colin Richmond, 108–22. Gloucester, 1987.

McSheffrey, Shannon. "Sexual Misconduct and the Regulation of Behaviour in the Wards in Late 15th-Century London." Unpublished paper presented at the Medieval and Tudor London Seminar, London, June 1994.

Mentzer, Raymond A., ed. *Sin and the Calvinists: Morals Control and the Consistory in the Reformed Tradition*. Sixteenth Century Essays and Studies, vol. 32. Kirksville, Mo., 1994.

Mitterauer, Michael. "Servants and Youth." *Continuity and Change* 5 (1990): 11–38.

Sozialgeschichte der Jugend. Frankfurt, 1986.

Moeller, Bernd. *Imperial Cities and the Reformation: Three Essays*. Ed. and trans. H. C. Erik Midelfort and Mark U. Edwards, Jr. Philadelphia, 1972.

Mollat, Michel. *The Poor in the Middle Ages: An Essay in Social History*. Trans. Arthur Goldhammer. New Haven, Conn., 1986.

Mollat, Michel, ed. *Études sur l'Histoire de la Pauvreté*. 2 vols. Paris, 1974.

Morrill, John. "The Ecology of Allegiance in the English Revolution." *Journal of British Studies* 26 (1987): 451–67.

Morris, W. A. *The Frankpledge System.* New York, 1910.

Muchembled, Robert. *Popular Culture and Elite Culture in France, 1400–1740.* Trans. Lydia Cochrane. Baton Rouge, La., 1985.

Muldrew, Craig. "Interpreting the Market: The Ethics of Credit and Community Relations in Early Modern England." *Social History* 18 (1993): 163–83.

Oestreich, Gerhard. *Strukturprobleme der frühen Neuzeit.* Berlin, 1980.

Orme, Nicholas. "The Culture of Children in Medieval England." *Past and Present* 148 (1995): 48–88.

Owen, Dorothy M. "Ecclesiastical Jurisdiction, 1300–1550: The Records and Their Interpretation." *Studies in Church History* 11 (1975): 199–221.

The Records of the Established Church in England, Excluding Parochial Records. London, 1970.

The Oxford English Dictionary. 2nd edn., 20 vols., ed. J. A. Simpson and E. S. C. Weiner. Oxford, 1989–.

Ozment, Steven E. *The Reformation in the Cities: The Appeal of Protestantism to Sixteenth-Century Germany and Switzerland.* New Haven, Conn., 1975.

Palmer, Robert C. *The County Courts of Medieval England.* Princeton, N.J., 1982.

English Law in the Age of the Black Death, 1348–1381. Chapel Hill, N.C., 1993.

Patten, John. "Patterns of Migration and Movement of Labour to Three Pre-Industrial East Anglian Towns." In *Migration and Society in Early Modern England,* ed. Peter Clark and David Souden, 77–106. London, 1988.

Pelling, Margaret. "Old Age, Poverty, and Disability in Early Modern Norwich." In *Life, Death, and the Elderly,* ed. M. Pelling and R. M. Smith, 74–101. London, 1991.

Phythian-Adams, Charles. *Desolation of a City: Coventry and the Urban Crisis of the Late Middle Ages.* Cambridge, 1979.

Phythian-Adams, Charles, ed. *Societies, Cultures and Kinship, 1580–1850.* Leicester, 1993.

Pollard, A. W., and G. R. Redgrave, comps. *A Short-title Catalogue of Books Printed in England, Scotland and Ireland and of English Books Printed Abroad, 1475–1640.* 2nd edn. rev. & enl. by W. A. Jackson, F. S. Ferguson, and K. F. Pantzer in 3 vols. London, 1976–91.

Poos, L. R. *A Rural Society after the Black Death: Essex, 1350–1525.* Cambridge, 1991.

"Sex, Lies, and the Church Courts of Pre-Reformation England." *Journal of Interdisciplinary History* 25 (1995): 585–607.

Prodi, Paolo, and Carla Penuti, eds. *Disciplina dell'anima, disciplina del corpo e disciplina della societa tra medioevo ed eta moderna.* Bologna, 1994.

Raftis, J. A. *A Small Town in Late Medieval England: Godmanchester.* Toronto, 1982.

Warboys: Two Hundred Years in the Life of an English Mediaeval Town. Toronto, 1974.

Razi, Zvi. *Life, Marriage and Death in a Medieval Parish.* Cambridge, 1980.

Razi, Zvi, and Richard Smith, eds. *Medieval Society and the Manor Court.* Oxford, 1996.

Richardson, R. C. *Puritanism in North-West England: A Regional Study of the Diocese of Chester to 1642.* Manchester, 1972.

Riddy, Felicity. "Mother Knows Best: Reading Social Change in a Courtesy Text." *Speculum* 71 (1996): 66–86.

Rokkan, Stein. "Dimensions of State Formation and Nation-Building." In *The Formation of National States in Western Europe*, ed. Charles Tilly, 562–600. Princeton, N.J., 1975.

Roper, Lyndal. *The Holy Household: Women and Morals in Reformation Augsburg*. Oxford, 1989.

    Oedipus and the Devil: Witchcraft, Sexuality and Religion in Early Modern Europe. London, 1994.

Rosen, Adrienne. "Winchester in Transition, 1580–1700." In *Country Towns in Pre-Industrial England*, ed. Peter Clark, 143–95. New York, 1981.

Rubin, Miri. *Charity and Community in Medieval Cambridge*. Cambridge, 1987.

    "The Poor." In *Fifteenth-Century Attitudes*, ed. Rosemary Horrox, 169–82. Cambridge, 1994.

Rudd, David P. "The Involuntarily Poor in English Religious Writings from the Late Middle Ages to 1600." University of Lancaster Ph.D. thesis, 1992.

Scanlon, Larry. *Narrative, Authority and Power: The Medieval Exemplum and the Chaucerian Tradition*. Cambridge, 1994.

Scarisbrick, J. J. *The Reformation and the English People*. Oxford, 1984.

Scase, Wendy. *"Piers Plowman" and the New Anti-Clericalism*. Cambridge, 1989.

Schilling, Heinz. *Civic Calvinism in Northwestern Germany and the Netherlands*. sixteenth Century Essays and Studies, vol. 17. Kirksville, Mo., 1991.

Schofield, Roger, and E. A. Wrigley. "Infant and Child Mortality in England in the Late Tudor and Early Stuart Period." In *Health, Medicine and Mortality*, ed. Charles Webster, 61–95. Cambridge, 1979.

Sharpe, J. A. *Crime in Early Modern England, 1550–1750*. London, 1984.

    Crime in Seventeenth-Century England: A County Study. Cambridge, 1983.

    "Defamation and Sexual Slander in Early Modern England: The Church Courts at York." Borthwick Institute of Historical Research Papers, no. 58. York, 1972.

    "'Such Disagreement Betwyx Neighbours': Litigation and Human Relations in Early Modern England." In *Disputes and Settlements: Law and Human Relations in the West*, ed. John Bossy, 167–87. Cambridge, 1983.

    "Witchcraft and Women in Seventeenth-Century England: Some Northern Evidence." *Continuity and Change* 6 (1991): 179–99.

Sheail, John. "The Regional Distribution of Wealth in England as Indicated in the Lay Subsidy Returns of 1524/5." University of London Ph.D. thesis, 1968.

Skipp, V. *Crisis and Development: An Ecological Case Study of the Forest of Arden, 1570–1674*. Cambridge, 1978.

Slack, Paul A. *Poverty and Policy in Tudor and Stuart England*. London, 1988.

    "Social Policy and the Constraints of Government, 1547–58." In *The Mid-Tudor Polity, c.1540–1560*, ed. J. Loach and R. Tittler, 137–58. London, 1980.

Smith, Richard Dean. "Social Reform in an Urban Context: Colchester, Essex, 1570–1640." University of Colorado Ph.D. thesis, 1996.

Smith, Richard M. "Demographic Developments in Rural England, 1300–1348: A Survey." In *Before the Black Death*, ed. Bruce M. S. Campbell, 25–77. Manchester, 1991.

    "Kin and Neighbors in a Thirteenth-Century Suffolk Community." *Journal of Family History* 4 (1979): 219–56.

Spufford, Margaret. "Puritanism and Social Control?" In *Order and Disorder in Early Modern England*, ed. Anthony Fletcher and John Stevenson, 41–57. Cambridge, 1985.

Spufford, Margaret, ed. *The World of Rural Dissenters: 1520–1725*. Cambridge, 1995.

Stallybrass, Peter, and Allon White. *The Politics and Poetics of Transgression*. Ithaca, N.Y., 1986.

Stoyle, Mark. *Loyalty and Locality: Popular Allegiance in Devon During the English Civil War*. Exeter, 1994.

Tawney, R. H. *Religion and the Rise of Capitalism*. London, 1926.

Thirsk, Joan. *Agricultural Regions and Agrarian History in England, 1500–1750*. Basingstoke, 1987.

Thomas, Keith. "Cleanliness and Godliness in Early Modern England." In *Religion, Culture and Society in Early Modern Britain*, ed. Anthony Fletcher and Peter Roberts, 56–83. Cambridge, 1994.

Tilly, Charles, ed. *The Formation of National States in Western Europe*. Princeton, N.J., 1975.

Tillyard, E. M. W. *The Elizabethan World Picture*. London, 1943.

Todd, Margo. *Christian Humanism and the Puritan Social Order*. Cambridge, 1987.

Todd, Margo, ed. *Reformation to Revolution: Politics and Religion in Early Modern England*. London, 1995.

Uhart, Marie-Claire. "The Early Reception of Piers Plowman." University of Leicester Ph.D. thesis, 1988.

Underdown, David. "The Chalk and the Cheese: Contrasts Among the English Clubmen." *Past and Present* 85 (1979): 25–48.

   Fire from Heaven: The Life of an English Town [Dorchester] in the Seventeenth Century. New Haven, Conn., 1992.

   "Regional Cultures? Local Variations in Popular Culture During the Early Modern Period." In *Popular Culture in England, c. 1500–1850*, ed. Tim Harris, 28–47. New York, 1995.

   "A Reply to John Morrill." *Journal of British Studies* 26 (1987): 468–79.

   Revel, Riot, and Rebellion: Popular Politics and Culture in England, 1603–1660. Oxford, 1985.

   "The Taming of the Scold: The Enforcement of Patriarchal Authority in Early Modern England." In *Order and Disorder in Early Modern England*, ed. Anthony Fletcher and John Stevenson, 116–36. Cambridge, 1985.

The Victoria County Histories (= *The Victoria History of the Counties of England*). Various places, various dates.

The Victoria County History of York, East Riding. Vol. I. Ed. K. J. Allison. London, 1969.

von Friedeburg, Robert. "Reformation of Manners and the Social Composition of Offenders in an East Anglian Cloth Village: Earls Colne, Essex, 1531–1642." *Journal of British Studies* 29 (1990): 347–83.

   Sündenzucht und sozialer Wandel: Earls Colne (England), Ipswich und Springfield (Neuengland) c. 1524–1690 im Vergleich. Stuttgart, 1993.

Walter, John, and Roger Schofield, eds. *Famine, Disease and the Social Order in Early Modern Society*. Cambridge, 1989.

Weber, Max. *The Protestant Ethic and the Spirit of Capitalism*. Trans. Talcott Parsons. New York, 1958.

Wenig, Scott A. "The Ecclesiastical Vision and Pastoral Achievements of the Progressive Bishops Under Elizabeth I, 1559–1579." University of Colorado Ph.D. thesis, 1994.

Wenzel, Siegfried. *The Sin of Sloth: Acedia in Medieval Thought and Literature.* Chapel Hill, N.C., 1960.

Williams, Raymond. *Marxism and Literature.* Oxford, 1977.

Woodcock, Brian L. *Medieval Ecclesiastical Courts in the Diocese of Canterbury.* Oxford, 1952.

Woods, Robert. *Forging a Culture of Law and Order: The Justices of the Peace in England, 1470–1537.* Forthcoming.

Wrightson, Keith. *English Society, 1580–1680.* London, 1982.

"The Puritan Reformation of Manners, with Special Reference to the Counties of Lancashire and Essex, 1640–60." University of Cambridge Ph.D. thesis, 1973.

"The Social Order of Early Modern England." In *The World We Have Gained,* ed. L. Bonfield, R. M. Smith, and K. Wrightson, 177–202. Oxford, 1986.

"Two Concepts of Order: Justices, Constables and Jurymen in Seventeenth-Century England." In *An Ungovernable People,* ed. John Brewer and J. Styles, 21–46. London, 1980.

Wrightson, Keith, and David Levine. *Poverty and Piety in an English Village: Terling, 1525–1700.* Paperback, Oxford, 1995 (orig. publ. New York, 1979).

Wrigley, E. A., and R. S. Schofield. *The Population History of England, 1541–1871: A Reconstruction.* London, 1981.

Wunderli, Richard M. *London Church Courts and Society on the Eve of the Reformation.* Cambridge, Mass., 1981.

Zell, Michael. *Industry in the Countryside: Wealden Society in the Sixteenth Century.* Cambridge, 1994.

Index

Cambridge Studies in Population, Economy and Society in Past Time

Titles available in paperback are marked with an asterisk

M